THE FEMINISM OF UNCERTAINTY

THE FEMINISM OF UNCERTAINTY

A Gender Diary

Ann Snitow

DUKE UNIVERSITY PRESS
Durham and London, 2015

© 2015 Duke University Press
All rights reserved
Designed by Kristina Kachele
Typeset in Quadraat Pro by Copperline

Library of Congress Cataloging-in-Publication Data Snitow,
Ann Barr, 1943–
The feminism of uncertainty : a gender diary / Ann Snitow.
pages cm
Includes bibliographical references and index.
ISBN 978-0-8223-5860-2 (hardcover : alk. paper)
ISBN 978-0-8223-5874-9 (pbk. : alk. paper)
ISBN 978-0-8223-7567-8 (e-book)
1. Feminism—United States. 2. Feminism. 3. Snitow, Ann
Barr, 1943– 4. Feminists—United States—Biography.

I. Title.
HQ1426.S615 2015
305.420973—dc23
2015006353

to the past and future feminists

CONTENTS

Acknowledgments ix
Introduction: The Feminism of Uncertainty: I 1

Part I CONTINUING A GENDER DIARY
1 A Gender Diary 21
2 Critiquing a Gender Diary 59

Part II MOTHERS/LOVERS
3 Introduction to Mothers/Lovers 71
4 Dorothy Dinnerstein: Creative Unknowing 80
5 From the Gender Diary: Living with Dorothy Dinnerstein (1923–1992) 93
6 Changing Our Minds about Motherhood: 1963–1990 97
7 The Sex Wars in Feminism: Retrenchment versus Transformation 123
8 The Poet of Bad Girls: Angela Carter (1940–1992) 139
9 Inside the Circus Tent: Excerpts from an Interview with Angela Carter, 1988 148
10 The Beast Within: Lady into Fox and A Man in the Zoo, by David Garnett 153

Part III THE FEMINIST PICARESQUE
11 Introduction to the Feminist Picaresque 159
12 Occupying Greenham Common 163
13 Feminist Futures in the Former East Bloc 191
14 Feminism Travels: Cautionary Tales 204
15 Who are the Polish Feminists? (Slawka) 216
16 "Should I Marry Him?" Questions from Students 228

17   The Peripatetic Feminist Activist/Professor Spends One Day
        in a Small City in Albania 238
18   Certainty and Doubt in the Classroom: Teaching Film in
        Prison 241

Part IV REFUGEES FROM UTOPIA
19   Introduction to Refugees from Utopia 273
20   Remembering, Forgetting, and the Making of
        The Feminist Memoir Project 275
21   The Politics of Passion: Ellen Willis (1941–2006) 293
22   Returning to the Well: Revisiting Shulamith Firestone's
        The Dialectic of Sex 297

Part V THE FEMINISM OF UNCERTAINTY
23   Introduction to the Feminism of Uncertainty 307
24   Life Sentence: My Uncertainty Principle 310
25   Doubt's Visionary: Doris Lessing 316
26   Utopia, Downsized: A Farrago 328
27   The Feminism of Uncertainty: II 330
        Appendix: Publication History 335
        Bibliography 339
        Index 355

A photo gallery appears after page 264.

ACKNOWLEDGMENTS

In the acknowledgments after each piece collected here, I've named the many who helped me in so many ways, over so many years. I thank them all again for a lifetime of intense conversations, actions taken together, and then rethought. How exciting it's been—and continues to be.

This collection could never have come together without Katie Detwiler, whose technical skills and warm intellectual company have made this project delightful rather than onerous. A number of friends have been marvelous critical readers. They have helped me, encouraged me, rescued me. I thank, for their good ear, brilliant edits, and long empathy with my doings: Cynthia Carr, Rachel Blau DuPlessis, Susan Faludi, Evelyn Frankford, Daniel Goode, Karen Hopenwasser, Judith Levine, Henry Shapiro, Meredith Tax, Leonore Tiefer, and Carole Vance. I thank, too, for their support and skill, my editors at Dissent: Michael Walzer, Judy Walzer, Michael Kazin, and Maxine Phillips.

Alan Snitow and Deborah Kaufman have been fellow travelers for years. Discussions with them have enriched all I do.

I thank Nanette Rainone, creator of the radio show "Womankind," on WBAI-FM New York, for being the best and most helpful boss I have ever had and for giving me the opportunity to talk about feminism for hours and hours on the radio, 1970–1979.

No one who writes personal essays today should omit a thank you to Phillip Lopate, champion of the form, inspiring practitioner, generous reader.

These are the members of my first consciousness-raising group, 1969–1970, the founding group of New York Radical Feminists called the Stanton-Anthony Brigade: Minda Bickman, Diane Crothers, Shulamith Firestone,

Martha Gershun, Anne Koedt, Cellestine Ware, and of my long-term CR group (1974–ca. 1992), called The Sex Fools or the Third Street Circle, depending on our mood: Ros Baxandall, Bonnie Bellow, Cynthia Carr, Judy Coburn, Shaelagh Doyle, Karen Durbin, Deirdre English, Sally George, Brett Harvey, M. Mark, Irene Peslikis, Alix Kates Shulman, Katie Taylor, Ellen Willis. What superb company you have been. Our rich conversations and your loyal friendship over all these years have been pure gold.

To the many women active in the Feminist Anti-Censorship Taskforce (FACT) and the writers, editors, and designers of Caught Looking: Feminism, Pornography, and Censorship: How would I have gotten through the perilous feminist sex wars without you? Thank you. And thank you, too, for the buoyant company of all those who banded together in No More Nice Girls; we dressed up and marched our feet off trying to protect the right to abortion for all women.

Elzbieta Matynia, director of The New School's summer program in Poland, "Democracy and Diversity" (1992–present), created a teaching and learning environment more effective than any I have known; I thank her for my precious time in Krakow and Wroclaw, twenty summers which have been the wellspring of some of the essays here. I thank, too, Hana Cervinkova, who warmly supported the school with tactical brilliance.

The members of the Network of East-West Women are a constant support and inspiration to my ongoing writing and activism. I can name only a few here from East Central Europe whom I met early on and whose inspiration sealed my love for feminist work in the region: Sonja Licht, Slawka Walczewska, Malgorzata Fuszara, Malgorzata Tarasiewicz (Director of NEWW), Lepa Mladjenovic, Roma Ciesla, Beata Kozak, Barbara Limanowska, Wanda Nowicka, Bozena Jawien. Thank you, too, to the many students from the region who are now friends and colleagues. To the many U.S.-based members of the Network: You were its mainstay from the start, and I am in the process of writing about you and will thank you one by one. What a wild ride we had together in the years right after 1989.

To Cynthia Carr, Amber Hollibaugh, and Gayle Rubin, thank you for excellent advice about what an essay collection can be. To Aviva Goode, Bill Eis, and Bruce Kennedy: Thank you for helping me sort out the details of publishing. To Alice Gavin and Stephanie Damoff: Thank you for careful and thoughtful editorial assistance. To Julienne Obadia and Beth Weiman: Thank you for wonderfully rescuing me from freefall post-Katie.

To all who joined together in Take Back the Future (2002–2006) during the dreadful George W. Bush years: Thank you for your heartening company in those dark times, and thanks particularly to Drucilla Cornell, who helped found the group, and to Judith Levine, who partnered in keeping it going. Your ideas about activism are a constant resource.

I thank Eugene Lang College and The New School for giving me a supportive, fascinating, university home since 1986. I've learned much from my colleagues there and want particularly to acknowledge all those who helped me bring Gender Studies back to the university (twice). You are so many I can only mention here those who were there at the beginning in 1986: the late Janet Abu-Lughod, Seyla Benhabib, Louise Tilley, Vera Zolberg—and, later, Rayna Rapp, our first Gender Studies and Feminist Theory director (1994). You have all been magnificent colleagues, with just the right mixture of dedication and humor to sustain us for what turned out to be a long haul. I've had the good fortune to co-teach several courses—about feminism, race, the 1960s, and the Left—with my colleague, Victoria Hattam. Thank you for how much I learned and for the lovely structures we built in our efforts to understand civil rights and women's liberation. I've had an extraordinary reader in my colleague, Kate Eichhorn. Thank you for hours of exchanges about modern women's movements; your questions have inspired (more and more) work.

Thank you to the New York Institute for the Humanities, who gave a home to the seminar I ran there from 1982 to 1994, "Sex, Gender, and Consumer Culture." This group generated an extraordinary amount of creative work during the years we talked together.

I am grateful to the Institut für die Wissenschaften vom Menschen in Vienna, where I was in residence for an interesting semester, 1999–2000, and to the J. William Fulbright Foreign Scholarship Board, which made me a Fulbright Specialist and supported one of my trips to Albania.

I am so grateful to my colleagues in Gender Studies at the Jagiellonian University in Krakow (Beata Kowalska), at the Central European University in Budapest (Nancy Stepan, Joanna Regulska, and Jasmina Lukic), at the Belgrade Women's Studies Center (Dasa Duhacek), at Babes-Bolyai University in Cluj (Eniko Magyari-Vince), at the University of Bucharest (Mihaela Miroiu), at Masaryk University in Brno (Iva Smidova), at Maria Curie-Skłodowska University in Lublin (Tomek Kitlinski), at Warsaw University (Agnieszka Graff), at the European University of Tirana (Ermira Danaj), and many others for inviting me to talk to your students. These visits have been landmarks in my feminist teaching in East Central Europe. We all share a sense of surprise: No one expected that the Gender Studies programs you developed would ever exist.

I thank Laura Micham and the Sallie Bingham Center for Women's History and Culture at Duke University's Rubenstein Library for offering my papers and audio tapes a place in their extraordinary archive of feminist activism. With her dedication and kindness, Laura raised my valuation of the piles of material generated in a messy activist life.

At Duke University press I thank the amazing Ken Wissoker, the kind and ever-helpful Elizabeth Ault, Amy Ruth Buchanan, Kristina Kachele, and Sara Leone. Thank you to the two anonymous readers who warmly supported this book and helped to make it better. My wonderful indexer, Julienne Obadia, has turned the categories in this book into poetry. Thank you.

At Sloan Kettering Memorial Hospital, I thank Dr. Jason Konner; his directness, brilliance, and warm support made so many things possible. Dr. Phillip Bukberg has also been my without whom nothing. And nothing at all would be possible without Susan Hefner.

I have written a number of these pieces where the phone and domestic distractions couldn't reach me, in cafés. These secret hideouts can only work when the staff welcomes writers who sit drinking coffee for hours. So thank you to Dominique Ansel and his staff, to Rosa at the Café Dante, and to everyone at Hiroko's.

Finally, my love and deep gratitude to Daniel Goode—composer and clarinetist. I feel so lucky: "She shall have music wherever she goes. . . ." Thank you for the delights of our busy, crazy, happy life together.

November 2014

INTRODUCTION

The Feminism of Uncertainty: I

Utopia, Activism, Uncertainty

To my initial surprise, I have been able to make a short list of preoccupations that have marked the thirty-five years of writing gathered here. First, as I reread these essays, now clustered together to form new patterns, everywhere I find the belief in the importance of imagining a better world—call it utopian yearning. But also everywhere here, this hopefulness collapses into utopia's common twin, ironic skepticism. This combination is wonderfully recorded in a typical remark of my parents' generation: "A new world is coming"—their dream of socialism—words followed over the years with ever-darkening laughter: "We should live so long." Next, running throughout, I find the assumption that, for me, feminist activism is necessary. (No doubt this is a choice, but it hasn't felt like one.) Finally, also all through, I hear a thrumming, inescapable, and sometimes much valued tone of uncertainty, an acceptance of the blundering in the dark that is part of all activism.

Everyone who engages in the tragicomedy of activism will negotiate the stretch between speculative desire and the shortfall of action in her or his own way. Happy endings require that one set sail toward a near enough horizon and keep one's eyes off the inevitable: failure, confusion, and the falling out of comrades. There is no right way to balance these things, and this book is not meant to be exemplary. What it does offer is a variety of descriptions of how one person has tried to locate feminism in her life—in situations that keep changing.

I have acted (and written) with passionate conviction while constantly wondering where such actions lie in larger schemes of things. Like Doris Lessing, a novelist whom I have treasured in all her phases, I am subject to disconcerting shifts in my perception of scale. Today we marched against recent homophobic violence in Greenwich Village; tomorrow New York City is under water and men and women (if they are still so identified) are travelling over our momentary Bohemia in boats, gazing down with incomprehension at our ragged neighborhood through thirty feet of water. Does anything feminist activists once did shape what these travelers of the future are saying and doing?

As my friend V. says, who cares? For her, the only thing that matters is to be vital in one's own moment. The after-lives of our thoughts or acts are of no consequence. Since our being and intentions cannot be remembered or retrieved, what we do can never confidently be assigned a long-term value, pernicious or benign. Forget the future, V. says, as the future will forget us. But, then, V. is not an activist.

I became a feminist activist in 1969. My first consciousness-raising meeting in the fall of that year—quite by chance and thanks to the urgings of my friend Cellestine Ware—turned out to be the founding of New York Radical Feminists. There's no counting the number of meetings that followed. (Once, a friend going in the other direction on the street called out to me in alarm: "Oh, dear. Am I missing a meeting?") Many have recorded what that time felt like: a love affair, a revelation, a little click of the lens that refocused everything. So now I was a feminist for life. But what would this mean? The particular rush I experienced in those first months couldn't maintain itself for two breaths. Sisterhood crumbled at a touch, weakened by differences of race, class, and political traditions, and also by damaged selves and the "tears of things." Our astonishing and bracing rage at patriarchy was necessary but insufficient for the long haul.

From 1969 onward, polemics and reviews poured from me, but all that is absent from this collection because it was champagne with a fizz that soon went. Though I didn't know it then, behind all that frenzy I was searching for ways to do feminist writing, teaching, and activism that would be resilient enough to sustain this love I felt for the women's liberation movement into a future I might happily inhabit. This book includes a sampling of my writing between 1978 and 2014. These pieces seem to me to explore a feminism I hope can endure yet be flexible enough to turn and turn about, through the shape-shifting of history, while remaining linked to my early utopian feminist desires, desires which linger even when they seem far to seek.

It would be easy to say that some ineluctable logic and beauty I discovered in my early encounters with feminism cured primal wounds and fueled my continuous engagement. And, to be sure, that would be one piece of the story—though one can't help remarking that many women, even some who desperately need change, have seemed impervious to this allure. I suspect, rather, that to understand such a relentless commitment, I would need a longer narrative, a trip further back to my girlhood, when I had no conscious feminist ideas whatsoever—though perhaps I already had what I might recognize now as feminist feelings.

> *The family breakfast table: My mother and father are sitting at the head and foot of this small table, I and my younger brother between them, say 10 and 5 years old. Our parents are both reading* The New York Times, *my father placid, enjoying his usual burnt toast with marmalade, my mother, increasingly agitated. She reads out something—probably about the evil of racism or the injustice of poverty or the stupidity of the government—and here is her often-repeated remark, which has mattered so much: "Something must be done!"*

Something must be done? Such a call to action requires quite a lot of unpacking. For a (newly) middle-class woman, the child of restless, unfulfilled, and socially powerless immigrants, a woman who observed with longing her father's exits from home to meet other men at the Working Men's Circle while her gifted mother stewed at home, a woman who became a communist in 1933 and passed in the late 1940s into anxious post-McCarthy retreat, a woman who then reinvented radical politics for herself hidden in this solid suburban scene, such words have many, layered meanings. What could this still-hungry mother of mine have imagined we at that table should or could do?

My father, also the child of struggling immigrants, and with progressive values himself, had no expectation that he could change the world; he was delighted to be part of it and, starting from scratch, to succeed on its terms. But on my mother's side the inheritance is clear: Changing the world is an absolute duty; and—though this part was never voiced—such work is also a deep pleasure, offering a path into a significant life. Looking back at this primal scene, the founding scene of "politics" for both my brother and me, I see how essential the Left-wing utopian dreams of my parents' generation were to us both. But the source of my feminism also makes an appearance at that breakfast table. Creative as my mother was in finding ways "to do something," she was also constantly balked in her efforts to be an active, public being. She was, alas, merely a woman. When, finally, Women's Liberation took wing in all directions, her anger fused with mine; feminism was simply it for both of us, the best salve for our wounded hearts.

Guilt was an element in our activism too, of course. After all, how could we be sitting at this well-stocked table while so many we read about were suffering? But such guilt is well-trodden ground. And even in *extremis*, activism is not inevitable; some do, some do not. Let me return to family states of mind that were more productive than guilt in my activist life—and perhaps in the lives of others—the naïveté of utopian wishes and the vaunting desire for a life of consequence.

No activism is possible without naïveté, some faith in action in spite of rational assessments of what can actually be done. And, also, no activism without some grandiosity, some earnest belief in the value of making an unseemly display. It's easy to see activism as a fool's game, a piece of self-expressive insistence with no clear promise of bringing change—though a move to activism is always, itself, change. I think of the many years I worked to bring Gender Studies into full reality in a hostile or indifferent university environment, where feminism was seen as the height of unsophistication; I think of the early days of my work in postcommunist Eastern Europe where fine people (for example, the great Polish dissident Adam Michnik) laughed when they heard I was a feminist organizer. So silly was feminism that hostility wasn't even necessary. One had to be willing to seem ridiculous, extreme, grotesque. One had to be naïve enough to imagine that something could—and must—be done in this obviously impossible environment.

One way to make sense of this story of unwavering engagement, and to give it a meaningful arc, would be to assume that one moves from the innocent belief that one can direct change and the grand certainty that one is right, to critique, to knowledge of complexity, and to humility. But, for me at least, that is not how it has been at all. Of course one hopes to benefit from second thoughts, more experience, critical analysis—even from growing wisdom. One strives to understand scale, to recognize that even the most successful organizing is but a piece, of a piece, of a piece of larger events one can seek (but rarely expect) to shape—events that break apart into an infinite diversity of narratives. But all my years of activism have also been shot through with moments when I denied impotence and indulged in gormless hope, states of mind that sustained me through actions that came to little (like our theory/action group Take Back The Future's endless marches against the U.S. attack on Iraq, 2002–2006), and actions that may well have contributed in some solid way to valuable political shifts (like a bunch of friends sitting in the rain at Zuccotti Park trying to add "feminism" to the mix in the first astonishing weeks of the massive uprising known as Occupy Wall Street, 2011).

Recently, a friend told me, "Occupy is finished." But how can she know? Occupy aspires to be everywhere; look for it under your boot soles. Occupy's inventive, dispersed actions brought back into open, loud expression both rage at injustice and utopian hopefulness, feelings that had long been suppressed in public life. The energy that came from this return is incalculable. Skepticism about Occupy Wall Street is easy to justify, but rising expectations have a long reach.

My entry into feminist organizing in East Central Europe, described in several essays in this collection, depended on the entirely mistaken idea that the shock of postcommunism would awaken an idealism and political intensity similar to that of 1968 in the United States, a time of revelation I longed to revisit. This ignorance gave way to knowledge and disillusion at once, but it was too late. I was hooked by the entirely different desires and fears arising for new friends in actually existing postcommunism; I stayed to slog along with them in the messy *vrai*. But no move to a linear narrative is intended here, no direct line from wishful fantasy to sober truth. Recognizing limitation is sensible but it is also inadequate. Embarrassing as I sometimes find it, I don't want to dismiss the value of the initial thrilling illusion; my ignorant excitement was determinative, and its ghost lingers in the work I continue to do in my activist travels in East Central Europe.

Uncertainty. Embracing uncertainty—since I can never get far beyond it—is both my temperament and the political aesthetic I can still sustain without tasting ashes. My field is literature, and the form I've been using for many years is the personal essay. What Doris Lessing has called "the small personal voice" is both a way of knowing and of exposing how little one knows. In these essays I have tried to offer unsettling details to mess up big stories with smaller ones.

At the end of her life, and in her most pained, apocalyptic mood, the feminist psychologist I have written about in this collection repeatedly, Dorothy Dinnerstein, saw uncertainty as our species' only hope. Human beings can't know if we can or will choose to save ourselves from ourselves. Uncertainty on this point is our best goad, both for acting, and for imagining a future.

Like many activists I know, I have written episodically, and I feel some consternation about the gaps. Why did I never write about my fifteen years in a small, consciousness-raising group; or about the smashing initial success of the Abortion Project that helped bring that right to New York in 1970 and the total failure of raising the same issue fifteen years later in Nicaragua; or about helping to start Gender Studies programs in various U.S. universities and, later, in Budapest, Krakow, and Kyrgyzstan? It's easier to understand why I never reflected in print about my premovement choice to work on the Edwardians—my subject for years as a PhD student of literature—the end product a (horribly lengthy) study of modern irony: *Ford Madox Ford and the Voice of Uncertainty*. (How unconsciously, comically revealing to use the word "uncertainty" in the title of two seemingly unrelated—but at some depth perhaps connected?—books.)

What can I offer now to get back the texture of those early, unrecorded days of feminist organizing? Here's a flash of memory:

> *I've been dispatched to organize a consciousness-raising group—the political form common to feminist action then—on New York's Upper West side. The twelve or so women in the room are nervous, but, in the wild zeitgeist of 1970, they intuit that they want this—whatever it is. I explain what these weekly discussions might do: encourage separation from the daily pressure to conform; suggest startlingly new subjects for thought and action; connect women to each other in entirely new ways; support new identities like lesbian, or divorced woman, or woman mad as hell—undermining shame.*
>
> *One woman is by far the most voluble and challenging. She asks me question after question, throwing doubt on feminism as possibly absurd, hopeless, divisive. At first, I keep answering as best I can. After all, these worries have some heft. But suddenly I realize that the boyfriend she keeps mentioning is in the room; these questions are his mean jabs at her nascent feminist feelings. Desperately, she is asking me to put words in her mouth to take home. I stop offering answers, dropping a claim to authority that feels false. Instead, I turn myself into her collaborator, analyzing and criticizing the world from which these phantom questions come. I am handing her a tray of destabilizing ideas she might be able to serve up to her disparaging lover.*
>
> *The meeting changes, becomes a discussion of the hostility they all expect to encounter beyond this room. The group is now established, and I move on to something else—at a speed that is urgency, but also youth.*

I find I want to add in retrospect: Youth, and the often-foolish certainties of youth. Our rising expectations were, as the boyfriend said, absurd—but also creative. The baby boom generation's dreams of total change, fostered by the careening growth of the postwar years in the United States, often led to success, which then some misread as the usual pace of victory. The brilliance and daring of the civil rights movement showed the way, and other movements joined in the expansion of hope.

The revival of feminism in the United States was a zone of invention. When we started, the books we needed to read were out of print—and most had yet to be written, and are still being written now. Any historical record of women's past resistance to prejudice, insult, and invisibility was absent from public memory. Women's suffering—of violence, of humiliation—was unremarked and unremarkable. An aspiring woman's ambitions were risible. One had to discover confidence without supporting evidence. Congress was virtually an all-male space, and so was the newspaper, the doctor's office, the union; leaders were almost always—and expected to be—male, including those in radical movements. The first job was to denaturalize this enveloping reality, to bring it back into history—and into struggle.

From the beginning I could see that feminism was a polyglot undertaking. In the early 1980s when I did my first international feminist actions, the multiplicity of feminist ideas and projects became even more obvious. Movements for gender justice offered wildly divergent accounts of themselves. But this instability added to the fascination. And, for me, at that point, maintaining such excitement was key. The loss of momentum in U.S. feminist activism in the 1980s threatened me with sadness and loss. I had committed myself and had to rethink the possible during those acute backlash years.

So, like many other feminists of that time, I left town. I went to the women's peace camp on Greenham Common in England (1983, 1984) and sat in the dirt with feminists of very different traditions. As we huddled in our plastic tents and around our campfires, feminists visited us from all over the world. Wandering from gate to gate of a huge missile installation, we were like a peripatetic philosophy school, arguing constantly. The fundamental differences among women couldn't have been made more obvious. But unlikely alliances kept forming. At Greenham, differences in identity, ideas, and political aesthetics could sometimes be productive.

Back home in New York, I was very active in what became known as the feminist sex wars of the 1980s. The powerful outburst of feminist rage against pornography in those years struck me as an overheated reaction to the obvious news that sexism would be around for a very long time. Male violence hadn't significantly changed, but now we had brought it out into the open for all to see. Antipornography feminists were expressing their shock at male resistance to women's liberation: Men are violent! Their sexual fantasies are disgusting! Sex is violence! These constructions of male sexuality struck me as the outcries of deeply disappointed people, who had hoped for so much more from feminist revolution. I worked for a number of years to counter what might almost be called a feminist sex panic: by participating in the planning group, convened by Carole Vance, of the Barnard Conference IX on sexuality (1982); by editing, with Christine Stansell and Sharon Thompson, *Powers of Desire: The Politics of Sexuality* (1983); by running a seminar at the New York Institute for the Humanities, "Sexuality and Consumer Culture" (1982–1994); and by working in the activist group, the Feminist Anti-Censorship Taskforce, (FACT, 1982–1986). Also in these years, I was writing about what core feminist problems and possible strategies were being obscured by a monolithic analysis of male sexuality. In a number of my reviews and articles from this period (I've included a typical one here, "The Beast Within," and several studies of Angela Carter), I was trying to explore in literary criticism the sensibility we were developing at the Barnard Conference and in FACT. We were discussing the variety and the common unreadability of desire in both men and women and calling for more exploration, less censure.

It felt particularly thankless to have to criticize other feminists as committed as oneself for taking the feminist movement in what I saw as a moralistic and self-defeating direction. Antipornography activists seemed to have no such qualms; they proclaimed the feminist groups that criticized them as *not* feminist by definition; in one confrontation, I was heckled as a Nazi. One can't help remarking that internecine fights are often the hottest—because of the tearing apart of what is also—in some ways—connected, and because other more powerful enemies are further off, indifferent, even harder to imagine as subject to change. Though we did angrily deconstruct the words of Ronald Reagan, we couldn't make much of a dent in what he was doing. For us, his victory in 1980 ushered in decades of reaction. The antipornography position seemed to us to recapitulate and fuel a growing repressive and self-righteous atmosphere.

For better and worse, the sex wars seem to have been unavoidable. They revealed some of the deep differences among feminists and clarified the limitations of feminist discourse on sexuality. They pointed to the need for greater freedom of inquiry in what Freud called the most ragged aspect of human personality. But important as I think our quest was for less repression in those dark times and for a more exploratory and open feminist conversation about sexuality, the internal rift had its costs.

Luckily for me during this period of difficult and repetitive discourse war among feminists, I was also carrying on a continuous conversation with the psychologist Dorothy Dinnerstein. I had interviewed her about her book, *The Mermaid and the Minotaur: Sexual Arrangements and Human Malaise*, in 1977. From then until her death in 1992, our endless talk branched and branched. Talking to Dorothy was, like Greenham, an ambulatory school. Her friends and students walked and talked with her along the palisades near her house and around the military installation at Seneca Falls in upstate New York, taking part in the ongoing women's peace camp there. Along the beaches of a Caribbean island, we walked, we talked, and she taught me to put on a mask and gaze for hours at life under the sea, a world I revisit whenever I can. How to see more and more—and differently—this is what the luminous Dorothy Dinnerstein had to teach.

Exchanges with Dorothy were free and speculative. She had a little loose love for all the world. When we went to see one of the early anti-Vietnam War movies, *Platoon*, I left the theater bubbling with outrage: That wasn't really an antiwar film as promised at all! The final images are all about male heroism—which only comes from being damaged and enlightened by war. The hero has come through, chastened but a Man. It's war that makes real men, etc., etc. After my fulminations were exhausted, Dorothy said, "Poor men." I said, "Poor men!?" "Yes," she said, "because they're so obedient." I was nonplussed. Why this of all the possible critical reactions after seeing this irritating film? "Well, in order to satisfy their fathers and each other they feel that they have to line up, armor themselves, and march off with their brothers to kill or be killed. Very few say no, though more have begun resisting in recent years, perhaps a symptom of a breakdown in gender rigidity." This train of thought seems obvious to me now. But back then, thinking about male insecurity, compliance, and passivity (traits on which women supposedly had a monopoly) opened up new questions, leading to an imaginative shift. Censoring pornography in order to discipline men seemed more and more off the mark. And the term "sexual deviance" became meaningless, an expression of fear about all sexuality.

On yet another track in these years, and very late in the game, I was considering having a baby, possibly influenced by a new pronatalism in my aging feminist generation, a shift in atmosphere that disturbed me and was suddenly everywhere—not only outside feminism's reach but also within. Dorothy had written about "the chagrins of the nursery" and here I was—my partner and I as ambivalent as ever—trying for motherhood, ultimately without success. This mixture of desire and doubts about that desire, oddly joined with the sex war struggles of the same period, gave rise to the section of this book, "Mothers/Lovers."

The years and years that feminists of my generation spent trying to get, then trying to keep, the right to abortion isn't recorded in the essays here. This demand had originally been a mere gateway to our wishes, and it was enraging, but also stupefying, to have to ask for something so basically and obviously just as, for example, funding for Medicaid abortions, which was lost in 1976, only three years after our Supreme Court victory in *Roe vs. Wade*. Much later, there I was again in our zap street theater group, No More Nice Girls, still asking for abortion—this time using satire and costumes to keep ourselves going. The pain, boredom, and humiliation of such repetitions seem to me to be largely unrecorded in feminist writing, though in 1923 Carrie Chapman Catt famously expressed the horror of such redundancy when she described efforts to get women the vote:

> To get the word male . . . out of the Constitution cost the women of the country fifty-two years of pauseless campaign. During that time they were forced to conduct fifty-six campaigns of referenda to male voters; 480 campaigns to urge Legislatures to submit suffrage amendments to voters; forty-seven campaigns to induce state constitutional conventions to write woman suffrage into state constitutions; 277 campaigns to persuade state party conventions to include woman suffrage planks; thirty campaigns to urge presidential party conventions to adopt woman suffrage planks in party platforms, and nineteen campaigns with nineteen successive Congresses.

By the end of the 1980s, I recall: Exhaustion.

Then, in 1989, came the days of wonder. Whole populations were freeing themselves from totalitarian rule with hardly a shot fired. The excitement invaded politics worldwide and, on the Left, a political location in which I still securely if combatively reside, shock ruled. The end of Western communism broke apart the Left thinking of over a century. We were all in disarray, writing books with titles like *After the Fall*. My reaction was to go right over there.

This move, made as I've said in ignorance, in a fantasy of new beginnings (but there are no new beginnings—cancel that absurd, redundant phrase) began an important new phase of my activist life. In 1991, I cofounded the nongovernmental organization, the Network of East-West Women (NEWW), and in 1992 I began teaching a graduate course about "gender" every summer in Poland in Elzbieta Matynia's brilliant school, "Democracy and Diversity." We set out to educate—and learn from—a whole new kind of person, one living, suddenly, amazingly, in postcommunism. What, we were all curious to know, was "postcommunism" going to look like—globally and day-to-day? Nothing has been more difficult or more intense than working with the brave and inventive—and the sometimes isolated or openly insulted—feminist activists of East Central Europe. Stoned by skinheads on gay pride marches, viciously attacked by the Catholic Church, often viewed as monsters in their own communities, these friends continue to propose a feminism to me both familiar and constantly new.

During all these years of activism, I've been a college professor—of literature and of gender studies. Why "gender studies," a controversial term? Some have feared that this newer name will once again make "women" disappear, a reasonable worry given the long history of such erasures. I have been a part of a number of collectives struggling to define and establish "Women's Studies" or "Women's and Gender Studies" or "Gender and Sexuality Studies" or, to include in this account an unusual effort at refinement, a "Gender Studies and Feminist Theory" program at The New School. (This MA program was canceled; some professors criticized feminist theory as bourgeois.) I prefer the term "Gender Studies" because, with Myra Jehlen, I am particularly interested in thinking about the line-drawing and blurring that goes on among various gender positions. Feminists have a positive stake in confronting the anxieties gender crossings arouse. In the face of backlash, using the word "gender" signals the possible value of this indeterminacy.

Has teaching students about gender been another form of feminist activism? I would like to maintain a distinction. There's nothing to be gained either by fusing theory and practice or by putting them in competition. At the same time, in repeating, loaded feminist debates, I hear a recurring glitch, a recalcitrant something that reminds me of the enduring divides I describe in "A Gender Diary." A constant wrangling about theory versus practice is endemic to our current social/political/institutional situations. We might as well embrace the complexity in current tensions between thought and action, and the ways in which we are often motivated—or forced—to move back and forth. Feminists in the university face a special dilemma. We have to trim to fast shifts in the shape of our schools, institutions which are, these days, endlessly stressed and over-stretched, constantly reorganizing themselves to sell their intangible wares and survive. The feminist professor must claim to have created fresh and innovative new turns of thought for each review period. She bites the hand that feeds her by critiquing the prevailing structures of knowledge, but she also knows she mustn't bite too hard. Given the difficulty of the stance "Gender Studies" in the university—who, after all, are its subjects, who its objects?—feminist professors are travelers between their roots in a great social movement and their equally important role as critics able to stand outside that fray, to create room for contemplation. In our insecure identity as both insiders and outsiders, at our best, we are among the most brilliant survivors in a tottering academic system.

I have navigated these dangerous waters with various personal solutions. (Activists once too idealistically said there are no personal solutions in a collective struggle.) It took years to get gender included as a category of study in my university. Balancing in air, I had to do this work while still insisting that any static concept of "feminist knowledge" offered no solid place to stand. In response to this dilemma, I have had a scattered academic life—only one foot in the academy, and the other—well, who can say where, given my picaresque activist career? Meanwhile, some of my colleagues in the university worry: Can teaching students and writing brilliantly about gender and race, as they do, count as politics? Is intellectual work and teaching *enough*? My response is: Why not? There's no authority to define "enough," and no one can determine the multiplier effect of our different locations. For now, no current utopian dream of synthesis (my usual temptation) can collapse what I see as a creative and uneven proliferation of feminist actions and theoretical speculations.

When the activist and the theorist are the same person, as they often are, these differences abide within. And, of course, these individual subjectivities are not stable or unitary—a common insight among theorists, but one that doesn't always carry over into the space they (we) give each other for ambivalence or self-contradiction.

Finally, writing, imagining, theorizing, doing—all are, at some level, practice. Nonetheless, granting them their differences widens the space for feminism to thrive. Though the activist spectacle is itself a thought experiment, the theorist knows all the ways in which the activist may be naïve, choosing wrong targets, chanting misleading words, foolishly imagining changes that are undertheorized or ill-conceived. (I shudder at the memory of certain signs I've carried at demonstrations. Note to self: Irony doesn't work on placards.) As the theorist knows, if wishes were horses, the poor would ride. There's that gap the theorist thinks about all the time, between wishes and horses, while the activist rushes on with no time to write it all down or to correct direction.

Over the years, in the gender studies classroom, I've come to worry about our graduate students' encounter with the theory/practice debates. Feminism is their legacy, but their brilliant education is constituting them as infinitely skeptical subjects. How can one be a feminist, they wonder, when one has learned about the movement's past and present gross over-simplifications, about all the blinkered feminist moments—of racism, of positivism, of collusion with neo-liberalism and neo-colonialism? Should feminism be outgrown as a flawed artifact of bourgeois culture? After all this piercing, relevant critique, how can they do intellectual work intended to have an impact on women's lot without seeming to regress, to abandon knowledge of feminism's checkered history? How can feminism, the movement, the commitment, survive so much thoughtful deconstruction, so much knowing?

I offer students an example of how different modes can coexist and how historical opportunities for change may not line up with what one thinks one ideally should be doing. I have both cofounded an international non-governmental organization and written a savagely critical article about such international NGOs, pointing out the many limitations of these cross-border projects, and the on-the-ground reasons why one is often stuck with this flawed form. The analytic work of feminism continues at an ever-changing angle to the buoyancy of activist projects.

I try to reassure these serious feminist students that it can all be inside one life: One acts and is unavoidably disappointed. One sees the pitfalls and tries—and often fails—to avoid them. Out of my particular temperament comes this small suggestion: "Don't fear the lack of a good fit between thought and action. The distance between what you should do and what you can always yawns wide. Why assume a monolithic, coherent model for your own subjectivity when you are becoming so sophisticated about the patchwork of all consciousness?"

In recent years, feminism in the academy has taken many important and suggestive turns. These critiques have meant much to me, particularly the work on intersectionality, on queer theory, on the importance of affect to politics, on eco-politics and posthumanism, on the rich possible uses of our history, often to be reencountered in archives. In response, I have often changed my thinking about what and how to teach and about what organizing should—or can—be done. The essays collected here reflect different moments in this constant reassessment. Because feminism is a portmanteau term, describing varied long-term collective enterprises in which the building blocks—subjectivity, experience, nature, culture—are always being rethought and reengaged in daily living, a flat identity "feminist" can only be a general marker of changing interests and desires.

Dear Students, I would say, people who imagine change are of divided mind. Since there is no leader, no credentialing authority, no gatekeeper to say "No entry here; you're not a real feminist," fortunately and unfortunately, feminism can't maintain a fixed stance and must always struggle for always-shifting affiliations and aesthetics. So—criticize away. Feminists need and will always have agonistic relationships not only with the world but among themselves. Don't swamp with paralyzing doubt what might be your small piece of the larger, evolving project. Feminism is a sensibility, subject to constant revision, but very portable. Even as you change, you can take it with you.

To The Archive

> Utopianism is always addressed to the future, so when
> feminists wrote those revolutionary words in 1970, surely
> they were meant for us, the later generations.
> —Kate Eichhorn

> Take my life. But don't take the meaning of my life. —Joanna Russ

> . . . time makes what was mute talk. —Henry Shapiro

> The living and the dead can move back and forth as they like.
> —Austerlitz, W. G. Sebald

> . . . The will to remember . . .
> —Joan Nestle describing the moving force and multiple
> powers of the Lesbian Herstory Archives

A few years ago, a university bought my papers. Twenty-two boxes left the house—tapes of radio shows (now, amazingly, digitized), meeting notes, handwritten talks, women's movement ephemera—from the U.S. in the 70s and onward, and from the first independent women's movements in East Central Europe since 1989. There's easily as much again still sitting in my apartment, all of it promised in the years ahead.

The difference this has made to me is remarkable. A deep shift: I feel rescued.

> Urgent group email. F.R. has died, and her books and papers are sitting on a
> curb in Greenwich Village, waiting for the garbage truck. Hurry, someone, to
> pick up this stuff. But it turns out we all continue to be desperately busy. No
> one comes.

Before all those dusty files went to the archive, I feared collecting essays written over thirty-five years. The danger, I thought, would lie in melancholy—

both mine and the reader's. The voices of earlier selves would put me to shame and eager enthusiasms frozen on the page would remind me of possibly jejune passions that motivated me from my first political action, a ban-the-bomb vigil on the Cornell quadrangle in 1961—and onward for five decades. Could the essays I chose—published in such disparate and sometimes obscure places, at such different times, with such different motives—add to each other, travel, change their meaning in new combinations? Or would time prove a thief and rob them of all resonance in the now? Though others will have to answer such questions, the process of selection has taught me much. The way this book has been organized follows a train of thought about what categories have remained salient for me in the ups and downs of a long feminist history.

> A Gender Studies meeting in the mid-nineties: I've just been introduced to one of our new graduate students. When she hears my name, she gasps and blurts out "You're history!" Of course she immediately hears herself and rushes to apologize since, whether a specter from the past or not, I am still sitting there, one of the professors in her program. The concept "generations" may be misleading. In fact we are in this undertaking, call it feminism, together—changeable as it will no doubt prove to be.

Teaching over decades, I have noticed the truth of Doris Lessing's observation that ideas move through societies like tides. There was the time in the early 1970s when I could disparage romantic fantasies to flocks of young students who greeted my skepticism with eager delight. Then, suddenly, as if a gong had sounded and hopes for new forms of fantasy had evaporated, my irony at the expense of romance fell dead in the theater of the classroom. Students looked uncomprehending, or anxious, or rejecting. To my shock, my tone of only a year before had turned out to be the language of another country, a bygone era. Expectations were closing down and it was becoming harder for young women to imagine autonomy as a source of pleasure rather than of shame or loneliness.

After some years of this sometimes-galling eclipse, again the times turned. Journalists and researchers started calling me because "I was history," and this new attention heartened me, however little, I told myself, that I actually cared about it. The glitterati came, and asked me questions that touched me deeply: "How did you make demonstrations happen?" I thought it odd that they had no idea of this, and then realized their brilliant machines and devices gave them means of assembling their large networks in ways that are entirely different from the movement-building structures of the 1970s. To their wonderment, we had made an extremely durable social revolution before the invention of the Internet.

Because I have sustained a political passion like feminism through changing landscapes at home, through far-flung travels, through quite different stages of my life, I have taken a particular tour through the vagaries of time. But before the beautiful mess of the archive, all this material seemed trapped in a flattened seam of history. I felt pegged: "Second Wave Feminist," "Socialist Feminist," "Peace Movement Feminist," "Anti-Antipornography Feminist" otherwise known to journalists as the "Pro-Sex Faction" (what hilarious nomenclature). I now think that the depression I was feeling was symptomatic of an actively regressive construction of time and history: the zeitgeist at the height of backlash was obliterating what had earlier felt thrillingly diverse. Backlash sought to *impose* linearity on stories that were never linear—so that feminism could be given an end. I felt superannuated and sorrowful and, as the feminist affect theorists so wittily say, such depression should sometimes be recognized as a political, not a private, feeling. (I want one of those wonderful buttons these feminists wear at demonstrations: "Depressed? Maybe it's political.")

When Rachel Blau DuPlessis and I sent out our call for activist memoirs around 1992, a collection that became *The Feminist Memoir Project*, we were trying to save a generation from an oblivion that seemed to be swiftly overtaking us, and at the same time, to take apart the idea that feminist activists in the United States in the 60s and 70s were in any sense a "generation" at all. They were never a single, coherent group or engaged on a central project. Feminist activists who had invented an astonishing variety of antisexist acts when such rebellions seemed new, were being shoveled together into a single group, the Second Wave, then criticized for movement exclusions, then slated—all together—to be conveniently forgotten. This narrowing of narratives deeply upset us, and we sought accounts of activist life from those early days—across differences of race, class, sexualities, local contexts, and diversities of both survival needs and utopian wishes. *"Take my life. But don't take the meaning of my life."* Which I would amend: Dear Young Feminists, interpret "the meaning" of our lives as you will, and as you need.

It helped that I had a young colleague, Kate Eichhorn, who wanted to hear such memories, with their feelings and contexts attached, and without apology. She was studying the informal creation of zines made by young Riot Grrrls in the 90s, and she found earlier feminist texts collaged there—a connection, a recognition, an appropriation, sometimes perhaps a turn or return. The curiosity she and many others have shown in what her book calls "the archival turn in feminism" has brought water to what I feared would become a desert. No one can know what seeds future feminists will want to nurture or transplant from this garden. But my earlier dead-end feeling? Gone. Thank you.

The essays collected here are time-marked. Beyond some cutting of redundancies and some line editing, I haven't revised them; they are not meant to offer an end point of accumulated feminist understanding. Because of their specificity, they are (somewhat) safe from certain crimes of anachronism, and reveal particular patterns and emphases in discourse that are otherwise nearly irretrievable. (Foucault's "law of the sayable.") Gradually, while choosing and arranging these essays, and inspired by conversations with young feminists who are already poking around in my archive, I began to feel that the concept "dated" was dated.

The essays represent (relatively) still points in a steady flow of activity, while the archive has no framing devices, no conscious pattern. Often, I suspect, the archive registers what one has chosen to forget and what must therefore be assembled by others (those fizzy, early polemics are no doubt in there in various drafts!). I feel both dismembered and connected to an unreadable future. There's a sort of freedom in having no idea what is in those boxes of air checks, agendas, rough drafts. The essays are mine, but the archive is, ultimately, for others to mull over. The material to be discovered there is potentially new; these bits and pieces await. . . . Well, I can't imagine who you will be.

Having my papers in the archives is a state of fluidity in time that I never dreamed of—and I feel all the anxieties and hopes that accompany stories without endings. I'm happy to have managed whatever distillation I could in the essays here. But I value, too, the flowing water not contained in jars.

2014

I

CONTINUING A GENDER DIARY

I

A GENDER DIARY

*In the early days of this wave of the women's movement, I sat in a weekly
consciousness-raising group with my friend A. We compared notes recently:
What did you think was happening? How did you think our own lives were going
to change? A. said she had felt, "Now I can be a woman; it's no longer so
humiliating. I can stop fantasizing that secretly I am a man, as I used to, before I
had children. Now I can value what was once my shame." Her answer amazed me.
Sitting in the same meetings during those years, my thoughts were roughly the
reverse: "Now I don't have to be a woman anymore. I need never become a mother.
Being a woman has always been humiliating, but I used to assume there was no
exit. Now the very idea 'woman' is up for grabs. 'Woman' is my slave name;
feminism will give me freedom to seek some other identity altogether."*

On its face this clash of theoretical and practical positions may seem absurd,
but it is my goal to explore such contradictions, to show why they are not
absurd at all. Feminism is inevitably a mixed form, requiring in its very nature such inconsistencies. In what follows I try to show first, that a common
divide keeps forming in both feminist thought and action between the need
to build the identity "woman" and give it solid political meaning and the
need to tear down the very category "woman" and dismantle its all-too-solid
history. Feminists often split along the lines of some version of this argument, and that splitting is my subject. Second, I argue that though a settled
compromise between these positions is currently impossible, and though a
constant choosing of sides is tactically unavoidable, feminists—and indeed
most women—live in a complex relationship to this central feminist divide.
From moment to moment we perform subtle psychological and social negotiations about just how gendered we choose to be.

This tension—between needing to act as women and needing an identity not overdetermined by our gender—is as old as Western feminism. It is at the core of what feminism is. The divide runs, twisting and turning, right through movement history. The problem of identity it poses was barely conceivable before the eighteenth century, when almost everyone saw women as a separate species. Since then absolute definitions of gender difference have fundamentally eroded, and the idea "woman" has become a question rather than a given.

In the current wave of the movement, the divide is more urgent and central a part of feminism than ever before. On the one hand, many women moved by feminism are engaged by its promise of solidarity, the poetry of a retrieved worth. It feels glorious to "reclaim an identity they taught [us] to despise." (The line is Michelle Cliff's.) Movement passion rescues women-only groups from contempt; female intimacy acquires new meanings and becomes more threatening to the male exclusiveness so long considered "the world."

On the other hand, other feminists, often equally stirred by solidarity, rebel against having to be "women" at all. They argue that whenever we uncritically accept the monolith "woman," we run the risk of merely relocating ourselves inside the old closed ring of an unchanging feminine nature. But is there any such reliable nature? These feminists question the eternal sisterhood. It may be a pleasure to be "we," and it may be strategically imperative to struggle as "we," but who, they ask, are "we"?[1]

This diary was begun to sort out my own thoughts about the divide. I have asked myself, is the image of a divide too rigid, will it only help to build higher the very boundaries I seek to wear down? Yet I keep stumbling on this figure in my descriptions of daily movement life. Perhaps the problem is my own. But others certainly have shared the experience of "division." Maybe the image works best as a place to start, not as a conclusion. A recurring difference inside feminism seems to lie deep, but it is also mobile, changing in emphasis, not (I'm happy to say) very orderly.

Take as an example my checkered entries about the women's peace movement. A number of feminists, myself included, felt uneasy about the new wave of women-only peace groups of the early 1980s. As feminist peace activist Ynestra King characterized the new spirit: "A feminist peace sensibility is forming; it includes new women's culture and traditional women's culture."[2] Some saw such a fusion between traditional female solidarity and new women's forms of protest as particularly powerful. Others felt that the two were at cross-purposes. Might blurring them actually lead to a watering down of feminism? The idea that women are by definition more nurturant, life giving, and less belligerent than men is very old; the idea that such gender distinctions are social, hence subject to change, is much more recent, fragile, counterintuitive, and contested. Can the old idea of female specialness and the newer idea of a female outlook forged in social oppression join in a movement? And just how?

> A study group met for a time in 1983 to talk about women's peace politics.[3] I was the irritating one in our group, always anxious about the nature of our project. I was the one who always nagged, "Why a women's peace movement?"
>
> I argued with a patient Amy Swerdlow that women asking men to protect the children (as Women Strike for Peace asked Congress in 1961) was a repetition of an old, impotent, suppliant's gesture. Men had waged wars in the name of just such protection. And besides, did we want a world where only women worried about the children?[4] "So what's your solution?" the good-tempered group wanted to know. "Should women stop worrying about the children? Who trusts men to fill the gap?" Amy described how the loving women, going off to Washington to protest against nuclear testing, filled their suburban freezers with dinners so their families would miss them less.
>
> I tried to explain the source of my resistance to the motherly rhetoric of the women's peace movement. During the 1960s, some of us had angrily offered to poison men's private peace, abort men's children. We proposed a bad girl's exchange: We'd give up protection for freedom, give up the approval we got for nurturance in exchange for the energy we'd get from open anger.
>
> Of course, I knew what the group would ask me next, and rightly, too: "Whose freedom? Which rage? Isn't abandoning men's project of war rage enough? And is women's powerlessness really mother's fault?" Although I reminded the group that the new wave of feminists never blamed motherhood as much as the media claimed, we did run from it, like the young who scrawled the slogan on Paris walls in 1968: "Cours, camarade, le vieux monde est derriére toi." (Run, comrade, the past is just behind you.)

This scene is caricature, but it begins to get at the mood of our group. Fractious, I was always asking the others if they didn't agree that peace is assumed to be a women's issue for all the wrong reasons. I argued that if there is to be no more "women-only" when it comes to emotional generosity or trips to the laundry, why "women-only" in the peace movement? Maybe the most radical thing we could do would be to refuse the ancient women-peace connection? The army is a dense locale of male symbols, actions, and forms of association, so let men sit in the drizzle with us at the gates of military installations. Even if theorists emphasize the contingent and the historical and say that peace is an issue that affects women *differently* from men because of our different social position, we are trapped again in an inevitably over-simplified idea of "women." Are *all* women affected the same way by war? Or is class or age or race or nationality as important a variable? What do we gain, I asked the group, when we name the way we suffer from war as a specifically *women's* suffering? And so it went.

Until one day Ynestra King tactfully suggested that perhaps I was seeking a mixed group to do my peace activism. (Mixed is a code word for men and women working together.) I was horrified. We were laughing, I'm pleased to recall, as I confessed myself reluctant to do political work in mixed groups. The clichés about women in the male Left making the coffee and doing the xeroxing were all literally true in my case. (I blame myself as well; often I chose those tasks, afraid of others.) Only by working with women had I managed to develop an intense and active relationship to politics at all. Not only had my political identity been forged in the women-only mold, but the rich networks I had formed inside feminism were the daily source of continued activism. My experience of the women-only peace camp at Greenham Common, England was to become a source of continued political energy and inspiration. Women-only (the abstraction) was full of problems; women-only (the political reality in my life) was full of fascination, social pleasure, debates about meaning in the midst of actions taken, even sometimes, victories won.

The political meaning of these sides changes, as does the place they hold in each woman's life. But no matter where each feminist finds herself in the argument about the meaning of women-only, all agree that in practical political work, separate women's groups are necessary. Whatever the issue, feminists have gained a great deal by saying, "We are 'women,' and this is what 'women' want." This belief in some ground of shared experience is the social basis from which any sustained political struggle must come.

Even feminists like myself, anxious about any restatement of a female ideal—of peacefulness or nurturance or light—are constantly forced in practice to consider what activists lose if we choose to say peace is *not* a women's issue. We keep rediscovering the necessity to speak specifically as women when we speak of peace because the female citizen has almost no representation in the places where decisions about war and peace are made—the Congress, the corporation, the army.

In 1979, President Jimmy Carter fired former congresswoman Bella Abzug from her special position as co-chair of his National Advisory Commission for Women because the women on the commission insisted on using that platform to talk about war and the economy. These, said the President, were not women's issues; women's role was to support the President. Carter was saying in effect that women have no place in general social debate, that women, as we learned from the subsequent presidential campaign, are a "special interest group."

What a conundrum for feminists: Because women have little general representation in Congress, our demand to be citizens—gender unspecified—can be made only through gender solidarity; but when we declare ourselves separate, succeed, for example, in getting our own government commission, the President turns around and tries to make that power base into a ghetto where only certain stereotypically female issues can be named. So, however separate we may choose to be, our "separate" has to be different from his "separate," a distinction it's hard to keep clear in our own and other minds, but one we must keep trying to make.

This case may seem beside the point to radicals who never vested any hope in the federal government in the first place. But the firing of Bella Abzug was a perfect public embodiment of the puzzle of women's situation. The idea that "women" can speak about war is itself the unsettled question, requiring constant public tests. It is no coincidence that Bella Abzug was one of the organizers of Women Strike for Peace in 1961. She must have observed the strengths and weaknesses in the public image of mothers for peace; then, on the coattails of feminism, she tried to be an insider, a congresswoman presumably empowered to speak—as a woman, or for women, or for herself—on any public topic. People with social memory were able to witness the problem that arises for the public woman, no matter what her stance. Feminism is potentially radical in almost all its guises precisely because it interprets this injustice, makes the Abzug impasse visible. Once visible, it begins to feel intolerable.[5]

By traveling along the twisted track of this argument, I have made what I think is a representative journey, what feminist historians such as Joan Kelly and Denise Riley have called an "oscillation," which is typical of both feminist theory and practice.[6] Such oscillations are inevitable for the foreseeable future. In a cruel irony that is one mark of women's oppression, when women speak *as women* they run a special risk of not being heard because the female voice is by our culture's definition that-voice-you-can-ignore. But the alternative is to pretend that public men speak for women or that women who speak inside male-female forums are heard and heeded as much as similarly placed men. Few women feel satisfied that this neutral (almost always male) public voice reflects the particulars of women's experience, however varied and indeterminate that experience may be.

Caught between not being heard because we are different and not being heard because we are invisible, feminists face a necessary strategic leap of nerve every time we shape a political action. We weigh the kinds of powerlessness women habitually face; we choose our strategy—as women, as citizens—always sacrificing some part of what we know.

Because "separate" keeps changing its meaning depending on how it is achieved and in what larger context its political forms unfold, there is no fixed progressive position, no final theoretical or practical resting place for feminists attempting to find a social voice for women. Often our special womanness turns into a narrow space only a moment after we celebrate it; at other times, our difference becomes a refuge and source of new work, just when it looked most like a prison in which we are powerless. And finally, although women differ fundamentally about the meaning and value of "woman," we all live partly in, partly out of this identity by social necessity. Or as Denise Riley puts it, "Women are not women in all aspects of their lives."[7]

Peace is *not* a women's issue; at the same time, if women don't claim a special relationship to general political struggles, we will experience that other, more common specialness reserved for those named women: We will be excluded from talking about and acting on the life and death questions that face our species.

Names for a Recurring Feminist Divide

In every case, the specialness of women has this double face, though often, in the heat of new confrontations, feminists suffer a harmful amnesia; we forget about this paradox we live with. Feminist theorists keep renaming this tension, as if new names could advance feminist political work. But at this point new names are likely to tempt us to forget that we have named this split before. In the service of trying to help us recognize what we are fated—for some time—to repeat, here is a reminder of past taxonomies.

Minimizers and Maximizers

The divide so central as to be feminism's defining characteristic goes by many names. Catharine Stimpson cleverly called it the feminist debate between the "minimizers" and the "maximizers."[8] Briefly, the minimizers are feminists who want to undermine the category "woman," to minimize the meaning of sex difference. (As we shall see, this stance can have surprisingly different political faces.) The maximizers want to keep the category (or feel they can't do otherwise), but they want to change its meaning, to reclaim and elaborate the social being "woman," and to empower her.

Radical Feminists and Cultural Feminists

In *Daring to Be Bad: A History of the Radical Feminist Movement in America, 1967–1975*, Alice Echols sees this divide on a time line of the current women's movement, with "radical feminism" more typical of the initial feminist impulse in this wave succeeded by "cultural feminism." Echols's definition of the initial bursts of "radical feminism" shows that it also included "cultural feminism" in embryo. She argues that both strains were present from the first—contradictory elements that soon proclaimed themselves as tensions in sisterhood. Nonetheless, the earlier groups usually defined the commonality of "women" as the shared fact of their oppression by "men." Women were to work separately from men not as a structural ideal but because such separation was necessary to escape a domination that only a specifically feminist (rather than mixed, Left) politics could change. Echols gives as an example Kathie Sarachild, who disliked the women's contingents at peace marches against the Vietnam War: "Only if the *stated* purpose of a women's group is to fight against the relegation of women to a separate position and status, in other words, to fight for women's liberation, only then does a separate women's group acquire a revolutionary character. Then separation becomes a base for power rather than a symbol of powerlessness."[9]

On the other side stands Echols's category, "cultural feminism." In her depiction of the divide, the cultural feminist celebration of being female was a retreat from "radical feminism": "It was easier to rehabilitate femininity than to abolish gender."[10] She offers as a prime example of the growth of cultural feminism the popularity of Jane Alpert's "new feminist theory," published in *Ms.* magazine in 1973 as "Mother Right":

Feminists have asserted that the essential difference between women and men does not lie in biology but rather in the roles that patriarchal societies (men) have required each sex to play. . . . However, a flaw in this feminist argument has persisted: *it contradicts our felt experience of the biological difference between the sexes as one of immense significance.* . . . The unique consciousness or sensibility of women, the particular attributes that set feminist art apart, and a compelling line of research now being pursued by feminist anthropologists all point to the idea that *female biology is the basis of women's powers.* Biology is hence the source and not the enemy of feminist revolution.[11]

Echols concludes that by 1973, "Alpert's contention that women were united by their common biology was enormously tempting, given the factionalism within the movement."[12]

Ironically, then, the pressure of differences that quickly surfaced in the women's movement between lesbians and straight women, between white and black, between classes, was a key source of the new pressure toward unity. The female body offered a permanence and an immediately rich identity that radical feminism, with its call to a long, often negative struggle of resistance, could not.

As her tone reveals, in Echols's account, "radical feminism" is a relatively positive term and "cultural feminism" an almost entirely negative one. As I'll explain later, I have a number of reasons for sharing this judgment. Finally, though, it won't help us to understand recurring feminist oppositions if we simply sort them into progressive versus reactionary alignments. The divide is nothing so simple as a split between truly radical activists and benighted conservative ones, or between real agents for change and liberal reformers, or between practical fighters and sophisticated theorists. The sides in this debate don't line up neatly in these ways. Maximizers and minimizers have political histories that converge and diverge. But a pretense of neutrality won't get us anywhere either. I'm describing a struggle here, and every account of it contains its overt or covert tropism toward one side or the other.

Essentialists and Social Constructionists

We have only to move from an account of movement politics to one of feminist theory in order to reverse Echols's scenario of decline. In academic feminist discussion, the divide between the "essentialists" and the "social constructionists" has been a rout for the essentialists. Briefly, essentialists (like Alpert, above) see gender as rooted in biological sex differences. Hardly anyone of any camp will now admit to being an essentialist, since the term has become associated with a naive claim to an eternal female nature. All the same, essentialism, like its counterpart, cultural feminism, is abundantly present in current movement work. When Barbara Deming writes that "the capacity to bear and nurture children gives women a special consciousness, a spiritual advantage rather than a disadvantage," she is assigning an enduring meaning to anatomical sex differences. When Andrea Dworkin describes how through sex a woman's "insides are worn away over time, and she, possessed, becomes weak, depleted, usurped in all her physical and mental energies . . . by the one who occupies her," she is asserting that in sex women are immolated as a matter of course, in the nature of things.[13]

Social construction—the idea that the meaning of the body is changeable—is far harder to embrace with confidence. As Ellen Willis once put it, culture may shape the body, but we feel that the body has ways of pushing back.[14] To assert that the body has no enduring, natural language often seems like a rejection of common sense. Where can a woman stand—embodied or disembodied—in the flow of this argument?

Writing not about gender in general but about that more focused issue of bodies and essences, sexuality, Carole Vance has raised questions about the strengths and vicissitudes of social construction theory. She observes that the social constructionists who try to discuss sexuality differ about just what is constructed. Few would go so far as to say that the body plays no part at all as a material condition on which we build desire and sexual mores. But even for those social constructionists who try to escape entirely from any a priori ideas about the body, essentialism makes a sly comeback through unexamined assumptions. For example, how can social constructionists confidently say they are studying "sexuality"? If there is no essential, transhistorical biology of arousal, then there is no unitary subject, "sexuality," to discuss: "If sexuality is constructed differently at each time and place, can we use the term in a comparatively meaningful way? . . . Have constructionists undermined their own categories? Is there an 'it' to study?"[15]

In the essentialist-versus-social constructionist version of the divide, one can see that one term in the argument is far more stable than the other. Essentialism, such as Jane Alpert's in "Mother Right," assumes a relatively stable social identity in "male" and "female," while as Carole Vance argues, social construction is at its best as a source of destabilizing questions. By definition, social construction theory cannot offer a securely bounded area for the study of gender; instead it initiates an inspiring collapse of gender verities.

Cultural Feminists and Post-Structuralists

The contrast between more and less stable categories suggests yet another recent vocabulary for the feminist divide. In "Cultural Feminism versus Post-Structuralism: The Identity Crisis in Feminist Theory," Linda Alcoff puts Echols's definition of "cultural feminism" up against what she sees as a more recent counterdevelopment: feminist post-structural theory. By speaking only of "the last ten years," Alcoff lops off the phase of "radical feminism" that preceded "cultural feminism" in movement history, leaving the revisionist image of extreme essentialism (such as Mary Daly's in *Gyn/Ecology*) as the basic matrix of feminist thought from which a radical "nominalism" has more recently and heroically departed, calling all categories into doubt.[16] It is no accident that with attention to detail, Alice Echols can trace a political decline from "radical feminism" to "cultural feminism" between 1967 and 1975, while Linda Alcoff can persuasively trace a gain in theoretical understanding from "cultural feminism" to "post-structuralism" between 1978 and 1988. Put them together and both narratives change: Instead of collapse or progress, we see one typical oscillation in the historical life of the divide.

These two accounts are also at odds because they survey very different political locations: Echols is writing about radical feminist activism, Alcoff about developments in academic feminist theory. Though political activism has developed a different version of the central debate from that of the more recent academic feminism, both confront the multiple problems posed by the divide. Nor will a model that goes like this work: *thesis* (essentialism, cultural feminism), *antithesis* (post-structuralism, deconstruction, Lacanian psychoanalysis), *synthesis* (some stable amalgam of women's solidarity that includes radical doubts about the formation, cohesion, and potential power of the group).

Instead, the divide keeps forming *inside* each of these categories. It is fundamental at any level one cares to meet it: material, psychological, linguistic. For example, U.S. feminist theorists don't agree about whether post-structuralism tends more often toward its own version of essentialism (strengthening the arguments of maximizers by recognizing an enduring position of female Other) or whether post-structuralism is instead the best tool minimalists have (weakening any universalized, permanent concept such as Woman).[17] Certainly post-structuralists disagree among themselves, and this debate around and inside post-structuralism should be no surprise. In feminist discourse a tension keeps forming between finding a useful lever in female identity and seeing that identity as hopelessly compromised.

I'm not regressing here to the good old days of an undifferentiated, under-theorized sisterhood, trying to blur distinctions others have usefully struggled to establish, but I do want to explore a configuration—the divide—that repeats in very different circumstances. For example, in an earlier oscillation, both radical feminism and liberal feminism offered their own versions of doubt about cultural feminism and essentialism. Liberal feminists refused the idea that biology should structure women's public and sometimes even their private roles. Radical feminists saw the creation and maintenance of gender difference as the means by which patriarchs controlled women.[18] Though neither group had the powerful theoretical tools later developed by the post-structuralists, both intimated basic elements in post-structuralist work: that the category "woman" was a construction, a discourse over which there had been an ongoing struggle; and that the self, the "subject," was as much the issue as were social institutions. To be sure, these early activists often foolishly ignored Freud; they invoked an unproblematic "self" that could be rescued from the dark male tower of oppression; and they hourly expected the radical deconstruction of gender, as if the deconstruction of what had been constructed was relatively easy. Nonetheless, radical, philosophical doubts about the cohesion of "woman" have roots that go all the way down in the history of both liberal and radical feminism.

Recently I asked feminist critic Marianne DeKoven for a piece she and Linda Bamber wrote about the divide for the Modern Language Association in 1982. "Feminists have refined our thinking a great deal since then," she said. Yes, no doubt; but there is not much from the recent past that we can confidently discard. In fact, the Bamber-DeKoven depiction of the divide remains useful because we are nowhere near a synthesis that would make these positions relics of a completed phase. One side of the divide, Bamber says in her half of the paper, "has been loosely identified with American feminism, the other with French feminism."

But in fact these labels are inadequate, as both responses can be found in the work of both French and American feminists. Instead of debating French vs. American feminism, then, I want to define the two poles of our responses nonjudgmentally and simply list their characteristics under Column A and Column B.

Column A feminism is political, empirical, historical. A Column A feminist rebels against the marginalization of women and demands access to "positions that require knowledge and confer power." A Column A feminist insists on woman as subject, on equal pay for equal work, on the necessity for women to be better represented in political life, the media, history books, etc. Column A feminism assumes, as Marks and de Cour-tivron put it, "that women have (always) been present but invisible and if they look they will find themselves."

The Column B feminist, on the other hand, is not particularly interested in the woman as subject. Instead of claiming power, knowledge and high culture for women, Column B feminism attacks these privileged quan-tities as "phallogocentric." . . . The feminine in Column B is part of the challenge to God, money, the phallus, origins and ends, philosophical privilege, the transcendent author, representation, the Descartian cogito, transparent language, and so on. The feminine is valorized as fragment, absence, scandal. . . . Whereas the Column A feminist means to occupy the center on equal terms with men, the Column B feminist, sometimes aided by Derrida, Lacan, Althusser, Levi-Strauss, and Foucault, subverts the center and endorses her own marginality.[19]

No doubt Bamber and DeKoven would restate these terms now in the light of eight more years of good, collective feminist work, but I am trying to write against the grain of that usually excellent impulse here, trying to suggest a more distant perspective in which eight years become a dot.

Alcoff is only the latest in a long line of frustrated feminists who want to push beyond the divide, to be done with it. She writes typically: "We cannot simply embrace the paradox. In order to avoid the serious disadvantages of cultural feminism and post-structuralism, feminism needs to transcend the dilemma by developing a third course."[20] But "embracing the paradox" is just what feminism cannot choose but do. There is no transcendence, no third course. The urgent contradiction women constantly experience between the pressure to be a woman and the pressure not to be one will change only through a historical process; it cannot be dissolved through thought alone.

This is not to undervalue theory in the name of some more solid material reality but to emphasize that the dualism of the divide requires constant work; it resists us. It's not that we can't interrupt current patterns, not that trying to imagine our way beyond them isn't valuable, but that such work is continual.[21] What is more, activists trying to make fundamental changes, trying to push forward the feminist discourse and alter its material context, don't agree about what sort of synthesis they want. Nor can activists turn to theorists in any direct way for a resolution of these differences. Activism and scholarship have called forth different readings of the divide, but neither of these locations remains innocent of the primary contradiction. There is no marriage of theoretical mind and activist brawn to give us New Feminist Woman. The recognition that binary thinking is a problem doesn't offer us any immediate solution.

In other words, neither cultural feminism nor post-structuralism suggests a clear course when the time comes to discuss political strategy. Though we have learned much, we are still faced with the continuing strategic difficulty of *what to do*. As Michèle Barrett puts it: "It does not need remarking that the postmodernist point of view is explicitly hostile to any political project behind the ephemeral."[22] The virtue of the ephemeral action is its way of evading ossification of image or meaning. Ephemerally, we can recognize a possibility we cannot live out, imagine a journey we cannot yet take. We begin: The category "woman" is a fiction; then, post-structuralism suggests ways in which human beings live by fictions; then, in its turn, activism requires of feminists that we elaborate the fiction "woman" as if she were not a provisional invention at all but a person we know well, one in need of obvious rights and powers. Activism and theory weave together here, working on what remains the same basic cloth, the stuff of feminism.

Some theorists like Alcoff reach for a synthesis, a third way, beyond the divide, while others like Bamber and DeKoven choose instead the metaphor of an inescapable, irreducible "doubleness"—a word that crops up everywhere in feminist discussion. To me, the metaphor of doubleness is the more useful: it is a reminder of the unresolved tension on which feminism continues to be built. As Alice Walker puts it in her formal definition of a "womanist" (her word for a black feminist): "Appreciates and prefers women's culture, women's emotional flexibility . . . committed to survival and wholeness of entire people, male and female. Not a separatist, except periodically, for health."[23]

This is not to deny change but to give a different estimate of its rate. Mass feminist consciousness has made a great difference; we have created not only new expectations but also new institutions. Yet, inevitably, the optimism of activism has given way to the academic second thoughts that tell us why our work is so hard. For even straightforward, liberal changes—like equal pay or day care—are proving far more elusive than feminists dreamed in 1970. We are moving more slowly than Western women of the late twentieth century can easily accept—or are even likely to imagine.

Motherists and Feminists

If the long view has a virtue beyond the questionable one of inducing calm, it can help feminists include women to whom a rapid political or theoretical movement forward has usually seemed beside the point—poor women, peasant women, and women who for any number of reasons identify themselves not as feminists but as militant mothers, fighting together for survival. In a study group convened by Temma Kaplan since 1985, Grass Roots Movements of Women, feminists who do research about such movements in different parts of the world, past and present, have been meeting to discuss the relationship among revolutionary action, women, and feminist political consciousness. As Meredith Tax described this activism:

> There is a crux in women's history/women's studies, a knot and a blurry place where various things converge. This place has no name and there is no established methodology for studying it. The things that converge there are variously called: community organizations, working-class women's organizations, consumer movements, popular mass organizations, housewives' organizations, mothers' movements, strike support movements, bread strikes, revolutions at the base, women's peace movements. Some feminist or protofeminist groups and united front organizations of women may be part of this crux. Or they may be different. There is very little theory, either feminist or Marxist, regarding this crux.[24]

The group has been asking: Under what class circumstances do women decide to band together as women, break out of domestic space, and publicly protest? What part have these actions actually played in gaining fundamental political changes? How do women define what they have done and why? Does it make any sense to name feminist thinking as part of this female solidarity? Is there reason to think some kind of feminist consciousness is likely to emerge from this kind of political experience? Is the general marginality of these groups a strength or a weakness?

Almost all the women we have been studying present themselves to the world as mothers (hence, "motherists") acting for the survival of their children. Their groups almost always arise when men are forced to be absent (because they are migrant workers or soldiers) or in times of crisis, when the role of nurturance assigned to women has been rendered impossible. Faced with the imperatives of their traditional work (to feed the children, to keep the family together) and with the loss of bread, or mobility, or whatever they need to do that work, women can turn into a military force, breaking the shop windows of the baker or the butcher, burning the pass cards, assembling to confront the police state, sitting in where normally they would never go—on the steps of the governor's house, at the gates of the cruise missile base.

As feminists, it interested us to speculate about whether the women in these groups felt any kind of criticism of the social role of mother itself, or of the structural ghettoization of women, or of the sexism that greets women's political efforts. As Marysa Navarro said of the women she studies, the Mothers of the Plaza de Mayo, who march to make the Argentine government give them news of their kidnapped, murdered children: "They can only consider ends that are mothers' ends."[25] The surfacing of political issues beyond the family weakened the Mothers of the Plaza de Mayo. Some wished to claim that party politics don't matter and that their murdered children were innocent of any interest in political struggle. Others felt political activism had been their children's right, one they now wished to share. These argued that their bereavement was not only a moral witnessing of crime and a demand for justice but also a specific intervention with immediate and threatening political implications to the state.

This kind of difference has split the mothers of the Plaza de Mayo along the feminist divide. To what extent is motherhood a powerful identity, a word to conjure with? To what extent is it a patriarchal construction that inevitably places mothers outside the realm of the social, the changing, the active? What power can women who weep, yell, mourn in the street have? Surely a mother's grief and rage removed from the home, suddenly exposed to publicity, are powerful, shocking. Yet as Navarro also points out, the unity of this image was misleading; its force was eventually undermined by differences a group structured around the monolith "mother" was unable to confront.

But, finally, to give the argument one more turn, many Plaza de Mayo women experienced a political transformation through their mothers' network. No group can resolve all political tensions through some ideal formation. The mothers of the disappeared, with their cross-party unity, have been able to convene big demonstrations, drawing new people into the political process. Women can move when a political vacuum develops; by being women who have accepted their lot, they can face the soldiers who have taken their children with a sense of righteous indignation that even a usually murderous police find it hard to dispute. On whatever terms, they have changed the political climate, invented new ways to resist state terrorism.

Using examples like these, the Grass Roots study group gave rise to a particularly poignant exploration of the feminist divide. In each member's work we saw a different version of how women have managed the mixed blessing of their female specialness. Actions like bread riots are desperate and ephemeral, but also effective. With these street eruptions, women put a government on notice; they signal that the poor can be pushed no further. It is finally women who know when the line has been crossed to starvation. But what then? Prices go down; the women go home—until the next time.

Women's movements for survival are like fire storms, changing and dissolving, resistant to political definition. We asked: Would a feminist critique of the traditional role of women keep these groups going longer? Or might feminist insights themselves contribute to the splits that quickly break down the unity shared during crisis? Or, in yet another shift of our assumed values, why shouldn't such groups end when the crisis ends, perhaps leaving behind them politicized people, active networks, even community organizations capable of future action when called for? If the Left were to expand its definition of political culture beyond the state and the workplace more often, wouldn't the political consciousness of women consumers, mothers, and community activists begin to look enduring in its own way, an important potential source of political energy? Perhaps, our group theorized, we are wrong to wish the women to have formed ongoing political groups growing out of bread riots or meat strikes. Maybe we would see more if we redefined political life to include usually invisible female networks.

The more we talked, the more we saw the ramifications of the fact that the traditional movements were collectivist, the feminist ones more individualistic. Women's local activism draws on a long history of women's culture in which mutual support is essential to life, not (as it often is with contemporary urban feminists) a rare or fragile achievement. The community of peasant women (or working women, or colonized women, or concerned mothers) was a given for the motherists; crisis made the idea of a separate, private identity beyond the daily struggle for survival unimportant. Here was another face of the divide: Collectivist movements are powerful, but they usually don't raise questions about women's work. Feminism has raised the questions, and claimed an individual destiny for each woman, but remains ambivalent toward older traditions of female solidarity. Surely our group was ambivalent. We worried that mothers' social networks can rarely redefine the terms of their needs. And rich as traditional forms of female association may be, we kept coming on instances in which the power of societies organized for internal support along gender lines was undermined by the sexism of that very organization.

For example, historian Mrinalini Sinha's research describes how the Bengali middle class of nineteenth-century India used its tradition of marrying and bedding child brides as a way of defining itself against a racist, colonial government.[26] The English hypocritically criticized Bengali men as effeminate because they could not wait. Bengali men answered that it was their women who couldn't wait: The way to control unbounded female sexuality—in which, of course, the English disbelieved—was to marry women at first menstruation.

In Sinha's account one rarely hears the voices of Bengali women themselves, but the question of which sexism would control them—the English marriages of restraint or the Bengali marriages of children—raged around these women. Neither side in the quarrel had women's autonomy or power at heart. Both wanted to wage the colonial fight using women as the symbolic representative of their rivalry. Because Bengali men wanted control of their women just as much as the English wanted control of Bengali men, the anticolonial struggle had less to offer women than men. In general, our group found that sexism inside an oppressed or impoverished community—such as rigidity about gender roles, or about male authority over women, or about female chastity—has cost revolutionary movements a great deal. Too often, gender politics goes unrecognized as an element in class defeat.[27]

Our group disagreed about the women's solidarity we were studying: Was it a part of the long effort to change women's position and to criticize hierarchy in general, or did motherist goals pull in an essentially different direction from feminist ones? And no matter where each one of us found herself on the spectrum of the group's responses to motherist movements, no resolution emerged of the paradox between mothers' goals and the goals of female individuals no longer defined primarily by reproduction and its attendant tasks. We saw this tension in some of the groups we studied, and we kept discovering it in ourselves. (Indeed, some of us were part of groups that used motherist rhetoric, as Ynestra King and I were of women's peace networks, or Amy Swerdlow had been of Women Strike for Peace.)

Drawing hard lines between the traditional women's movements and modern Western feminist consciousness never worked, not because the distinction doesn't exist but because it is woven inside our movement itself. A motherist is in some definitions a feminist, in others not. And these differing feminisms are yoked together by the range of difficulties to be found in women's current situation. Our scholarly distance from the motherists kept collapsing. The children's toy exchange network that Julie Wells described as one of the political groupings that build black women's solidarity in South Africa couldn't help striking us urban women in the United States as a good idea.[28] We, too, are in charge of the children and need each other to get by. We, too, are likely to act politically along the lines of association our female tasks have shaped. We sometimes long for the community the women we were studying took more for granted, although we couldn't help remarking on the ways those sustaining communities—say of union workers, or peasants, or ghettoized racial groups—used women's energy, loyalty, and passion as by right, while usually denying them a say in the group's public life, its historical consciousness.

Culture offers a variety of rewards to women for always giving attention to others first. Love is a special female responsibility. Some feminists see this female giving as fulfilling and morally powerful. Others see it as a mark of oppression and argue that women are given the job of "life," but that any job relegated to the powerless is one undervalued by the society as a whole. Yet in our group there was one area of agreement: Traditional women's concerns—for life, for the children, for peace—should be everyone's. Beyond that agreement the question that re-creates the feminist divide remained: How can the caring that belongs to "mother" travel out to become the responsibility of everyone? Women's backs hold up the world, and we ached for the way women's passionate caring is usually taken for granted, even by women themselves. Some Western feminists, aching like this, want above all to recognize and honor these mothers who, as Adrienne Rich writes, "age after age, perversely, with no extraordinary power, reconstitute the world."[29] Others, also aching, start on what can seem an impossible search for ways to break the ancient, tireless mother's promise to be the mule of the world.

Equality and Difference

By now anyone who has spent time wrangling with feminist issues has recognized the divide and is no doubt waiting for me to produce the name for it that is probably the oldest, certainly the most all-encompassing: "equality" versus "difference." Most feminist thought grapples unavoidably with some aspect of the equality-difference problem at both the level of theory and of strategy. In theory, this version of the divide might be stated: Do women want to be equal to men (with the meaning of "equal" hotly contested),[30] or do women see biology as establishing a difference that will always require a strong recognition and that might ultimately define quite separate possibilities inside "the human"?

Some difference-feminists would argue that women have a special morality, or aesthetic, or capacity for community that it is feminism's responsibility to maximize. Others would put the theoretical case for difference more neutrally and would argue that woman, no matter *what* she is like, is unassimilable. Because she is biologically and therefore psychologically separable from man, she is enduring proof that there is no universally representative human being, no "human wholeness."[31] In contrast, the equality-feminists would argue that it is possible for the biological difference to wither away as a basis for social organization, either by moving men and women toward some shared center (androgyny) or toward some experience of human variety in which biology is but one small variable.

Difference theory tends to emphasize the body (and more recently the unconscious where the body's psychic meaning develops); equality theory tends to deemphasize the body and to place faith in each individual's capacity to develop a self not ultimately circumscribed by a collective law of gender. For difference theorists the body can be either the site of pain and oppression or the site of orgasmic ecstasy and maternal joy. For equality theorists neither extreme is as compelling as the overriding idea that the difference between male and female bodies is a problem in need of solution. In this view, therefore, sexual hierarchy and sexual oppression are bound to continue unless the body is transcended or displaced as the center of female identity.

At the level of practical strategy, the equality-difference divide is just as ubiquitous as it is in theory. Willingly or not, activist lawyers find themselves pitted against each other because they disagree about whether "equal treatment" before the law is better or worse for women than "special treatment," for example, in cases about pregnancy benefits or child custody. (Should pregnancy be defined as unique, requiring special legal provisions, or will pregnant women get more actual economic support if pregnancy, when incapacitating, is grouped with other temporary conditions that keep people from work? Should women who give birth and are almost always the ones who care for children therefore get an automatic preference in custody battles, or will women gain more ultimately if men are defined by law as equally responsible for children, hence equally eligible to be awarded custody?)[32] Sometimes activists find themselves pressured by events to pit the mainstreaming of information about women in the school curriculum against the need for separate programs for women's studies. Or they find themselves having to choose between working to get traditionally male jobs (for example in construction) and working to get fair pay in the women-only jobs they are already doing.

One rushes to respond that these strategic alternatives should not be mutually exclusive, but often, in the heat of local struggles, they temporarily become so. No matter what their theoretical position on the divide, activists find themselves having to make painfully unsatisfactory short-term decisions about the rival claims of equality and difference.[33]

Regrettably, these definitions, these examples flatten out the oscillations of the equality-difference debate; they obscure the class struggles that have shaped the development of the argument; they offer neat parallels where there should be asymmetries. Viewed historically, the oscillation between a feminism of equality and one of difference is a bitter disagreement about which path is more progressive, more able to change women's basic condition of subordination.

In this history each side has taken more than one turn at calling the other reactionary and each has had its genuine vanguard moments. "Difference" gained some working women protection at a time when any social legislation to regulate work was rare, while "equality" lay behind middle-class women's demand for the vote, a drive Ellen DuBois has called "the most radical program for women's emancipation possible in the nineteenth century."[34] At the same time, bourgeois women's demands that men should have to be as sexually pure as women finessed the divide between difference and equality and gave rise to interesting cross-class alliances of women seeking ways to make men conform to women's standard, rather than the usual way round—a notion of equality with a difference.[35] As DuBois points out, it is difficult to decide which of these varied political constructions gave nineteenth-century women the most real leverage to make change:

> My hypothesis is that the significance of the woman suffrage movement rested precisely on the fact that it bypassed women's oppression within the family, or private sphere, and demanded instead her admission to citizenship, and through it admission to the public arena.[36]

In other words, at a time when criticism of women's separate family role was still unthinkable, imagining a place outside the family where such a role would make no difference was—for a time—a most radical act.

Equality and difference are broad ideas and have included a range of definitions and political expressions. Equality, for example, can mean anything from the mildest liberal reform (this is piece-of-the-pie feminism, in which women are merely to be included in the world as it is) to the most radical reduction of gender to insignificance. Difference can mean anything from Mary Daly's belief in the natural superiority of women to psychoanalytic theories of how women are inevitably cast as "the Other" because they lack penises.[37]

Just now equality—fresh from recent defeats at the polls and in the courts—is under attack by British and U.S. theorists who are developing a powerful critique of the eighteenth- and nineteenth-century roots of feminism in liberalism. In what is a growing body of work, feminists are exploring the serious limitations of a tradition based on an ideal of equality for separate, independent individuals acting in a free, public sphere—either the market or the state. This liberalism, which runs as an essential thread through Anglo-American feminism, has caused much disappointment. Feminists have become increasingly aware of its basic flaws, of the ways it splits off public and private, leaves sexual differences entirely out of its narrative of the world, and pretends to a neutrality that is nullified by the realities of gender, class, and race. A feminism that honors individual rights has grown leery of the liberal tradition that always puts those rights before community and before any caring for general needs. Liberalism promises an equal right to compete, but as bell hooks puts it: "Since men are not equals in white supremacist, capitalist, patriarchal class structure, which men do women want to be equal to?"[38]

These arguments against the origins and tendencies of equality-feminism are cogent and useful. They have uncovered unexamined assumptions and the essential weakness in a demand for a passive neutrality of opportunity. But there are cracks in the critique of equality-feminism that lead me back to my general assertion that neither side of the divide can easily be transcended. The biggest complaint against a feminist demand of "equality" is that this construction means women must become conceptual men, or rather that to have equal rights they will have to repress their biological difference, to subordinate themselves in still new ways under an unchanged male hegemony.[39] In this argument the norm is assumed to be male and women's entry into public space is assumed to be a loss of the aspects of experience they formerly embodied—privacy, feeling, nurturance, dailiness. Surely, though, this argument entails a monolithic and eternal view both of public space and of the category "male." How successfully does public space maintain its male gender markers, how totally exclude the private side of life? (The city street is male, yet it can at times be not only physically but also conceptually invaded, say, by a sense of neighborhood or by a demonstration of mass solidarity.)[40] Does male space sometimes dramatically reveal the fact of women's absence? How well does the taboo on public women hold up under the multiple pressures of modernity? Even if public and private are conceptually absolutes, to what extent do individual men and women experience moments in both positions?

Or, if one rejects these hopeful efforts to find loopholes in the iron laws of gender difference, the fear that women will become men still deserves double scrutiny. Is the collapse of gender difference into maleness really the problem women face? Or are we perhaps quite close to men already at the moment when we fear absorption into the other?

None of this is meant as a refutation of the important current work that brings skepticism to the construction of our demands. When health activist Wendy Chavkin notes that making pregnancy disappear by calling it a "disability" is one more way of letting business and government evade sharing responsibility for reproduction, she is right to worry about the invisibility of women's bodies and of our work of reproduction of which our bodies are one small part. When philosopher Alison Jaggar gives examples of how male norms have buried the often separate needs of women, she is sounding a valuable warning. When critic Myra Jehlen describes how hard it is for the concept of a person to include the particular when that particular is female, she is identifying the depth of our difficulty, men's phobic resistance to the inclusion of women into any neutral or public equation.[41]

Nonetheless, I want to reanimate the problem of the divide, to show the potential vigor on both sides. On the one hand, an abstract promise of equality is not enough for people living in capitalism, where everyone is free both to vote and to starve. On the other, as Zillah Eisenstein has pointed out in The Radical Future of Liberal Feminism, the demand for equality has a radical meaning in a capitalist society that claims to offer it but structurally often denies it. Feminism asks for many things the patriarchal state cannot give without radical change. Juliet Mitchell's rethinking of the value of equality-feminism reaches a related conclusion: When basic rights are under attack, liberalism feels necessary again. At best, liberalism sometimes tips in action and becomes more radical than its root conceptions promise. Certainly, no matter which strategy we choose—based on a model of equality or of difference—we are constantly forced to compromise.[42]

It's not that we haven't gotten beyond classical liberalism in theory but that in practice we cannot live beyond it. In their very structure, contemporary court cases about sex and gender dramatize the fact of the divide, and media questions demand the short, one-sided answer. Each "case," each "story" in which we act is different, and we are only at moments able to shape that difference, make it into the kind of "difference" we want.[43]

The Divide Is Not a Universal

After having said so much about how deep the divide goes in feminism, how completely it defines what feminism is, I run the risk of seeming to say that the divide has some timeless essence. In fact, I want to argue the opposite, to place Western feminism inside its two-hundred-year history as a specific possibility for thought and action that arose as one of the possibilities of modernity.

When Mary Wollstonecraft wrote one of the founding books of feminism in 1792, *A Vindication of the Rights of Women*, she said what was new then and remains fresh, shocking, and doubtful to many now: that sex hierarchy—like ranks in the church and the army or like the then newly contested ascendancy of kings—was social, not natural. Though women before her had named injustices and taken sides in several episodes of an ancient *quarrelle des femmes*, Wollstonecraft's generation experienced the divide in ways related to how feminists experience it now. At one and the same time she could see gender as a solid wall barring her way into liberty, citizenship, and a male dignity she envied, and could see how porous the wall was, how many ways she herself could imagine stepping through into an identity less absolute and more chaotic.

Modern feminists often criticize her unhappy compromise with bourgeois revolution and liberal political goals, but if Wollstonecraft was often an equality-feminist in the narrowest sense, eager to speak of absolute rights, of an idealized male individualism, and to ignore the body, this narrowness was in part a measure of her desperation.[44] The body, she felt, could be counted on to assert its ever-present and dreary pull; the enlightenment promised her a mind that might escape. She acknowledged difference as an absolute—men are stronger—and then with cunning, she offered men a deal:

> Avoiding, as I have hitherto done, any direct comparison of the two sexes collectively, or frankly acknowledging the inferiority of women, according to the present appearance of things, I shall only insist that men have increased that inferiority till women are almost sunk below the standard of rational creatures. Let their faculties have room to unfold, and their virtues to gain strength, and then determine where the whole sex must stand in the intellectual scale.[45]

Wheedling a bit, Wollstonecraft made men the modest proposal that if women are inferior, men have nothing to fear; they can generously afford to give women their little chance at the light. This is a sly, agnostic treatment of the issue of equality versus difference. Experimental and groping spirit, Wollstonecraft *didn't know* how much biological difference might come to mean; but that she suffered humiliation and loss through being a woman she did know, and all she asked was to be let out of the prison house of gender identity for long enough to judge what men had and what part of that she might want.

When Wollstonecraft wrote, difference was the prevailing wind, equality the incipient revolutionary storm. She feared that if women could not partake in the new civil and political rights of democracy, they would "remain immured in their families groping in the dark." To be sure, this rejection of the private sphere made no sense to many feminists who came after her and left modern feminists the task of recognizing the importance of the private and women's different life there, yet it is a rejection that was absolutely necessary as one of feminism's first moves. We in turn have rejected Wollstonecraft's call for chastity, for the end of the passionate emotions "which disturb the order of society";[46] we have rejected her confidence in objective reason and her desire to live as a disembodied self (and a very understandable desire, too, for one whose best friend died in childbirth and who was to die of childbed fever herself), but we have not gotten beyond needing to make the basic demands she made—for civil rights, education, autonomy.

Finally, what is extraordinary in *A Vindication* is its chaos. Multivalent, driven, ambivalent, the text races over most of feminism's main roads. It constantly goes back on itself in tone, thrilling with self-hatred, rage, disappointment, and hope—the very sort of emotions it explains are the mark of women's inferiority, triviality, and lascivious abandon. Though its appeals to God and virtue are a dead letter to feminists now, the anger and passion with which Wollstonecraft made those appeals—and out of which she imagined the depth of women's otherness, our forced incapacity, the injustice of our situation—feel thoroughly modern. Her structural disorganization derives in part from a circular motion through now familiar stages of protest, reasoning, fury, despair, contempt, desire.[47] She makes demands for women, then doubles back to say that womanhood should be beside the point. Her book is one of those that mark the start of an avalanche of mass self-consciousness about gender injustice. So, in the midst of the hopeful excitement, the divide is there, at the beginning of our history.

If the divide is central to feminist history, feminists need to recognize it with more suppleness, but this enlarged perspective doesn't let one out of having to choose a position in the divide. On the contrary, by arguing that there is no imminent resolution, I hope to throw each reader back on the necessity of finding where her own work falls and of assessing how powerful that political decision is as a tool for undermining the dense, deeply embedded oppression of women.

By writing of the varied vocabularies and constructions feminists have used to describe the divide, I do not mean to intimate that they are all one, but to emphasize their difference. Each issue calls forth a new configuration, a new version of the spectrum of feminist opinion, and most require an internal as well as external struggle about goals and tactics. Though it is understandable that we dream of peace among feminists, that we resist in sisterhood the factionalism that has so often disappointed us in brotherhood, still we must carry on the argument among ourselves. Better, we must actively embrace it. The tension in the divide, far from being our enemy, is a dynamic force that links very different women. Feminism encompasses central dilemmas in modem experience, mysteries of identity that get full expression in its debates. The electricity of its internal disagreements is part of feminism's continuing power to shock and involve large numbers of people in a public conversation far beyond the movement itself. The dynamic feminist divide is about difference; it dramatizes women's differences from each other—and the necessity of our sometimes making common cause.

A Gender Diary: Some Stories, Some Dialogues

If, as I've said, the divide offers no third way, no high ground of neutrality, I certainly have not been able to present this overview so far without a constant humming theme beneath, my own eagerness to break the category "woman" down, to find a definition of difference that pushes so far beyond a settled identity that "being a woman" breaks apart.

Though sometimes I have found the theoretical equality arguments I have described blinkered and reactive, when it comes to strategy, I almost always choose that side, fearing the romance of femaleness even more than the flatness and pretense of undifferentiated, gender-free public space.

I suspect that each one's emphasis—equality or difference—arises alongside and not after the reasons. We criticize Wollstonecraft's worship of rationality, but how willing are we modern ones to look at the unconscious, the idiosyncratic, the temperamental histories of our own politics? It is in these histories—private, intellectual, and social—that we can find why some women feel safer with the equality model as the rock of their practice (with difference as a necessary condition imposed on it), while other women feel more true to themselves, more fully expressed, by difference as their rock (with equality a sort of bottom-line call for basic reforms that cannot ultimately satisfy).

Why do I decide (again and again) that being a woman is a liability, while others I know decide (again and again) that a separate female culture is more exciting, more in their interests, more promising as a strategic stance for now than my idea of slipping the noose of gender, living for precious moments of the imagination outside it? An obvious first answer is that class, race, and sexual preference determine my choices, and surely these play their central part. Yet in my experience of splits in the women's movement, I keep joining with women who share my feminist preferences but who have arrived at these conclusions from very different starting points.

This is not to understate the importance of class, race, and sexual preference but merely to observe that these important variables don't segment feminism along the divide; they don't provide direct keys to each one's sense of self-interest or desire nor do they yield clear directions for the most useful strategic moves. For example, lesbian and straight women are likely to bring very different understandings and needs to discussions of whether or not women's communities work, whether or not the concept is constricting. Yet in my own experience, trust of women's communities does not fall out along the lines of sexual preference. Instead, up close, the variables proliferate. What was the texture of childhood for each one of us? What face did the world beyond home present?

In the fifties, when an earlier, roiled life of gender and politics had subsided and the gender messages seemed monolithic again, I lived with my parents in the suburbs. My mother's class and generation had lived through repeated, basic changes of direction about women, family, and work, and my own engaged and curious mother passed on her ambivalent reception of the world's mixed messages to me in the food. With hindsight, I can see that of course gender, family, and class weren't the settled issues they seemed then. But the times put a convincing cover over continuing change. Deborah Rosenfelt and Judith Stacey describe this precise historical moment and the particular feminist politics born from it:

> The ultradomestic nineteen fifties [was] an aberrant decade in the history of U.S. family and gender relations and one that has set the unfortunate terms for waves of personal and political reaction to family issues ever since. Viewed in this perspective, the attack on the breadwinner/homemaker nuclear family by the women's liberation movement may have been an

overreaction to an aberrant and highly fragile cultural form, a family system that, for other reasons, was already passing from the scene. Our devastating critiques of the vulnerability and cultural devaluation of dependent wives and mothers helped millions of women to leave or avoid these domestic traps, and this is to our everlasting credit. But, with hindsight, it seems to us that these critiques had some negative consequences as well. . . . Feminism's overreaction to the fifties was an antinatalist, antimaternalist moment.[48]

I am the child of this moment, and some of the atmosphere of rage generated by that hysterically domestic ideology of the fifties can now feel callow, young, or ignorant. Yet I have many more kind words to say for the reaction of which I was a part in the early seventies than Rosenfelt and Stacey seem to: I don't think the feminism of this phase would have spoken so powerfully to so many without this churlish outbreak of indignation. Nothing we have learned since about the fragility of the nuclear family alters the fundamental problems it continues to pose for women. It is not really gone, though it is changing. And although feminism seeks to preside over the changes, other forces are at work, half the time threatening us with loneliness, half the time promising us rich emotional lives if we will but stay home—a vicious double punch combination. In this climate, feminist resistance to pronatalism—of either the fifties or the nineties—continues to make sense.

It's hard to remember now what the initial feminist moves in this wave felt like, the heady but alarming atmosphere of female revolt. As one anxious friend wondered back then, "Can I be in this and stay married?" The answer was often "no," the upheaval terrifying. Some of us early ones were too afraid of the lives of our mothers to recognize ourselves in them. But I remember that this emotional throwing off of the mother's life felt like the only way to begin. Black women whose ties to their mothers were more often a mutual struggle for survival rarely shared this particular emotion. As Audre Lorde has said, "Black children were not meant to survive,"[49] so parents and children saw a lifeline in each other that was harder for the prosperous or the white to discern. The usually white and middle-class women who were typical members of early women's consciousness-raising groups often saw their mothers as desperate or depressed in the midst of their relative privilege. Many had been educated like men and had then been expected to become . . . men's wives. We used to agree in those meetings that motherhood was the divide: Before it, you could pretend you were just like everyone else; afterward, you were a species apart—invisible and despised.

But if motherhood was despised, it was also festooned—then as now—with roses. Either way, in 1970, motherhood seemed an inevitable part of my future, and the qualities some feminists now praise as uniquely women's were taken for granted as female necessities: Everyone wanted the nice one, the sweet one, the good one, the nurturant one, the pretty one. No one wanted the women who didn't want to be women. It's hard to recover how frightening it was to step out of those ideas, to resist continuing on as expected; it's hard to get back how very naked it made us feel. Some of the vociferousness of our rhetoric, which now seems unshaded or raw, came partly from the anxiety we felt when we made this proclamation, that we didn't want to be women. A great wave of misogyny rose to greet us. So we said it even more. Hindsight has brought in its necessary wisdom, its temporizing reaction. We have gotten beyond the complaint of the daughters, have come to respect the realities, the worries, and the work of the mothers. But to me "difference" will always represent a necessary modification of the initial impulse, a reminder of complexity, a brake on precipitate hopes. It can never feel like the primary insight felt, the first breaking with the gender bargain. The immediate reward was immense, the thrill of separating from authority.

> Conversation with E. She recalls that the new women's movement meant to her: You don't have to struggle to be attractive to men anymore. You can stop working so hard on that side of things. I was impressed by this liberation so much beyond my own. I felt the opposite. Oppressed and depressed before the movement, I found sexual power unthinkable, the privilege of a very few women. Now angry and awake, I felt for the first time what the active eroticism of men might be like. What men thought of me no longer blocked out the parallel question of what I thought of them, which made sexual encounters far more interesting than they had once been. Like E., I worried about men's approval less, but (without much tangible reason) my hopes for the whole business of men and women rose. For a brief time in the early seventies, I had an emotional intimation of what some men must feel: free to rub up against the world, take space, make judgments. With all its hazards this confidence also offered its delight—but only for a moment of course. The necessary reaction followed at once: Women aren't men in public space. There is no safety.
>
> Besides, I had romanticized male experience; men are not as free as I imagined. Still, I remember that wild if deluded time—not wanting to be a man but wanting the freedom of the street. The feminist rallying cry "Take Back

the Night" has always struck me as a fine piece of movement poetry. We don't have the night, but we want it, we want it.

Another memory of the early seventies: An academic woman sympathetic to the movement but not active asked what motivated me to spend all this time organizing, marching, meeting. (Subtext: Why wasn't I finishing my book? Why did I keep flinging myself around?)

I tried to explain the excitement I felt at the idea that I didn't have to be a woman. She was shocked, confused. This was the motor of my activism? She asked, "How can someone who doesn't like being a woman be a feminist?" To which I could only answer, "Why would anyone who likes being a woman need to be a feminist?"

Quite properly my colleague feared woman-hating. She assumed that feminism must be working to restore respect and dignity to women. Feminism would revalue what had been debased, women's contribution to human history. I, on the other hand, had to confess: I could never have made myself lick all those stamps for a better idea of what womanhood means. Was this, as my colleague thought, just a new kind of misogyny? I wouldn't dare say self-hatred played no part in what I wanted from feminism from the first. But even back then, for me, womanhating—or loving—felt beside the point. It was the idea of breaking the law of the category itself that made me delirious.

The first time I heard "women" mentioned as a potentially political contemporary category I was already in graduate school. It was the mid-sixties and a bright young woman of the New Left was saying how important it was to enlist the separate support of women workers in our organizing against the Vietnam War. I remember arguing with her, flushed with a secret humiliation. What good was she doing these workers, I asked her, by addressing them and categorizing them separately? Who was she to speak so condescendingly of "them"? Didn't she know that the inferior category she had named would creep up in the night and grab her, too?

I'm ashamed now to admit that gender solidarity—which I lived inside happily, richly every day in those years—first obtruded itself on my conscious mind as a threat and a betrayal. So entirely was I trapped in negative feelings about what women are and can do that I had repressed any knowledge of femaleness as a defining characteristic of my being.

I can see now that women very different from me came to feminist conclusions much like my own. But this is later knowledge. My feminism came from the suburbs, where I knew no white, middle-class woman with children who *had a job or any major activities beyond the family. Yet, though a girl, I was promised education, offered the pretense of gender neutrality. This island of illusions was a small world, but if I seek the source for why cultural feminism has so little power to draw me, it is to this world I return in thought. During the day, it was safe, carefully limited, and female. The idea that this was all made me frantic.*

S. reads the gender diary with consternation. In Puerto Rico, where she grew up, this fear of the mother's life would be an obscenity. She can't recognize the desire I write of—to escape scot free from the role I was born to. Latina feminists she knows feel rage, but what is this shame, she wants to know. In her childhood both sexes believed being a woman was magic.

S. means it about the magic, hard as it is for me to take this in. She means sexual power, primal allure, even social dignity. S. became a feminist later, by a different route, and now she is as agnostic about the meaning of gender as I am. But when she was young, she had no qualms about being a woman.

After listening to S., I add another piece to my story of the suburbs. Jews who weren't spending much of our time being Jewish, we lived where ethnicity was easy to miss. (Of course it was there; but I didn't know it.) In the suburbs, Motherhood was white bread, with no powerful ethnic graininess. For better and worse, I was brought up on this stripped, denatured product. Magical women seemed laughably remote. No doubt this flatness in local myth made girls believe less in their own special self, but at the same time it gave them less faith in the beckoning ideal of mother. My gifted mother taught me not the richness of home but the necessity of feminism. Feminism was her conscious as well as unconscious gift.

It is not enough for the diary to tell how one woman, myself, came to choose—again and again—a feminism on the minimalizers' side of the divide. Somehow the diary must also tell how this decision can never feel solid or final. No one gets to stay firmly on her side; no one gets to rest in a reliably clear position. Mothers who believe their daughters should roam as free as men find themselves giving those daughters taxi fare, telling them not to talk to strangers, filling them with the lore of danger. Activists who want women to be very naughty (as the women in a little zap group we call No More Nice Girls want women to be) nonetheless warn them there's a price to pay for daring to defy men in public space.[50] Even when a woman chooses which shoes she'll wear today—is it to be the running shoes, the flats, the spikes?—she's deciding where to place herself for the moment on the current possible spectrum of images of "woman." Whatever our habitual position on the divide, in daily life we travel back and forth, or, to change metaphors, we scramble for whatever toehold we can.

Living with the divide: In a room full of feminists, everyone is saying that a so-called surrogate mother, one who bears a child for others, should have the right to change her mind for a time (several weeks? months?) after the baby is born. This looks like agreement. Women who have been on opposite sides of the divide in many struggles converge here. Outraged at the insulting way one Mary Beth Whitehead has been treated by fertility clinics, law courts, and press. She is not a "surrogate," we say, but a "mother" indeed.

The debate seems richer than it's been lately. Nobody knows how to sort out the contradictions of the new reproductive technologies yet, so for a fertile moment there's a freedom, an expressiveness in all that's said. Charged words like "birth" and "mothering" and "the kids" are spilling all around, but no one yet dares to draw the ideological line defining which possibilities belong inside feminism, which are antithetical to it. Some sing a song of pregnancy and birth while others offer contrapuntal motifs of child-free lesbian youth, of infertility, all in different keys of doubt about how much feminists may want to make motherhood special, different from parenting, different from caring—a unique and absolute relation to a child.

But just as we're settling in for an evening that promises to be fraught, surprising, suggestive, my warning system, sensitive after twenty years of feminist activism, gives a familiar twitch and tug. Over by the door, one woman has decided: Surrogacy is baby-selling and ought to be outlawed. All mothering will be debased if motherhood can be bought. Over by the couch, another woman is anxiously responding: Why should motherhood be the sacred place we keep clean from money, while men sell the work of their bodies every day? Do we want women to be the special representatives of the moral and spiritual things that can't be bought, with the inevitable result that women's work is once again done without pay?

Here it is then. The metaconversation that has hovered over my political life since 1969, when I joined one of the first women's consciousness-raising groups. On the one hand, sacred motherhood. On the other, a wish—variously expressed—for this special identity to wither away.

Only a little later in the brief, eventful history of this ad hoc Mary Beth Whitehead support group, a cleverly worded petition was circulated. It quoted the grounds the court used to disqualify Whitehead from mother-hood—from the way she dyed her hair to the way she played patty-cake—and ended: "By these standards, we are all unfit mothers." I wanted to sign the petition, but someone told me, "Only mothers are signing." I was amazed. Did one have to be literally a mother in order to speak authentically in support of Whitehead? Whether I'm a mother or not, the always obvious fact that I am from the mother half of humanity conditions my life.

But after this initial flash of outrage at exclusion, I had second thoughts: Maybe I should be glad not to sign. Why should I have to be assumed to be a mother if I am not? Instead of accepting that all women are mothers in essence if not in fact, don't I prefer a world in which some are mothers—and can speak as mothers—while others are decidedly not?

To make a complicated situation more so: While I was struggling with the rights and wrongs of my being allowed to sign, several other women refused to sign. Why? Because the petition quoted Whitehead's remark that she knew what was best for her child because she was the mother. The nonsigners saw this claim as once again imputing some magic biological essence to mother-hood. They didn't want to be caught signing a document that implied that mother always knows best. They supported Whitehead's right to dye her hair but not her claim to maternal infallibility.

I saw the purity of this position, recognized these nonsigners as my closest political sisters, the ones who run fast because the old world of mother-right is just behind them. But in this case I didn't feel quite as they felt. I was too angry at the double standard, the unfair response to Whitehead's attempts to extricate herself from disaster. I thought that given the circumstances of here, of now, Mary Beth Whitehead was as good an authority about her still-nursing baby as we could find anywhere in the situation. It didn't bother me at all to sign a petition that included her claim to a uniquely privileged place. The press and the court seemed to hate her for that very specialness; yet they all relegated her to it, execrating her for her unacceptable ambivalence. Under such conditions she was embracing with an understandable vengeance the very role the world named as hers. Who could blame her?

Eventually, I signed the petition, which was also signed by a number of celebrities and was much reported in the press. It is well to remember how quickly such public moments flatten out internal feminist debates. After much feminist work, the newspapers—formerly silent about feminism's stake in surrogacy questions—began speaking of "the feminist position." But noth-ing they ever wrote about us or our petition came close to the dilemma as *we had debated it during the few intense weeks we met. Prosurrogacy and antisurrogacy positions coexist inside feminism. They each require expression, because neither alone can respond fully to the class, race, and gender issues raised when a poor woman carries a child for a rich man for money.*

Over time I've stopped being depressed by the lack of feminist accord. I see feminists as stuck with the very indeterminacy I say I long for. This is it then, the life part way in, part way out. One can be recalled to "woman" anytime—by things as terrible as rape, as trivial as a rude shout on the street—but one can never stay inside "woman," because it keeps moving. We constantly find ourselves beyond its familiar cover.

Gender markers are being hotly reasserted these days—U.S. defense is called "standing tough" while the Pope's letter on women calls motherhood woman's true vocation. Yet this very heat is a sign of gender's instabilities. We can clutch aspects of the identity we like, but they often slip away. Modern women experience moments of free fall. How is it for you, there, out in space near me? Different, I know. Yet we share—some with more pleasure, some with more pain—this uncertainty.

1989

Acknowledgments

I am indebted to the hard-working readers of an earlier draft, who are nevertheless not to blame for the times I have failed to profit from their excellent advice: Nancy Davidson, Adrienne Harris, Temma Kaplan, Mim Kelber, Ynestra King, Susana Leval, Eunice Lipton, Alix Kates Shulman, Alan Snitow, Nadine Taub, Meredith Tax, Sharon Thompson, and Carole Vance.

A shorter version of this article ("Pages from a Gender Diary") appeared in *Dissent* (Spring 1989); a longer version ("A Gender Diary") is in *Rocking the Ship of State: Toward a Feminist Peace Politics*, ed. Adrienne Harris and Ynestra King (Boulder, Colo.: Westview Press, 1989).

Notes

1. The "we" problem has no more simple solution than does the divide itself, but in spite of its false promise of unity, the "we" remains politically important. In this piece, "we" includes anyone who calls herself a feminist, anyone who is actively engaged with the struggles described here.

2. MARHO Forum, John Jay College, New York, March 2, 1984. For feminist critiques of the new peace activism see Bishop and Green, eds., *Breaching the Peace: A Collection of Radical Feminist Papers* and Snitow, "Holding the Line at Greenham."

3. Lourdes Benería and Phyllis Mack began the study group, which was initially funded by the Institute for Research on Women at Rutgers University. Other members were: Dorothy Dinnerstein, Zala Chandler, Carol Cohn, Adrienne Harris, Ynestra King, Rhoda Linton, Sara Ruddick, Amy Swerdlow.

4. See Swerdlow, "Pure Milk, Not Poison" in *Rocking the Ship of State*. (This book grew from the study group above.)

5. Abzug and Kelber, *Gender Gap*. According to Kelber, Carter was outraged that the women of the commission were criticizing his social priorities; they were supposed to be on his side. Most of the commission resigned when Carter fired Abzug. When he reconstituted the commission somewhat later, the adjective "national" had been dropped from its name and it became the President's Advisory Commission for Women, with restricted powers and no lobbying function.

6. "In the United States, we oscillate between participating in, and separating from, organizations and institutions that remain alienating and stubbornly male dominant." (Kelly, "The Doubled Vision of Feminist Theory," 55). Also see Riley, *War in the Nursery*.

7. Riley, talk at the Barnard Women's Center, New York, April 11, 1985.

8. Stimpson, "The New Scholarship about Women."

9. Echols, *Daring to Be Bad*, 81.

10. Echols, *Daring to Be Bad*, 273.

11. Echols, *Daring to Be Bad*, 270.

12. Echols, *Daring to Be Bad*, 273.

13. Deming, "To Those Who Would Start a People's Party," 24, cited in Echols, *Daring to Be Bad*, 272; Dworkin, *Intercourse*, 67. Dworkin is not a biological determinist in *Intercourse*, but she sees culture as so saturated with misogyny that the victimization of women is seamless, total, as eternal in its own way as "mother right."

14. Willis, remarks at the NYU Symposium on the publication of Snitow, Stansell, and Thompson's *Powers of Desire: The Politics of Sexuality*, New York, December 2, 1983.

15. Vance, "Social Construction Theory," 164.

16. Alcoff, "Cultural Feminism Versus Post-Structuralism," especially 406.

17. Linda Alcoff sees post-structuralism as anti-essentialist; in contrast, in *Feminist Studies* 14, no. 1 (Spring 1988), the editors Judith Newton and Nancy Hoffman introduce a collection of essays on deconstruction by describing differences *among* deconstructionists on the question of essentialism as on other matters.

18. See New York Radical Feminists, "Politics of the Ego: A Manifesto for N.Y. Radical Feminists." The vocabulary of the manifesto, adopted in December 1969, seems crude now, with its emphasis on "psychology" jejune, but the document begins with the task feminists have taken up since—the analysis of the interlocking ways in which culture organizes subordination.

19. Bamber and DeKoven, "Metacriticism and the Value of Difference" (paper, MLA panel "Feminist Criticism: Theories and Directions," Los Angeles, December 28, 1982).

20. Alcoff, "Cultural Feminism versus Post-Structuralism," 421.

21. One might make a separate study of third-course thinking. Sometimes this work is an important and urgent effort to see the limiting terms of a current contradiction, to recognize from which quarter new contradictions are likely to develop. Third-course writing at its best tries to reinterpret the present and offer clues to the future. (English theorists have called this prefigurative thinking.) But often this work runs the risk of pretending that new terms resolve difficulties, and, more insidiously, it often falls back covertly into the divide it claims to have transcended. I admire, although I am not always persuaded by, the third-course thinking in such pieces as Miles, "The Integrative Feminine Principle in North American Radicalism." I have more doubts about pieces such as Ferguson, "Sex War" and Philipson, "The Repression of History and Gender: A Critical Perspective on the Feminist Sexuality Debate." These essays claim a higher ground, "a third perspective" (Ferguson, 108), that is extremely difficult to construct; their classifications of the sides of the divide reveal a tropism more unavoidable than they recognize.

22. Barrett, "The Concept of 'Difference.'" 34.

23. Walker, *In Search of Our Mother's Gardens*, xi (epigraph). Also see, for example, Kelly, "The Doubled Vision of Feminist Theory"; and Rich, "Compulsory Heterosexuality and Lesbian Existence," 6off. Rich also uses the metaphor of the continuum to describe the range in women's lives among different levels of female community. Jane Gallop describes Julia Kristeva's effort to think beyond dualism: "A constantly double discourse is necessary, one that asserts and then questions" (Gallop, *The Daughter's Seduction*, 122).

24. Meredith Tax, "Agenda for Meeting at Barnard, May 3, 1986," 1. Members of the study group, convened at the Barnard Women's Center: Margorie Agosin, Amrita Basu, Dana Frank, Temma Kaplan, Ynestra King, Marysa Navarro, Ann Snitow, Amy Swerdlow, Meredith Tax, Julie Wells, Marilyn Young.

25. Marysa Navarro, Grass Roots Meeting, May 3, 1986. Also see Christian, "Mothers March, but to 2 Drummers."

26. Sinha, "The Age of Consent Act"; and Sinha, "Gender and Imperialism."

27. At the Grass Roots study group, Julie Wells and Anne McClintock offered the example of Crossroads in South Africa, a squatter community of blacks largely maintained by women but finally undermined by, among other things, a colonialism that placed paid black men in charge. Also see descriptions of ways in which women become connected with revolutionary movements in Molyneux, "Mobilization Without Emancipation?"; Kaplan, "Women and Communal Strikes in the Crises of 1917–1922"; and Kaplan, "Female Consciousness and Collective Action."

28. Wells, "The Impact of Motherist Movements on South African Women's Political Participation."

29. Rich, "Natural Resources," 67.

30. Alison M. Jaggar gives an account of the contemporary feminist debate about the meaning and value of the demand for "equality" in Jaggar, "Sexual Difference and Sexual Equality." For some general accounts of the debate, also see Donovan, *Feminist Theory*; Eisenstein, *Contemporary Feminist Thought*; Eisenstein and Jardine, eds., *The Future of Difference*; Eisenstein, *Feminism and Sexual Equality*; Mitchell, *Women's Estate*; Mitchell and Oakley, eds., *What is Feminism?* The debates about Carol Gilligan's *In a Different Voice* often turn on the equality-difference problem. See Broughton, ed., *New Ideas in Psychology* and his "Women's Rationality and Men's Virtues"; Kerber et al., "On *In a Different Voice*"; and Benhabib, "The Generalized and the Concrete Other." Similarly, the feminist response to Illich, *Gender*, has tended to raise these issues. See, for example, Benería, "Meditations on Ivan Illich's *Gender*."

31. The phrase "human wholeness" comes from Friedan, *The Second Stage*, and the concept receives a valuable and devastating critique in Jehlen, "Against Human Wholeness."

32. For the pregnancy issue, see Bertin, "Brief of the American Civil Liberties Union et al."; Chavkin, "Walking a Tightrope: Pregnancy, Parenting, and Work"; Vogel, "Debating Difference"; Bird and Holland, "Capitol Letter"; Williams, "Equality's Riddle"; Kay, "Equality and Difference." For the custody issue, see Bartlett and Stack, "Joint Custody, Feminism and the Dependency Dilemma"; Chesler, *Mothers on Trial*; Weitzman, *The Divorce Revolution*. The work of Nadine Taub, director of the Women's Rights Litigation Clinic, School of Law, Rutgers/Newark, has frequent bearing on both issues and on the larger questions in equality-difference debates. See Taub, "Defining and Combatting Sexual Harassment"; Taub, "Feminist Tensions"; Taub, "A Public Policy of Private Caring"; Taub and Williams, "Will Equality Require More Than Assimilation, Accommodation or Separation from the Existing Social Structure?" The burgeoning feminist work on the new reproductive technologies also reproduces the divide. For complete references to all aspects of these debates, see Taub and Cohen, *Reproductive Laws for the 1990s*.

33. If I had to come up with an example of a feminist strategy that faced the power of the divide squarely yet at the same time undermined the oppression the divide represents, I'd choose recent feminist comparable worth legislation. Humble and earthshaking, comparable worth asserts two things: First, because women and men do different work, the concept "equal pay" has little effect on raising women's low wages; and, second, if work were to be judged by standards of difficulty, educational preparation, experience, and so on (standards preferably developed by workers themselves), then antidiscrimination laws might enforce that men and women doing work of comparable worth be paid the same. (Perhaps nurses and auto mechanics? Or teachers and middle managers?) The activists who have proposed comparable worth have singularly few pretentions. They are the first to point out that on its face, the proposal ignores the work women do in the family, ignores the noneconomic reasons why women and men have different kinds of jobs, ignores what's wrong with job hi-

erarchies and with "worth" as the sole basis for determining pay. Yet this little brown mouse of a liberal reform, narrow in its present political potential and limited by its nature, has a touch of deconstructive genius. Without hoping to get women doing men's work tomorrow, the comparable worth model erodes the economic advantages to employers of consistently undervaluing women's work and channeling women into stigmatized work ghettoes where pay is always lower. With comparable worth, the stigma might well continue to haunt women's work, but women would be better paid. Men might start wanting a "woman's" job that paid well, while women might have new psychological incentives to cross gender work categories. Who knows, perhaps stigma might not catch up as categories of work got rethought and their gender markers moved around. And if the stigma clung to women's work, if men refused to be nurses even if nurses were paid as well as construction workers, a woman earning money is an independent woman. She can change the family; she can consider leaving it. Comparable worth asserts the divide, yet, slyly, it goes to work on the basic economic and psychological underpinnings of the divide; it undermines the idea that all work has a natural gender. See Evans and Nelson, *Wage Justice*. The mixtures of progressive and conservative impulses that have characterized both sides of the divide at different moments get a nuanced reading from Nancy F. Cott in her historical study of American feminism, *The Grounding of Modern Feminism*.

34. DuBois, "The Radicalism of the Woman Suffrage Movement," 128.

35. See, for example, Walkowitz, *Prostitution and Victorian Society*, 128.

36. DuBois, "The Radicalism of the Woman Suffrage Movement," 128.

37. See Daly, *Gyn/Ecology*. Maggie McFadden gives an account of this range in her useful taxonomy piece, "Anatomy of Difference." Adrienne Harris has pointed out to me that essentialism comes and goes in feminist psychoanalytic discussions of the penis: "The concept slips, moves in and breaks apart."

38. hooks, "Feminism," 62.

39. Taken together, Alison Jaggar's essays on the equality-difference debate offer a poignant (and I think continuingly ambivalent) personal account of how one feminist theorist developed doubts about the equality position. See Jaggar, "Sexual Difference and Sexual Equality"; Jaggar, "Towards a More Integrated World"; Jaggar, "Sex Inequality and Bias in Sex Differences in Research."

40. See, for example, Stansell, *City of Women*.

41. For Chavkin, Jaggar, and Jehlen see notes 30, 31, 32, and 39 above.

42. Eisenstein, *The Radical Future of Liberal Feminism*; Mitchell, "Women and Equality."

43. The feminist scandal of the Sears case offers a particularly disturbing example of the divide as it can get played out within the exigencies of a court case. See Milkman, "Women's History and the Sears Case"; and Scott, "Deconstructing Equality-Versus-Difference." In her introduction to *Feminism and Equality*, Anne Phillips offers a useful instance of how, in different contexts, the feminist ambivalence about liberalism emerges; she observes that in the United States, feminism began with equality models that revealed their inadequacy in practice, while in Britain, feminists began

with a socialist critique of liberal goals that their own disappointments have modified in the equality direction.

44. See the now classic restoration of Mary Wollstonecraft by Juliet Mitchell, "Women and Equality." Also see two more recent, subtle readings of Wollstonecraft: Yeager, "Writing as Action"; Kaplan "Wild Nights". An instance of Wollstonecraft's contemporaneity: Linda Nochlin makes precisely her arguments about gender; Nochlin sees it as a variable changeable as class or vocation in her groundbreaking essay, "Why Have There Been No Great Women Artists?"

45. Wollstonecraft, *A Vindication of the Rights of Woman*, 35.

46. Wollstonecraft, *A Vindication of the Rights of Woman*, 5, 30.

47. Firestone, *The Dialectic of Sex*, strikes me as offering the best instance of this mixture of tones in contemporary feminism. Firestone dedicates her book to de Beauvoir, but her political fervor comes much closer to Wollstonecraft's.

48. Rosenfelt and Stacey, "Second Thoughts on the Second Wave," 351.

49. Lorde, "The Transformation of Silence into Language and Action."

50. Since the Hyde Amendment restricting Medicaid abortions in 1976, No More Nice Girls has done occasional, ad hoc street events in New York City to dramatize new threats to women's sexual autonomy.

2

CRITIQUING A GENDER DIARY

Binaries

The most enduring disagreement about the "Diary" has been between those who see me as having finally succumbed to an iron binary, and those who see me as having finally gotten out of that strict order into a more dynamic, historically contingent representation of what I call in the piece, "the divide."

I used to respond to those who thought the "Diary" was based on a reductive binary by elaborating further on my doubts about transcendence. Many readers have suggested "third ways," a synthesis beyond divide thinking, and I have often liked their constructions, while still insisting that, in some larger sense, third way thinking is not a quick path out of the basic tensions I've named. As the literary critic Barbara Johnson puts it, binaries do need to be confronted; they do necessarily "play the role of the critical fall guy. . . . [But] the very impulse to 'go beyond' is an impulse structured by a binary opposition between oneself and what one attempts to leave behind."[1]

Part of my point about the divide was precisely its reductiveness, its many limitations as a basis for thinking about women's identity as political actors. The reductiveness of the divide is related to the reductiveness of that cultural production, "women," the endurance of the idea that they—far more than men—are limited and relative creatures.

In *Only Paradoxes to Offer*, Joan Scott places the abiding (rather than timeless) strength of the divide as part of the history of Western modernity. To see why women's movements oscillate between constructing and deconstructing "woman" requires, says Scott, "reading the repetitions and conflicts of feminism as symptoms of contradictions in the political discourses that produced feminism."[2] Feminism, then, is a response. To understand this is to understand feminism's dependency on other systems of meaning, to rid oneself of the misleading illusion that feminism stands alone as a complete world view—an idea that hides the very dynamics feminism needs to know and change. Feminism arises to trouble the sleep of Western men who claim to have achieved "democracy," "equality," and "liberty." Male domination of women is much older than these claims, but these particular conversations—the feminisms of modernity—are responses to social and political revolutions that offered individuality and freedoms to women with one hand and, with the other, snatched them away. Contemporary liberals, social democrats, advocates of open civil societies who bemoan the limitations or divisiveness of identity politics, need to think again. In key respects, identity politics takes form from democratic liberalism's promises and short falls.

I would put it now: The divide is a recurring contradiction common in many modern political movements, a tension which itself gives rise to narratives of power. Like all traditionally recurring, powerful constructions, "the divide" has a paradoxical energy. It provides groups with ways to organize themselves and at the same time it conforms to received ideas. "The divide" is, among other things, an expression of a theoretical and social impasse; it is difficult to get beyond it to the new thinking all my "third way" critics so rightly long for. To describe the divide is not to love it, but it is to respect it as more than an ephemeral manifestation. Whatever status one finally chooses to grant binaries—and however productive it is to recognize current terms as subject to change through political action—deconstruction comes hard.

Metaphors

Escape. For all these cautions about how long changes in depth structure take, there's still something radical and attractive in people's resistance to the "Diary's" metaphor of "the divide" that I don't want to lose. I find in some old notes from a talk Gayatri Spivak gave: "All metaphors are bad"—one of the typical provocations I love in her work. Of course, what follows in the notes is a tissue of poetry, though no single metaphor holds. She is elusive, telegraphic, escaping the prison of each metaphor though the door of the next. She goes faster and faster, because "all metaphors are bad," but there's no way to give them up, no such thing as nakedness.

Though I didn't mean "the divide" as a fixity, and though I tried to demonstrate my metaphor's instabilities, all the same, spatial images like "the divide" or falsely concrete names reinforce themselves. They beg to be repeated. My colleague Heidi Krueger told me that, reading the piece, she felt "bludgeoned by polarity." Oh, dear.

Efforts to break out are valuable and push the envelope. For example, supporting third way thinking, feminist philosopher Sonia Kruks criticized "the divide" of the "Diary" by wondering if individuals don't indeed construct their own enduring synthesis; she suggested that new subjectivities are places where third way thinking develops. Similarly, resisting the overdetermined, static quality of the divide metaphor, Barbara Balliet suggested what I think is so, that my description gives "a false wholeness to these positions," that the situation is less a story of division than, in Balliet's alternative metaphor, of "proliferation." In a related insight, Don Scott wondered if by now the categories of the divide aren't in the process of emptying out, on the way to disappearing—as new resistances to gender take form. Linda Gordon observed, in a thoughtful note to me, that only some of the many divisions in feminism "are dichotomous." She also pointed out what I thought was implied, but perhaps not clearly enough, that in the "Diary," I was sometimes identifying the same "divide" called by different names, while at other times I was describing genuinely different feminist constructions, which may not be as analogous as I thought. The divide's conceptual disorderliness and my own may need further separating out.[3]

Still others worried that my particular depiction of the divide obscured the centrally important dynamics of race, class, and sexual preference, which they saw as the more enduring depth structures of "division." For example, Maud Lavin kept writing "context" in the margins, seeing the divide as too abstract a proposition for the social complexity of feminism as lived in different moments, different racial and class configurations. In discussions of the divide, it's always important to ask *cui bono* about any characterization of conflict. In a similar request for context, Julie Abraham asked how the divide position would be of any use in parsing the epigram: "I don't want to be a woman but I do want to be a lesbian." (On a dare, let me try: in this witty formulation, one politics of identity is being rejected and another substituted—but with the larger destabilizing effect of dragging bits and pieces of identity into the realm of choice, play, pleasure. In maximizing a gendered *choice*, one moves the more static concept "gender identity" off center, to a place where *being* a woman is not the point but *choosing* a woman is.)

To loosen the constraints of the metaphor "the divide," I wish to offer a rival metaphor: "loopholes," means of escape. I long for moments when the daily, oppressive pressure on women both to be and not be "women" transmogrifies into some state that's not so maddening or so overdetermined. I welcome all evidence that the whole equality-difference tension is outworn, emptying out, with no resonance for a new generation. Avaunt to metaphors that constrain more than they serve. Queer dissolves definitions.

Feminists may need to seek a less stable and static picture of our conflicts, but should we worry, too, that the open-ended flexibility we so eagerly substitute for the binary might itself be easily co-opted, rigidified, and internalized as a pressure constantly to change ourselves, in a new construction of female lability and compliance? Might "flexibility" be women's new job, the new doubleness—or proliferation—required of us by changes over which our politics can barely be said to preside? For all that I want swift movement, flexible identities, free fall, and pleasurable masquerade, I also want to apply skepticism to these metaphors, too.

Experience

The diary entries here are not meant as precise examples of the divide; they are instead emotionally shaded accounts of daily political life. There is, however, nothing raw about them, nothing meant to claim a special status as the real. Rather, they are as instrumentally deployed as all the other writing in the "Diary." I wrote those sections because I wanted a level of disorder which changes in form can provide, but any use of memoir opens another can of worms, the large question feminists continue to debate: What is the status of "experience"? What value do I place on the "diary" element of "A Gender Diary"? What did I hope for from it?

As I recall it, in my consciousness-raising group in New York City in 1970, we all believed in the truth of "experience"—*tout cours*. Women had a range of specifically "women's experiences" but, suborned by men's lack of interest or general contempt or hostility, we had paid poor attention to these experiences of ours; we hadn't discussed them among ourselves, we hadn't elevated them to acceptable cultural subject matter; often we had barely named them, or we were using *their* names: "whore," "dog," "depressed menopausal housewife." Women's historical record, women's daily activities, women's angle of vision—all were "hidden" or "silenced." This was the language of then.

Of course, even "then," quite different women were reporting quite different experiences. Indeed, the discovery of variety as well as unity was part of consciousness-raising's power, and, as I said in the diary, different women took different ideas about what "woman" means away from the circle. In retrospect, I see that they were also thinking differently about what sort of enterprise it is to name new "experiences." They thought about where "experience" comes from according to quite different (not always consciously recognized) intellectual traditions. Some had science as their model: Women's authentic experience was there; new questions would reveal it (not create it). Others put power at the center: Men, the stronger class, controlled the prevailing definitions of "women's experience" and circumscribed women's actual social opportunities. In this construction, women had so far failed to become a group, to rebel, because they suffered from false consciousness. Men had hidden them from themselves and limited them by force. But there was a material truth about women's oppression, which women could know and from which they could construct a group—and a rebellion.

In yet another related materialist account, the early women's liberation group, Redstockings, developed what they called "the prowoman line": What a woman reports about herself is all the authenticity there is, and no one has any further right of interpretation. This assertion of women's rationality and rejection of women's duped complicity was a remarkable starting point, a radical rejection of the available interpretative languages. Believers in the prowoman line recognized women as colonized but decided to listen to them attentively anyway—for some difference, some grain of independence which must be there, just because men cannot be everywhere and all at once. Somehow, women, too, are active players. Women's interests are different from men's; therefore, they have a different reality to report, develop, and defend. However it may look, women are always already acting out of their own necessity, their own best interests in a bad situation. (One famous example was makeup: Was wearing makeup an example of how brainwashed women were—slaves to fashion and men's approval? No, said the prowoman line: Makeup is war paint. Men have the power and the money and women seek their approval out of a rational assessment of what one needs to do to survive.)

So, in the early days of the second wave, the keyword "experience" did a lot of skewing around. Nonetheless, through all this ruck of newly forming ideas, the issue of women as reporters of experience—as beings with our own subjectivity—was always front and center in our talk. Developing the terms for women to describe their experience, and the independent politics to extend and change that experience—these were the main things we thought we were doing. Did we ever go so far as to say that in our small feminist groups we were *inventing* new experiences for women? I don't remember it that way. This level of sophistication came later—with the crucial theoretical advantages of deconstruction, and its accompanying anxieties over whether or not there remain any shared grounds for women's solidarity. Rather than disparage an earlier self, or drown knowledge of our early moves in self-criticism, let me urge instead that these early, philosophically naive constructions of "experience" were tremendously productive.

The struggle to cobble together the available ideas about what one is and what is happening can lend one a certain pride of authorship. The pace, the constant pressure to reinvent oneself in modernity expands opportunities for resistance. People are always describing themselves to themselves, but this always colonized cultural activity is also—forgive my reach for what I can't be sure of through these metaphors—half-baked, threadbare, a thinking on one's feet. What's unsatisfying in current scripts pushes us to tell the story again.

So, now I would put it: Down with a belief in "experience" as a source of independent meaning, of hidden truth, of sturdy reality. But viva "experience" as mess, a garment woven in culture but always poorly stitched together—a hybrid well recorded, sometimes, in diaries.

In 1970, I began a weekly radio series on *Womankind* (WBAI New York) about women's diaries and letters. When I try to get into the head I had in 1970 as I developed the series, which ran for several years and which included discussions and excerpts from all kinds of texts, from slave narratives to the letters of Jane Carlyle, from the diaries of plantation mistresses to journal entries written by a friend, Gail Kuenstler, only weeks before being aired, I hear a kind of excited babble, which was a typical noise then. The founding idea of the series was that women had often written in marginal literary forms that expressed their displacement from the cultural center. Combining what was in the air, I saw women as silenced, but also, mysteriously, indirectly, as speakers. At the moment I introduced the subject of form, I was noticing conventional limitations in what women wrote, but at the same time, I was placing fervent hope in the hidden rebellions of expressiveness I sought to discover in private writing. Any expectations of encountering experience in the raw soon died, but my intent in airing "experience" as a mobilizing and complex fiction lived. I read the diaries as women's claim to own their experience, sometimes even as a formal battle cry. The claim to own the account of one's life was a possible if steep path out—into social visibility, hence into a changed social landscape. The women I discussed had often used diaries as forms of escape from being nothing; at the same time, writing diaries felt safe. No one would hold these scribblers' feet to the fire. No one would even bother to complain of any lack of coherent framing devices, system, design, ambition.

One of the series's main themes was about the erasure of women's texts, the burnings by relatives and by women themselves—because what women scribbled wasn't important, not something to preserve; or because women's scribbles tell secrets; or because purging what women say is an act of purification. (The A. of "A Gender Diary" burned her childhood journals on her wedding day.)

My radio shows deplored women's marginality, but they also expressed exasperation about how women joined men in immolating themselves. I empathized and complained about women's lack of confidence, the quaver I sometimes detected in their authorial voices, their fear of being found out. The radio series changed, moving from discussions of diaries of the past to my call for listeners to send me their private writings, which I would— triumphantly!—make public. In response, I received a current diary from a woman living in the suburbs with husband and kids, also in an active culture of wife-swapping; isolated, she was pickled in passion, rage, and despair. She called herself only "Mary Occupant" of a suburban address. In 1971, her rich text interested me primarily for the way it was shot through with self-hatred, illustrated by this short excerpt from near the end of the several volumes she sent—much of which we aired:

> Keeping a journal has not, I feel, really "helped" me in any way. Instead of making me know my own mind, it has made me feel that my mind is a fragmented maelstrom of conflicting ideas and opinions.

How differently I read this now. Excuse me, "Mary Occupant," if I ever patronized you. Living in day-to-day busyness with husband, children, the new sexualized consumerisms, the fast arrival of popularizing texts about liberation, you felt that your mind was "fragmented." Male authority was incoherent, too. The rules were in precipitous motion, and the men in Mary O.'s frenzied life sent mixed messages that drove her half-mad with confused yearning and existential dread. Hail to Mary O., who knew her own mind as well as anybody, and who was buried and miserable and didn't know her own mind at all.

The shift, the constant circling and retelling, these are part of the search for the loopholes, for the places where, denied subjectivity, colonized by negative images or controlling narratives, people generate (incipiently) new narratives anyway.

I no longer believe in acts of autonomous self-creation in the way I did in

1970. At the same time, perhaps out of that same gormless optimism that made me one of those earlier activists in the first place, I do believe in loopholes. The theorists whose work has chastened my earlier confidence in the benign possibilities in political organizing have also provided me with precious new material to cobble together into "feminism."

1998

Thank you to the following who discussed "A Gender Diary" with me in wonderful conversations: Julie Abraham, Barbara Balliet, Linda Gordon, Heidi Krueger, Sonia Kruks, Maud Lavin, Don Scott. Thank you, too, to Gail Kuenstler and to Mary Occupant (a pseudonym) for allowing me to read and air their unpublished diaries.

As I read these excerpts now, in 2013, from a long "Afterword to A Gender Diary," which I wrote in 1998, I hear the backlash atmosphere of that time. Feminism was on the defensive. In 1998 my university, The New School for Social Research, canceled its only-four-years-old MA in Gender Studies and Feminist Theory. When students protested, the provost of that year explained to them that gender as a category of academic inquiry was a fad.

Since my university is almost as resistant as ever, why do I feel so much less defensive today in 2013? Old age confirms the wisdom of the "Diary," its recognition of oscillation and of failure as an inevitable element in all political success. I no longer fear feminism's death. Of course it dies a thousand deaths, but women keep demanding autonomy, which seems to be a reliably offensive provocation. Just claiming independence for the subject position "woman" continues to drive people wild with rage, leading to a desire to repress, which has the usual result.

In the backlash years, rage, once the fusing emotion of feminism, was more often the property of those who feared feminism. They said outrageous things, for example that women should die in childbirth rather than have an abortion, or that only willing women can become pregnant through rape. In reaction, in 2012, there was another turn: Women who had forgotten all about feminism or had never even heard about it felt wonder as they recognized this sea of misogyny in which women continue to swim. "Teach the fish to question the water" was one of our feminist sayings in the 1960s.

Tone and context change, which is why I maintain my confidence in diaries, as reports from a particular time and place. A diary is a literary form, a creation of voice, the product of a private process of selection. It has been most of all in literature that I can see the ambiguity and uncertainty that properly surround my single-minded passion for feminism.

2013

Notes

1. Johnson, *The Critical Difference*, xi.
2. Scott, *Only Paradoxes to Offer*, 3.
3. These comments were all made in conversation.

II

MOTHERS/LOVERS

3

INTRODUCTION TO MOTHERS/LOVERS

From my first burst of intense activism, say 1969 to 1979, what I mainly recall is a prevailing feeling shared across all sorts of different feminist groups, a mixture of outrage and hope hard to recapture now. Sexism, racism, capitalism were all under attack on many fronts; we expected everything was going to change. I remember sitting on the train home after hours of talking to women, truly at ease in a public place for the first time in my entire life, breathing deeply, taking as much space as I wanted. Have we written enough about how erotic these new freedoms sometimes felt? Most of us were young of course, but that can't fully explain the general atmosphere of passion set free, the literal embodiment of the name the movement had then: "Women's Liberation."

Beginning in 1980, my memories change. Instead of a blur of excitement and continuous, tumbling revelation, my activities and ideas separate out into quite different strands. I am amazed that these intense engagements were all going on more or less at the same time, from fighting backlash to building women's studies programs; from participating in the heterogeneous women's peace movement to urgently criticizing the feminist antipornography movement. Looking back, I seem to have been living in a number of narratives at once, like a character in avant garde fiction. Discourse shift must have been daily, and feminist activists must have been learning or inventing new languages by the hour. I associate these different feminist projects with different people, aesthetics, locations, emotions. This was a time of constant transitions, compartmentalizations, glossolalia.

Early on, fault lines in U.S. feminist movements along race, class, and sexual difference had rendered "sisterhood" a utopian wish, far from the reality of the many movement reproductions of social inequalities. But in the acute backlash years of the 80s and 90s, tensions multiplied with the loss of movement momentum and the dwindling of opportunities to grow and win. Time slowed down. Anger at differences and exclusions continued, but a new feminist alienation took many forms beyond these frames. Disappointment was often directed into internal movement struggles, and uncertainty about the feminist future lowered all boats. In this section, "Mothers/ Lovers," the slash is meant to indicate strain among fundamentally different strategies and desires in this period.

Years of talking to Dorothy Dinnerstein made me self-conscious about something that I already felt and knew with some distress, the depth of human ambivalence—mine and everyone's. (I've included in this section an account of feminist ambivalence about motherhood.) Dorothy was forgiving about how we human beings fail to see what we are doing to the planet. After all, we hardly understand the implications of our clever inventions. But she was urgent about the need for adults to grow up and fully grasp our dangerous situation. In our discussions, male violence was cast as a complex species adaptation now threatening us all with death. Dorothy crafted a subtle etiology of the hatred of women, which feminists could use as a basis for rethinking motherhood, fatherhood, and the problem of care in general. The asymmetrical relations between women and men created deep structures of difference—but these, she argued, have always been subject to change. It is this confidence in the lability of human beings that makes Dorothy Dinnerstein's work so deeply suggestive for feminism.

Two of the pieces in this section describe Dinnerstein's arguments in *The Mermaid and the Minotaur: Sexual Arrangements and Human Malaise* (1976). The word "malaise" captures her evocative understanding of us creative and destructive human beings—full of passion and constantly driven by insecurity and regret. Working with Dorothy, I wondered what other U.S. feminists had been saying about motherhood. Here I include that research, "Changing Our Minds about Motherhood: 1963–1990," with a timeline, as evidence: Feminist ideas about the good life—whether choosing motherhood or not— mutate radically with the times. But throughout we seem to find it hard to theorize the mixed toxicity and loveliness of being mothers. And do we want men to have this rich and often difficult experience, too—or not? Some feminists see men as incapable of the day-to-day care of their children; Dinnerstein argues for the crucial importance of their learning how.

It was while dwelling in this broadly speculative atmosphere that I first heard about the new feminist antiviolence movement. Exciting! Relevant to what I was thinking then about how feminist activism might change the culture of male violence and misogyny. What would a new antiviolence movement do beyond the work of important institutions we were already creating, like battered women's shelters, rape crisis centers, and reform of the police and the courts? These were necessary but not sufficient and were already being appropriated by hospitals and a justice system not overseen by feminists or managed with feminist sensibility. Indeed, we needed more—but exactly what?

In San Francisco in 1976, feminist organizing against violence (Women Against Violence Against Women—WAVAW) had early transmogrified into a group with a different emphasis (Women Against Violence in Pornography and Media—WAVPM). At the same time, I, too, was writing about women's sexuality, media, and pornography: "Mass Market Romance: Pornography for Women is Different" (*The Radical History Review*, 1979) was an early example of what became a flood of feminist academic work on popular culture, in this case Harlequin Romances; "The Front Line: Notes on Sex in Novels by Women, 1969–1979" (*Signs*, 1980) was a survey that showed how little women felt free to write about sex at all. I had also just begun working with Christine Stansell and Sharon Thompson on an anthology, *Powers of Desire: The Politics of Sexuality* (Monthly Review Press, 1983). We were looking for any help, any language, for talking about women's sexuality—and men's. For example, was romantic love a mechanism of women's oppression? Did men have similar yearnings—what for? Was it even useful to talk about what "women" want or what "men" want? Why assume that sexuality and the range of difference in sexual desires would necessarily be organized along gender lines?

In our quest, we found little material to work with. Taboo clustered thick around all our themes. Our publisher told us to beware: we would mostly get smut. But Carole Vance gave us a more on-target warning: "People will do anything to escape this topic. Don't settle for pieces about menstruation and breastfeeding, when what you want is new thinking about sexuality." We tried to focus on sex, but we saw, too, that the borders of this subject were hard to establish and contested. Shame was one barrier to this conversation, and ignorance of each other's sexual lives another. We considered our book as merely a beginning in what would need to be a long and open-ended exploration.

In this state of interested unknowing, in 1979, I went with my women's group, which we sometimes called "The Sex Fools," to an antipornography conference and march through Times Square. Modeled on California's WAVPM, this was the founding of the New York-based group Women Against Pornography (WAP). Given all that has passed since on the contested ground of feminist work on sexuality, that sunny day seems like a key moment, containing in miniature so much that was to follow. Two friends—Marty Pottenger and Katie Taylor—criticized this focus for feminist organizing from the first and gave out a dissenting leaflet to the marchers as we streamed along the porn zone of 42nd Street. Their flier reminded us that there were working women on every corner we passed. The mayor of New York City saw them as sleazy and expendable, and this march seemed to join him. We were part of his clean up, contributing to the larger, steady move toward clearing out "undesirables" and making the city ready for realtors. What support were we offering prostitutes and sex workers, some of whom were organizing on their own behalf? As Adrienne Rich asked, with whom were we going to cast our lot?

At the conference that followed the march, these fault lines became even clearer. In clusters in the corridors, many began to express dismay. At first I couldn't believe that other feminists were saying that pornography was a major cause of violence against women. I could think of so many others, for example arising from the growing work of feminist psychologists and historians. This reductive idea of cause and effect seemed absurd. Besides, there were so many different kinds of sexual material out there—not to mention the slew of other images, decorous pictures of women with their clothes on, that showed them as inferior and in need of constant instruction from men.

In 1981, Carole Vance chose "towards a politics of sexuality" as the possible subject of the yearly Barnard Conference, The Scholar and The Feminist IX. Barnard convened a planning group, and Vance had to persuade us that sexuality should indeed be our topic. All year, we discussed women and sexuality in an exploratory mode, trying to avoid any unexamined assumptions about the sexuality of either "men" or "women." The explosion at the conference, April 24, 1982, is well known; readers can find the gory details in Vance's careful account in her epilogue to the first edition and her introductory piece to the second of *Pleasure and Danger: Exploring Female Sexuality* (1984, 1992).

Perhaps I can encapsulate some of the anger and aggression expressed at the conference by antipornography activists by describing the tee shirts Women Against Pornography wore as they marched back and forth before the gates of Barnard College, picketing the conference: On the front—"For

Feminist Sexuality," and on the back—"And Against SM [sadomasochism]." But it was the Barnard planning committee's goal to ask the very question which WAP activists seemed to think had a foregone answer: What might we mean by a "feminist sexuality"? This simple message on a tee shirt seemed to imply that there were proper limits to sexual feelings and behavior, which all right-thinking feminists would know and choose to guide their sexual lives. Those who openly questioned such boundary-setting at the conference, or who were proposing entirely different questions and frameworks, were called perverts and betrayers of feminism, labels that damaged lives and careers in the years that followed.

In fact, we in the planning group had often been startled to hear about each others' ideas and desires, tastes and taboos. We speculated about where our different pleasures and prohibitions came from. Social and political identity seemed to be a part of sexuality, but the correlations didn't line up neatly: The femme confessed to liking being on top. The tough girl, along with the general majority, preferred being on the bottom. It turned out that the markers "lesbian" and "straight" didn't tell us all that much, and differences in sexual mores along race and class lines were also unpredictable, often contradicting stereotypes.

We wondered what sexual landscapes different women might design if they had more sexual safety, confidence, and agency. Perhaps the familiar lines between public men and private women divided up sexual space as they did the social and political worlds. Did it then follow that changing current maps of the public and the private would change sexualities? Or was sex a different territory and not necessarily bounded by the social? What feminist politics could we imagine that could actually change desire? Questions. Questions.

Carole Vance's iconic formulation, that women in patriarchy will always be calculating their sexual actions, balancing between "pleasure and danger," has entered the language without attribution and captures the openness of these meetings. Some crumbs from these conversations can be gleaned from Vance's "Diary of a Conference on Sexuality," meant as the conference program, and then confiscated by the Barnard administration a few days before the meeting, in a crescendo of anxiety organized by antipornography activists. This was just the kind of shutdown we conference planners had hoped to forestall. I think one could say that this conference was the beginning of what came to be called "the feminist sex wars."

In the early 80s, friends used to ask me why I was bothering with this fight over sexual representation, which they called "sleaze." Why did I care? One said, "A plague on both your houses." But this common image of the feminist sex wars as having two fully articulated "sides" obscures the stages of the sex wars as I understand them. First came the new and passionate antipornography initiative. No doubt, like many others, these feminists missed the movement intensity of the early 70s. Regrettably, however, they achieved the revival of earlier excitement by emphasizing a form of outrage that could all too easily gain public traction in a deeply conservative time. I have often wondered whether antipornography activists recognized or worried about how closely the targets they chose and the language they employed for their campaign mapped onto nineteenth-century feminist purity crusades and onto the then fast-growing right-wing furor about "immorality," the loss of "respect" for women, the "decay" of the family, the "murder" of the "innocent" fetus, etc. Certainly, their antipornography writings show no signs of concern that they were reproducing repressive, punitive definitions of sexuality that might hurt any number of individuals and groups.

It was this slippage into an older idea of female virtue and male vice that disturbed a number of feminists. We sharply criticized the drawing of a line between good girls and bad girls, between sweet, sensual, "egalitarian" sex and hot, driven, patriarchal, "subordinating" sex; we saw the effort to eliminate or control pornography as a strategic wrong turn. Surely this was a move away from feminism's earlier ideas of erotic exploration and sexual freedom for women—even in a patriarchy.

Proceeding cautiously, we believed with Gayle Rubin that feminists have no special claim to knowledge about sexuality, about behaviors and feelings inflected by gender but not necessarily determined by it. In spite of insisting on this indeterminacy, we rejected the idea of "compromise" or "moderation" in our confrontation with antipornography thinking; we saw the over-simple account of sexuality in the new antipornography movement as threatening to the future of feminist work. The idea that the popular image of feminism for a new generation would be that male sexuality was, *tout court*, "violence" had tragic dimensions. Was protection our best hope? For me, and I believe many others, the definition of feminism as the building of walls, in the false hope that such defenses would end male violence, was desolating.

I feel even more today than I felt then that it was urgent to push back against the imputation that feminists see women as the passive victims of male sexuality. Those of us who were trying to put together a reasoned response to the new movement saw men's violence against women as a complex, multicaused behavior that went beyond the sexual, certainly beyond sexual images. We, too, wanted radical changes in male sexual culture, but in this new, falsely polarized atmosphere it was hard to express rage about male violence without being pulled into the antipornography vortex. In effect, the antipornography movement largely closed down a more wide-ranging feminist conversation about both sexuality and violence. We didn't want to add credibility to the already-existing right wing antivice campaigns; stigmas on sex and increasing repressions were everywhere, and we already had plenty of evidence that more policing would not create the security we needed or make the liberatory changes we wanted. This was a defining moment for what I continue to claim as "radical feminism."

In the months after the Barnard Conference in 1982, it became clear that antipornography feminism was on a roll. In 1983, Catharine MacKinnon and Andrea Dworkin drafted their proposal for an ordinance in Minneapolis to make the production or selling of pornography actionable if it fulfilled a series of definitions so broad as to include all sorts of images, for example, if it showed a part rather than the whole of a woman's body. This extraordinary prohibition alone would have indicted a wide and indiscriminate swath of sexual images and texts, from art to sex education manuals already under attack by some religious groups.

In 1984, in an atmosphere of real alarm about where feminist activism was going, a number of feminists convened FACT (the Feminist Anti-Censorship Taskforce), an action group to organize opposition to these new definitions of feminism and specifically to oppose versions of the ordinance whenever they appeared—including those sponsored by right-wing legislators riding high in the Reagan years and happy to join feminists in the legal, state repression of what they called "immorality" or "the degradation of women."

FACT activists didn't see all pornography as "degrading" to women. To me, the word "degrading" was a constant irritant. How can an image "degrade"? I was always complaining about the implications of this word, as if women can automatically be shamed by representations or even misrepresentations of their sexuality. How strange were these times, so far away from the kind of speculative discussions many feminists were having in other voices, other rooms.

In the midst of the struggle to counter the antipornography ethos, some members of FACT decided to edit a small book of the articles we were writing and the talks we were giving nonstop. An editorial group formed (Kate Ellis, Nan D. Hunter, Beth Jaker, Barbara O'Dair, and Abby Tallmer) and worked with three artists in FACT (Hannah Alderfer, Beth Jaker, and Marybeth Nelson). The texts of *Caught Looking: Feminism, Pornography, and Censorship* (1986) are polemics, histories, and analyses. Taken alone, they are a useful record of FACT's main arguments. But the artists turned the collection into much more: a powerful collage of words and images that is still circulating in the world, a distinguished instance of collective, political art.

Among my favorite things about the brilliant *Caught Looking* was its position in our historical moment. We, and many others, had challenged the legality of all the versions of the ordinance, and if the Supreme Court had taken on the case and had reversed a lower court's decision that the statute was unconstitutional, we could have been a first test of whether a serious publication, laced with images from the history and current variety of the genre, pornography, could be considered actionable under this dangerously vague law. By this point, the amazing first generation of feminist lawyers were fully engaged, including FACT member Nan Hunter, and had written FACT's amicus brief. In 1986, we all breathed a sigh of relief when—unfortunately for reasons so different from our multiple objections—it was settled that the Ordinance was unconstitutional on First Amendment grounds.

The pieces I've included in Mothers/Lovers from the glut we all produced, trying to reclaim what we saw as the deeply radical and liberatory potential of feminism, are representative of two modes I used then for entering this discussion. First, my analysis of the antipornography position, "The Feminist Sex Wars: Retrenchment Versus Transformation." Second, several of many literary reviews from this period of *Sturm* and *Drang*. My piece about David Garnett's human-to-animal fables was meant to sneak up on more unstable ideas of sexuality than the prevailing feminist discourse allowed. The two pieces here about Angela Carter, including reviews and an interview, also were meant to point to transgressive and radical alternatives. This great feminist writer was taking apart sexual mores by altering all the old scripts.

Finally, I want to include in this note on the years of Mothers/Lovers a tribute to Carole S. Vance. Vance's leadership has always been quiet and her fundamental role in conceptualizing what we sometimes sardonically called the anti-antipornography position is often overlooked. She claims that the Barnard Planning Group, the Sexuality Conference IX that followed, the founding of the Feminist Anti-Censorship Taskforce, and a number of other inventive initiatives were all collective endeavors. Indeed they were. But all collectives have organizers who bring the group together and establish the conditions for making creative political interventions. This was Carole. As the many who value her focused, brilliant interventions will recognize, she never gives herself the credit that is her due.

In the end, FACT's basic analysis of why feminist campaigns against pornography are misdirected and politically damaging to Women's Liberation were largely accepted in the feminist theory world. Much interesting work on sexual images and meanings was produced in the academy in the 1980s and continues, and queer theory has radically questioned former boundaries around sexual identities and desires. In the larger U.S. context, however, what was originally antipornography movement rhetoric has gone mainstream and continues to corner the language for describing the root sources of violence against women. In fact, women's autonomy—as sexual beings and as citizens—continues to be fought over everywhere in the world, using many fast-changing discourses.

The work continues. Women face terrible repression, violence, and patriarchal policing all over the world. Feminists must seek solutions that honor women's agency and confront the many social structures that overdetermine the oppression of women. Valuing sexual freedom for women is central to this fight. Just now, women in India are demonstrating in the streets against recent, brutal rapes, claiming "the right to loiter." Women need chances to seek pleasure in spite of all the dangers.

2014

4

DOROTHY DINNERSTEIN

Creative Unknowing

When I first read *The Mermaid and the Minotaur* in 1977, a bright light went on in the world. There, at last, in gorgeous, three-dimensional detail someone had described the inner workings of the gender injustices that had burned me all my life.

Why and how did the book make such a difference to many like me who read it in the late seventies? To get at its initial impact one would need, first, to remember, or imagine, the decades before the revival of feminism. Misogyny was the very air we breathed then: "In the long years before second-wave feminism, women and girls were unquestioningly belittled. Daily insulted without remark. Definitely tracked away from achievement. Aggressively ignored or ignorantly aggressed upon. Assumed as helpers, and when unhelpful, called bitches or witches. Humiliation seemed fitting and pride made one faintly ridiculous."[1]

The great outburst of indignation against this common state of affairs that revived an activist feminism in America had already peaked and was losing some momentum by the time *Mermaid* first appeared. The many women who had risen up on the high roll of that passion had barely had time to sort out where our mass explosion of rage came from—or what we were going to make of it in the long term. Deeply enlivened as I had felt by the new reading of the world that feminism offered, my delight and activist work had often been accompanied by a shadowy, unformed anxiety: "But there is something wrong with women. There is something distasteful about them (us)."

For example, armored by feminism as I supposedly was, I could still find myself: in a magazine store, exclaiming with enthusiasm to my lover about some article I had found, "Hey, look at this," and crumbling entirely at his ordinary/extraordinary answer: "Don't give me orders!" Why was I ashamed by his absurd response? After all, I had been merely lively, active, reaching out with a peremptory confidence for friendly company. In fact, I would never have had the nerve—had I had the desire—to boss. Yet nothing felt more familiar than this shame, this cowed acceptance of the fact that my lover—and by extension, men in general—found my energy unseemly and overwhelming. Feminism, so hopeful and utopian, had made promises of transformation through the exercise of nineteenth-century virtues like knowledge and will and effort. Meanwhile, little daily episodes like the one in the magazine store were wearing me down and crippling my new feminist resistance.

To my amazement and deep relief, Dorothy Dinnerstein had written about what I wordlessly felt: "The stone walls that activism runs into have buried foundations."[2] The book offered a full anatomy of the men who run the world yet fuss like threatened children when women with less worldly power say "Boo." Such men, she argues, are continuing their endless acts of separation from the ruler of their infancy, mother. Women, too, are complicit in the daily injustices they suffer since they, too, distrust the mother in themselves.

Dinnerstein offered a subtle, revealing account of the deals men and women have traditionally struck with each other, including what was for me the first intelligible, usable explanation for women's shamed acquiescence in male power, and our ambivalence about our own uses of force. She saw the female monopoly of infant care as decisive in all the gender asymmetry of social life that follows. It is a woman who introduces us to the world before we can recognize her as a limited, mortal being like ourselves. Struggling out from under the control of this first alluring, seemingly all-powerful person is the biggest fight we ever fight. Exhausted, we fling ourselves out of the sea full of mermaids onto the dry land of minotaurs who roar and strut but who nonetheless seem much more tamable and rational in contrast to the mother still stalking in an infantile layer of our personality.

Dinnerstein argues that male power in the public sphere feels right, even when terrible; at least male tyranny stands on the firm ground of adult mastery and will; at least it seems solid in its denial of absurdity, limitation, and death. For the most part, public projects are carried on without the constant modifying influence of doubts. One boldly builds the bomb: one doesn't let anxiety about how to stow radioactive garbage slow one down. Worrying about the waste products of human efforts is somebody else's job, and that irritating, nagging somebody is a woman. ("Don't give me orders!") Men agree to build the world while women agree both to support them in this struggle and to give vent, like harmless jesters, to the knowledge both sexes have that "there is something trivial and empty, ugly and sad, in what he does."[3] A proverb records this bargain: Men must work and women must weep.

In spite of feminism's extraordinary energy and collective will, which did indeed change so much, hatred and fear of women is entrenched, pervasive within us as well as without. The Mermaid and the Minotaur didn't rescue me from this fact, or from my vulnerability to policing by men, but Dinnersteinian knowledge shifted the burden, making my common womanish feelings of self-doubt, foolishness, inconsequence into a shared—perhaps an alterable—condition.

Such a public airing of women's often unconscious, usually private griefs went a long way toward explaining where the powerful rage of feminism comes from in our time. The ancient symbiosis between men and women, with its traditional divisions of labor, was never fully consensual, never reliable. In modernity, the old arrangements show increasing strain. Women notice and suffer from this crisis more. They are now supposed to do both men's and women's traditional work, an emotional and physical overload neither honored nor supported by the culture. Because they are the ones who were dependent on that symbiosis to recognize themselves as valuable and whole, they feel bitter when men retreat from the traditional responsibilities of the old bargain. But finally, however much they depended on it, women lost more under the old regime, sacrificing sexual impulse and worldly freedom. From that dear old familiar system's decay they have the least to lose.

Dinnerstein's evocation of the age-old arrangements between men and women often approaches poetry. In her circuitous prose, she re-creates the familiar pull of culturally rich versions of the heterosexual past, the dance in the village square, the men kicking and shouting and twirling women whose job it is to admire and magnify male strength. This dance, the old quadrille, lingers in our unconscious, however much we consciously reject its certainties. She argued that our asymmetrical gender arrangements are among the common neuroses by which we have traditionally glued ourselves together—always precariously. Dinnerstein looked for the depth structures that hold the dance in place, even as it becomes a *danse macabre*, and found the near universal fact of female-dominated infancy. As long as childhood is ruled by mother alone, she argued, the child will revenge itself on her and on her surrogate, mother nature, in a more and more technically proficient expression of infantile disappointment, in unreasonable, murderous assaults that our life web cannot long sustain.

The many psychoanalytic and scientific insights that coalesced in Dinnerstein's grand argument were not news. Her founding assumptions were in Freud, in Ruth Benedict (she had considered becoming an anthropologist), in Melanie Klein, in Simone de Beauvoir, in Norman O. Brown, in Herbert Marcuse, and in her great teachers, the gestalt psychologists Wolfgang Kohler, Max Wertheimer, and Solomon Asch (whose Social Psychology was a central source for all she thought). But in spite of her warmly acknowledged indebtedness, Dinnerstein was the first to combine a full recognition of the difficulty of the gender conundrum with a full belief in the possibility of changing what she called "sexual arrangements and human malaise." She offered an account of a deeply embedded, unconscious and enduring complexity without cancelling the possibility of a purposeful struggle for change. For feminists, this was water in the desert.

It felt new that Dinnerstein both saw the difficulty and imagined ways out. Her ambition was dazzling: Men could learn to nurture. Women could outgrow the existential cowardice of dependence and take on world building. Children could face the terrifying fact that both men and women are limited and limiting. They could outgrow the grief of learning early that their parents are merely human, not mythic-monstrous mermaids or heroic-destructive minotaurs. They could look somewhere else for the charms of transcendence and defilement. They could know more about their inevitable sorrows. They could grow up.

How wildly romantic it all sounds as I describe Dinnerstein's argument twenty-three years after I first read it. Though belief in the social construction of our gender arrangements is now taken for granted, very few current thinkers write sweeping scenarios for social change like those in *Mermaid*. Which leads one to ask where such ideas came from, and what their after history is likely to be.

Dorothy Dinnerstein was born in 1923 in New York City, in a then teeming, poor, Jewish neighborhood of the Bronx, where, at family dinner tables, so many of that culture group known as the New York intellectuals sharpened their debating skills and built up their big thoughts about revolutionary change. Leftists and modernists more likely to discuss Lenin-versus-Trotsky than religion, they were nonetheless deeply influenced by older Jewish beliefs in the power of study and debate to bring moral truths to bear on everyday life. Finding the right answers mattered because figuring out the internal dynamics of change offered opportunities—hard to grasp, perhaps, but always there.

I have a few notes Dorothy scrawled in longhand about her father and mother:

When I was maybe 5, [my mother] said God was not a big person in the sky but a "little bit of everything," i.e., everything that is is in part sacred. Yet she herself embodied the grunginess, the shitty, mean quality of all reality. [My father], timidly and in his glimmering-across-distance way, was the one who conveyed the elusive omnipresence of grace, the always-evaporating halo of sacredness surrounding and suffusing ordinary event. Still, he submitted to the authority of her meaner, more "practical," more "normal," more "necessary" vision. . . .

Maybe a couple of years later (1929 or 30?) I learned that they were faithful Norman Thomas socialists. . . . Also, they were pacifists: war wrong. . . . Amazing event (Was I 12? Was it 1935?) re movie "All Quiet on the Western Front" when I had my big agonized revelation war would come and seize our lives soon: [my mother] was arguing at me for spoilsport agitation on a festive outing. [My father], I sensed even then, knew I was right but wouldn't stand up for me. . . .

It must have been in the last year of [my father's] life—1948—that he told me of his young psychoses. [Nathan Dinnerstein had a nervous breakdown as a soldier in World War I. He obsessed for hours, drawing a "mystic symbol uniting all world religions. . . ." His plan was to drop letters instead of bombs on the Germans "which would make them *see*."] [Notes from 1982]

In dreams began responsibilities. Dinnerstein was one on whom nothing was lost. Out of her mother's mundane materiality and her father's potent/impotent mix of vision, fantasy, and despair she began early to build her theories of how people parcel themselves out, dividing up the various capabilities that lie in being human. The Big Questions meet the smaller social imperative to narrow one's sights to having a pleasant day at the movies. People choose the piece of life to which they will orient their attention, but there is nothing fixed about this. People change their focal length all the time—or at least they can. Life can feel sacred or not. One grandmother focused on the Friday night candles; the other spent months alone, ostensibly opening or closing the family retreat in the Catskills, but actually sinking into a great independent solitude. This second grandmother, "Shana Esther," so dignified, so lacking in the usual female sense of domestic duty, was Dorothy's ego ideal. She saw that men and women didn't fit well into their slots and early concluded that the whole system is less solid and stable than it seems.

One invents oneself out of the available materials. Reality is something a person shapes from the perceptual field. The possible perceptual range was always her urgent question: "I was sleeping," said the four-year-old Dorothy to her grandfather. "How do you know you were sleeping?" she recalled his asking, and remarked that this was "a very respectful question to ask a child."[4]

She became a psychologist, initially an empiricist, working with Kohler, Wertheimer, and Asch. Except for one luminous and premonitory article in a psychoanalytic journal about Hans Christian Andersen's "Little Mermaid" (a story of a little girl who, against the odds of the gender system, tries to become more fully human), Dinnerstein's professional publications before Mermaid were records of her laboratory experiments on perception, memory, and thinking.

She knew Mermaid was different, and she imagined her scientist colleagues asking what on earth a nice laboratory psychologist like Dorothy could be doing, writing a mess of indefensible statements like this. On one of those author information sheets publishers send to their writers, she acknowledged herself a split being (her great theme) and wrote that with Mermaid she was starting to assert her other half: "This split follows from the fact that some of the problems in which I am interested lend themselves to clean, elegant little laboratory studies while others do not."[5]

But such absolute antinomies were Dorothy's enemies; she never let them stand for long. And, indeed, reading as an amateur through her experimental pieces, I find her differing from Harvard's S. S. Stevens on the subject of context and perception; she is interested in how "the wider context can affect the character of some local piece of what we experience as reality." In a letter to her in 1965, Stevens is cool, dismissing her ambitions: "The context problem with which you are wrestling is rather hopeless, isn't it?"[6]

Hopeless? Dinnerstein was always interested in this question: How much can we hope to know about ourselves? Human self-reflexivity is our curse and genius. Stevens was arguing that context introduces bias and distortion; it's better to neutralize context effects to do good science. Dinnerstein cared about method and precision, too, but she wanted nonetheless to study that mess, "context." She distrusted the drawing of lines, the blinkering of observation: just this complex and no further. Indeed, such deceptive neatness was the danger toward which she directed her final work, about the complex variability of human sentience. She wanted to get at "the flexible responsiveness of the nervous system to the available stimulus array, a responsiveness which enables the perceiver to extract the optimal amount of experience, of exercise for his perceptual capacities, and of useful information, out of each situation in which he finds himself."[7]

In all her work, Dinnerstein was tracking human "flexible responsiveness," the way we can shift the frame to extend our capacities to think and know. At the same time, she always saw human perception, memory, and thinking as full of the perversions that come from our rage at limits. What clever, dangerous, lazy animals, split between our delight at how much we can positively know and do, and our reluctance to live, since we know we must die. Dinnerstein was a great observer of human ambivalence, weaving Freud and the other influences on her adult life together with the various family voices in which great dreams for a socialist future met cautious, ironic, immigrant doubts about everything. *Mermaid* is a conversation with all of her mentors; she is grateful, but she confronts them: Why did they not seek to know human "flexible responsiveness"? Why did they not see that gender can change, and with it the way we live gender scripts, the way we confront nature and death?

Dinnerstein comes from a time when great utopian hopes were jostled but not dismantled by great traumas of violence and failure. (At the end of *Mermaid*, she offers in the super-fluidity of her descriptive powers, full and revealing portraits of her parents' generation, of her own, and of the New Left, whose rages she deeply understood.) In the early 1980s, at the height of the antinuclear movements of that dangerous time, many young women flocked to Dorothy to ask her what she thought the prospect was for peace, good sense, an end to a destructiveness suddenly gone global. Never did she answer the same way twice. On the one hand, pessimism was in order. Human beings are hopelessly angry, their common condition. On the other hand, optimism was in order. We cannot really know just what our limits are. Doubt can be applied as easily to doom as to survival. Human flexible responsiveness might well lead to the necessary, enormous changes at the last minute before the poisoning of the world.

At age 69 Dorothy Dinnerstein died in a car crash on a rainy day just a few blocks from her house in New Jersey. She was alone in the car and no one else was hurt. She had been a distinguished professor of psychology at Rutgers Newark for thirty years, and was now emeritus. For several years her memory had been going and she had heroically tried to keep her mind working while sharply noting in painful diary entries what she was so expert at observing, the vagaries of perception, "the soft spots or cracks . . . in the human sense of reality."[8] On whatever level of consciousness it occurred, she resolved in an apocalyptic instant her escalating distress at her failing power to keep life's events in some kind of order. But right up until the end, in lighter moods, she could laugh with her friends about our great hopes for change and our false hopes for mastery. As at her childhood dinner table, we would talk, talk, talk, just for the pleasure of talking, always knowing it was probably fruitless to talk about deep changes in gender arrangements.

But, who knows? Maybe, she sometimes thought, something will come of it. She wrote *Mermaid*, she said, for the pleasure of setting in place a full description of how prevailing gender arrangements might be understood as keys to current human limitations, childishness, and rage. There's no reason to think knowing this will make any more difference to the world than earlier dreamers made by intoning that God is love. But, who knows? (And maybe that earlier call, too, was of use?) Whether or not it can fulfill its wild ambitions as a wake-up call to the species, *Mermaid* (along with the early movement texts of Juliet Mitchell, Nancy Chodorow, Jane Flax, Jean Baker Miller, and Adrienne Rich) stands as one of the founding texts of contemporary feminist psychology.

How could such a book slip out of print unremarked and disappear from social debates about gender and mothering in which it was initially so central? A few years after Dorothy's death, I was an outside examiner at her last doctoral student's thesis defense. The event brought together people with a variety of relationships to both Dorothy herself and to her work. Questions were raised about whether or not Dorothy's ideas had dated. Would she have written differently if she had lived to read the new work about the biological bases of sex difference? "Yes," said one of the men who had worked with Dorothy for years, "what is the scientific status of Dorothy's work now?" At that moment I was much struck by the passive stance of this question. In academia, the work that endures is the work that others choose to engage. Surely the answer to Dorothy's continued usefulness and importance lay with us in that room. Did we still argue with her in our articles, find her formulations descriptive and suggestive—or not? In fact, few of the men in the room had taken on the disruptive and disturbing challenges of the argument in *Mermaid*. Some spoke of biology as destiny as if Dorothy had never confronted relevant questions about the maternal body. But, in fact, she always granted biological science a large place in her speculations and had been much influenced by some of these very colleagues at Rutgers, among them her late husband, Daniel Lehrman, who studied the mutual interdependence between biological and social influences on the behavior of birds. Her theory is based in the science they all shared, from Lehrman's observations of the plasticity of animal behavior, to her other colleagues' studies of the far greater range of human social invention. She acknowledged biological limits without believing scientists could easily determine what those limits are, since those scientists are themselves unstable amalgams of body and context.

This exchange at Rutgers dramatized some of the problems in *Mermaid's* ongoing life as a classic. The book is misread. Or it is not read. Or it is ignored, pushed to the edge of consciousness, where we harbor things that we half know but that are unwelcome.

For example, inside feminist debates, *Mermaid* is often faulted for not being angry enough at men, not blaming them enough for their coercive violence, not separating enough from their (patriarchal) theories. Odd. *Mermaid* says men have reached the end of their traditional rope and are risking us all in a mad dash toward species death. Is this not blame? But Dinnerstein sees them as so far gone in their work of armoring themselves and staving women off that they are unlikely to stop what they are doing, no matter how much women nag and carp. Hence, it is women who will have to take more responsibility. Dinnerstein criticizes women for the multiple ways they have of sidestepping this task, since her expectations for new male initiatives to limit human recklessness are very low indeed.

Another charge the book often faces is that it is culture bound and ahistorical, that it describes heterosexual women in nuclear families in the West as if their situation were a timeless universal. Dinnerstein has been criticized as not sensitive enough to difference, for example, being unaware of how lesbian existence or sexual arrangements in other cultures offered exceptions to her argument. In fact, she anticipated these charges and went to great lengths in the book to respond to them. First, she acknowledged her location and its limits. Then she insisted that at the intrapsychic level at which she was speaking, the fact of mother-dominated infancy trumped other variables. The near universal female monopoly over infant care has indeed been treated by Freud and others as unchangeable—but not by Dorothy. In contrast to most of her mentors, Dinnerstein insisted on bringing childrearing practices into history. She believed their universality was contingent, not inevitable, and argued that human beings are constantly rebelling against such depth structures, which are inherently unstable. Nonetheless, she was theorizing beyond conventional ideas of difference, toward a shared politics that includes a respect for its own origins in a preverbal, unconscious life. Far from ahistorical, the book winds up to an apocalyptic vision: she saw recent history, say since 1945, as a time of accelerating danger, a near end to species life. We are moving fast—either toward a recognition that we must rein in our mad impulses, or toward doom. I suppose predicting an imminent end of history could be called ahistorical, but history, particularly recent Western history, is one of the things Dinnerstein writes about best.

Yet another charge: The book blames mothers. If this criticism of *Mermaid* were less frequent I'd easily dismiss it as a simple misreading of Dorothy's complex sentences, of the way she often takes on the voice of the unconscious so it can be heard. But so many readers conflate Dinnerstein's account of how infants see the mother with what she thinks the powers of the mother actually are that there must be a real problem here. Somehow Dinnerstein's description of how a monster mother is stalking around in all our heads is taken as her idea of who the mother really is. Of course, she intends us to take away just the opposite, that real mothers are flawed, mortal, struggling beings who are usually doing their best while in the fantasy life of their small children they are all-powerful providers, the great Goddess Kali, maker and destroyer of worlds. Perhaps the conflation of these two merely shows how hard it is to keep them apart even in our adult minds—and this is just Dinnerstein's point.

Mermaid is often dismissed as hard to read. The sentences are intricate and the structure spiraling and self-referential. But there is no way to avoid the clear argument no matter where you enter or exit the maze. In fact, *Mermaid* explores its core point in such depth and breadth that somewhere in its pages a reader almost inevitably meets him or herself—if he or she only keeps reading. Dinnerstein's prose is powerful and relentless, though like all good art, the book can sustain many levels of reading. When an entire book explores the idea that no one wants to listen to women's fears and warnings, perhaps one may be permitted to wonder if "not-reading" might be the very symptom under discussion.

A few weeks before Dorothy died, she and I went together to a lecture by an eminent feminist. There was much intelligent but unsurprising talk—about work, day care, the continued absence of women in government. Dorothy listened and came along for the coffee after, a polite elder stateswoman, honored but not actively invited to join the academic dance. (Dorothy's lack of interest in the mores of academia, its rituals, rewards, and associations, was notorious. Certain it is that among her friends she would have been the one least likely to be angry or surprised that her book was out of print.) Once we were alone, I offered a penny for her thoughts. She was discouraged: the eminent feminist and her distinguished audience had given no evidence that they had taken on her argument in *Mermaid*. They had never even mentioned changing childrearing arrangements so men would be centrally involved too.

I don't think she was right that feminists hadn't heard her argument. But by the late 1980s, feminists had long stopped hoping for change at this deep, structural level. In the United States, they sought state support for mothers— but wistfully, as a lost cause, and they were so tired of asking for male help that they had collapsed into their old ambivalence about whether they really wanted men involved after all. Dorothy herself had lost heart in those backlash times and had withdrawn some of her interest in feminism, disliking how the movement sometimes isolated gender as if the category could be separated from the great theme that interested her—species survival. In these times of doubt she would argue: Gender changes slowly, against deep resistance, while our species is killing itself fast. She would ask: Might some other way into the maze work better? Certainly the muting of both feminist rage and feminist hope corresponds with *The Mermaid and the Minotaur*'s disappearance from the bookstore.

But this is too dark an account of Dinnerstein's readers. A generation of feminist psychologists continue to converse with *Mermaid*. Nancy Chodorow, Jane Flax, Teresa Brennan, Marianne Hirsch, Hester Eisenstein, Adrienne Harris, Louise Taylor, Mari Jo Buhle, and Jessica Benjamin take Dinnerstein on, pushing beyond her account of women's failed subjectivity and enterprise toward other possible scenarios for childhood interaction and growth. With the reprinting of *Mermaid*, new readers can decide for themselves what is useful in this extraordinary book.

Each generation has its own aesthetics of action, its own relationship to individual and group engagement. In the ten years Dorothy Dinnerstein was incubating *Mermaid*, 1966–1976, the United States was in an apocalyptic mood. Dorothy used this language of crisis and apocalypse. She, too, dreamed of big, sweeping, basic shifts in the human capacity to choose life, to stop pouring poison down the village wells of all the world. But this sweeping voice is now quite out of style. Generalizations about the human condition remind some readers of an empty liberal universalism, which in some guises is rhetorical, hypocritical, and racist. In the current political climate as I write in 1999, "apocalypse" doesn't get at the kinds of danger people are imagining. Instead, new kinds of power are creeping into position here and there, needing no big bombs to herald their stealthy arrival. The global politics that Dorothy Dinnerstein's idea of peace calls for is on the agenda but still hard to imagine. There is a conceptual vacuum where once there was a very specific fear of The End.

Luckily, though, the value of Dorothy Dinnerstein's argument does not depend on its apocalyptic atmosphere. Her observations are detailed and resonant enough to educate very different kinds of movements to the dangers of the gender division of labor. The unjust and destructive asymmetries of gender she describes will continue to shape private and public lives as a post–cold war world unfolds its new banners, social practices, and political lines of control and force. Dinnerstein's accounts of our incapacity to outgrow our hatred of mother remain descriptive and harrowing, while her dream of male-female reconciliation, of a rational coming to terms with the inevitability of our irrationality, breathes out a hopefulness about human malleability that is as necessary as ever.

What became The Mermaid and the Minotaur was only a small piece of what Dorothy had in mind when she started writing. Gender was originally intended as but one example of how our wayward, gifted species has cobbled meanings and mores together, always precariously and with uneven consequences. Other examples were to have been religious belief ("Sex, Eros, and Spirit" was one of her courses at Rutgers) and an examination of the strange line we draw between work and play. The larger argument was meant to create in us a more mature recognition that we are alone here; we are the makers of history and the caretakers of a wild nature that now depends on our growing up, knowing ourselves, and learning self-restraint if that nature is to survive.

At her death, she was writing the book that was to explore these larger intentions, "Sentience and Survival: Mobilizing Eros," which was already clear in outline, a study of the layered, discontinuous nature of human consciousness. It was to be a full catalogue of the mental strategies we use to give us a sense of mastery and an analysis of how these choices so often mislead us, dangerously misdirecting our attention from what we urgently need to know. It is the constant move in scale from intimacy to grandeur that makes both Mermaid and the plan for "Sentience" so evocative. Dorothy saw religion and ritual as ways we develop mental flexibility by moving from our immediate present to the contemplation of first and last things beyond the boundaries of our single life.

Dorothy disliked the idea of memorials, no doubt because she was against grandiosity and fuss. Ignoring her wishes on this one point her daughter, Naomi Miller, and the rest of us held a memorial for Dorothy anyway—a wonderful day, except for her unbearable absence.

It was like the last scene in a play by Shakespeare: the twins come up and are recognized for what they are—the male one with his strut and sword, the female one with her seemingly trivial love of butterflies and her politely suppressed secret knowledge of the limitations of her self-important lover. The men said what a good scientist Dorothy Dinnerstein was, how hard-headed. (One could almost pluck from the air the floating phrase "thought-like-a-man.") The women retold tales Dorothy had loved about the triumph of eros over thanatos, like the one about a woman who falls off an ocean liner and, some hours later, when they discover she's gone and turn back, they find her because she's still swimming.

Though everyone remembered the beautiful Dorothy whose luminous presence had seduced us into changing so much, the men and women spoke so differently that the effect was comic, a parody of the great book. Could it be that this enactment of gender, in these particular, loved, long-observed people, was where Dorothy had gotten all those far-reaching ideas! The scene closed with music. In that moment we all—both men and women—knew ourselves with a fullness, and felt a generosity toward each other that had not necessarily been in the cards. *The Mermaid and the Minotaur* offers forbearance for our limits while demanding that we take responsibility for them. This is a balance never to be fully achieved, always changing—the very stuff of life.

1999

Notes

1. Rachel Blau DuPlessis and Ann Snitow, "The Feminist Memoir," in *The Feminist Memoir Project: Voices from Women's Liberation*, 4.

2. Dinnerstein, *The Mermaid and the Minotaur*, 12.

3. Dinnerstein, *The Mermaid and the Minotaur*, 214.

4. Dorothy Dinnerstein, in conversation.

5. Dorothy Dinnerstein, publisher's author information sheet.

6. Snitow, personal files.

7. Snitow, personal files.

8. Dinnerstein, unpublished diary entry.

5

FROM THE GENDER DIARY

Living with Dorothy Dinnerstein (1923–1992)

> We are mermaids or minotaurs,
> only half human. We sense a
> monstrosity about ourselves.
> —Dorothy Dinnerstein

About the maladaptive relations between man and woman which Dorothy Dinnerstein describes, I, and we all, have much too much experience.

Take the following entry from my diary:

> A male friend I've known well for years turns out to have a daughter. This fact comes out because I happen to tell him about The Mermaid and the Minotaur; otherwise I might never have known of it.
>
> "How old is your daughter?"
>
> My friend casts his head back and makes counting gestures with his fingers. Then he says, with some surprise, "She must be about six now!" My friend doesn't think of his daughter as a secret; a perfect repression obviates the need for secrets. After making one hospital visit shortly after she was born, he has never seen his daughter again.
>
> To me this fact is so stunning that I would like to take Dinnerstein's ideas about the loss we all sustain through the absence of our fathers during our first introduction to life and carve them with a cleaver on my friend's smooth and empty heart.

Another, pre-Dinnerstein memory from the diary: A man I used to love once confided in me that he didn't think I would be a whole person, ever, if I didn't have a child. In my journal I wrote the following fantasy:

I am pregnant. (My lover dislikes birth control; it offends his potency, which my pregnancy proves.) I give him a choice: an abortion or he keeps the baby, not hiring some other woman to nurse it but taking care of it himself. Hating abortion far worse than birth control, he takes the second alternative. A daughter is born. When my lover brings my daughter to visit me, the baby cries and he is forced to interrupt himself to go and pick her up. The baby's schedule keeps him from taking trips or making money. I have a good job so I give him child support and I say, "A few more years like this, having the experiences of women, and you'll be the wisest man in America." For the first time he begins to understand me. I stay away and don't mind that my daughter cries on the rare occasions I see her; after all, it's a wise child that knows its blood mother if that mother has the freedom to go away and lacks the usual guilt to make her stay. Meanwhile, my lover is bringing up my daughter. This experience is the only one that could make him into a fit companion.

At the time I made this journal entry, I knew only that my lover had said something unforgivable, and, worse, something against which I was powerless to defend myself. Now, reading Dinnerstein has clarified these emotions: I had half thought I was a whole human being; my friend reminded me that to him I was not. My friend was afraid of me as an autonomous creature, his mother disturbingly off the leash and on the rampage in the world. My lover told me I would not be a complete human being without the experience of motherhood. I wrote to contradict him, to claim that it is he who needs this experience in order to be completely human.

These angry fantasies come naturally during our era of breakdown in what Dorothy Dinnerstein saw as our asymmetrical sexual arrangements. The female desire to carve a political tract on the unresponsive male heart, of taking the baby back from father (from patriarchal control) and never letting him come near it again, or the self-defeating fantasy of giving a child away—these extremities are the products of desperation, dizzy efforts to correct an increasingly pathological imbalance in the roles of the sexes.

The two stories I have told are Dinnersteinian fables. In the first we see a man who forgot the existence of his daughter. Her needs can have no modifying influence on what he does in the world. He is Dinnerstein's minotaur, "mindless, greedy." He has escaped from mother, and from the mother in himself.

The women in this first story are almost invisible: one is the mother who has been left alone with her child; the other is the frustrated writer. Neither really knows how to beard the minotaur in his far-off den. They are Dinnerstein's mermaids, able to love the child but too socially powerless to do more than impotently rage at its father.

In my second story, the mother is now so furious that she refuses to become Dinnerstein's "treacherous mermaid, seductive and impenetrable representative of the dark and magic underwater world from which our life comes."[1] She tries to become like the man in the first story; she leaves her child, ignores it when it cries. The woman in this story is the revolutionary, running fast because the old world is just behind her. But to enter the male realm, which is free from the chagrins of the nursery, she must sacrifice other parts of herself. She outruns her own strengths; she exhausts herself. She needs to be nurtured by the love and support of the man and of the child she has left behind, just as for generations they both have flourished by being nurtured by her.

In the world Dinnerstein describes and in the world of my stories, there is not as yet a well-established middle ground where the minotaur's world-building project and the nurturant mother can meet. In her interest in the extremes, mermaid and minotaur, Dinnerstein is not saying there is no such middle ground in our actual social life between these mythic, half-human roles. (In fact, she always insists that actual men and women do not, and luckily cannot, fit comfortably or neatly into these sexual divisions.) Rather she is using the myths as metaphors to illustrate the barriers we put between ourselves and change: Dinnerstein is showing us the boxes, so we can see how much time we actually spend outside them.

1978

When I met Dorothy I was a swimmer. She taught me (and most of her friends) to snorkel. After hours of gazing at the fish, Dorothy would make cold-eyed observations about our own species. This was the joy of being with Dorothy at the seashore.

By the end of her life, Dorothy expected very little from human consciousness in the way of a massive move toward peacemaking and preservation. But her skepticism extended to her own apocalyptic side. One thing we know, she would say, is that we don't know what will happen. *Mermaid* approaches the apocalypse, the death of the species, but stops at the brink of prophecy, both impressed and horrified by the range of human capacity. Dorothy believed in human action—people are always doing!—but she saw this ceaseless activity from a great distance, as species vitality, wonderful and dreadful, creative communication and world war. And these things weren't separable, they were part of the same undertaking. For me this confusion of human motives was the hardest thing to learn, and the thing I most craved to know.

One day (when I was a lot younger) I accused Dorothy of speaking apocalyptically but not really believing her dire words. After all, were we not enjoying our days at the beach? If she believed what she was saying, surely she would be devoting every second to spreading the word: Repent, the end is at hand. Our actions were inconsistent! What were we doing on this island, staring at fish for hours?

Her response scuttled sideways like a crab. The beautiful beach. The death of the species. At the same time that we talk about the end of the world, we also enjoy this talking, the fascinating exercise of our faculties, like birds singing from tree to tree. And rather than feeling moral disgust at this mixture, Dorothy saw it simply as Our Situation, the kind of creatures we are. We enjoy the walk along a possibly (not inevitably) dying ocean. That things die is part of why we love them, though it would be a triumph if we could foster their life, love death less. Death and mayhem are inescapable, but we needn't always give them first place, trumping everything. Pleasure and hope are the very things which might motivate us to save ourselves. (In an anecdote she loved, a young man decides to kill himself, jumps off a high bridge, changes his mind in the air, straightens his body out into a dive and survives.) Human ambivalence. Dorothy embodied it shamelessly. She understood it, loved it, despaired over it, studied it.

Before I knew Dorothy, I feared my divided mind. It felt like lying, or stupidity, or inauthenticity. Dorothy greeted the divided mind. We love the world, and we don't. We want to act and do, and we don't. We feel pleasure and delight and, almost in the same instant, we don't. The freedom to take that wonderful-horrible mental life seriously was the gift she gave. She gave freedom—which insight always offers—and though she knew how rarely she or I or anyone can use this gift, still she found ways to keep giving it in amazingly full measure right up until she died.

1993

Notes

1. Dinnerstein, *The Mermaid and the Minotaur*, 5.

6

CHANGING OUR MINDS ABOUT MOTHERHOOD

1963–1990

I've just emerged from a bout of reading, a wide eclectic sampling of what this wave of U.S. feminism has had to say about motherhood. My conclusions are tentative, and there's another study that I've learned arises directly out of this one—a study of how feminists have misread our own texts on this subject. My reading came as the end point of a year and a half of infertility treatments, and although I see now how heavy that experience lies on my own readings, perhaps my misreadings, I've also come to see that *anyone* doing this work is likely to worry about where to stand. I want to criticize the pervasive pronatalism that has so shaped my recent experience—a pronatalism not only in the culture at large but also inside feminism—but this desire inevitably raises the question: Who is allowed to criticize pronatalism, to question the desire for children? The mothers might feel it disingenuous to take on this task; they have their children after all. And the childless are bound to feel that their critique is a species of sour grapes. Certainly, women like me who have tried so hard to have babies late might well feel sheepish and hypocritical about mounting a heavy critique of pronatalism. Will the lesbian community speak up with unembarrassed enthusiasm for the child-free life? Not now. Far more typical at the moment is the recent book *Politics of the Heart: A Lesbian Parenting Anthology*. (Although I find there Nancy D. Polikoff's question to the community: "Who is talking about the women who don't ever want to be mothers?" Her answer: "No one."[1]) In one of the best collections of essays about the decision to mother I've found, *Why Children?*, the editors say they searched for mothers unhappy with motherhood and they found them, but they could not get these mothers to write (Dowrick and Grundberg, 1981). The dissatisfied mothers feared hurting their children if they admitted how little they had liked mothering. And what about the mothers who had children against their will? Are they in a position to complain? Not really, once again: it will hurt the children to know they were unwanted. Besides, women have made an art of turning these defeats into triumphs; women have made a richer world out of their necessities. And so the children rarely hear a forthright critique of how women come to mother in a patriarchy—although, of course, they usually know all about it at one level or another, and guilt is left to fill in the holes of the story.

Women with children and women without them have been bristling at each other for years over the question of authenticity. The fight over the Equal Rights Amendment was a national example of this kind of warfare, but even inside feminism there's no particularly friendly entry point for this discussion. Which speaker has the necessary experience, hence the authority, to speak? Mothers can say they've seen both sides, can make judgments about what motherhood is like. Initiates, they are the ones who can measure the true dimensions of the choice. It's harder to imagine what the non-mothers can tell about their condition. One rises each morning to children—and often, of course, all through the night—but does one rise to the counter-condition—Ah, another day without children? The two conditions are not precisely parallel. And each one has its own narrative taboos.

What I want to argue is that feminism set out to break both taboos—those surrounding the experiences of the mothers and of the nonmothers, but for reasons I find both inside our U.S. movement and even more in the society in which that movement unfolded, in the long run we were better able to attend to mothers' voices (or at least to begin on that project) than we were able to imagine a full and deeply meaningful life without motherhood, without children. Finally, in the defensive Reagan years, feminist ambivalence and guilt about blaming mothers, and our ambivalence about becoming mothers ourselves, toned down and tuned out a more elusive discussion of what choice might mean if there were really two imaginable lives for women—with and without children.

Building a supportive culture for both the mothers and the nonmothers is a crucial feminist task, but in the rising national babble of pronatalism in the 1980s, listening to the mothers was a project subtly susceptible to co-optation. Meanwhile, although I certainly felt that feminism was my shield at the infertility clinic, and that the often desperate women I met there were relatively lucky to be experiencing this loss of a baby now, when feminism is in the air, when middle-class married women work, when the birth rate is 1.9 children per woman, not the 3.7 of 1956, nonetheless feminist culture didn't seem to be producing alluring images or thinkable identities for the childless. What feminist idea about independence of work or political life seemed bracing enough to counter the yearning miasma of the infertility clinic? Could one turn to the feminist critique of the new reproductive technologies? Middle class and well informed, the women in infertility support groups (set up by the national organization, Resolve) had already intimated most of the useful social and medical feminist analysis in books like Andrea Eagan's, Barbara Katz Rothman's, Gina Corea's, and Barbara Stanworth's. Certainly, we all knew we were test animals (for example, record-keeping was the major undertaking at the clinic I attended), but this knowledge of the downsides of medicalization had little bearing on the questions of our desire and need. Where was the feminist critique of our motivation? Why were we such eager consumers of twice-daily injections of pergonal, and mood-altering progesterone?

In 1970, feminism would have been quite hostile to these extreme undertakings, but that can't help anyone now. Indeed, it may well be that that earlier reaction to the pressure to mother was so historically specific that it can have no direct descendants. Young women now can be angry about the threat to abortion without feeling the terrible claustrophobia about the future my generation felt as children of the 1950s. All the same, historical shifts like these cannot fully explain the current flaccidity of the critique of motherhood in feminism. Surely we can't claim that young women have made peace with mothers, or that mothers now have social services or more help, so where has the rage gone? Why does the pronatalism of our period flourish with so little argument from us, the feminists?

To answer questions like these, I've begun to construct a time line of feminism on motherhood. Although the record is complex, and although my generalizations are often contradicted by important exceptions, I see three distinct periods along the line. First, 1963 (Friedan, of course) to about 1974—the period of what I call the "demon texts," for which we have been apologizing ever since. Second, 1975 to 1979, the period in which feminism tried to take on the issue of motherhood seriously, to criticize the institution, explore the actual experience, theorize the social and psychological implications. In this period, feminists began on the project of breaking the first of the two taboos I mentioned earlier—the taboo on mothers' own descriptions of the fascination and joy of mothering (even in a patriarchy) and also the pain, isolation, boredom, murderousness.

By 1979, in a massive shift in the politics of the whole country, some feminist work shifts, too, from discussing motherhood to discussing families. Feminism continues to anatomize motherhood, but the movement is on the defensive. Certain once-desired changes recede as imaginable possibilities. In this period, feminists speak of "different voices" and "single mothers by choice"; the feminist hope of breaking the iron bond between mother and child seems gone, except in rhetorical flourishes, perhaps gone for good in this wave.

I'm going to try—briefly—to substantiate this periodization, but first a reminder: precision about generations and locations is particularly important in a discussion of motherhood. And each person has her own point of entry on this line. Nonetheless, the line has its own power to impose similar conditions, pressures, meanings on women of different ages, races, classes. The particular piece of feminist intellectual history I'm exploring here follows quite closely the trajectory of the baby-boom generation, what demographers call the mouse in the python, a large bulge traveling down the decades.

This bulging generation is very powerful and continues to set its own rules. Its late childbearing has made an upward blip on the generally descending graph of births per thousand. Its experiences disproportionately influence the social atmosphere. When it has babies, the stores are flooded with baby food. The culture this group creates, including the culture of feminism, shapes the era I'm describing here. For the young, the next bit of the line remains a mystery. Current debates about the feminist refusal to pathologize motherhood along race lines, the multiple meanings of black teenage pregnancy, and the low rate of marriage and fertility among college students—all give hints of how women may now be renaming or experimenting with the placement of children in their life cycles. It's a cheerful thought that many readers will have experiences that don't correspond to this outline.

Period 1: 1963 to about 1975

Nineteen sixty-three is the year of *The Feminine Mystique*. The inadequacies of that book are well known. For example, in *From Margin to Center* (1984), bell hooks flips Friedan's story of the home-bound misery of the suburban housewife: for black women of the same period, paid work (which Friedan recommends for middle-class women) was usually drudgery, alienated work; work in the home seemed far more satisfying. Many have criticized Friedan's classism, racism, homophobia, her false universals. But Friedan herself has ignored all this and criticized *The Feminine Mystique* on different grounds altogether. In *The Second Stage* (1981), Friedan blames her earlier book for being antifamily, for trying to pry women away from children, and for overemphasizing women as autonomous individuals. In fact, *The Feminine Mystique* is rather mild on these points; it says nothing most feminists wouldn't agree to today about the need for women to have some stake in the world beyond their homes.

The Feminine Mystique is the first of my demon texts, by which I mean books demonized, apologized for, endlessly quoted out of context, to prove that the feminism of the early seventies was, in Friedan's words of recantation, "strangely blind." She excoriates her earlier self for thinking too much about "women alone, or women against men," but not enough about "the family."[2] In retrospect, it's an amazing thing that books in the early seventies dared to speak of "women alone, or women against men." It was, plain and simple, a breakthrough. Yet we've been apologizing for these books and often misreading them as demon texts ever since.

The most famous demon text is Shulamith Firestone's *The Dialectic of Sex: The Case for Feminist Revolution* (1970). This book is usually the starting point for discussions of how feminism has been "strangely blind" about motherhood. Certainly, there are few of its sentences that Firestone would leave unmodified if she were writing with the same intent today. Her undertheorized enthusiasm for cybernetics, her self-hating disgust at the pregnant body ("Pregnancy is barbaric"), her picture of the female body as a prison from which a benign, nonpatriarchal science might release us have all dated. Her call for an end to childhood—although more interesting, I think, than scoffers have been prepared to grant—doesn't resonate with any experience of children at all. Finally, though, it's her tone we can't identify with, the sixties atmosphere of freewheeling, shameless speculation. Part of the demonizing of this text arises out of a misreading of genre. *The Dialectic of Sex* is an example of utopian writing. (Some of this atmosphere has now been reclaimed—at least for academic feminism—in such work as Donna Haraway's [1985] "Manifesto for Cyborgs.")

Besides this tendency by feminists as well as nonfeminists to misread the tone and genre of *The Dialectic of Sex*, everyone colludes in calling it a mother-hating book. Search the pages; you won't find the evidence. I find instead:

> At the present time, for a woman to come out openly against motherhood on principle is physically dangerous. She can get away with it only if she adds that she is neurotic, abnormal, childhating and therefore "unfit." . . .

This is hardly a free atmosphere of inquiry. Until the taboo is lifted, until the decision not to have children or not to have them "naturally" is at least as legitimate as traditional childbearing, women are as good as forced into their female roles.[3]

In other words, Firestone's work is reactive and rhetorical. The point is always "smash patriarchy," not mothers.

Of course, there are real demon texts more deserving of critique inside feminism, callow works like a few of the essays in the collection *Pronatalism: The Myth of Mom and Apple Pie* (Peck and Senderowitz, 1974), which reject childbearing in favor of having unsoiled white rugs and the extra cash to buy them. There's also some panic during this period about the new term then, the "population explosion." An ecology influenced by feminism has reinterpreted this material for us since, but some of the early essays talk as if once again it's up to women to populate the world properly, this time by abstaining from a killing *overproduction* of children.

But, inside feminism, such moments are rare. Instead I found extreme rhetoric meant to break the inexorable tie between mothers and children. For example, Lucia Valeska in "If All Else Fails, I'm Still a Mother": "All women who are able to plot their destinies with the relative mobility of the childfree should be encouraged to take on at least one existing child. . . . To have our own biological children today is personally and politically irresponsible."[4] In the demonizing mode it's easy to hear this as a party line with biological mothers as self-indulgent backsliders. I hear in it, too, an effort to imagine a responsibility to kids which is not biological. The early texts are trying to pull away from the known and, like all utopian thinking, they can sound thin, absurd, undigested. But mother-hating? No.

The real demon texts I've found in my first period are works of social science outside feminism like the Moynihan report of 1965 on the so-called "tangled pathology" of the black family. Mother really is named as the problem there, and the cure? More power for fathers![5] Black feminists often have to wrestle with this text when they set out to write about their motherhood experience. Ambivalence about the culture of black mothering is hard to express in the same universe where one has also to find ways to contradict the Moynihan report. Attacks on the black family and lack of protection for black children makes mothering heroic, a slap in the face of white supremacy. As Audre Lorde put it, these children weren't "meant to survive," so managing to mother them is a deep contribution to the beloved community.[6]

Finally, in my search for early feminist mother-hating what I found was—mostly—an absence. In the major anthologies like *Sisterhood is Powerful*, *Women in Sexist Society*, and *Liberation Now!* there are hardly any articles on any aspect of mothering.[7] Nothing strange, really, about this blindness. The mouse had only just started down the python; most of the writers were young.

The exceptions, such as several articles in Leslie Tanner's *Voices from Women's Liberation* (1970), offer a program that is unexceptionable even today—for example, Vicki Pollard's "Producing Society's Babies" or the much reprinted "On Day Care" by Louise Gross and Phyllis MacEwan.[8] This second piece argues mildly that women shouldn't just want day care because it will liberate them, but also because day care is good for kids, too. The assumption in this short, initial period is that women's liberation should come first.

The revisions between the *Our Bodies/Ourselves*, which was a newsprint booklet in 1971 and the glossy tome, *Ourselves and Our Children*, of 1978 reveals, I think, the hidden dynamics of our alienation from that earlier time. Under the section "Pregnancy," the early version says such things as: "We, as women, grow up in a society that subtly leads us to believe that we will find our ultimate fulfillment by living out our reproductive function and at the same time discourages us from trying to express ourselves in the world of work." Only after pages and pages of reassurance that "we as women can be whole human beings without having children" does the 1971 text finally ask, "What are the positive reasons for having children?"[9] The feminism of 1970 established a harsh self-questioning about a motherhood that formerly had been taken for granted.

But soon, very soon, this peremptory and radical questioning was misread as an attack on housewives. This has been as effective an instance of divide-and-conquer as I know. By the late seventies, both the mothers and the non-mothers were on the defensive. What a triumph of backlash, with internal dynamics that have been fully explored by Faye Ginsburg (1989) and others, feminists seeking to understand the special bitterness among women in our era.

The rewriting of the material on whether or not to have a child, in the *Ourselves and Our Children* of 1978, carries me into my second period, 1976 to 1980.

Period 2: 1976–1980

The 1978 text couldn't be more different from the earlier version of *Our Bodies/Ourselves*. It acknowledges that "until quite recently" having a baby wasn't really considered a decision, but then goes on to assume that all that has changed, ending with this gee-whiz sentence: "Now almost 5 percent of the population has declared its intentions to remain child-free."[10]

This is a liberal text, celebrating variety without much concern for uneven consequences. Both people who have decided to have children and people who have decided against are quoted at some length, but the effect is false symmetry, with no dialectic tension. The proliferation of people's reasons here is useful and instructive, an effort to get at difference, but the structural result is an aimless pluralism, a series of life-style questions, no politics.

But if in my description of *Ourselves and Our Children* I'm using the word liberal pejoratively, this my second period is also liberal in the best sense of the word: a time of freer speech, wider inquiry, a refusal of orthodoxy, an embrace of the practical reality. In these years the feminist work of exploring motherhood took off, and books central to feminist thinking in this wave were written, both about the daily experience of being a mother and about motherhood's most far-reaching implications.

Nineteen seventy-six alone saw the publication of Adrienne Rich's *Of Woman Born*, Dorothy Dinnerstein's *The Mermaid and the Minotaur*, Jane Lazarre's *The Mother Knot*, and Linda Gordon's *Woman's Body, Woman's Right*. Also in that year, French feminism began to be a power in American feminist academic thinking. *Signs* published Helene Cixous's "The Laugh of the Medusa," which included these immediately controversial words: "There is always within [woman] at least a little of that good mother's milk. She writes in white ink."[11] Mysteries and provocations—which introduced a flood!

My Mother/Myself (1977), Nancy Friday's book, popularized the motherhood discussions in feminism, though it has often been criticized as essentially a daughter's book. Julia Kristeva split the page of *Tel Quel* down the middle in that year in "Love's Heretical Ethics"; she was digging for the semiotic, the mother language of the body before speech. And 1978: Nancy Chodorow's *The Reproduction of Mothering* and Michelle Wallace's *Black Macho and the Myth of the Superwoman*. These books were events. The intellectual work of feminism has its renaissance in these years. Not only does this period give rise to important work but also to fructifying debate.

Rachel DuPlessis introduced the brilliant special issue of *Feminist Studies* on motherhood in 1978 with an encomium to Rich's *Of Woman Born*. She honored what Rich was trying to do—to pry mothering away from the patriarchal institution, *motherhood*. But then, DuPlessis went on to worry that Rich might be overreacting, overprivileging the body. DuPlessis wrote, "If, by the process of touching physicality, Rich wants to find that essence beyond conflict, the place where all women necessarily meet, the essence of woman, pure blood, I cannot follow there."[12] Discussions like these inaugurate our continuing debates about essentialism, the body, and social construction.

DuPlessis says she won't discuss practical politics, but she does ask the larger political question that nags throughout the period but is rarely addressed: Which construction of motherhood is productive for feminist work? If we take Dinnerstein at her word, we're trying to get men to be mothers. If we follow Rich, our energies move toward building a female culture capable of the support not only of women but also of their children. Neither author would put these implications so baldly, without shading. Yet these texts create rival political auras, and feminist theory is still far from sorting out the implications for activism of this great period of groundbreaking work.

It's important to add that, in this period, in 1976, the first Hyde Amendment was passed; we lost Medicaid abortion. Abortion—the primal scene of this wave, won, to our amazement, in 1973—was only affordable for all classes for *three* years before this barely established right began slipping away again. While feminist thinkers were elaborating on the themes of motherhood, that other question—whether or not mothering is to remain a female universal—was slipping, slipping away. Feminist work of this period largely ignores the subject of my second taboo, the viability of the choice not to mother. Meanwhile the New Right was mounting a massive offensive against all efforts to separate women and mothering.

Period 3: 1980-1990

My second period ends—and my third begins—with the important threshold article by Sara Ruddick in 1980, "Maternal Thinking." This piece pushed the work of the late seventies to some logical conclusions. Ruddick took seriously the question of what women actually *do* when they mother. She developed a rich description of what she called "maternal practice" and "maternal thinking." A whole separate study deserves to be made of how this much-reprinted article has been read, reread, misread, appropriated into a variety of arguments. Ruddick herself says that the implications for feminism of her splendid anatomy of mothering are unclear. Is motherhood really a separable practice? Are its special features capable of translation into women's public power? Does motherhood have the universality Ruddick's work implies? Does the different voices argument (also developed by Carol Gilligan in 1982) lead to a vigorous feminist politics?

This is not even the beginning of a proper discussion of Ruddick, but for my purposes here, it's important to point out that Ruddick herself says that her book is not really about what feminism should say or do about mothering. Rather, it provides one of the best descriptions feminism has of *why* women are so deeply committed to the mothering experience, even under very oppressive conditions. Ruddick's work is a song to motherhood—multiphonic, without sugar—but still a song. "Maternal Thinking" is the fullest response since Adrienne Rich to the call to end my first taboo, the taboo on speaking the life of the mother.

It leaves my other taboo untouched, but this might well have seemed benign neglect in any other year but 1980. It was not part of Ruddick's intention to publish her work in the same year Ronald Reagan was elected, yet the meeting of the twain is, I think, part of this small history of U.S. feminism on motherhood.

Ruddick argues—with much reason—that hers is a specifically anti-Reagan text: it includes men as mothers; it includes lesbians as mothers; it demands public support for women's work. But it is extremely difficult to do an end-run around Reaganism by a mere proliferation of family forms. The Left tried it; feminism tried it; everyone failed. (I'm thinking of Michael Lerner's Friends of Families organizing between about 1979 and 1982. I'm thinking of NOW's National Assembly on the Future of the Family in November of 1979. I'm thinking of Betty Friedan's retreat in *The Second Stage* of 1981.) As Barbara Ehrenreich and others pointed out, the word "family" was a grave in which the more autonomous word "women" got buried.[13] The problem with defining any cohabiting group as family and leaving it at that was the disappearance of any discussion of power within that group. Arlie Hochschild's *The Second Shift* (1989) reaffirms what we already intimate from experience: women, not families, continue to do almost all domestic work.

My time line for the eighties is a record of frustration, retrenchment, defeat, and sorrow. Out of the Baby M case in 1986–87 in which a so-called surrogate mother battled for and lost custody of the child she had carried but contracted away before birth, comes Phyllis Chesler's *Sacred Bond* (1988), the very title unthinkable a decade earlier. Certainly, things weren't going our way, and the studies to prove it poured out. In 1985 we get Lenore Weitzman's frightening figures about what happens to women after no-fault divorce, and in 1986 Phyllis Chesler on the injustice of child-custody laws, including feminist-initiated reforms.

1986: My peak year for backlash at least partially internalized by feminism, gives us Sue Miller's novel *The Good Mother* and Sylvia Ann Hewlett's *A Lesser Life*. *A Lesser Life* concerns itself with the horrendous struggles of working mothers, that is, of most mothers now. Hewlett, once a self-defined feminist, is now against the ERA and sees nothing but liberal blarney in legal equality models. In this particularly mean season, in which mothers do everything without social supports, Hewlett wants protection. She simply can't imagine social support for childrearing except as special programs for women, whom she assumes will be the main ones responsible for children forevermore. Hewlett blames feminism for not making demands on the state. Of course feminists did make them. Our failure to win is a complex, historical event Hewlett oversimplifies. Further, one might argue that Hewlett's assumption, that women will inevitably do most of the childrearing, is broadly shared by the men in power, too, and that this attitude itself is one reason it is hard to coerce the state to do the work.

There are exceptions to backlash thinking on the eighties timeline, of course, although several turned out to be books and articles published elsewhere (I find my line doesn't work outside the United States). Kathleen Gerson's *Hard Choices: How Women Decide About Work, Career, and Motherhood* (1985) tried to get at how profoundly women's lives are being changed by work. Sacred bond or not, women are simply spending less of their lives on mothering, more and more on a variety of other things. This book was among the very few I found that tried to address my second taboo, to take seriously the idea that women may well come to see mothering as one element in life, not its defining core. However raggedly, the women Gerson interviewed are already living out basically new story lines, making piecemeal changes over which feminism must struggle to preside.

Also during this period have come the great books on abortion: Rosalind Petchesky's *Abortion and Woman's Choice* and Kristen Luker's *Abortion and the Politics of Motherhood* in 1984 and Faye Ginsburg's *Contested Lives* in 1989. But on the political front it's been some time since feminists demanding abortion have put front and center the idea that one good use to which one might put this right is to choose not to have kids *at all*. Chastised in the Reagan years, pro-choice strategists—understandably—have emphasized the right to wait, the right to space one's children, the right to have each child wanted. They feared invoking any image that could be read as a female withdrawal from the role of nurturer.

Broad societal events like the steady rise of divorce and women's increasing workplace participation collide with women's failure to get day care, child support, fair enough custody laws, changes in the structure of a work day and a typical work life, and finally any reliable, ongoing support from men. Our discouragement is, in my view, the subtext of most of what we have written about motherhood in the past decade. I think women are heartbroken. Never has the baby been so delicious. We are—in this period of reaction—elaborating, extending, reinstitutionalizing this relation for ourselves. Mary Gordon writes in *The New York Times* book review (1985): "It is impossible for me to believe that anything I write could have a fraction of the importance of the child growing inside me."[14] A feminist theorist tells me she is more proud of her new baby than of all her books.

I don't mean to criticize these deep sentiments but to situate them. They are freely expressed now; in 1970, feminist mothers, like all mothers, were briefly on the defensive, and ecstatic descriptions of mothering were themselves taboo. But now, since 1980, that brief past, with whatever its excesses or limitations, feels long gone. Even the still acceptable project of elaborating the culture of motherhood tends now to leave out the down part of the mother's story—her oppression, fury, regrets. One can't speak blithely of wanting an abortion anymore nor skeptically about the importance of motherhood. In the 1980s we have apologized again and again for ever having uttered what we now often name a callow, classist, immature, or narcissistic word against mothering. Instead, we have praised the heroism of women raising children alone, or poor, usually both. We have embraced nurturance as an ethic, sometimes wishing that men would share this ethic without much hoping they will, and we have soldiered on, caring for the kids (in the United States, more first children were born in 1988 than in any year on record), and continued to do 84 percent of the housework. Complaints now have a way of sounding monstrous, even perhaps to our own ears. For here the children are, and if we're angry, in backlash times like these it's easy for feminism's opponents to insist that anger at oppression is really anger at children or at mothers. The New Right has been brilliant at encouraging this slippage, making women feel that being angry at the present state of mothering will poison the well of life. Guilt complicates feminist rage—and slows down feminist activism. There is the mother's guilt toward her children, and the non-mother's guilt that she has evaded this mass sisterhood now elaborated for us all as full of joy and pain, blood and passion, that she has evaded the central life dramas of intimacy and separation described so well in feminist writing about motherhood.

So, in conclusion, what? I hope it's clear that it's no part of my argument to say women shouldn't want children. This would be to trivialize the complexity of wishes, to call mothering a sort of false consciousness—a belittling suggestion. Women have incorporated a great deal into their mothering, but one question for feminism should surely be: Do we want this presently capacious identity, mother, to expand or to contract? How special do we want mothering to be? In other words, what does feminism gain by the privileging of motherhood? My reading makes more obvious than ever that feminists completely disagree on this point—or rather that there are many feminisms, different particularly on this point. And here's another viper's nest: Do feminists want men to become mothers, too, that is, to have primary childcare responsibilities?

Again, the feminist work on this point veers wildly, is murky. Women disagree about what we should want—also about what we can get—from men. bell hooks thinks we're afraid to let men know how really mad we are, afraid to finally confront them. That may be one reason we falter, but there are others: Women ask, for example, "Can men really nurture?" And behind that doubt, or that insult, hides our knowledge of what psychological power mothers have. Why give that up, we may well ask? I suspect that in addition, in our period, women are eager to establish that we don't really need men. This wave of feminism was a great outburst of indignation, and it's important to us to feel that men are no longer necessary, particularly since lots of men are gone before the baby is two. In so far as patriarchy means the protective law of the father, patriarchy's over.

I find a great cynicism among us about ever getting men's help, or the state's. Because we have won so few tangible victories, women tend to adopt a sort of Mother Courage stance now—long suffering, almost sometimes a parody of being tireless.

But it occurs to me that, finally, this picture I'm painting is much too bleak. One can ask other questions that hint at a more volatile situation altogether. In spite of the low spirits of recent movement history, actually, we are living in a moment in which women's identities are extremely labile and expanding. How do we feminists greet and interpret the fact that women are voting with their feet, marrying later, using contraception and abortion, and having fewer children? Do we look forward to some golden age when parental leave, childcare, and flextime will have helped women so much that the birthrate will rise again? Such a thought seems buried in the current feminist piety about abortion, that we want not only the right to abort but also the right to have children, etc. A worthy thought, but one that has not yet been fully examined. Are we to consider the lowered birthrate merely one more proof that women are so over-worked they're ready to drop, or might there be some opportunities for very different desires and choices buried in these broad demographic changes?

Under what banner are we going to fly our demands for mothers? I like best the gender-neutral constructions of this cohort of the brilliant feminist lawyers. Yet, as they would be first to point out, gender-neutral demands—for parenting leaves, disability, gender-blind custody—have their short-term price. We give up something, a special privilege wound up in the culture-laden word "mother" that we will not instantly regain in the form of freedom and power. We're talking about a slow process of change when we talk about motherhood; we're talking about social divisions that are still fundamental. Giving up the exclusivity of motherhood is bound to feel to many like loss. Deirdre English called this "the fear that feminism will free men first."[15] Men will have the power of the world *and* the nurturant experience, the centrality to their children. Only a fool gives up something present for something intangible and speculative; in Jack and the Beanstalk, Jack exchanges the cow for a couple of beans. But even if we can't yet imagine our passage from here to there, from control over motherhood to shared, socialized parenthood, couldn't we talk about it, structure demands? An epigram keeps forming in my mind: "Just because you can't have something doesn't mean you don't want it or shouldn't fight for it."

Let me end with a cautionary analogy: In the nineteenth century, feminism's *idée fixe* was the vote. We won it, but it was hard to make it mean something larger than mere voting, to make it into a source of public authority for women. In our wave, the *idée fixe* has been abortion. If we're lucky, and if we work very hard, we may win it. But just like with the vote, there will be much resistance to letting the right to abortion expand to its larger potential meaning. We seem—this time around—to really want abortion. And this right carries within it the seed of new identities for women.

Postscript

On April 30, 1991, I made a visit, kindly arranged by Hester Eisenstein, to the State University of New York at Buffalo, where a wonderful group addressed the question of the time line.

The younger women in the room reported that they were under acute pressure to have children—and soon. We older ones felt consternation: What form does the pressure take? "Medical. The media, doctors, other women all tell us that if we don't have children, we're opening ourselves to all kinds of diseases like endometriosis and uterine cancer."

Dispirited about the current atmosphere, we compared this threat with the nineteenth-century idea that if women went to college, their uteruses would shrivel up as their brains developed. At the same time, we noted for the record the problem with the counter-claim sometimes made by feminism that all medical limits set in a patriarchy are merely corrupt, that without patriarchy we could control our bodies. This misleading promise led some to assume late babies were no problem at all, and contributed to the very atmosphere which has brought so many women to put faith in erratic and experimental technologies which promise this elusive control.

In yet another turn of the argument, we worried that some recent feminist critiques of birth technology ignore advances on which we've come usefully to rely. Claire Kahane went so far as to wonder if some sectors of the ecology movement, by romanticizing "the natural," had added to the pressures the younger women in the room were feeling to do "the natural" thing.

We moved on to men: Are men trying to break in upon the mother-child dyad with the new birth technologies, or with lawsuits against women who smoke, drink, or take crack while pregnant? If the mother is the enemy of the fetus, the state becomes the paternal rescuer. These thoughts led us to question just how paranoid we wanted to be: Male appropriations are legion and female skepticism is justly epidemic, but how, then, to leave the path open for men to make a more progressive move toward joining women and children?

Certainly, men still fade out of most motherhood discussions. For example, several reported that their college alumni magazines were flooded in the mid-1980s with reports from career women who didn't want to go to work anymore, who wanted to stay home with their kids. This was the new "choice" of the middle class. What made this potentially rich option for variety and change ominous besides its unrepentant class-bound character was the utter lack of this "choice" for men. The "Mommy track" as it was called in the United States was a revised work trajectory that would include time for children. Revolutionary if it were a rethinking of work for everyone, this corporate plan became a symbol of the continuing divide between male and female life-stories—with motherhood the signpost at the crossroads.

Thank you to the feminists of Buffalo.

In other responses, several women have questioned my observation that the U.S. time line of feminism on motherhood won't work for other countries. Marti Scheel writes that in the case she knows, West Germany, the line works if one starts three to five years later, as the baby boom was delayed there. Of course, I'd like to know what other readers outside the United States think.

Greetings from New York.

1992

Timeline: U.S. Feminism on Motherhood: 1963–1990

Compiled by Ann Snitow and Carolyn Morell

Key: All items are feminist or feminist-related unless marked ★. Items marked ★ are relevant articles and events.

1963   Friedan, Betty. *The Feminine Mystique*. New York: W. W. Norton, 1963.

1964   Rossi, Alice. "Transition to Parenthood." *Journal of Marriage and Family* 1, no. 30 (1964): 26–39.

1965   ★Moynihan, Daniel Patrick. "The Negro Family: The Case for National Action." Washington D.C.: United States Department of Labor, http://www.dol.gov/dol/aboutdol/history/webid -meynihan.htm.

1969   Pollard, Vicki. "Producing Society's Babies." *Women: A Journal of Liberation* (Fall 1969). Reprinted in *Voices From Women's Liberation*, edited by Leslie B. Tanner, 193–98. New York: Signet Books, 1970.

Willis, Ellen. "Whatever Happened to Women? Nothing, That's the Trouble." *Mademoiselle*, September 1969, 150, 206–209.

1970   Firestone, Shulamith. *The Dialectic of Sex*. New York: William Morrow, 1970.

Tanner, Leslie, ed., *Voices From Women's Liberation*. New York: Signet Books, 1970.

1971   Boston Women's Health Collective. *Our Bodies, Ourselves*. Boston: New England Free Press, 1971.

Peck, Ellen. *The Baby Trap*. New York: Pinnacle Books, 1971.

★Comprehensive Child Development Act of 1971, S. 1512, 92nd Congress (1971).

1973   Radl, Shirley. *Mother's Day is Over*. New York: Charterhouse, 1973.

★Gilder, George. *Sexual Suicide*. New York: Quadrangle Books, 1973.

★Roe v. Wade. The Supreme Court guarantees the abortion right.

1974   Bernerd, Jessie. *The Future of Motherhood*. New York: The Dial Press, 1974.

Mitchell, Juliet. *Psychoanalysis and Feminism: Freud, Reich, Laing, and Women*. New York: Pantheon Books, 1974.

Peck, Ellen, and Judith Senderowitz. *Pronatalism: The Myth of Mom and Apple Pie*. New York: Thomas Y. Crowell, 1974.

1975   Hammer, Signe. *Daughters and Mothers, Mothers and Daughters*. New York: Quadrangle Books, 1975.

Valeksa, Lucia. "If All Else Fails, I'm Still a Mother." *Quest* 1, no. 3 (Winter 1975): 52–64.

1976   Chodorow, Nancy, and Susan Cantratto. "The Fantasy of the Perfect Mother." *Social Problems* 23, no. 2 (1976): 54–75.

Cixous, Helene. "The Laugh of the Medusa." *Signs* 1, no. 4 (Summer 1976): 875–93.

Dinnerstein, Dorothy. *The Mermaid and the Minotaur: Sexual Arrangements and Human Malaise.* New York: Harper & Row, 1976.

Gordon, Linda. *Woman's Body, Woman's Right: Birth Control in America.* New York: Grossman Publishers, 1976.

Lazarre, Jane. *The Mother Knot.* New York: McGraw-Hill, 1976.

Rich, Adrienne. *Of Woman Born: Motherhood as Experience and Institution.* New York: W. W. Norton, 1976.

Russo, N. F. "The Motherhood Mandate." *Journal of Social Issues* 32, no. 3 (1976): 143–54.

*Hyde Amendment of 1976 ending Medicaid-funded abortions.

1977   Friday, Nancy. *My Mother/Myself: The Daughter's Search for Identity.* New York: Delacorte Press, 1977.

Joffe, Carole. *Friendly Intruders: Childcare Professionals and Family Life.* Berkeley: University of California Press, 1977.

Klepfisz, Irena. "Women Without Children/Women Without Families/Women Alone." 1977. Reprinted in *Dreams of an Insomniac: Jewish Feminist Essays, Speeches, and Diatribes,* 3–14. Portland, OR: Eighth Mountain Press, 1990.

Kristeva, Julia. "Love's Heretical Ethics." *Tel Quel* 74 (Winter 1977): 39–49.

Rossi, Alice. "A Biosocial Perspective on Parenting." *Daedelus* 106, no. 2 (1977): 1–31.

*Lasch, Christopher. *Haven in a Heartless World.* New York: Basic Books, 1977.

1978   Boston Women's Health Collective. *Ourselves and Our Children: A Book by and for Parents.* New York: Random House, 1978.

Chodorow, Nancy. *The Reproduction of Mothering: Psychoanalysis and the Sociology of Gender.* Berkeley: University of California Press, 1978.

DuPlessis, Rachel Blau. "Washing Blood." Introduction to "Toward a Feminist Theory of Motherhood." Special issue, *Feminist Studies* 4 no. 2 (June 1978): 1–12.

Hoffner, Elaine. *Mothering: The Emotional Experience of Motherhood after Freud and Feminism.* New York: Doubleday, Inc., 1978.

Wallace, Michele. *Black Macho and the Myth of the Superwoman*. New York: The Dial Press, 1978.

1979   Arcana, Judith. *Our Mother's Daughters*. Berkeley, CA: Shameless Hussy Press, 1979.

CARASA (Committee for Abortion Rights and Against Sterilization Abuse). *Women under Attack: Abortion, Sterilization Abuse and Reproductive Freedom*. New York: CARASA, 1979.

Chesler, Phyllis. *With Child: A Diary of Motherhood*. New York: Thomas Y. Crowell, 1979.

Petchesky, Rosalind, ed. "Workers, Reproductive Hazards and the Politics of Protection." Special issue, *Feminist Studies* 5, no. 2 (Summer 1979).

Friedan, Betty. "Feminism Takes a New Turn." *The New York Times*, August 26, 1979.

Lerner, Michael. "Friends of Families." Organizing drive, California, c. 1979–82.

Lorde, Audre. "Man Child: A Black Lesbian Feminist's Response." *Conditions: Four* 2, no. 1 (Winter 1979): 30–61.

NOW "National Assembly on the Future of the Family" Conference, New York, NY, November 1979.

"The Scholar and the Feminist VI: The Future of Difference." Conference. Barnard College, New York, NY, April 1979.

Willis, Ellen. "The Family: Love It or Leave It." *The Village Voice*, September 17, 1979, 29–35.

1980   Badinter, Elizabeth. *Mother Love: Myth and Reality*. New York: Macmillan, 1980.

Ehrensaft, Diane. "When Men and Women Mother." *Socialist Review* 10, no. 4 (Summer 1980): 49.

Eisenstein, Hester, and Alice Jardine, eds. *The Future of Difference*. Boston: G. K. Hall, 1980.

Marks, Elaine, and Isabelle De Courtivron, eds. *New French Feminisms: An Anthology*. Amherst: University of Massachusetts Press, 1980.

Oakley, Ann. *Becoming a Mother*. New York: Schocken Books, 1980.

———. *Women Confined: Toward a Sociology of Childbirth*. New York: Schocken Books, 1980.

Ruddick, Sally. "Maternal Thinking." *Feminist Studies* 6, no. 2 (Summer 1980): 342–67.

Weisskopf, Susan Contratto. "Maternal Sexuality and Asexual Motherhood." *Signs* 5, no. 4 (Summer 1980): 766-82.

1981   Bridenthal, Renate, Joan Kelly, Amy Swerdlow, and Phyllis Vine. *Household and Kin: Families in Flux.* New York: The Feminist Press, 1981.

Brown, Carol. "Mothers, Fathers, and Children: From Private to Public Patriarchy." Reprinted in *Women and Revolution,* edited by Lydia Sargent, 239–67. Boston: South End Press, 1981.

Dowrick, Stephanie, and Sibyl Grundberg. *Why Children?* New York: Harcourt Brace Jovanovich, 1981.

Friedan, Betty. *The Second Stage.* New York: Summit Books, 1981.

Hirsch, Marianne. "Mothers and Daughters: A Review." *Signs* 7, no. 1 (1981): 200–22.

Lorber, J., R. L. Coser, A. S. Rossi, and N. Chodorow. "On The Reproduction of Mothering: A Methodological Debate" *Signs* 6, no. 3 (1981): 482–514.

O'Brien, Mary. *The Politics of Reproduction.* New York: Routledge, 1981.

*Ronald Reagan's draconian Family Protection Act proposed.

1982   Barrett, Michèle, and Mary McIntosh. *The Anti-Social Family.* London: Verso, 1982.

Gilbert, Lucy, and Paula Webster. *Bound by Love: The Sweet Trap of Daughterhood.* Boston: Beacon Press, 1982.

Gilligan, Carol. *In a Different Voice: Psychological Theory and Women's Development.* Cambridge: Harvard University Press, 1982.

Lerner, L. "Chodorow's Reproduction of Mothering: An Appraisal." *The Psychoanalytic Review* 69, no. 1 (1982): 151.

Rothman, Barbara Katz. *In Labor: Women and Power in the Birth Place.* New York: W. W. Norton, 1982.

Thorne, Barrie, and Marilyn Yalom. *Rethinking the Family: Some Feminist Questions.* New York: Longman, 1982.

*ERA defeated.

1983   Dally, Ann. *Inventing Motherhood: The Consequences of an Ideal.* New York: Shocken Books 1983.

Daniels, Pamela, and Kathy Weingarten. *Sooner or Later.* New York: W. W. Norton, 1983.

Diamond, Irene, ed. *Families, Politics and Public Policy: A Feminist Dialogue on the State.* New York: Longman, 1983.

Folbre, Nancy. "Of Patriarchy Born: The Political Economy of Fertility Decisions." *Feminist Studies* 9, no. 2 (Summer 1983): 261–84.

Porter, Nancy. "Documenting Experience, Building Theory: Two Books on Mothering." *Women's Studies Quarterly* 7 (Winter 1983): 44.

Riley, Denise. *War in the Nursery: Theories of the Child and the Mother.* London: Virago, 1983.

1984 Allen, Jeffner. "Motherhood: The Annihilation of Women." In *Mothering: Essays in Feminist Theory*, edited by Joyce Trebilcot, 215–30. Totowa: Rowman and Allanheld, 1984.

Alpert, Judith L., Mary-Joan Gerson, and Mary Sue Richardson. "Mothering: The View from Psychological Research." *Signs* 9, no.3 (1984): 434–53.

Arditti, Rita, Renate Duelli-Klein, and Shelley Minden. *Test-Tube Women: What Future for Motherhood?* London: Pandora Press, 1984.

Boston Women's Health Collective. *The New Our Bodies, Ourselves: A Book by and for Women.* New York: Touchstone/Simon & Schuster, 1984.

Delphy, Christine. *Close to Home: A Materialist Analysis of Women's Oppression.* Amherst: University of Massachusetts, 1984.

Folbre, Nancy. "The Pauperization of Motherhood: Patriarchy and Public Policy in the United States." *Review of Radical Political Economics* 16, no. 4 (Winter 1984): 72–88.

Gerson, Mary-Joan. "Feminism and the Wish For a Child." *Sex Roles* 7 (September 1984): 389–99.

Giddings, Paula. *When and Where I Enter: The Impact of Black Women on Race and Sex in America.* New York: William Morrow, 1984.

Greer, Germaine. *Sex and Destiny: The Politics of Human Fertility.* New York: Harper and Row, 1984.

hooks, bell. "Revolutionary Parenting." Reprinted in bell hooks, *From Margin to Center.* Boston: South End Press, 1984.

Luker, Kristen. *Abortion and the Politics of Motherhood.* Berkeley: University of California Press, 1984.

Petchesky, Rosalind. *Abortion and Women's Choice: The State, Sexuality, and Reproductive Freedom.* New York: Longman, 1984.

Rapp, Rayna. "The Ethics of Choice: After My Amniocentesis, Mike and I Faced the Toughest Decision of our Lives" *Ms.*, April 1984, 97–100.

Sevenhuijsen, Selma, and Petra de Vries. "The Women's

Movement and Motherhood." In *A Creative Tension: Key Issues of Socialist Feminism: An International Perspective from Activist Dutch Women*, edited by Anja Meulenbelt, Joyce Outshoorn, Selma Sevenhuijsen, and Petra de Vries, 9–25. Boston: South End Press, 1984.

Simons, Margaret A. "Motherhood, Feminism, and Identity." *Women's Studies International Forum* 7, no. 5 (1984): 349–59.

Trebilcot, Joyce, ed. *Mothering: Essays in Feminist Theory*. Totowa: Rowman & Allanheld, 1984.

1985 Corea, Gena. *The Mother Machine: Reproductive Technologies from Artificial Insemination to Artificial Wombs*. New York: Harper and Row, 1985.

Gerson, Kathleen. *Hard Choices: How Women Decide about Work, Career, and Motherhood*. Berkeley: University of California Press, 1985.

Gittins, Diana. *The Family in Question*. London: Macmillan, 1985.

Haraway, Donna. "A Manifesto for Cyborgs: Science, Technology, and Socialist Feminism in the 1980s." *Socialist Review* no. 80 (1985): 65–108.

Pies, Cheri. *Considering Parenthood*. San Francisco: Spinsters Book, 1985.

Renvoize, Jean. *Going Solo: Single Mothers by Choice*. Boston: Routledge and Kegan Paul, 1985.

Schulenberg, Joy. *Gay Parenting: A Complete Guide for Gay Men and Lesbians with Children*. New York: Anchor Press/Doubleday, 1985.

Weitzman, Lenore J. *The Divorce Revolution: The Unexpected Social and Economic Consequences for Women and Children in America*. New York: Free Press, 1985.

Zelizer, Viviana. *Pricing the Priceless Child: The Changing Social Value of Children*. New York: Basic Books, 1985.

1986 Atwood, Margaret. *The Handmaid's Tale*. Boston: Houghton Mifflin, 1986.

Barrett, Michèle, and Roberta Hamilton. *The Politics of Diversity: Feminism, Marxism, and Nationalism*. London: Verso, 1986.

Chesler, Phyllis. *Mothers on Trial: The Battle for Children and Custody*. Seattle: Seal Press, 1986.

Ferguson, Ann, ed. "Motherhood and Sexuality." Special issue, *Hypatia* 1, no. 2 (Fall 1986).

Gerson, Kathleen. "Emerging Social Divisions among Women:

Implications for Welfare State Politics." *Politics and Society* 15, no. 2 (1986): 213–24.

Heron, Liz. "Motherhood . . . To Have or Have Not? In *Changes of Heart: Reflections on Women's Independence*, 177–218. Boston: Pandora Press, 1986.

Hewlett, Sylvia Ann. *A Lesser Life: The Myth of Women's Liberation in America*. New York: William Morrow, 1986.

Kantrowicz, Barbara. "Three's a Crowd." *Newsweek*, September 1, 1986, 68–76.

Mairs, Nancy. "On Being Raised By a Daughter." In *Plaintext*. Tuscon: University of Arizona Press, 1986.

Ms. Editors. Theme of issue: "When to Have Your Baby." *Ms.* (December 1986).

Omolade, Barbara. "It's a Family Affair: The Real Lives of Black Single Mothers." *Village Voice*, July 16, 1986.

Rothman, Barbara Katz. *The Tentative Pregnancy: Prenatal Diagnosis and the Future of Motherhood*. New York: Viking, 1986.

*Fleming, Anne Taylor. "The American Wife." *New York Times Magazine*, October 26, 1986.

*McBroom, Patricia A. *The Third Sex: The New Professional Woman*. New York: William Morrow, 1986.

1987   Eagan, Andrea. *The Newborn Mother: Stages of Her Growth*. New York: H. Holt, 1987.

Ehrensaft, Diane. *Parenting Together*. New York: Free Press, 1987.

Genevie, Louis E., and Eva Margolies. *The Motherhood Report: How Women Feel About Being Mothers*. New York: Macmillan, 1987.

Gleve, Katherine. "Rethinking Feminist Attitudes Towards Motherhood." *Feminist Review* 25 (Spring 1987): 38–45.

Martin, Emily. *The Woman in the Body: A Cultural Analysis of Reproduction*. Boston: Beacon Press, 1987.

Omolade, Barbara. "The Unbroken Circle: A Historical and Contemporary Study of Black Single Mothers and Their Families." *Wisconsin Women's Law Journal* 3 (1987): 239–74.

Petchesky, Rosalind. "Fetal Images." *Feminist Studies* 13, no. 2 (1987): 263–92.

Pollack, Sandra, and Jeanne Vaughan, eds. *Politics of the Heart: A Lesbian Parenting Anthology*. Ithaca: Firebrand Books, 1987.

Pruett, Kyle. *The Nurturing Father: Journeys Toward the Complete Man*. New York: Warner Books, 1987.

Rosenfelt, Deborah, and Judith Stacey. "Second Thoughts on the Second Wave." *Feminist Studies* 13, no. 2 (1987): 341–61.

Segal, Lynne. "Back to the Nursery." *New Statesman*, February 1, 1987.

————. *Is the Future Female? Troubled Thoughts on Contemporary Feminism*. New York: Peter Bedrick Books, 1987.

Editor unknown. "Motherhood is Political: The Ideal vs. The Real." Special issue, *Sojourner* (1987).

Spallone, Patricia, and Lynn Steinberg. *Made to Order: The Myth of Reproductive and Genetic Progress*. New York: Pergamon Press, 1987.

Stanworth, Michelle, ed. *Reproductive Technologies: Gender, Motherhood and Medicine*. Minneapolis: University of Minnesota Press, 1987.

*The "Baby M" case.

*Smilgis, Martha. "Here Come the Dinks." *Time Magazine*, April 20, 1987, 75.

*Wattenberg, Ben J. *The Birth Dearth: What Happens When People In Free Countries Don't Have Enough Babies?* New York: Pharos Books, 1987.

1988   Aguero, Kathi, Marea Gordett, and Ruth Perry. "Mothering and Writing: A Conversation." *Women's Review of Books* 5, no. 10/11 (July 1988): 29–30.

Benjamin, Jessica. *The Bonds of Love: Psychoanalysis, Feminism, and the Problem of Domination*. New York: Pantheon Books, 1988.

CARASA (Committee for Abortion Rights and Against Sterilization Abuse). *Women Under Attack: Victories, Backlash, and the Fight for Reproductive Freedom*. Edited by Susan E. Davis. Athene Series, no. 7. Boston: South End Press, 1988 (Expanded Reprint).

Chesler, Phyllis. *Sacred Bond: The Legacy of Baby M*. New York: Times Books, 1988.

Eisenstein, Zillah R. *The Female Body and the Law*. Berkeley: University of California Press, 1988.

Epstein, Cynthia Fuchs. *Deceptive Distinctions: Sex, Gender, and the Social Order*. New Haven, CT: Yale University Press, 1988.

Grabucher, Marianne. *There's a Good Girl: Gender Stereotyping in the First Three Years of Life: A Diary*. Translated by Wendy Philipson. London: Women's Press, 1988.

Herman, Ellen. "Desperately Seeking Motherhood." *Zeta*, March 1988, 73–76.

Quindlen, Anna. "Mother's Choice." *Ms*, February 1988, 55, 57.

Weideger, Paula. "Womb Worship." *Ms*, February 1988, 54, 56.

Weinberg, Joanna. "Shared Dreams: A Left Perspective on Disability Rights an Reproductive Rights." In *Women with Disabilities*, edited by Adrienne Asch and Michelle Fine, 297–305. Philadelphia: Temple University Press, 1988.
*Family Support Act (Workfare).

1989   Douglas, Susan J. "Otherhood." *In These Times* (September 1989): 12–13.

Edwards, Harriet. *How Could You? Mothers without Custody of Their Children*. Berkeley, CA: Crossing Press, 1989.

Ferguson, Ann. *Blood at the Root: Motherhood, Sexuality, and Male Dominance*. London: Pandora Press, 1989.

Gerson, Deborah. "Infertility and the Construction of Desperation." *Socialist Review* 19, no. 3, (July/September 1989): 45–64.

Ginsburg, Faye D. *Contested Lives: The Abortion Debate in an American Community*. Berkeley: University of California Press, 1989.

Hirsch, Marianne. *The Mother-Daughter Plot: Narrative, Psychoanalysis, and Feminism*. Bloomington: Indiana University Press, 1989.

Hochschild, Arlie. *The Second Shift*. London: Viking Penguin, 1989.

Olivier, Christiane. *Jocasta's Children: The Imprint of the Mother*. New York: Routledge, 1989.

Purdy, Laura M., ed. "Ethics and Reproduction." Special issue, *Hypatia* 4, no. 3 (Fall 1989).

Rothman, Barbara Katz. *Recreating Motherhood: Ideology and Technology in a Patriarchal Society*. New York: W. W. Norton, 1989.

Ruddick, Sally. *Maternal Thinking: Towards a Politics of Peace*. Boston: Beacon, 1989.

Sevenhuijsen, S., and Carol Smart, eds. *Child Custody and the Politics of Gender*. New York: Routledge, 1989.

1990   Arnup, Katherine, Andree Levesque, and Ruth Roach Pierson. *Delivering Motherhood: Maternal Ideologies and Practices in the 19th and 20th Centuries*. New York: Routledge, 1990.

Chamberlayne, Prue. "The Mother's Manifesto and Disputes over 'Mutterlichkeit.'" *Feminist Review* no. 35 (Summer 1990): 9–23.

Cole, Ellen, and Jane Price Knowles, eds. *Woman-Defined Motherhood*. Binghamton: Harrington Park Press, 1990.

Ehrensaft, Diane. "Feminists Fight (for) Fathers." *Socialist Review* 20, no. 4 (October-December 1990): 57–80.

Finger, Anne. *Past Due: A Story of Disability, Pregnancy, and Birth.* Seattle: Seal Press, 1990.

Gordon, Tuula. *Feminist Mothers.* New York: New York University Press, 1990.

Kaminer, Wendy. *A Fearful Freedom: Women's Flight from Equality.* Reading, MA: AddisonWesley, 1990.

Morell, Carolyn MacKelcan. "Unwomanly Conduct: The Challenges of Intentional Childlessness." PhD diss., Bryn Mawr. Published in 1994 by Routledge.

O'Barr, Jean, Deborah Pope, and Mary Wyer, eds. *Ties that Bind: Essays on Mothering and Patriarchy.* Chicago: University of Chicago Press, 1990.

Rapping, Elayne. "The Future of Motherhood: Some Unfashionably Visionary Thoughts." In *Women, Class, and the Feminist Imagination,* edited by Karen V. Hanson and Ilene J. Philipson, 537–48. Philadelphia, PA: Temple University Press, 1990.

Sandelowski, Margarete. "Fault Lines: Infertility and Imperiled Sisterhood." *Feminist Studies* 16, no. 1 (Spring 1990): 33–51.

White, Evelyn C., ed. *The Black Women's Health Book: Speaking for Ourselves.* Seattle: Seal Press, 1990.

Wilt, Judith. *Abortion, Choice, and Contemporary Fiction: The Armageddon of the Maternal Instinct.* Chicago: University of Chicago Press, 1990.

1992

Notes

1. Polikoff, "Lesbians Choosing Children: The Personal is Political." In *Politics of the Heart,* 49.

2. Friedan, *The Second Stage,* 70–71.

3. Firestone, *The Dialectic of Sex,* 189–90.

4. Valeska, "If All Else Fails, I'm Still a Mother," 61.

5. Moynihan, "The Negro Family: The Case for National Action."

6. Lorde, "A Litany for Survival." In *The Black Unicorn,* 255–56.

7. Morgan, Robin ed. *Sisterhood is Powerful: An Anthology of Writings from the Women's Liberation Movement.* New York: Vintage Books, 1970. Gornick, Vivian and Barbara K. Moran, eds. New York: Signet Books, 1971. *Women in Sexist Society: Studies in Power*

and *Powerlessness.* Anonymous eds. *Liberation Now!: Writings from the Women's Liberation Movement.* New York: Dell Books, 1971.

8. Pollard, "Producing Societies Babies," 193–98; Gross and MacEwan, "On Day Care," 199–207.

9. Boston Women's Health Collective, *Our Bodies/Ourselves,* 73, 76.

10. Boston Women's Health Collective, *Ourselves and Our Children,* 17.

11. Cixous, "The Laugh of the Medusa," 876–93.

12. DuPlessis, "Washing Blood," 11.

13. See as an example, Ehrenreich, "What is Socialist Feminism?," 76.

14. Gordon, "On Mothership and Authorhood," *New York Times,* February 10, 1985, Sunday Book Review, http://www.nytimes.com/1985/02/10/books/on-mothership-and-authorhood.html.

15. English, "The Fear That Feminism Will Free Men First," 477–83.

7

THE SEX WARS IN FEMINISM

Retrenchment versus Transformation

This piece is drawn from a talk that was given to a number of groups between March and September 1983 in response to a growing movement among feminists to identify pornography as dangerous to women. Andrea Dworkin and Catharine MacKinnon then proposed their antipornography Civil Ordinance which tried to put into law the claim that "pornography is central in creating and maintaining the civil inequality of the sexes."¹ In February 1986, the Ordinance was declared a violation of First Amendment rights by the U.S. Supreme Court. The questions remain: How should feminists who want to change sexual culture think about pornography? In which activist direction can we seek a sexual liberation for women that is quite different from the neutral, unembellished promise of the First Amendment?

There is a storm brewing in the women's liberation movement over sexual politics. This is not to say the women's movement is by any means limited to the current debates about pornography. But when a woman today goes searching for the feminism she's heard about, that has called her, she is likely to encounter the antipornography movement, with its definition of sex and sexual imagery as continuous zones of special danger to women. Of late, this has been one burning tip of feminism where energy and feeling collect.

These heated feelings recall the passions that fueled the early days of the present wave of feminism, that fueled the pro-abortion movement and the women's health movement—both also about that contested terrain, the female body. As a veteran of those years, I remember how empowering that anger was, how it opened the eyes and cleansed the blood. We must indeed act out of what we feel or be cut off from the deepest sources of energy and political authenticity.

Nonetheless, I want to argue here that we need to know more about these feelings, or else run the risk of creating a strategy likely to move us away from the very things we say we desire. I want to argue that, in general, today's antipornography campaigns achieve their energy by mobilizing a complex amalgam of female rage, fear, and humiliation in strategic directions that are not in the long-term best interests of our movement. A politics of outrage—which can be valuable and effective—can also seriously fail women in our efforts to change the basic dynamics of the sex-gender system.

Both in Canada and the United States, feminists are moving in the forefront of new political alliances pledged to combat pornography through legal means. Canadians have emphasized municipal bylaws, licensing, and reforms to the Criminal Code, while U.S. antipornography activists are trying to use civil rights legislation as the basis of civil suits. These U.S. laws—now being proposed and tested in court—would allow an individual to claim damages if a public utterance could be defined as "the sexually explicit subordination of women."[2] What does it mean in Mulroney's Canada or Reagan's America to demand new legal means to regulate public sexual imagery? How have we come to this strategic and theoretical point in the history of feminist thinking and activism about men's and women's sexuality?

All that I think about activism centered on the symbolic terrain of the sexual has developed in the atmosphere of the remarkable new work of feminist historians and theorists such as Carl Degler, Ellen DuBois, Barbara Epstein, Kate Ellis, Linda Gordon, Mary Hartman, Carroll Smith-Rosenberg, Gayle Rubin, Carole Vance, and Judy Walkowitz.[3] They provide a frame through which I see women's present efforts to gain sexual autonomy. This work suggests that though there were exceptions, most of the North American activist women who spoke of the importance of sex in the course of the nineteenth century spoke of how hard it was for women to gain control of their bodies within marriage—to control pregnancy. In this effort, middle-class women struggled to establish themselves as moral authorities. Even some of the most radical nineteenth-century activists accepted a general moral scheme in which men were sexual predators, fallen women were victims, and married, middle-class women were sexually pure.

In other words, the vast majority of nineteenth-century feminists accepted a model of society that not only assumed that men and women live in separate spheres, do different social tasks, but also that they have essentially different sexual and moral natures. Vulnerable on many fronts, nineteenth-century women chose organizing strategies to gain protection that *confirmed* gender differences.

If one narrows one's focus to these women, to the last major wave of feminism in the nineteenth century, male and female can look like two fixed, clearly defined categories, almost like two species. But as soon as one draws back and takes a longer view, these sharply defined gender distinctions begin to blur and shift. In the West in the last 150 years or so, the idea that gender is a particularly clear or useful principle by which to organize social life has been steadily eroded. We continue to cling to gender identity, of course—who, we wonder, would we be without it?—but gender keeps changing on us. Take, for example, the mothers of the young women who initiated the present wave of the women's movement. Born into a world where women couldn't vote, either forced to work or discouraged from working, depending not on gender but on class, rushed into the factories during World War II, then out of them again when the real men came home, this generation of women experienced—within one lifetime—four or five fundamentally different versions of what a woman is and does. They had reason to whisper into their daughters' ears that a woman might need to be any number of things.

Each wave of feminism has come a bit closer to facing this frightening malleability of gender. At the start of the present women's movement, we flirted with this idea as never before. Though Anne Koedt wrote in the germinal essay, "The Myth of the Vaginal Orgasm,"[4] that female sexuality was utterly different and out of synchronization with male, other theorists, such as Shulamith Firestone (*The Dialectic of Sex*), were saying the opposite, that gender and sexuality were separable, that sex could be set free from the old gender boundaries, that birth control and the chance of economic independence outside the family were going to make a tremendous difference, were going to change what *being a woman can mean*. For a brief, heady moment, women as different as Koedt and Firestone joined to proclaim the right to demand a sexuality more centered on female pleasure. Though consciousness-raising groups discussed rape and spent long sessions detailing "what men do to us around sex," their predominant mood was one of hope: we felt we could fight our oppression effectively.

But gradually the mood of the women's movement changed and its organizing shifted in emphasis. In general, there was a move away from insisting on the power of self-definition—think of the Lavender Menace, or the early celebration of the vibrator, or the new heterosexual imperative that one should demand from men exactly what one wanted sexually—to an emphasis on how women are victimized, how all heterosexual sex is, to some degree, forced sex, how rape and assault are the central facts of women's sexual life and central metaphors for women's situation in general. How did a sector of the movement come to say that violence and rape are the fundamental causes of sexism, rather, for example, than child-rearing practices or economic inequalities? Why did the many powers of men to control women in a complex and heterogeneous society such as our own get telescoped into the single power of the male fist?

My answers to these questions are speculative and the following generalizations are not meant to imply that all antipornography campaigns have the same sources, content, or political goals. Nor do I want to overstate the shift in movement priorities. Nearly all the current formulations of sexual issues in this wave of feminism were already present in the intense intellectual melee of 1969 to 1972. The changes are of emphasis, of visibility, of strategy. We are faced now with the task of exploring the various strands of the ideological web we've been weaving all along, discovering and facing the contradictions that are inevitable in a movement as rich, as broadly based, as our own. There are many variables here—both inside and outside the dynamics of our own political groups.

Let me take it as emblematic and not a coincidence that in the United States pornography became a much-publicized focus for feminist organizing around 1977, the year after the U.S. Supreme Court began seriously to undermine the right to abortion it had only established in 1973. By ruling that women could not use Medicaid funds for abortions, the court returned abortion to the status of privilege for those who can afford it. This failure of movement momentum got publicity, while at the same time the Equal Rights Amendment to the U.S. Constitution, which would have rendered hundreds of discriminatory laws illegal, was beginning to run into serious political trouble. The popular backlash against the political program of feminism was in full swing, with the New Right stealing media attention and gaining clout as a powerful, growing lobby.

In spite of a mass-based women's movement, by the late '70s it was also plain that women were not making economic gains. Though token women were appearing in high places, most women without economic support from men continued to live in poverty, a situation that has steadily undermined the allure of feminist enthusiasm for female independence. Without public support for day care and other family services, the working woman had reason to see her job not as a new access to power, but as one more instance of exploitation. Feminists have mounted a campaign against the "feminization of poverty," and, here and there, the fact that working women put in a double day has been acknowledged, but no social movement has yet succeeded in significantly altering this unfairness.

In such a political climate, feminists felt disappointment and frustration: How could it be that, in spite of the vitality of our movement, change was so much slower than we had hoped? The lively antipornography campaigns of this period are one expression of a general discouragement among women, and among all progressive movements during this period of backlash. The terms the antipornography movement uses to describe women's condition betray a loss of heart about women's ability to challenge men's power directly.

In this time of backlash, some feminists seem to be reasoning that if the state is impervious to our attacks, perhaps we can compel its unchecked strength to our service. Maybe, this argument goes, the masculine power structure that resisted the ideology of equality will listen more attentively to the ideology of difference. The antipornography movement posits a male sexual drive that is intrinsically violent, different in kind from a more consensual and loving female sexual nature. If equality and gender-blind institutions are unobtainable, if they are fantasies of sameness that bury women's particular sexual and psychological condition and obscure the phobic male reaction to women, then, these feminists reason, why continue demanding equality? Why not demand instead specific recognition in law and custom of women's special nature and vulnerability?

The logic of this argument is compelling, but it collapses a theoretical tension that was clear and vibrant earlier, a tension between recognizing the specific situation of women with all the strengths that proceed from it and, at the same time, attacking the female role, the female myth. In other words, female difference, the special culture of women, is a source of movement strength and authenticity while the idealization of femaleness tends to undermine the movement's power to challenge the status quo. Though some antipornography theorists pay lip service to this distinction between women and the abstraction, Woman, almost all opt for a politics that defines male and female as relatively fixed, timeless categories. For these theorists, history is nothing but a record of female frustration and sexual slavery. Things are going badly now because for women they always go badly. For these feminists, only a profound and enduring difference between the sexes seems an adequately powerful explanation of why changes we wish for are so slow in coming.

One reason, then, why the antipornography movement became a focus of feminist energy in the late '70s lies in its claim to explain the recalcitrance of the male power structure. And at the same time that external events seemed to mock earlier feminist high expectations, internal movement difficulties also made this emotionally vivid, symbolic campaign attractive. We had created revolutionary institutions, battered women's shelters, rape crisis centers, and the women who worked in them began to explore the complexity of female victimization. We learned from them not only about the variety of ways in which men brutalize women but also about how women internalize this oppression, weakening our capacity to resist. The women's movement set out to name male crimes formerly invisible—rape, wife battering, sexual harassment—and at first this naming was power in itself. For example, sexual harassment at work used to be socially invisible; it was accepted as a natural event, never seen as an injustice. Now, after years of effective feminist political action, in many an administrator's drawer lies a plan for what to do with a sexual harassment charge.

But rather than seeing this as a step forward in economic and social power, however small, our movement began to be frightened by what it had brought to light. Visibility created new consciousness, but also new fear—and new forms of old sexual terrors: sexual harassment was suddenly *everywhere*; rape was an *epidemic*; pornography was a violent polemic against women. It was almost as if, by naming the sexual crimes, by ending female denial, we frightened ourselves more than anyone else.

Pornography became the symbol of female defeat: Look, they hate us, we could say, pointing to a picture. Far less colorful instances of male dominance surround us: institutionalized sexism that needs no lurid, not to mention stigmatized, representations of naked women to make itself felt. But this engrained system of masculine power has proved far harder to attack.

Antipornography theory offers relief in the form of clear moral categories: there are victims and oppressors. As in the nineteenth-century debates on sex, lust is male, outrage female. But why should such solid, high boundaries between the genders comfort modern feminists? One reason must be our own uncertainties and anxieties about the present fluidity of gender imagery and identity. Nor are these anxieties unjustified: There is no guarantee that shifting gender definitions are in themselves progressive, leading inevitably to increased flexibility and choice. Nonetheless, in the midst of disturbing change, we must recognize, too, our opportunities—and celebrate our triumphs. In spite of backlash and our own failures, the women's movement has made enduring changes in how everyone thinks about women.

Instead of recognizing that the new visibility of women's sexual victimization is a great leap forward, some feminists are drawing energy from the assertion that women's situation is fast deteriorating. They have, I believe, lost sight of the larger historical truth: the women of the nineteenth century *belonged* to their husbands or fathers. Under such conditions, wife beating and marital rape could barely be conceived of as crimes.

Our situation is profoundly different. Women are flooding into public space. Exploitation, new forms of sexual anomie, backlash, phobic resistance from men, new impediments to women's autonomy are all inevitable; but we must not misinterpret these as defeats, nor lose heart about our long-term ability to change the state, nurture our own institutions, and protect ourselves without restricting ourselves.

The antipornography movement has attracted women from many sectors of women's liberation. But this unity has a high price, for it requires that we oversimplify, that we hypothesize a monolithic enemy, a timeless, universal, male sexual brutality. When we create a "them," we perform a sort of ritual of purification: There are no differences among men or women—of power, class, race. All are collapsed into a false unity, the brotherhood of the oppressors, the sisterhood of the victims.

In this sisterhood, we can seem far closer than we are likely to feel when we discuss those more basic and problematic sources of sexual mores: ethnicity, church, school, and family. We are bound to disagree once we confront the sexual politics implicit in these complex social institutions, but from just this sort of useful debate will come the substance of a nonracist feminist concept of sexual freedom. Sometimes, ironically, our drive toward a premature feminist unity through female outrage has led to scapegoating inside the women's movement, as if we were already agreed about which sexual practices belong beyond the feminist pale. I find such internal attacks particularly terrifying now at a time when sexual minorities are increasingly harassed by the state. Given the sexual ignorance, fear, and oppression in a sex-negative society, it is a false hope that feminist unity can rely on a premature agreement on sexual expression.

What *are* the feminist grounds of unity in a discussion of pornography, or of women's sexual freedom in general? Feminists on all sides of this debate share the desire to "take back the night"; to own our sexual selves; to express these selves in images of our own choosing. We share a feminist anger about women's sexual exploitation and a desire to leave the impress of this feeling—our recognition of profound injustices that reach to the core of identity—upon the consciousness of the world.

We also share the belief that sex is primarily a social, not biological, construction; hence social power relations have everything to do with who can do what to whom sexually. Since sex is social, we agree that its symbolic representation is important, that the imagery of sex is worth feminist analytical attention. We agree, too, that in sex, as in everything, women are sometimes right to fear: misogyny permeates our social life and men dominate women. But finally, and significantly, we disagree about the best route to liberation—or even to safety.

Present antipornography theory, rather than advancing feminist thinking about sexuality, continues sexist traditions of displacement or distortion of sexual questions. Instead of enlarging the definition of sexual pleasure to include a formerly invisible female subjectivity, antipornography thinking perpetuates an all too familiar intellectual legacy, one that defines male arousal as intrinsically threatening to female autonomy. Once again, women's experience fades into the background while men fill the foreground. Antipornography theory limits this focus further by collapsing a wide range of sexually explicit images into only one thing: violence against women.

But feminists have little to gain from this narrowing idea of what pornographic imagery contains. A definition of pornography that takes the problem of analysis seriously has to include not only violence, hatred, and fear of women, but also a long list of other elements, which may help explain why we women ourselves have such a mixture of reactions to the genre. (I have heterosexual porn in mind here, but some of this description applies to other types of pornography; generally, porn is a much more varied genre than antiporn activists acknowledge.)

Pornography sometimes includes elements of play, as if the fear women feel toward men had evaporated and women were relaxed and willing at last. Such a fantasy—sexual revolution as *fait accompli*—is manipulative and insensitive in most of the guises we know, but it can also be wishful, eager, and utopian.

Porn can depict thrilling (as opposed to threatening) danger. Though some of its manic quality comes from women-hating, some seems propelled by fear and joy about breaching the always uncertain boundaries of flesh and personality.

Hostility haunts the genre, but as part of a psychodrama in which men often imagine themselves women's victims. Mother is the ultimate specter and women, too, have moments of glee when she is symbolically brought low.

Some pornography is defiant and thumbs a nose at death, at the limitations of the body and nature, indeed at anything that balks the male (perhaps potentially the female?) will.

The Feminist Anti-Censorship Taskforce book committee put together a collection of articles FACT members wrote against any censoring of sexual material called *Caught Looking: Feminism, Pornography, and Censorship*.

The book was illustrated by the kind of pornographic images that might well be censored if the Minneapolis Anti-Pornography Ordinance, passed in the city of Indianapolis in 1984, had been accepted as law by the U.S. Supreme Court.

Caught Looking was intended to pair theory with a mini-history of the wide range of images actually available in various pornographic traditions.

The artists who chose the images and designed the collection were: Hannah Alderfer, Beth Jaker, and Marybeth Nelson.

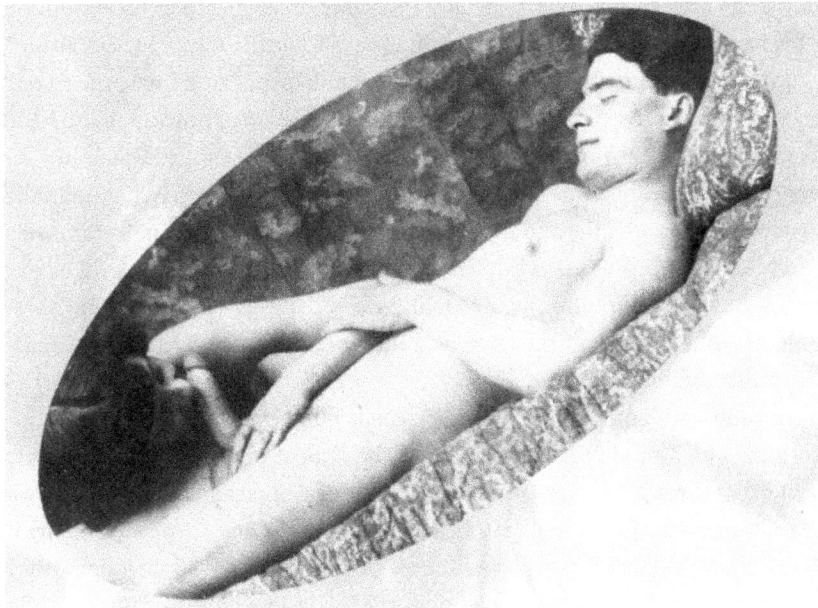

Porn offers men a private path to arousal, an arousal that may be all too easily routed by fear or shame.

Though pornography often centers emotionally on dramas of dominance and submission, anyone who has looked at the raging dependence or the imagined omnipotence of a one-year-old has reason to doubt that patriarchy is the only source of our species' love/hate relationship to the emotions of power and powerlessness. Pornography is infantile then, but "infantile" is a word we use as a simple negative at the risk of patronizing some of our own sources of deep feeling. In many of the guises we know, such infantile feelings give rise to images of the brutal or the coldly murderous; in others, however, childishness can be more innocently regressive, potentially renewing. As Kate Ellis and others have argued, we can indulge in fantasies of childish omnipotence without having these define the entire field of our consciousness or intentions. Particular deep feelings may be neither valuable nor liberating, but they demand understanding; they cannot be sanitized through mere will.

Ridden with authoritarian fantasies as it is, pornography also flouts authority, which no doubt in part explains its appeal to young boys. Certainly while porn remains one of their few sources of sexual information we should not marvel at the importance of the genre. But porn as we know it is, of course, a miserably skewed source of information. While it does offer taboo, explicit images—however distorted—of the bodies of women, the

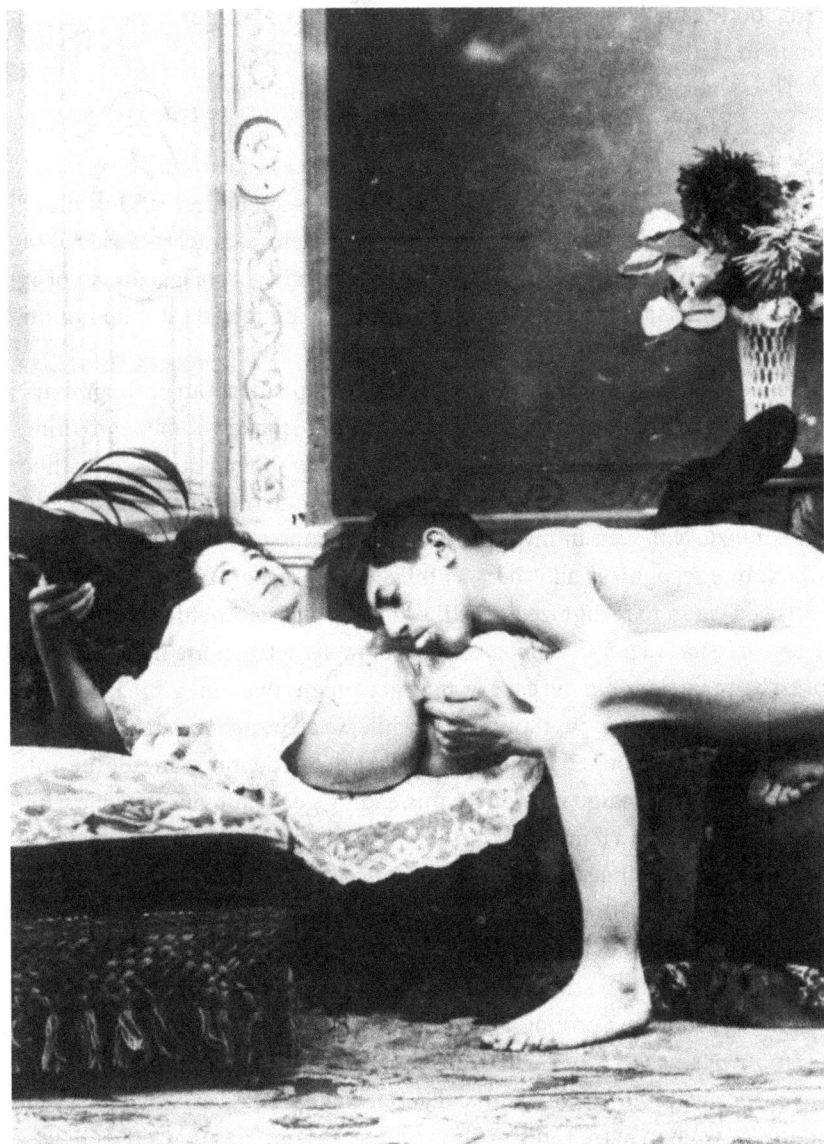

male body usually remains invisible. Since men control porn, they can continue to conceal themselves from inquisitive female eyes.

The same people who want sex education removed from schools now join feminists in the fight against porn. If this odd alliance prospers, we will hear the crash of successive doors closing in the faces of curious but isolated children. In the present political context, pieties about protecting children are passive and reactive; we are not protecting them so much as abandoning them to silence. Pornography as we know it requires a social context of ignorance and shame that present feminist campaigns against it do nothing to alter.

Finally, antipornography theory's central complaint about pornography is that it is objectifying and fragmenting. The genre makes women into things for male pleasure and takes only that part of the woman that pleases without threat. Once again, the danger of objectification and fragmentation depends on context. Not even in my most utopian dreams can I imagine a state in which one recognizes all others as fully as one recognizes oneself (if one can even claim to recognize oneself, roundly, fully, without fragmentation). The real issue is a political one. Antipornography activists are right to see oppressive male power in the gaze of men at women: Women cannot gaze back with a similar, defining authority. But, while we all want the transformed sexuality that will be ours when we are neither dependent nor afraid, the antipornography campaign introduces misleading goals into our struggle when it intimates that in a feminist world we will never objectify anyone, never take the part for the whole, never abandon ourselves to mindlessness or the intensities of feeling that link sex with childhood, death, the terrors and pleasures of the oceanic. Using people as extensions of one's own hungry will is hardly an activity restrained within the boundaries of pornography, nor is there any proof that pornography is a cause rather than a manifestation of far more pervasive imbalances of power and powerlessness.

Antipornography activists argue that pornography is everywhere, both the source of woman hatred and its ultimate expression. This is an effort to have it both ways: Woman-hating is everywhere, but the source of that hatred is specific, localized in pornography, the hate literature that educates men to degrade women. The internal contradiction here is plain. If misogyny is everywhere, why target its sexual manifestation? Or if misogyny collects around the sexual, why is this so? Why assume that the cordoning off of particular sexual images is likely to lessen women's oppression? This overemphasis placed on sex as cause is continuous with the very old idea that sex is an especially shameful, disturbing, guilt-provoking area of life. To accept rather than struggle against the idea that sex is dangerous and polluting is to fear ourselves as much as the men who rape and hurt. We need to be able to reject the sexism in porn without having to reject the realm of pornographic sexual fantasy as if that entire kingdom were without meaning or resonance for women.

Without history, without an analysis of complexity and difference, without a critical eye toward gender and its constant redefinitions, without some skepticism about how people ingest their culture, some recognition of the gap—in ideas and feelings—between the porn magazine and the man who reads it, we will only be purveying a false hope to those women whom we want to join us: that without porn, there will be far less male violence; that with less male violence, there will be far less male power.

In the antipornography campaign, the thing we have most to fear is winning, for further legal control of pornography would, first, leave the oppressive structures of this society perfectly intact, even strengthened, and, second, leave us disappointed, since crimes against women are not particularly linked to pornography and indeed have many other highly visible sources.

Women will be victimized while we lack power. But even now we are not completely powerless. In fact, we are in the midst of complex power negotiations with men all the time. One of the basic themes of porn is the taming of the beast, Woman, who if not bound, will grab; if not gagged, will speak. Pornography's fantasy penis is meant to tame the little bitch as it rarely can in real life.

However silenced and objectified we may be in the prevailing culture, we are not *only* silenced, not *only* objectified. Porn cannot fully define the situation in which we find ourselves. It symbolizes some, but not all, of our experiences—with men, with sexuality, with culture. In the liberation struggles of the '60s, American radicals insisted that everything is connected: what was happening in Vietnam was connected to what was happening in imperialist America. In the analysis and rhetoric of the antipornography movement, this tendency is carried to a distorting extreme. Instead of seeing connections among very different elements in our culture, some antipornography activists conflate things, see them all running together down a slippery slope. Pornography leads to rape, which leads to rape of the land, which leads to international imperialism.

I'm not arguing that these things are not connected, only that by connecting them too quickly, too seamlessly, through the evocative power of metaphor, we fail to see the all-important differences. We must make distinctions of kind and of degree. For it is in the places where things don't fit together neatly that we can best insert our political will toward change.

If we leave this discussion in the realm of moral absolutes, of slippery slopes on the road to sin, we have chosen a rhetorical strategy that can arouse and enrage but that cannot lead us to a position beyond the old moral categories of female righteousness.

Ironically enough, the slippery slope model isolates sex from all other issues, since all other issues collapse into sex, are only sex. Once again, differences, varieties of power and powerlessness, get lost in a false unity. A frame is drawn around women's sexual exploitation, and we are told this is the whole picture, the essence, the core truth. Women's sexual suffering becomes women's sexuality itself.

We do particular injury to feminist work by conflating sex with violence. This is to cede precious territory to the political opponents of feminism. It may be the female legacy of shame and fear that makes us accept this equation so quickly. Is it in our interests—not to mention in the interest of truth—to say that because husbands often rape wives, all marriage is rape? Or to say that women who reject this equation have been brainwashed by patriarchy? This is to deny women any agency at all in the long history of heterosexuality.

It is hard to imagine good organizing that can emerge from this insulting presumption. In her book *Right Wing Women*, antipornography theorist Andrea Dworkin argues that there are but two models for women's roles in society: the farm model and the prostitution model. Women are either fields to be plowed, cows to be milked; or they are meat to be bought. This is a pornographic reductionism of the role of women in history.

The antipornography worldview purports to solve several problems at once: it explains movement failure; it downplays what is unnerving in our successes; it reenergizes honorably weary activists; it reestablishes unity at a time when differences among women are increasingly visible and theoretically important. But, built on weak foundations, these political gains will not endure. When maleness is defined as a timeless quality, it becomes harder rather than easier to imagine how it can ever change. The politics of rage tapers off into a politics of despair—or of complacency—and gender, which at moments has seemed very fluid and variable, suddenly seems solid and reliable again. If, as Mary Daly generalized in *Gyn/Ecology*, footbinding in China and suttee in India and child molestation in Manitoba are all identical, seamless, essentially male acts, where is the break in this absolute tradition, the dynamic moment when female will can prevail?

Since one of the faults of antipornography theory is its misplaced concreteness, I can't be correspondingly specific about how I would go about working to alter the often limited, rapacious, or dreary sexual culture in which women—and also men—now live. There are a lot of questions to answer: Does a disproportionate amount of misogynistic feeling cluster around sex? Why? How deep does sexual phobia go? Is sex in fact an area of experience that will need to be seen as separate, with its own inner dynamic, even perhaps its own dialectic? If we reject the strategy of repression and banning, how *do* we raise self-consciousness and political consciousness about the aspects of porn that express sexual distress, derangement, hostility? (It does seem obvious to me that banning is a step in the opposite direction, away from learning, from unmasking, and toward a suppression that ignores meaning.) What is the actual content of porn and how is porn related to the broader questions of arousal? In other words, what makes something sexy, and what part does power play in the sexualization of a person or situation? Is it a feminist belief that without gender inequality all issues of power will wither away, or do we have a model for the future that will handle inequalities differently? Are there kinds of arousal we know and experience that are entirely absent in porn? How expressive is it of our full sexual range? How representative? How conventional and subject to its own aesthetic laws?

We must work to answer these questions, but we know a lot already. We know that women must have the right to abortion, to express freely our sexual preferences; that we must have the control of the structure and the economics of health care, day care, and our work lives in general. All these levels of private and social experience determine the degree of our sexual autonomy. The New Right is sure it knows what women's sexuality is all about. We must reject such false certainties—in both the feminist and New Right camps—while we set about building the nonrepressive sexual culture we hope for, one in which women's sexual expressiveness—and men's too—can flourish. In her essay "Why I'm Against S/M Liberation" (in *Against Sadomasochism*), Ti Grace Atkinson says, "I do not know any feminist worthy of that name who, if forced to choose between freedom and sex, would choose sex."[5] While women are forced to make such a choice we cannot consider ourselves free.

1985/1986

Acknowledgments

I thank my coeditors of *Powers of Desire: The Politics of Sexuality* (Monthly Review Press[6]), Christine Stansell and Sharon Thompson, and Carole Vance for many months of invaluable discussion. Nadine Taub helped me broaden and support my argument that disappointment is an unspoken theme of recent organizing, and Alice Echols was the first to develop the theme of false unities.

This piece is a talk that was delivered to a number of groups during 1983. Thanks to the following sponsoring organizations: Calgary Status of Women; the San Francisco Socialist School and Women against Violence in Pornography and the Media; the Fourteenth National Conference: Women and the Law; Lavender Left and Philadelphia Reproductive Rights Organization; New York University Colloquium on Sex and Gender.

Notes

1. From Dworkin-MacKinnon Minneapolis Antipornography Ordinance, reprinted in part in FACT, *Caught Looking*, 88.

2. FACT, *Caught Looking*, 88.

3. Carl N. Degler, *At Odds: Women and the Family in America from the Revolution to the Present*. Oxford: Oxford University Press, 1980. Barbara Epstein, *The Politics of Domesticity: Women, Evangelism, and Temperance in Nineteenth Century America*. Middletown, CT: Wesleyan University Press, 1981. Mary S. Hartman, *Victorian Murderesses: A True History of Thirteen Respectable French and English Women Accused of Unspeakable Crimes*. New York: Schocken, 1977. Ellen DuBois, "The Radicalism of the Women Suffrage Movement: Notes Toward the Reconstruction of Nineteenth-Century Feminism," *Feminist Studies* 3, no. 1/2 (1975): 63–71.

4. Koedt, "The Myth of the Vaginal Orgasm."

5. Atkinson, "Why I'm against S/M Liberation," 90–91.

6. Snitow et al., *Powers of Desire*.

8

THE POET OF BAD GIRLS

Angela Carter (1940–1992)

Sexual Freedom and Its Discontents:
Angela Carter's Postlapsarian Eve

Angela Carter, famous and much read in England, has come to American readers only piecemeal, almost as if American publishers see her as a wine that won't travel well. Demon fiction writer though she is, her first real U.S. *success d'estime* was for her feminist study of the Marquis de Sade, *The Sadeian Woman: And the Ideology of Pornography*. Even so, I remember the puzzled reviews of that book when it came out here in 1979. Most were grudgingly admiring, but taken together, they gave contradictory accounts of what the book said, agreeing only that Carter had somehow become besotted with de Sade and had misunderstood what a bad, bad man (or what a sad, sad man) he really was. One was totally unprepared, then, for the book itself:

> Sade's work concerns the nature of sexual freedom and is of particular significance to women because of his refusal to see female sexuality in relation to its reproductive function, a refusal as unusual in the later eighteenth century as it is now.[1]

In that year, in the United States, it was startling to hear a feminist voice so unapologetic for engaging the archenemy. *The Sadeian Woman* was misread for good reasons: It is a threatening book. Carter speculated in a number of unpleasant directions (can women be as monstrous as men?); she was flexible enough to contain opposites (an appreciation and a contempt for de Sade); and peremptory enough to read or willfully misread de Sade for her own subversive, emancipatory purposes. The book suggested a shameless and aggressively probing stance for a woman who would be the critic of male culture. It was phallic criticism consciously ironic about all phallic authority, and at its culminating moment it turned on its hero and excoriated him for making the mother figure in *Philosophy in the Boudoir* fall into a faint just before the moment of orgasm:

> He is as much afraid of freedom as the next man. So he makes her faint. He makes her faint because he can only conceive of freedom as existing in opposition, freedom as defined by tyranny.[2]

Hardly besotted with de Sade, Carter is bitterly disappointed that freedom has no savor for him unless the prohibited woman is in chains, unconscious of her sexuality. Just when he seemed to Carter so close to being a revolutionary pornographer, one who can see that everyone, even the mother, is sexual, and that anyone can cross the boundaries of gender and taboo, he lapses into the myths common in most pornography, reinstating the old rigidity, reasserting the safe laws of transgression. How much does the concept of freedom depend on the preexistence of prohibition? Carter tortures herself with this question in all her work. Meanwhile, to Carter's sorrow, the mother faints, the French Revolution fails, de Sade's freedom's just another word for naughty little boy.

No wonder the book caused consternation. It was an invention, a counterfiction to de Sade's, an intellectual interlude from a writer of extreme cunning who takes the imagination seriously as the place where we all tell stories to ourselves and where we can best see—inside the form itself—the structure of our own rules. Like most bad girls, Carter has a love/hate relationship to rules: She gives them their due, but defiantly demands a good time. Constantly at play, she writes fairy tales, Gothic horror stories, romances, phantasmagorical science fictions, allegories, fables—and her virtuosity at manipulating the laws of these conventional forms is dazzling. (She can skew them with irony or play them straight.) Reading a lot of Angela Carter at once is like being galloped on a child's hobbyhorse through the culture attic. You're choking on the fumes of greasepaint; you're startled as a bunch of waxwork Bluebeards, beasts, and beauties blunder into you; you're tangled in string by some grand puppeteer who jerks you around, then cuts the connection, leaving you free to play with whatever toy you want. You wind one up. It's a gorgeous tableau of a terrible, deep forest, where the Wolf and Little Red Riding Hood couple in the glittering dark. The whole thing sparkles and revolves, then runs down.

Certainly, Carter runs the risk of the true littérateur: How to resist the temptations of virtuosity? In an introduction to a marvelous essay, "Notes for a Theory of Sixties Style," in her collection of occasional pieces, Nothing Sacred, she disarms criticism by simply apologizing: "I note that [this essay] is over-written and over-literary, but a person can only walk the one way and that is the way I still walk."[3] Love me as I am, and don't hold it against me if what you love is an artifice; infinite variety is the best of a lover's tricks.

Sometimes called a pornographic writer, she is one only in a very special sense. Pleasure—and the fear that is so often pleasure's sauce—are her subjects, but the most exciting moments in her fiction are literary: the splendid verbal coups, the sensuous unfolding of the story line. She can write narrative turns of such beauty that you fall in love with the romance itself—forget the princess. Each book is a fresh experience in form and tone, a trip down the possible paths inherent in yet another style. Carter tries everything.

If you've no taste for the turns and twists and tricks of narrative for their own sake, Carter will pale on you too fast; you'll leave before she tells you her secrets. But secrets she has—often as rich as her prose. When she tells fairy tales, she chooses a fictional world ruled by the brutal economy of roles: pattern determines that little girls will run away and big wolves give chase. But the unconscious always erupts in a Carter story: Beauty falls in love with the beast *as a beast*; she doesn't want a prince. Neither freedom nor pleasure is rational or safe, though, ironically, both have their own determining structures, signaling the *angst* of entrapment inside patterns. (For these radiant retellings see The Bloody Chamber.)

A few of her more realistic pieces from an early volume, Fireworks, are moving precisely because the narrator wants so much to be authentic, to feel directly, and suffers the fate of the ironic and self-conscious, the fate of alienation from anything simple or sentimental. Carter's sophistication is curse and blessing. She can't go naked, no matter how many layers she strips off; a postlapsarian Eve, she is infernally knowing.

In the collection Saints and Strangers, Carter gives of her very best. The opening story, about Lizzie Borden ("The Fall River Axe Murders"), is particularly intricate in design. Carter assembles Lizzie's dreadful crime by picturing the Borden household at the moment before the family wakes on the fateful day in August 1892. In this atmosphere of unbearable imminence, Carter tours the sleeping house like an *hallucinée*. Her eyes like cameras, she witnesses each variable: the heat; Lizzie's menstrual blood; the experimental chemistry of unrefrigerated food; the circulation of boredom, madness, and money; relevant snatches of the past represented by the sparse objects in this miserly house. She passes through the constriction of locked doors to observe the architecture of the patriarchal family: father Borden and his captive womenfolk, wife, daughter, maid, each half swooning in sweat and unremembered dreams.[4]

But whenever this authorial omniscience seems too complete Carter draws back and reminds us of how she is straining to imagine these people. Explanations are all very well, but the author loses confidence as she gazes at an old photograph of Lizzie that "secretes mystery." Is Lizzie Borden utterly other—"as taut as the strings of a wind-harp from which random currents of the air pluck out tunes that are not our tunes"—or is she continuous with us, perhaps even a reasonable assassin, exacting a just retribution for the suppressed violence of her terrible, woman-wasting world?[5] By the end, Carter has let us see the ax, and the reasons Lizzie uses it, but the act itself need hardly be mentioned since, by now, the rival intensities of knowledge and mystery are so impacted that *everything* in the story cuts.

Freud broods over a psychological study like this, not only as a source of explanation but equally as a source of myth. In another fine story here, "Peter and the Wolf," Carter conflates a Freudian reading of a fairy tale with a rediscovery of the tale's original mystery. The story hangs in the balance between the power of the unconscious and the analysis of that power; Carter's art lies in her refusal to finally tip the scale to one side or the other:

> A girl from a village on the lower slopes [of the Alps] left her widowed mother to marry a man who lived up in the empty places. Soon she was pregnant. In October, there was a severe storm. The old woman knew her daughter was near her time and waited for a message but none arrived. After the storm passed, the old woman went up to see for herself, taking her grown son with her because she was afraid.
>
> From a long way off, they saw no smoke rising from the chimney. . . . There were traces of wolf-dung on the floor so they knew wolves had been in the house but left the corpse of the young mother alone although of her baby nothing was left except some mess that showed it had been born. Nor was there a trace of the son-in-law but a gnawed foot in a boot.
>
> They wrapped the dead in a quilt and took it home with them.[6]

Time passes; the old woman has other grandchildren, among them Peter, who at age 7 is taken above the timberline to tend the goats. A pack of wolves appears, "the thing he had been taught most to fear," among them a filthy, hairy little girl, obviously his lost cousin. The family captures this "marvel . . .

on all fours" and brings her down to the village. But her wildness is more terrible and absolute than they can encompass. In a frenzy she ruins the house, delivers a death wound to the grandmother and howls until the wolves rescue her in a marauding pack. Peter watches it all, including "the crevice of her girl-child's sex. . . . a flesh that seemed to open one upon another into herself, drawing him into an inner, secret place in which destination perpetually receded before him, his first, devastating, vertiginous intimation of infinity." After that, he turns to piety and books as a fence against the unknown. He studies until he is a "stranger" to the peasants of his village and they let him leave to become a priest.[7]

Down he comes from the mountains of his trauma and meets his cousin once again as she comes to drink at dawn from the river. He reacquaints himself with the power of her animal freedom, the oneness and grace that come from a perfect unconsciousness. This was what he had longed for all these years of pious self-abasement: sex without guilt, mortality without fear. His cry of "visionary ecstasy" startles the wolf-woman, who runs off, leaving him to continue his journey: "But what would he do at the seminary, now? For now he knew there was nothing to be afraid of. He experienced the vertigo of freedom." Under a "cool, rational sun," he gives one last look at the exotic mountain fastnesses now flattened like views on picture postcards. No longer circumscribed by old country tales, Peter is marked instead by the knowledge of one who has descended from the superstitious wilderness "into a different story."[8]

Carter never patronizes "the primitive, vast, magnificent, barren, unkind simplicity of the mountain." She sees through it, but often returns to it because, she says, "The Gothic tradition . . . retains a singular moral function—that of provoking unease." Always a radical, Carter insists that we count the power of the unconscious in our politics. If there are tyrants, she insists we examine our own hearts to find the unacknowledged place where we, too, love them.[9]

1986

A Footman at the Door: Angela Carter's Last Novel *Wise Children*

Angela Carter died of lung cancer on February 16, 1992 at age 51. For her committed readers, the loss was unbelievable. How could someone who was just in the middle of saying something so fascinating, rare, and deliciously funny, all at once be gone? Almost certainly—though we can't finally measure these things—her last novel, *Wise Children*, was written before she knew she was sick. On first reading, I thought it a farrago, a repeat of old turns under the circus top, familiar to her loyal fans.

But, though we've been with Carter on strings of occasions like this before—eccentric household dinners, carnivals, magic shows, birthday parties that careen out of control—that first reading was way off. After consideration, and still quite sure that Angela had no intention of writing herself an ending, I've come to see *Wise Children* as a complex philosophical work on the ambiguity of biological ties, on the family romance, on the theater generally (and Shakespeare in particular) and, above all, on pleasure.

To some degree, this second take is no surprise: Carter was always a demanding writer, abstract in her own rollicking way, allusive, a profoundly literary novelist of ideas. The ideas here arise out of the ever-surprising medium of one Dora Chance's raffish, also serious, attempt at writing her memoirs. She hopes for a best seller, for isn't her book about the theater, including behind-the-scenes glimpses of three generations of the gifted, beautiful, and famous, also fabulous clothes, five sets of theatrical twins, jokes, and magical endings like Shakespeare's romances? Even better, Dora herself, and her twin, Nora, are "illegitimate in every way."[10] Hers is a by-blow's story, written from the backstairs, the backstage, the dying music-hall tradition, the wrong side of the Thames, in Brixton. Like Shakespeare, gazing at everything from the Globe (which was also on the south side of the river, and which appears at the end of the novel in the form of a big birthday cake), Dora sees the high and the low, takes on their different voices, mixes them in one script. And she does Shakespeare one better, making not a mosaic of difference like his but a more promiscuous melting together; her people don't sort themselves out at the end but remain scrambled in a wild democracy—to the Bard unthinkable.

In a witty turn, Carter redefined "family romance" to mean a fiction in which a random set of people collude to love one another, to be one another's permanent destiny. "Family" becomes an idea, "love" an act of self-creation. It's not that Carter throws biology *out*, exactly. But she keeps edging the concept of family toward the fictional—and hilarity.

At the end of the novel, Dora and Nora, now 75, take on newborn twins, the next crop of family bastards. In their ecstasy at finally being parents they sing and dance in the street—

We can't give you anything but love, babies,
That's the only thing we've plenty of, babies[11]

As she cavorts and pushes the double baby carriage along, Nora glimpses her new narrative power: "We can tell these little darlings here whatever we like about their mum and dad."[12] Finally, biology is hearsay, a tale accepted on faith, based on the protestations of other people. (At the 1990 DIA Art Foundation forum on "critical fictions," Carter lamented the new genetic tests that threaten to put an end to this potential for duplicity.) Family is a drama that unfolds. Freud holds up one side of the curtain—the family romance—and the Bard the other: the romance of the discovery scene.

It was always Carter's work to retell these master accounts, the great tales, worm away at their plots, twist around their sentiments. Dora Chance dreams of destroying "the terms of every contract" and of setting "the old books on fire."[13] In Lear, the bastard is the villain. But in Wise Children, God stands up for bastards at last. For the late Shakespeare, an unspoiled identity lay in lawful paternity, sealed in the final embrace between true fathers and true daughters. For Carter, that line of true descent is forever branching, a family tree gone wild. In her version, the illegitimate get to inherit, too, and they are allowed Shakespeare's special gift in the comedies, happiness.

Dora and Nora's (possible) father is a pompous ass, who is always intoning that "the whole of human life" is to be found in the Bard.[14] Carter disagreed, and laughed at a culture that hypes Shakespeare, uses knowledge of him as a class marker, and commodifies him as a National Treasure. (In one great bit, a cat keeps pissing in a sacred urn of dirt from Stratford that is meant to be sprinkled as a benediction over a haywire Hollywood production of A Midsummer Night's Dream.)

Carter rewrites Shakespeare, parodies him, makes fun of his icons (the Chance sisters live on Bard Road), but she has no intention of giving up her romantic duet with plays she clearly knows in her very bones. The allusions come in cascades, with an incredibly agile range of effect. A bit of rosemary caught in Dora's teeth reminds her of Ophelia's rosemary for remembrance, opening the way to precious recollection. Elsewhere that same scene from Hamlet replays itself as farce, as the twins' goddaughter runs mad on television and exits calling, "Hey! Somebody call me a cab, right? A cab! Right away! . . . Goodnight, everybody! . . . Sleep tight. . . . Goodnight." Singing and dancing away, the Chance sisters faithfully give the audience their "helping of dark."[15]

The novel's mixture of silliness with homage to Shakespeare's power to enchant is very lovely. Carter dares what Shakespeare dares, his stunning reversals of fortune. The novel begins with a spring tempest and ends with the finding of the lost and with lovers meeting. This Shakespeare may be fractured, but it's beautiful.

Angela Carter sought a language for pleasure, a quest she took on very self-consciously as a feminist project. Pleasure was also to be for girls. Feminist critics call for this kind of writing, but the texts that actually deliver it are few. Carter's desires—ideological and literary, private and social—led her across current theoretical boundaries. Neither her polyglot word choices nor her deconstruction of myths precluded an indulgence, too, in old-fashioned closure—when she wanted that pleasure. She loved the old stories, partly because she could manipulate our nostalgia for them, but also because they delivered the goods—fantasy, distance, satisfaction, resolution. Pleasure with her was not always just a little further on, forever out of reach. She wanted it now; her writing celebrated the pre-Oedipal, the polymorphous, and the perverse.

The footman is at Nora and Dora's door with an invitation to a party, though on another day rather like this one, he will come with a black-edged message. Sorrow and death are always in the wings. Dora's story skips over the war because, alas, "it was no carnival."[16] Let others speak of the immovable sorrows we all face. Carter brought deep feeling to her knowledge that joy is important, fragile, more easily lost than anything. Hence entertainers have strange but precious work. The novel ends on Dora's thought, "Oh, what a joy it is to dance and sing!"[17] She is happy, but as she knows, a happy ending depends on knowing just when to stop.

1992

Notes

1. Carter, *The Sadeian Woman*, 1.
2. Carter, *The Sadeian Woman*, 132.
3. Carter, "Notes for a Theory of Sixties Style," 84.
4. Carter, "The Fall River Axe Murders," 9–31.
5. Carter, "The Fall River Axe Murders," 29, 31.
6. Carter, "Peter and the Wolf," 59.
7. Carter, "Peter and the Wolf," 59, 60, 63, 65.
8. Carter, "Peter and the Wolf," 66–67.
9. Carter, "Peter and the Wolf," 67; Carter, *Fireworks*, 133.
10. Carter, *Wise Children*, 11.

11. Carter, *Wise Children*, 231.
12. Carter, *Wise Children*, 230.
13. Carter, *Wise Children*, 222.
14. Carter, *Wise Children*, 14.
15. Carter, *Wise Children*, 47, 142.
16. Carter, *Wise Children*, 163.
17. Carter, *Wise Children*, 5 et passim.

9

INSIDE THE CIRCUS TENT

Excerpts from an Interview with Angela Carter, 1988

When I first published my interview with Angela Carter, I received a few angry letters. I had said Carter was a feminist, a Leftist, a radical critic of our times. Carter had acquired her own Jane-ites, the coterie of readers who sentimentalized and domesticated Jane Austen, making her safe—a cozy, charming piece of Englishry. The Carter-ites adored Angela for her magic, her style, her witch's cloak curiously wrought with signs and figures. She took them to fairyland. The feminist interviewer was a passionate admirer too, but of the Carter who laid down this credo in the middle of our two-hour talk:

> I am a child of my time. I'm from that generation that believed if you could actually find some way of making a synthesis of Marx and Freud you'd be getting towards a sort of universal explanation. Although I don't believe in universal explanations as such, I really don't see what's wrong with that.[1]

Carter is a necromancer who is hard at work "getting class right." She's a sleight-of-hand artist whose tricks arise from the unconscious. At the same time, she can do history with the accuracy of an *halluciné*. She's cunning and funny, tones which serve her well as she tries to slip parts of Freud and Marx together. Always fluent, Carter is hideously sophisticated about just what fluency can come to mean. Bravura toward cultural collapse? She is determined not to fiddle while we burn, but she fiddles and tries to show in this fiddling the burning—all very hard to do.

Angela Carter is tall, imposing, but she avoids being grand by wearing a denim skirt and a sweatshirt dotted with figures of Mickey Mouse. Her large face is delicate; the features work in different directions. Ask her a question, and obviously eager to answer, she nonetheless pauses a long time while you can almost hear her thoughts charging off at cross-purposes. Subtle, amused, a bit overwhelmed by a literary brio about which she is also skeptical, she hardly knows how to begin.

No direct approach got me anywhere in this interview. But Carter's insistence on the indirect method was more eloquent, finally. Her spirals pull in a lot of material. "It's difficult being a woman," she said. We were talking about writers:

> If I'm looking for American fiction that truly explicates to me what this extraordinary country is up to, I start off with Hawthorne and Melville. Melville I exempt from any sort of gender definition; I sort of think of him as being all things to all persons. [Naughty laughter, the feminist off the leash.] I think I know why this is so—because it is very difficult writing about a whole culture when one is in some sense in exile from it. . . . Women are marginalized. I sort of cope with this by deciding the margin is more important than the page.

We both mulled this over, still unsatisfied. What about the great, inclusive nineteenth-century women writers? George Eliot came up and we compared notes about *Middlemarch*. "It is a novel about the whole world and about the whole culture. And so it *can be done.* Do you know *The House of All Nations* by Christina Stead, which is a sort of Jacobean drama about international banking? Women aren't supposed to write that kind of novel. Stead is one of my favorite writers; I think she is really one of the great twentieth-century writers."

Of course Carter would love a writer who could be Jacobean about international banking. She, too, is mannered as she tackles the big subjects. We chewed over the great Stead novels for a while. Like Carter, she was a passionately political novelist who—for her own reasons, among them McCarthyism—worked indirectly.

"You know the Confucian proverb, 'The greatest eloquence is stuttering'? I always think of that with the later Christina Stead, even *The Man Who Loved Children*. She's starting to stutter there. That's *quite* badly written. [Gasps of daring.] Like Dreiser. The content is so important that style doesn't matter."

Stead's material was worldly, her domain far-flung. She lived and wrote, insider and outsider, in many cultures "as an international vagabond," a member of the "rootless shifting urban intelligentsia." Again an echo of Carter herself, who, for all her insistence that next to Stead she is a pastoral innocent, nonetheless spends much of her time living in foreign cities, a sojourner passing through university residencies, an observer on a wide world stage. She offered, "I don't believe in roots."

It was at this point that Carter produced her credo about Marx and Freud. Like Stead, though with different priorities and tools, she wants to get *everything* into her books. It is just that the definition of "everything" has changed.

Marx and Freud. These are the blocks we were playing with, we agreed, though we were laughing at how blunt and basic we were getting, after all this literary talk. Carter loves Freud. She thinks Americans tend to undervalue him because his capacity for moral ambiguity makes us too nervous. His treatment of children, for example: "He sees children as being full of contradictions." He has an "intense sense of their vulnerability and the impossibility of doing anything about it really." Children are "walking blindfolded on the edge of a precipice. Freud is capable of seeing them as trailing clouds of glory in the full Wordsworth way . . . *and* of being polymorphously perverse." He never wrinkles his nose at this mixture. Carter mimicked a Freud voice: "So the little girl wants to cut off her brother's willy; how interesting!"

"The American Freudians have found it hard to take on this whole package. In a funny way this is a Calvinist country, an either/or country. I always notice this when I come back here: the guys in the black hats and the guys in the white hats." Americans have sin, but she looks in vain for the remorse that generally goes with it. She muses on the difference between 42nd Street and London's sleazy district, Soho: "In Times Square, you really think your soul is in danger; in Soho, it's your wallet."

In England, sex is "raunchy." "Britain is a protestant country; it's puritanical; but we have no sense of sin. We think sex is *rude*; we don't think it's dirty or disgusting. It's rude, like children showing their bums. Though this isn't necessarily a healthy or adult way of looking at sex, it does mean that little boys aren't afraid that if they masturbate their willies are going to come off in their hands."

I asked Carter where the erotic is to be found among her categories. In her fairy tales, Beauty and the Beast end up on the floor together, and both have fur. "I am puzzled about my reputation for eroticism. Nobody ever asks me about it in England. [Comic grimace, poor old Britain.] It's all elastic twanging in England; that sound is the call to arms. I would have to adopt a French accent and say, 'But isn't it all part of life? Ze zensuality of everyday experience, ze zunshine, fruit, flowers, animals, ze presence of small children, ze warm tetch of flesh on flesh.'" [Delicious accent, silly as English sex.]

We were still circling: Marx and Freud, nationality and sex, style and its contents. Where were we? Back at the beginning, I had asked Carter about style. After an hour and a half, we had actually talked about it. I had tried to start small by reminding her of some essays she wrote in the '60s and '70s, where she traced the move from the hippie, "a beautiful explosion of sexually ambiguous silks and beads" to the more anxious women of 1975, with their "glazed, self-contained look typical of times of austerity." Carter had argued that in the '60s face paint wandered around, moving the glossy red wound from its sanctioned place; but the times changed. We had gone too far: "Scrub it all off and start again." She had ended one of those essays by remarking that the revival of red lipstick since the '60s indicates, above all, "that women's sense of security was transient."

So I asked her what she would say about style in the '80s. At a loss at first, she tried to persuade me she is no longer interested in style. But then the conversation got the better of her. Angela Carter is always interested in style.

We spoke about hippies and how their look persists, about punk, "an aesthetic of economic disaster." We were scornful about that "ghastly spectacle," French hippies, who never understood about "homemade." Like the good novelist she is, Carter gets the sequins right, the "flash" of the hippie waiter in the restaurant the night before, the "fancy dress" of people whose work is close to play and its opposite, the expensive, tailored style of yuppies with high salaries.

This is how our discussion about style began but by the end questions of style and politics fused in this very lovely moment as she tried to understand the different appeals of romanticism and rationality:

I was thinking about Blake, the long tradition of English radicalism. You can date it back to Milton, or back to *Piers Plowman*. It's all to do with dreamers. They fall asleep on the hillside and they have this visionary dream and they wake up again. . . .

Why is it that in Britain socialism has always been romantic and soft-edged and visionary? It's always been the dreamers—Blake and William Morris—dreamers of impossible dreams of beauty and wholeness. [Long pause.] And in France, it's *Lenin*. [Wild laughter—"I'm only formulating this now," she warned, and barreled on.] In Britain, and I expect also in America, socialism is soft, it's the soft option. It's to do with . . . Christianity. . . . Although Britain has had a tradition of socialism since the peasants' revolt, it's always like the blue mountains, something which will descend in a cloud. Whereas to Europe socialism is rationality—anticlerical.

You don't have to be *good* to be a socialist there; you have to be rational. Socialism is obvious when you think about it.

Here it is then—the thread, if there is one: Angela Carter has carried me from red lipstick to rival visions of liberation. Her socialism is dreamy. Her books offer play—of both words and flesh—and they offer ideas about history. Marx proposes; Freud interrupts. Under Carter's circus tent both are present—not perhaps in that impossible "synthesis," but in the imaginary space where writers try to have things, and to give their readers things we lack.

Why have I enjoyed this conversation so much? Because, as I see by the end, I have been in the presence of someone deeply happy, a dreamer fascinated by rationality, a stylist on a grand quest toward meaning. We rush out of Carter's hotel to meet the man she lives with (18 years younger than herself) and their son (five years old, born when she was 43) who are impatiently waiting beneath the fantasy clock at F.A.O. Schwartz.

1988

Note

1. See Snitow, "Angela Carter, Wild Thing: Conversations with a Necromancer," for the longer version of the interview.

THE BEAST WITHIN

Lady into Fox and A Man in the Zoo, by David Garnett

David Garnett is one of that mob of ghosts, the Bloomsbury crowd, who haunt the literary world with such persistence. As a child in the 1890s, he lived in the then untamed woods of Surrey with his distinguished parents, Edward, prescient publisher and critic, and Constance, translator of seventy volumes of great Russian fiction. As their roaming only child, he received books through the ear he turned toward them, wildness through the ear he turned away. Subsequently, he lived the London life of books and in a long career poured out novels, memoirs, literary appreciations, and translations, works for the most part sturdy but uninspired.

Briefly, though, in the kinetic 1920s, a fine miracle happened to David Garnett: He produced a cluster of novellas—among them Lady into Fox (1923) and A Man in the Zoo (1924)—which are mysteriously, permanently powerful. Only in these deceptively simple fables did he find a balance between his self-conscious inheritance of art and his secret love of disturbing wildness, between verbal sophistication and the equally interesting provocations of brute silence.

Lady into Fox is the story of the young and happily married Mr. and Mrs. Tebrick, who go out in the woods one day for a walk: "Hearing the hunt, Mr. Tebrick quickened his pace. . . . His wife hung back, and he, holding her hand, began to almost drag her. . . . She suddenly snatched her hand away from his very violently and cried out. . . . *Where his wife had been the moment before was a small fox, of a very bright red.*"[1]

This is the situation Garnett craves. The elegant wit laughs a bit at his own metaphor, is deliciously ironic on the theme of having a vixen for a wife. But the wild side of Garnett takes the whole thing entirely to heart. He stalks his metaphor down its own strange path: If one did have a fox for a wife, surely the sense of the ridiculous would be overwhelmed by feelings of love and loss? Garnett bestows on his Mr. Tebrick the good or bad fortune of remaining in love with his wife in her new condition.

At first, Mrs. Tebrick, too, seems eager to continue their solitary, confiding life together. She is ashamed of going naked and begs with her eyes to be dressed in a little jacket she used to wear. She drinks tea from a saucer and nibbles bread and butter from her husband's hand. In the early days, games of cards and reading aloud seem possible, but soon Mr. Tebrick notices that as he reads, his wife's eyes wander away and fix themselves avidly on a dove they have in a cage. Sorrowful and nervous, he tests her by buying a pet rabbit and leaving her alone with it for five minutes, only to return to find: "Blood on the carpet, blood on the armchairs and antimacassars, even a little blood spurtled on to the wall, and what was worse, Mrs. Tebrick tearing and growling over a piece of the skin and the legs, for she had eaten up all the rest of it."[2] Mr. Tebrick is devastated, considers murder and suicide, but his wife is sorry, comes fawning and begging, until finally she is in his arms and they shed tears, fox and man together. Reconciled, they spend the evening looking at views of Italy, Spain, and Scotland through the portable stereoscope which Mr. Tebrick specially adjusts for his beloved vixen's focal length.

Still, this can never be a peaceful household. The couple bicker—she wordlessly, though effectively, and he in a rage at her willfulness, her desire to break free and run wild. He calls her a "bad wild fox" and argues with her, all too familiarly, that "if I keep you confined it is to protect you."[3]

The seamless beauty of Lady into Fox lies in Garnett's success at having it all ways, his unabashed mixture of blood and grief with stereopticons. His satire on sly, hoydenish wives and on their eagerly repressive husbands never undermines the other side of the story, the fairy tale of fear and transformation. By taking everything literally, he achieves constant surprise, pushing us further and further into the world of animals, as Mr. Tebrick follows his lost, rebellious wife into the forest, discovers her litter of five by a new fox-husband, feels bitter jealousy, then finds he must continue to love. The fox world beckons, and Mr. Tebrick stops longing for the lost woman, his wife, and dwells instead on "the recollection of an animal. . . . His one hope now was the recovery of this beast."[4]

Garnett works through this same mixture of absurdity and love in the fable, A Man in the Zoo. Once again a couple goes walking, this time in the zoo; once again they are at odds. Josephine Lackett is always "considering the feelings of other people" while her love, John Cromartie, wishes her to separate from society, to consider only him. As they quarrel they stroll past rows of cages; with the grace of a gazelle, Garnett keeps changing narrative point of view, now standing outside with the lovers, now inside staring out through the eyes of a wolf, a fox, or a lion.

John is far too peremptory for his Josephine, who calls him "wild beast": "I might as well have a baboon or a bear . . . you ought to be shut up in the Zoo. The collection here is incomplete without you."[5] John takes her at her word and writes a delightfully solemn letter proposing himself as the missing link in the collection of the Royal Zoological Society. After only a slight hesitation, the Society installs him in a cage fitted out with objects from his native habitat, a table and chair, bookcases, and a reading lamp. The public comes to gaze, as do the chimpanzee on his left and the orang-outang on his right.

Allowed to wander around the zoo after closing, Mr. Cromartie finds the animals interesting; they in their turn recognize the distinction between him and the keepers; "They saw at once that he had come out of a cage."[6] He cares nothing for the crowds to whom he is a novelty, but he continues to suffer over the loss of Josephine.

It is Josephine who capitulates. She cannot rid herself of love for that beast, John. Against her will, she keeps gravitating toward the zoo in Regents Park, makes unaccustomed detours to places like Madame Tussaud's Wax Museum where she can give herself up "to the pleasure of gazing." Meanwhile, at home in the zoo, Mr. Cromartie has developed a relationship with a small, tessellated cat called a caracal: "They were equals in everything," both terribly proud, and alike, too, in the "untamed wildness of their tawny hearts."[7]

How can it end? Garnett pushes things, discovering more and more in the already outré. The Zoological Society, delighted with the stream of visitors to *homo sapiens*, installs yet another man, a talkative, bantering negro, in the next cage. The new Man in the Zoo speaks patronizingly of the other animals, a slight to his friends Cromartie cannot abide. Oh, how can it end? A man is always pursued by the world wherever he may go. Nor can he rest easily among animals; the increasingly jealous orang-outang finally gets his opportunity to maul Cromartie, bringing on the crisis.

In this Freudian daydream, animals and humans dance to the strange tune of their different but interlocking necessities. Mr. Cromartie loses a finger and once he lacks it, he's one step closer to his Miss Lackett, while she has admitted that he who bears "the Mark of the Beast" holds her attention, that she wants him more than the stuffy life beyond the bars, where, as Cromartie tells her, one "lives behind a mask in secret." Like Mr. and Mrs. Tebrick, these two form an animal pair only death can dissolve, a pair impervious to the fussy, chattering, ogling crowd. They are "bound up with each other"—for love is a terrible bondage—but Garnett feels their particular cage in life's menagerie offers, at least, the freedom of an aloof and private passion.[8]

When David Garnett was three years old, his father told him that an exotic Russian friend of the family had a princess for a mother "but that his father was a bear she had met in the forest." In these two uncanny tales, we are with Garnett inside the expansion of that disturbing but loved image, his primal scene, his maddening, phantom love affair. *Lady into Fox* might well have been written out of one smooth moment of rage at an erratic woman; and *A Man in the Zoo* might well have been written out of another such mood of bile, perhaps at an over-bred, too delicate female rejection. The wonder is that the sexual fury, the lonely, angry impulse, balloons outward as it does, like a magic bubble, into such fresh, free reaches of upper atmosphere. Both stories belong forever on the smallish shelf with the other great accounts of metamorphoses.

1986

Notes

1. Garnett, *Lady into Fox & A Man in the Zoo*, 6.
2. Garnett, *Lady into Fox & A Man in the Zoo*, 22.
3. Garnett, *Lady into Fox & A Man in the Zoo*, 21, 35.
4. Garnett, *Lady into Fox & A Man in the Zoo*, 44.
5. Garnett, *Lady into Fox & A Man in the Zoo*, 74.
6. Garnett, *Lady into Fox & A Man in the Zoo*, 84.
7. Garnett, *Lady into Fox & A Man in the Zoo*, 104.
8. Garnett, *Lady into Fox & A Man in the Zoo*, 121, 73, 129.

III

THE FEMINIST PICARESQUE

INTRODUCTION TO THE FEMINIST PICARESQUE

I want to embrace this in some ways absurd oxymoron: the feminist picaresque. I'll drop common associations that don't serve my purpose, but some of those naughty, rejected meanings of picaresque may linger on as irony. In my travels with feminism, I have been neither a rogue nor a maker of mischief—at least not by design. But sometimes I have been bumbling, wandering, disconnected, with no expectation—or intention—of being accepted. I'm not a criminal but I did smuggle U.S. dollars into Eastern Europe under my dress. I'm not a carefree rambler, but my trips have been roundabout, segmented, and my writings about these experiences have been anecdotal and often personal. Traveling with feminism has indeed been a quest for adventure. I'll drop the phallic image of the picaro, the sexual miscreant, traveling from place to place with a lance, but I will hold onto the more general description of one who is restless, willing to live for a time without any settled context, a sojourner who's always leaving.

My feminist work has deep thematic through-lines, but no single plot. New discoveries on my travels have changed my direction, which, in any case, was never straightforward. Some have found me a sympathetic outsider; a few pieces in this section record such happy encounters. Others have seen me as an uninvited visitor, whose story is disjointed and whose contact with those she visits is marginal, distorted, or beside the point. Some of those misconnections are recorded in this section, too.

The picaro often fails to know the rules, or if she knows them, she refuses to comply. Sometimes this merely confirms her irrelevance, but sometimes this wayward relationship to the mores of a particular time and place are of great use to those insiders who want to craft rebellions. The ignorant picaro can say and do what rooted activists cannot without paying an exorbitant home price. Feminists rightly criticize any obnoxious projection of their ideas onto others. But this constraint may well close off chances for real conversation. Is it more respectful to hide one's thoughts when in foreign territory? Or more respectful to imagine that one's hearers might well have related thoughts themselves, and in any case are capable of deciding to take or leave what the picaro says? The rogue visitor is sometimes disturbing or disruptive, but she is never the first to arrive, never able to offer a whole new story. Now everyone moves around, and the sojourner—responsible or not—is but one of a chorus of circulating global voices. Forget the silence and purity of first contact; that time is past.

In the early 1980s I started to travel with feminism. The slow down of feminist work in the United States in those years frightened me. I had to maintain energy and hope because I had committed myself, burned boats, tied my heart to the fortunes of feminism. So, continuing feminist work was necessary but what, day-to-day, would this mean? Like many other feminists of that time, I left home. I went to Greenham Common, England, where feminists of many different traditions were living around a U.S. cruise missile base in protest. As we sat in our plastic tents and around our campfires, feminists visited us from all over the world. We argued constantly. Feminism was becoming for me a peripatetic philosophy school. In my piece here about Greenham Common I try to give some of the range of those discussions. They changed me. The idea, "international feminism," expanded, became embodied in faces and actions, began to collect rich memories.

Activists from the United States are still properly worried about the colonizing potential inherent in our powerful position, our privileges of wealth, our increasingly dominant language, and our easy mobility. But in the 1980s, U.S. feminist internationalism matured; feminists made and responded to a wide range of critiques, and entered horizontal cross-border networks previously unimagined. Then, suddenly, at the end of the '80s, the political map of the world changed. To everyone's amazement, the Cold War ended—or so we thought. Revisiting the nuclear base at Greenham in the 1990s, I found the gates we had blocked in protest wide open, the reinforced airstrips chopped up, the soldiers all gone—though now we know how many other places they were soon to travel.

In 1990, the Yugoslav feminist writer Slavenka Drakulic put it to a bunch of U.S. feminists in New York that we were slackers who had never helped the repressed feminists in Eastern Europe during communism, and weren't doing anything to help them now—in their entirely new, dangerous, uncharted situation. This kind of provocation seems to have aroused this picaro's combative spirit. With Slavenka, I co-organized a conference where U.S. feminists were to meet East Central European women who—for a variety of reasons—identified as "feminists," too. Before I knew it, I became enmeshed, perhaps I should say enthralled, by the drama of swift change in the region.

My piece here, "Feminist Futures in the Former East Bloc," written early on in my East-West encounters, is a long list of reasons—sometimes contradictory, sometimes mutually reinforcing—why feminist ideas were homeless and often detested in postcommunism. The East Central European feminists who read the piece in the early 1990s—in English, then Russian, then Polish—were irritated and/or engaged by the case I made that their feminist work was on the edge of impossible—and very urgent.

By the time I wrote the second piece in this series of thought experiments about feminism in East Central Europe, "Feminism Travels: Cautionary Tales," I was well along in my fascination with questions of gender justice in the region. After our conference in 1991, I had helped found a nongovernmental organization (NGO), the Network of East-West Women, and "Cautionary Tales" offers another list, this time a catalog of all the ways NGOs are inadequate, weak, undemocratic, misleading, and unclear themselves about what they can and cannot do. I describe how NGOs can easily introduce all kinds of bad faith, useless competition, and distortion into the worlds where they work. I warn that "gender" is sometimes used as an exotic political import to obscure and abandon equally important questions of class and ethnicity. It felt right to sharply criticize what we were doing, but also right to keep working on the Network, trying to build local and international feminist community, talking, talking—and acting whenever we could. Some called us a "talking shop" and suggested that talking over dinner is not a movement. We argued back that women talking has been seen as trivial, but when men talk, it's called politics.

When I write about the Network and its always-fragile existence, I often think about a favorite book of mine, Bonnie Anderson's *Joyous Greetings: The First International Women's Movement, 1830–1860*. Anderson discovered an extraordinary web of relationships among feminists in the United States and all over Europe in the nineteenth century. In letters from jail cells or from children's nurseries, they heartened each other, strengthened each other's idea of what they were doing—demanding women's rights to own themselves, to be sexually free, to become citizens. They raised each others' spirits and so, I hope, do we in our Network, which has survived from 1991 until now.

After a brief biography of an extraordinary Polish feminist, Slawka Walczewska, the next pieces here give snapshots of my two decades of teaching about feminism in East Central Europe. Change in the region has been so dizzying that every two or three years we visiting professors were facing an entirely different culture. Our first students grew up under communism; now it's their parents who remember, and our young students are reinventing themselves in counterpoint to that quickly fading, recent past. It's been thrilling to watch this time-lapse movie, and sometimes, perhaps, to be a marginal image at the side of the frame, cheering, cajoling.

The last piece in "The Feminist Picaresque" is about a different—but at moments similarly destabilizing—teaching adventure. In 2011, I gave a course about film (and secretly about feminism) to men in a medium security prison. This time we all had some traits of the picaro, though without his mobility or freedom to make light of the strictures of the state. My students were living at the edge of legitimacy in a tense relationship both to law and resistance. They were, as the warden kept reminding me, "criminals." The divide between us was deep, but I tried to bend the rules in my students' favor, to imagine with them paths of escape.

My need for adventure is a case study: feelings of the uncanny, of disassociation, and of being lost save me from deadening repetition, discouragement, and burn out. With whatever strange mixture of narcissistic fantasy and the hardworking reality of slogging as an activist, I continue to travel with feminism.

12

OCCUPYING GREENHAM COMMON

I was gratified that Occupy Wall Street activists showed interest in my account of earlier political occupations in the 1980s and reprinted my piece about Greenham Common in their Occupy Gazette. I wrote the introduction below as a note to the Occupiers, calling for a new stage in occupation politics.

The piece below, written in 1984, about the occupation of the U.S. cruise missile base at Greenham Common, England, is not meant as a direct model for Occupy Wall Street (OWS) but as a reminder of an encouraging past. I have no doubt that the mass popular mobilizations of the 1980s, mostly in Europe, were an essential element in the collapse of Cold War militarism, though of course politicians continue to pretend otherwise, giving Ronald Reagan much of the credit. A vast, international public, cowed by nuclear fear for decades, made a radical turn, refusing to continue passive support for the specious idea that nuclear arms are a source of security.

It's taken a long time—and the shameless and obscene greed of a few—to stir the many to outrage once again. But here we are, joining in what we hope will become a mass refusal.

The occupation of the gates around Greenham Common—a demonstration that was rural, sprawling, and unmappable—established an ongoing symbolic place, which was able to inspire others to similar acts all over the world. To make the inconvenient journey to Greenham Common was to participate, to protest. Such physical, visible endurance was central to Greenham's power. I and thousands of others visited, year after year, until the Cold War was over and the base was abandoned.

What does place mean now in our era of dematerialization, virtual close-ness, speed of connection? I still see literal space as amazingly powerful and am ready to take a turn sitting in the drizzle at Zuccotti Park in New York. But perhaps the Greenham model of a years-long protest in a fixed place is now approaching the impossible. Back then we had fires when it got cold. Today, police techniques for surveillance and control are far more sophisticated and vicious, and the legal nets around public space have continually tightened in the so-called war against terror. The visible occupation of literal space de-pends on a system that eschews incarcerating protestors for decades, or that chooses not to machine gun them as the enemy. Grace Paley was heckled on picket lines: "They wouldn't let you do that in Russia." "Yeah," she used to reply, "In this country, we have civil rights. But what's the point if you never use them?"

These rights are eroding as I write this, perhaps making an earlier civil compact between government and citizens obsolete. The staging of political protest may need to move to different grounds—or should I say to new "plat-forms"? If we can't hold on to even a tiny tract of permanence, we'll simply have to find other forms of relentless presence.

Anyway, Greenham was never meant to be static; the goal was always pro-liferation, rhizomic development. At Christmas, 1986, artist Susan Kleckner decided to bring Greenham to New York with her "Window Piece." A differ-ent woman camped in a storefront window on West Broadway each week for almost a year. Women's Peace encampments also cropped up in those years and lasted several days in Madison Square Park and Battery Park. I remember being on rat patrol, so others could sleep.

Finally, a word about the expulsion of men from Greenham after the first nine months, described below. Among other things, this move essential-ized violence as male. With the men gone from the occupation, the map of violence could be unambiguous: peaceful female demonstrators outside the base confronted a male death machine on the other side of the wire.

It would be a great misunderstanding of how much good work feminist, queer politics has done in the almost thirty years since Greenham to think that we can or should draw such a simple diagram of good and evil again. But the fact that Occupy Wall Street is meant to include everyone doesn't offer any closure to the gender drama. Many have experienced OWS as a largely male space. Some women feel like tokens, less heard, less likely to be insid-ers in making decisions. Others have experienced sexual harassment.

Because the kinetic OWS keeps changing its population, its mores, its structures, its locations, no generalization about sexism can hold. But, dear friends, "men" and "women," since we're not going to take the short cut of gender separation this time around, constant vigilance is in order. Sexism can be subtle. Sexism can seem normal. (One young man of twenty-two told me that abortion is a minor issue, not worthy of Occupy Wall Street attention.) At Greenham, discussion of sexism and violence was unceasing, and these discussions should remain urgent for us now.

Whatever their differences, Greenham and OWS are alike in freeing political imagination, in setting loose an expressive, hopeful politics. No tents allowed on the ground? Let's hang them from helium balloons in the sky, as they did at Occupy Berkeley. Suddenly, the horizon is limitless.

December 10, 2011

Holding the Line at Greenham: Joyous Politics in Dangerous Times

I made my first trip to the women's peace encampment at Greenham Common in May 1984 partly to assure myself it was still there. After mass evictions in April, the press had announced with some glee that the continuous vigil at the U.S. cruise missile base was over at last. Certainly on my arrival in the freezing rain there seemed little enough evidence to contradict these reports.

When I reached the prosperous town of Newbury with a friend who had given me a lift from London, we couldn't at first even find the base, which our map said was a misshapen oval just outside the town. How could something nine miles around, bounded by a ten-foot fence, guarded by large contingents of the U.S. Air Force, the Royal Air Force, and the police be so quietly tucked away?

Finally a scrawled woman's symbol painted on the road gave us a clue. We went up to the plateau of land that was once "common" to all. And suddenly, the fence was right in front of us in the fog. The Greenham fence looks very serious—thick wire mesh topped by several feet of rolled barbed wire, all supported at frequent intervals by cement pylons. Ten feet farther inside are more rolls of barbed wire, forming a tangled second barrier rather like those on the battlefields of World War I. Inside the fence, we could just make out—through sheets of wire and rain—concrete runways, small bunker-like buildings, a treeless wasteland. One structure, rather like a giant, half-buried two-car garage, was, as I learned later, a missile silo.

But there were no women. Here was a gate, certainly, one of the nine where the women live, and before it several little humps of plastic, but the

Writing in my plastic bender (10 Million Women for 10 Days, September, 1984).
Photograph: Susan Kleckner.

Benders at Orange Gate. Photograph: © Paula Allen (original in color).

only people on view were a few policemen. A mile farther along and, finally, two women, standing beneath a twisted umbrella that they seemed to be holding more over the struggling fire than themselves. Two smallish women in the rain. Impossible. In silent agreement we drove on to yet another gate with again a huddle of plastic, an extinguished fire, a forlorn dereliction.

I finally understood: this was it. I asked to be dropped off back with those women with the umbrella and the fire. (You can't imagine what a depressing idea this was.) We drove back. I struggled into the waterproof boots my friend had lent me—absolute necessities as I soon discovered—and joined the women.

They were Donna and Maria. They were very, very wet. Maria's face was hidden under her sodden hood, though one could just manage to see she had a bad cold. Donna wished the world to know she was "fed up." Neither was interested in talking much. They seemed faintly aroused to hear that I had just come from New York, but as the day progressed I came to understand their lack of surprise. We stood there in the stinking nowhere and people stopped by in cars, visiting us from all over the world. If Greenham feels like the world's end, it is also a mecca, a shrine of the international peace movement.

Inventive, leaderless, a constantly rotating population of women have blocked the smooth functioning of this cruise missile base for three years now. In the great traditions of pacifism, anarchy, and English doggedness in adversity, they have entered the base, blockaded its gates, danced on its missile silos, made a mockery of its security systems, and inspired other people to set up peace camps elsewhere in Britain and all over the world—in Italy, for instance, and Australia, Japan, and the United States.

The camps were empty that first day because some of the women were exhausted; some in jail; some in New York suing Ronald Reagan; some at the cruise missile base in Sicily, helping the beleaguered women's peace camp there; some in Holland for a big government vote on NATO. After a few hours, Donna, too, left with one of the circumnavigating cars, off to Reading for a bath and a drink. Maria and I stayed where we were, which proved to be Indigo Gate. (The women have named their homes for the colors of the rainbow.) Although most of the women were gone, the Greenham peace camp was not shut down: at each gate several women were sticking it out in the rain. In fact, you can't really shut Greenham, even if you drag all the women away from all the gates. They come back or they go home, explaining that it hardly matters: "Greenham women are everywhere."

Back in 1981 when I first heard about the women's peace camp at Greenham Common, I was impressed but a little worried, too. Here was a stubborn little band of squatters obstructing business as usual at a huge military base. But the early media reports celebrated these women as orderly housewives and mothers who would never make this vulgar noise just for themselves but were naturally concerned about their children, innocent animals, and growing plants.

My feminist reaction was: not again. I had joined the women's liberation movement to escape this very myth of the special altruism of women, our innate peacefulness, our handy patience for repetitive tasks, our peculiar endurance—no doubt perfect for sitting numbly in the Greenham mud, babies and arms outstretched, begging men to keep our children safe from nuclear war.

We feminists had argued back then that women's work had to be done by men, too: no more "women only" when it came to emotional generosity or trips to the launderette. We did form women-only groups—an autonomous women's movement—but this was to forge a necessary solidarity for resistance, not to cordon off a magic femaleness as distorted in its way as the old reverence for motherhood. Women have a long history of allowing their own goals to be eclipsed by others, and even feminist groups have often been subsumed by other movements. Given this suspiciously unselfish past, I was uneasy with women-only groups that did not concentrate on overcoming the specific oppression of women.

And why should demilitarization be women's special task? If there's one thing in this world that won't discriminate in men's favor, it's a nuclear explosion. Since the army is a dense locale of male symbols, actions, and forms of association, let men sit in the drizzle, I thought; let them worry about the children for a change.

But even before going to Greenham I should have known better than to have trusted its media image. If the women were such nice little home birds, what were they doing out in the wild, balking at male authority, refusing to shut up or go back home? I've been to Greenham twice now in the effort to understand why many thousands of women have passed through the camps, why thousands are organized in support groups all over Britain and beyond, why thousands more can be roused to help in emergencies or show up for big actions.

What I discovered stirred my political imagination more than any activism since that first, intense feminist surge in the United States in the early 1970s. Though I still have many critical questions about Greenham, I see it as a source of fresh thinking about how to be joyously, effectively political in a conservative, dangerous time. Obviously this intense conversion experience is going to take some explaining.

Some of the women of Orange Gate, including some excellent cooks. We ate well at the 10 Million Women for 10 Days action. Photograph: Susan Kleckner.

When, in the summer of 1981, a small group of women from Cardiff in Wales decided to use their holidays to take a long walk for peace, they could choose from a startlingly large number of possible destinations. Unobtrusive, varying in size and purpose, more than one hundred U.S. military facilities were tucked away in the English countryside, an embarrassment of military sites available for political pilgrimage.

One U.S. base distinguished itself as particularly dreadful. Enormous, centrally located, but quietly carrying on incognito, the site was Greenham Common, outside the town of Newbury, where the U.S. Air Force was preparing for ninety-six ground-launched cruise missiles to be deployed in the fall of 1983. Because the cruise is small and deployed from mobile launch points on sea or land, and because it flies low, the cruise is hard to detect—transparently a first strike weapon.

To protest this new step in the arms race, the Welsh women set out to walk 120 miles due east to Newbury, only sixty miles out from London. They were a varied bunch, mostly strangers to each other—thirty-six women from very different class and political backgrounds, four men in support, and a few children. Their nine-day walk, which was ignored by the press, filled them with excitement and energy, and they were greeted warmly in the towns along the way.

By the time they reached Greenham, however, the media silence had become galling. Four women decided to chain themselves to the main gate of the base to force the world to take notice. This act of protest had children and grandchildren undreamed of by the original, quite humble, and politically inexperienced Greenham marchers. Teachers, farmers, nurses, and—yes—housewives, they had had no intention of staying at Greenham. But first the media took their time; then tents had to be set up and people informed. A few days spent in support of the chained women lengthened to a week, then two. Some campers had to leave, but others were just arriving.

The summer days began to give way to the chill damp of English winter. Perhaps it felt callow to give up protesting against nuclear disaster just because the afternoons were drawing in. Gradually, as the peace camp persisted—a small cluster of tents and caravans at the main gate of the base—one fact became plain: Greenham was tapping a great, hidden energy source for protest. There were enough women who were willing to give bits of time stolen from the work-that-is-never-done to keep a campfire perpetually burning on Greenham Common.

After initial amusement and tolerance, the missile base took alarm. Winter came but the women did not go away. On January 20, 1982, the nearby town of Newbury served notice on the camps of its intention to evict.

If ever the women had considered packing it in, this evidence that they were a real thorn in the side of the American military and its English support systems must have clinched matters. Prime Minister Margaret Thatcher told the world the women were irresponsible; she didn't like them one bit. The women began telling reporters, "We're here for as long as it takes"—the "it" left menacingly unspecific. Some may have meant only the local rejection of U.S. cruise missiles. But by this time even the opposition Labour party was beginning to consider the far more ambitious goal of unilateral disarmament as a serious English option.

The long-threatened eviction didn't come until late May 1982, when the camp was nine months old. By this time the women's community was firmly entrenched. The shifting population made even honest generalizations about the women difficult, while the press had long ended its romance with docile housewives and now made more insulting efforts to stereotype them (just middle-class ladies, just lesbians, just green-haired punks). The women themselves refused self-definition, other than to say that they were unified by their double commitment—to nonviolence and to direct action. Since they eschewed leaders as well as generalizations, there was no spokesperson to mediate between the world and the spontaneous acts of the group.

It is no doubt this very amorphousness that has made evicting the women so difficult. The police are taught to arrest the ringleader, but here there is none. Campers evicted from the Common land simply cross over to Ministry of Transport land, a strip alongside the road, or to Ministry of Defense Land. Evicted from there, they move back to council land. Constant evictions—sometimes daily—have become a central, shaping reality of Greenham life. Since no location there is legal, even the smallest acts of persistence acquire gravitas. For anyone, just visiting Greenham Common, sitting down on an overturned bucket at a campfire for a chat and tea, is an act of civil disobedience.

During my first visit, a two-day stay, I assumed that it was with grisly irony that the women had named the gates the colors of the rainbow. My time at Indigo was absurdly bleak and monochromatic. We struggled to keep the fire going; Maria (who, it turned out, was from Spain) performed a vegetarian miracle on a tiny, precariously tilted grill; we talked to the guards five feet from us on the other side of the fence about war, peace, men, women, weather, money; we slept in an ingenious but soaking handmade teepee,

A Greenham campsite. A house door has been wrested from domestic space and is now framing our campsite. Photograph: Susan Kleckner.

while outside an ever changing pair of guards patrolled with growling dogs under giant arc lamps which sizzled in the rain and lit up our dreams.

Greenham seemed mainly a passive test of endurance, though it was obvious, too, that instead of destroying the encampment, the stream of evictions has become a source of solidarity, resistance, and imagination. Where once gardens were planned, now a few flowers grow in a pram, easily rolled away at a moment's notice. Where once elaborate circus tents were pitched, now a cup on a stick holds up a makeshift roof. Those unprepossessing huddles of plastic I saw on my arrival were actually full of women, sheltering from the rain. These "benders" can look squashed and ugly from outside; but the bent branches that support the plastic are often still covered with leaves, making the inside a bower. When the bailiffs come with their big "chompers," they get a pile of soggy polyethylene, while the campers carry their few possessions across the road to safety. As soon as the bulldozers are gone, up go the plastic shelters once more.

Familiar domestic collages of blackened tea kettles, candles, corn flakes, bent spoons, chipped plates (never paper ones) lie around as if the contents of a house had been emptied into the mud, but here the house itself is gone. The women have left privacy and home, and now whatever acts of housekeeping they perform are in the most public of spaces up against the fence or road. Greenham is the ultimate housewife's nightmare: the space that

Some Greenham encampments were quite elaborate before evictions started.

can never be swept clean, ordered, sealed off, or safe. But as the mud blackens hands and the wood smoke permeates clothes and hair, the women of Greenham give up gracefully. (With thick irony I was offered the following suggestions: "Wood smoke is a pretty good deodorant." "Try washing the dishes in boiling water; it loosens things up a bit, under the fingernails.")

The evictions have further clarified the situation: this is life *in extremis*, life carried on where authority and custom do not mean it to be lived. There is only one source of water for all the camps. Only small and portable Robinson Crusoe contrivances have a chance. Greenham shreds the illusion of permanence and pushes those who live there into a naked, urgent present.

It is hard to imagine a better intellectual forcing ground for people struggling to grasp the full reality of the nuclear threat. Sitting at the fire, we discussed postindustrial society, postimperialist England, whether or not one should eat meat, the boundary between useful and irresponsible technical advances. Strewn around us were mixtures of very old technologies (how to make a fire with nothing but damp wood; how to cook everything on that fire—there is no electricity *anywhere* in the camps; how to build a shelter from bracken) and useful new ones (plastic protects everything; some women have fancy Gore-Tex sleeping bags or jackets because, though waterproof, they "breathe").

I told one woman who has lived at Greenham for two years that sometimes the camps looked to me as if World War III had already happened, as if we were rehearsing for life after the bomb, in a flat landscape where there will probably be plenty of bits of plastic and Velcro but no clean water, no electricity, nowhere to hide. She looked at me pityingly: "Greenham is a holiday camp next to what things would be like if these bombs go off."

Of course, of course. Still, Greenham is a grim reminder of how much effort the simplest acts of maintenance take once one has removed oneself from the house, the town, the city. People there are experimenting with self-governance in small communities; they are living with less, seeking new definitions of comfort and satisfaction.

Certainly that less is more seemed the message of my first visit. But on my second, Greenham revealed a whole new side. I arrived in delicate sunlight for an action called "10 Million Women for 10 Days" timed to coincide with NATO's vast maneuvers on the East German-West German border. This time instead of a wasteland I found a carnival, a cauldron of direct action, a wildly kinetic place. Circus tents were going up for the ten-day gathering and caravans offered free food. Strings of colorfully dressed women lined the road, walking clockwise and counterclockwise, in the great Greenham round. They had come to act.

Part of what makes the daily exhaustion of Greenham endurable for so many different kinds of women—and in such large numbers—is that contrary to first appearances, the place is a magnificent, exotic stage set for effective political gestures. Unlike other political demonstrations I have known, peace camp occupations are frames that can give form to hundreds of individual acts of resistance. Energy flows like light because of the immediacy of everything, the constant, imminent possibility for self-expression and group solidarity.

You are not only joining something larger than yourself but something that is continuously, inexorably taking its stand of militant witness and rebuke, even while you're sleeping, even when you're fed up and go off to spend a night in town, even when you're angry, confused, or at political loggerheads with every other woman in the place. Greenham is a springboard from which actions that would usually take months of laborious planning can be dreamed, discussed, and performed between night and morning.

Ideas for Greenham action can come from anywhere—something read in the paper, an image someone shares at the fire—and one such action made Greenham internationally famous, the "embrace the base" demonstration of December 12, 1982. The precipitating image—borrowed from the U.S.

Greenham women up against the fence—as always, discussing.

Women's Pentagon Action—was of women encircling the fence, surrounding it "with feelings of power and love." No one knew if enough women would come to stretch around the nine-mile perimeter, so the nervous few who had set the idea in motion told everyone to bring long scarves to use as connectors, just in case.

Somewhere between 30,000 and 50,000 came, more than enough to embrace the entire round. (Whatever the press says, the women are always uncountable: Greenham has no center, no single focus, no check-in point, no higher ground from which to gain an overview. The air force sent helicopters over each morning to count us when I was there, but this effort to get on top of things was a miserable failure.) To those who were there and the millions more who heard about it, the action seemed a miracle. The next day, 2,000 women blockaded all the entrances, and, two weeks later, on New Year's dawn, forty-four climbed the fence and began an hour's dance on the half-completed missile silos. On the anniversary of "embrace the base," the women tried another more hostile image of encirclement. Again 50,000 came, this time with mirrors they held up to the fence, reflecting its own dreary reality back on itself. At yet another carefully planned action, the women locked the soldiers inside by securing all the gates with heavy-duty bicycle locks. The increasingly frantic military police couldn't cut their way out and, finally, had to push one of their own gates down.

Cutting down the fence. Photograph: © Paula Allen (original in color).

But it is a distortion of Greenham activism to mention only these large and well-known events, which required an unusual amount of advance planning. In fact, nothing was more maddening for an old New Leftist like me than the effort to figure out where a Greenham action comes from—rather like trying to find out how a drop of dye travels through a gallon of water. Women told me: Well, this one had this idea. And we all had a meeting. (Who is this "all"? Whoever wanted to do an action.) Then some of us didn't like it. And we kept talking about it. We changed it a bit. We agreed to ask all our friends and their friends, by phone, by chain letter. We have a big network.

In some ways the women's peace encampment at Greenham Common is flamboyantly photogenic, a thrilling visual landscape, including both sweeping long lines of fence and cunning, small details. But, paradoxically, this scene can also drive a photographer mad since much of Greenham's meaning is actively, one might almost say programmatically, unphotogenic. Greenham's value system prescribes that no particular face shall have more recognition value than any other, no particular place any more vaunting centrality.

A world without hierarchies of space or time—this is the Greenham that has every intention of teasing and enraging any media that demand a controlled orchestration of event. Of late, the press has retaliated against the anarchy by trying to ignore this spontaneous stream of activist dramas. But this suppression of imagery can be but a partial success since no matter what happens there at any one place or moment, each event is also a dramatic representation of a continuous presence, in many places, moments. A particular act is easily ignored. (No one, for instance, reported fifty of us holding candles one night, waving and singing at a much-traveled crossroad—but hundreds driving by saw us.) Acts like these leave a subtle, cumulative record—including many small, privately remembered events—seemingly invisible but engraved in social memory.

Perhaps this is just to repeat the old saying, "The revolution will not be televised." The frustration of photographers is part of the point: the frame of the picture cuts off the sprawling symbolic landscape. The photographer who would represent Greenham is forced to become aware of the responsibility entailed in each act of selection, forced to recognize the limits of isolated anecdotes. Women gather at Greenham to be unpredictable, to do what they want, when they want, to act while balking at their culture's power to trap them once more inside the image of their act.

One of the brilliant structural inventions of the peace movement as a whole is its combination of small affinity groups with large networks. In the small group you are known, valued, listened to. These are the people you choose from the heart, the ones you want next to you if the police get rough. But instead of being an isolated enclave, the affinity group is linked to others in an international network, which shares some if not all the small group's goals. The Greenham network includes men as well as women, organized in a number of forms. Consensus is often possible in small groups that have worked together for a long time, while the network operates differently, joining people in coalitions where sharp disagreements are also acknowledged.

Most direct action at Greenham, though, is generated not from the larger network but within small affinity groups. An idea or image travels around the gates like wildfire. "Let's get up at 4:00 a.m. and shake a big stretch of fence down." "Let's have a vigil at the gate at sunset and call all the names of the people who wanted to be here but couldn't." "Let's confuse them by blockading the road a mile from the gate and creating such a traffic jam that they can't get to us to arrest us." Once, at Easter: "Let's dress up like furry animals and cover ourselves with honey, and break into the base." (No one arrested the women who did this one—maybe because they were too sticky?)

Or take the fence, that always-present reminder of an "outside" versus

Greenham Common fence. Photograph: Susan Kleckner.

"inside," a raggle-taggle band of colorful women who sing and dance and watch versus a gray-and-brown squad of soldiers who march and drill and watch. My first impression of this fence as something final and authoritative left me entirely unprepared for the women's view of it: they have simply rejected it as a legitimate boundary. Slipping under or cutting doors through the wire, they enter the base constantly, exploring, painting, filching frighteningly bureaucratic memos about nuclear war—symbolically undermining the concept "security." Hundreds have been arrested for criminal damage to the wire, yet women continue to enter the base routinely, in large numbers.

It is startling to learn just how much can be done by the carefully nonviolent who are also determined and militant and bent on obstruction. One demonstration called for women with bolt cutters (heavy wire clippers) to surround the fence and take the whole thing down. Thousands removed miles and miles of wire. Of course the fence is constantly repaired, shored up, rebuilt, but at any time or place you can come on a group working together rhythmically, like rowers, to shake it down again. The police rush over; the women rush away, laughing or ululating or singing, only to return the minute the coast is clear. Nine miles is a long front of vulnerability, and the police look and probably feel like fools as they sprint here and there, defending their barrier from women who never offer them much resistance, but never desist.

Decorating the fence. Photograph: © Paula Allen (original in color).

In one exceptional foray inside the base, a symbolic gesture became a literal obstruction when a camper painted a peace symbol on the convenient fuselage of what turned out to be the top-secret "Blackbird" spy plane. Her paint ruined its fabulously expensive titanium shield, but she was brought up on a minor charge—no doubt to avoid discussion in court about how vulnerable high technology is to sabotage and how easily women evade the authority of the base.

By now the fence can be quite beautiful, with its layers of history, its dense record of rival intentions. There isn't a yard that isn't cut, mended, woven with webs or dragons or God's eyes, painted, hung with objects like teething rings, pine cones, a pair of shoes, decorated with postcards, photographs ("Libby and her dog Zach, Seattle, WA"), pinned with messages: "To Lucy T. and all wimmin," or "Keep Britain tidy—remove cruise"; and once, to my shock, "To my dear son David, age 24, who gave his life in the miners' strike, 1984." Now the fence simply belongs to the women. They have taken it over.

For the first two years of its existence, the peace camp was an intense expression of one idea: cruise missiles shall not pass. But on November 14, 1983, the first missile-carrying transport planes arrived at the base. The defeat made it clear that cruise missiles at one particular English common in the Royal County of Berkshire are not really the point. Getting rid of the missiles remains a central goal, but the women now tend to spend more of their time thinking about a range of other matters: What kind of community makes nonviolent living possible? What is the optimum scale for human institutions? The old, often cozy or self-deprecating idea that there is a "little England" (as opposed to the imperial one) is acquiring some interesting new wrinkles at Greenham. The women are trying to imagine their country as smaller and its cooperative connection with the world beyond as larger.

Ever since deployment, the contrast they seek to make between human scale and U.S. megalomania has begun to take the form of a specific monitoring of cruise's comings and goings. The idea behind this particular missile system is that at times of alert, it can be taken from its silo, mounted, and ferried around the countryside to firing points that cannot be anticipated by the enemy. Mobility is of the essence, since the launchers are supposed to be unpredictably moving targets, ready to fire at a moment's notice.

In fact, the missiles travel in long convoys and the launchers themselves are wide and ponderous. Have you ever driven on small English country roads? I was held up for ten minutes near Greenham by a stalled motorcycle. The Greenham campers, those tireless witnesses of the physical facts, are derisive about the idea that the missiles are either swift or invisible.

While no small, unarmed group can prevent a cruise missile from poking its way out of the base, the Greenham women have easily managed to be a constant source of freshly invented obstructions. One told me: Since deployment, we've tried to maintain a night watch at all gates, to keep track of the convoys. I was terrified my first time. There was this little notice pinned to a tree, headed "What to do if cruise comes out." First you were to blow a whistle (also hanging on the tree) to wake the other gates. Then you were to walk to a distant phone box and activate the telephone-tree support system.

Part of the strategy behind tracking the missiles is to alert nearby towns that nuclear missile launchers (perhaps armed?) are rehearsing for World War III just up the lane. Women at the base attempt a blockade, while others arriving in cars scour the roads to find the convoy; they have succeeded in charting its course all but the first time.

Sound unlikely, absurd, useless? Absurdity is part of the women's point. They keep seeking new ways to dramatize a paradox: supposedly slick systems like cruise are fallible; but even if they weren't, it would be suicide to keep escalating war technology under the hypocritical policy "negotiate from strength." Nonviolent and resolutely low-tech, the women have almost certainly curtailed missile rehearsals with their constant vigilance. They are always being accused of weakening NATO and helping the Russians. When a policeman mutters that they are agents of the KGB, the women get really uproarious and sing (use an accelerating rhythm and, if your knees are good, dance a kazatsky):

We work for the Russians
At tuppence a day
They ask us to stay here
And that's why we stay
We drink lots of vodka
And that's why we're gay.
Hey.

In fact, as the women are demonstrating, the Soviets can easily know when the missiles leave the base. In tense times, why should they not misunderstand a rehearsal as an intention to make a secret launch? One needn't wait, though, for an atmosphere of international crisis; one can be nervous right now: once, the engine of a cruise launcher stalled and its clutch gave way. There they were, stranded nuclear launchers on the busy thoroughfare, A 339. The women point to the American soldiers who are the base's dirty little secret—the actual power behind the more visible Royal Air Force and police—the masterminds who have not yet worked out the bugged details of World War III. And they remind anyone who will listen: these Americans have bunkers inside for themselves and their families but not for you, oh, blithe passerby, not for you.

Sitting there at the gates of the base, the campers can see the rough beast of U.S. militarism slouching right toward them, but just facing it makes them feel more awake, less like comatose prey. Is Greenham only a place, then, where you can go, and feel that you've made a difference—but really you haven't? Is it an escape valve, where disaffected, radical, or anxious women can freely complain, taking themselves off their husbands' hands, the welfare rolls, and the streets? Is anybody listening?

Certainly Greenham's effectiveness is hard to measure. The powers that be—from Margaret Thatcher to NATO and even as far as the Kremlin—profess to be paying no attention to the women, nor to the mass European peace movement in general. But the women don't accept the powers that be, a stance that has earned them a grudging respect among their compatriots.

In this volatile political situation where the choices are so clear, the real audience for the obduracy of the Greenham campers is not the leadership of England or NATO, but the vast populations. E. P. Thompson, the great labor historian and respected peace activist, has said, "The decisions to develop new weapons—to deploy the SS-20 . . . to go ahead with cruise missiles—are taken by a few score people . . . secretively, behind closed doors, on both sides. But to check or to reverse any one of those decisions nothing will do except the voluntary efforts of hundreds of thousands."[1]

To turn around an arms race so richly fed by capital investment certainly a mass movement is essential, but what sort of mass? Greenham's effectiveness must be measured not only by the role it plays in mobilizing large numbers but also by the kind of political culture it has to offer those numbers.

By crude measurements—for example, polls—Greenham has made little statistical difference in how the English think about the nuclear threat. About half oppose the deployment of cruise missiles; a third approve; a sixth have no opinion. The loose entity "Greenham" is suspicious—loved, romanticized, hated, and scorned—precisely because it is capable of generating political experiences that are threatening, profound, and transformative.

Conservatives try to reassure themselves that the only women influenced are those already beyond the pale, the hags, the dykes, the freeloaders. What is continuously disconcerting to these observers is how this imagery half fits and half doesn't: Women who look "ordinary" in some respects suddenly make radical breaks with things as they are. They are housewife-witches or mother-lesbians who insist on walking the cracks of standard female identities.

Because they have agreed to differ among themselves, to act independently or in small bunches without having to get everyone's approval, difference is casually celebrated at Greenham. The women love to parody the contradictions that arise. They sing:

We're mostly vegetarian
Except when we're devouring men.

I met women of every class and generation, though very few black, Asian, or Indian women make their way there. There were Grannies against Cruise and striking miners' wives; there were a disproportionate number of professionals and intellectuals; there were both straight and lesbian women, with lesbian energy a great source of Greenham vitality and staying power; there were glorious flocks of young girls playing various forms of hooky, casting a cold, clear eye on their dim future in the present English job market. There were genuinely marginal women who would be on the dole, or in mental institutions, or in some other form of big trouble if Greenham weren't there.

Greenham is a melting pot, with all the false unities that can imply, but with the potential, too, for a new cosmopolitanism for feminist activism.

These women bring to the fire values forged in a variety of movements: they absolutely reject any leadership (like the anarchists, or like the feminist consciousness-raising groups some of them came from); they insist on non-violence (like the pacifist, Quaker, or other Christian groups some of them came from). They are ecologists, trade unionists, Labour party members, Campaign for Nuclear Disarmament (CND) activists, and refugees from a wide variety of Left groups.

These influences are a rich soil for Greenham, but the women have often burst out of those groups—especially the male-female ones—with frustration. Although the Greenham encampment was initiated by women, for the first months several men did live there. In February 1982, the women met separately and decided to ask these men to leave. Nothing in Greenham's history has caused as much furor and debate as this decision.

Why did the women ask the men to go? At Greenham one gets a variety of answers to this question. Some women say the first evictions were coming and they feared that the police would be more brutal if men were among the campers, and that the male campers themselves might respond with violence in defense of "their women." Others say that the women noticed the old divisions of labor creeping in. As one camper I interviewed had heard the story: "The men were beginning to take over the meetings but not pulling their weight as far as the chores were concerned." The women feared, too, that insofar as their resistance was militant and effective, the press would assume that this power came from the few men in the camp. Once more, women's acts would be invisible.

The Greenham women I talked to take great pains to point out that the purpose of Greenham is not to exclude men but to include women—at last. Though a few women there might still tell you women are biologically more peaceful than men, this view has been mostly replaced by a far more complex analysis of why women need to break with our old, private complicity with public male violence. No one at Greenham seems to be arguing that the always-evolving Greenham value system is inevitably female. The women recognize their continuity with the Quakers, with Gandhi, with the entire pacifist tradition, and with the anarchist critique of the state. At the same time, women, the Greenham campers believe, may have a separate statement to make about violence because we have our own specific history in relation to it. They also reject the structures or assumptions they are likely to find in mixed groups—where they feel their energies are deadened or co-opted. Greenham represents political opportunity for women. Greenham is open-ended.

A fast-flowing stream of ideas floods back from Greenham toward home, transforming the movements to which the women return on different terms. These other groups get flushed with some of the excitement of Greenham's creative pace. A Campaign for Nuclear Disarmament activist told me that CND takes a year to change a policy, while at Greenham, political ideas can get superseded by others through intense debate in a matter of days.

"Greenham" is now shorthand for a large complex of activities all over Britain and Europe, where other peace camps have been set up or where groups have formed in support. Though it is sometimes accused of being odd, isolated, and incommunicable, and though there's no hard evidence that it has changed mainstream politics, Greenham-ness has made a difference to the idea of how to be political in the diffuse style typical of all its works and days.

A whole activist generation was forged at Greenham, not of age but of shared practice. Greenham women are disobedient, disloyal to civilization, advanced in their ability to connect the dots of fragmented modern experiences. The movable hearth is their schoolroom, where they piece together a stunning if raffish political patchwork.

Before visiting Greenham, I had feared that its politics would prove simple-minded, that those absolutes, life and death, would have cast more complex social questions in the shade. How, for instance, could the old question "What do women want?" survive when the subject is Mutual Assured Destruction (MAD, U.S. military slang for nuclear deterrence). As Brenda Whisker wrote in *Breaching the Peace*, an English collection of feminist essays criticizing the women's peace movement, "I think that stopping the holocaust is easier than liberating women."[2] Hard words certainly, but understandable, solidified through bitter experience. While women and children are first, feminism continues to be last.

Elements of the Greenham intellectual environment feed such worries, but by the time I got to Greenham, a number of the radical feminist concerns in *Breaching the Peace* were already dated; Greenham consciousness had absorbed the critique and moved on.

Certainly many women do come to Greenham with no thought of feminism, speaking instead of quite other concerns—of God, of nature, of their grandchildren. Many come who would never have joined feminist groups, precisely because feminism seemed "selfish," aggressively women-only, threatening to a treasured, familiar female identity.

But once those women come to Greenham, a great deal happens to them there. During my two visits, I felt a rising bubble of excitement. The place is *about gender*; male and female are both forced by circumstances to caricature themselves. Greenham is a feminist laboratory. The experimental compounds may not be pure, but the mixed results are endlessly suggestive for anyone interested in how gender works, and in how women can change male power without seeking that power.

Some gender parables: The scene is a night at Green Gate. I am with Nesta King of the Women's Pentagon Action and with Janey Martin, a woman of nineteen who has been to Greenham a number of times and has cleverly helped us build our bender.

The general action this particular night seems to be fence shaking. Hundreds of women are gathered under the powerful lights, shaking, keening, singing, talking, strolling up and down the perimeter, which is very close to the silos just at this point.

Suddenly the police, who are usually very careful to pretend that this is all just female nonsense and no one on the base is very worried, lose their tempers. They form a line and walk us all steadily back from the fence. Somehow Janey, who is small and blond and delicate, doesn't move back fast enough. A policeman under less control than most, a very tall, hefty man who obviously feels like a lion taunted by mice, gives tiny Janey a sharp, mean push. She falls, frightened and startled, and—very much against her own political wishes in tranquility—springs up and gives him an angry push back. Useless, of course: he only gives her another fierce shove.

To my utter amazement, out of my mouth comes, very loudly: "Look, everyone, a huge man pushed little Janey. Aren't you ashamed, a big man like you?" Is *this* what's lurking in my mind? I'm horrified to encounter remnants of this very old story inside my feminist self. Do I really want to repeat that only a sissy pushes a girl, that girls aren't worth pushing, that it's only humiliating to shove them, no contest? Do I want to waste my political time trying to make men ashamed?

I did want to show up brute force as cruel, irresponsible, and finally useless, but the old gender exchange there at the fence was bound to obscure this more radical intention. Who was I—this outraged female, this moral mother hen? After all, what did I think we were doing? In spite of the singing, we meant business. We meant to criticize pushing people, to restrain ourselves from pushing back, but not to ask for the old forms of female quarter.

I wonder if women are having to learn at Greenham—with a difference—what men learn too early and carry too far: the courage to dare, to test reaction, to define oneself *against* others. Nonviolent direct action takes great courage. The big men on their horses or machines are doing as ordered—which is comfortable for them. In contrast, it can be truly terrifying to refuse to do what an angry, pushing policeman tells you to do. For women particularly, such acts are fresh and new and this cutting across the grain of feminine socialization is a favorite, daring sport of the young at the fence. Such initiations give women a revolutionary taste of conflict, lived out fully, in our own persons, with gender no longer a reliable determinant of the rules.

Certainly it is no use for women to turn self-righteous, as I had found myself doing—claiming a higher moral ground than men. On that ground, we are admired but ignored. As Dorothy Dinnerstein has argued in *The Mermaid and the Minotaur*, emotional women have traditionally been treated like court jesters that the king keeps around to express his own anxieties—and thus vent them harmlessly. A woman's body lying down in a road in front of a missile launcher has a very different symbolic resonance for everyone from that of a male body in the same position. Greenham's radical feminist critics wonder just what kind of peace a female lying down can bring. Won't men simply allow women to lie in the mud forever because the demonstrators themselves only underline men's concept of what is female (passivity, protest, peace) and what is male (aggression, action, war)?

Before I came to Greenham, I shared these worries. But at Greenham at its best, women's nonviolent direct action becomes not another face of female passivity but a difficult political practice with its own unique discipline. The trick—a hard one—is to skew the dynamics of the old male-female relationships toward new meanings, to interrupt the old conversation between overconfident kings and hysterical, powerless jesters. This will surely include an acknowledgment of our past complicity with men and war making and a dramatization of our new refusal to aid and assist. (I think of a delicious young woman I heard singing out to a group of also very young soldiers: "We don't find you sexy anymore, you know, with your little musket, fife, and drum.")

Perhaps some of the new meanings we need will be found buried in the old ones. If women feel powerless, we can try to share this feeling, to make individual men see that they, too, are relatively powerless in the face of a wildly escalating arms race. Naturally, this is a message men resist, but the women at Greenham are endlessly clever at dramatizing how the army shares their impotence: The army cannot prevent them from getting inside the fence or shaking it down. It cannot prevent them from blockading the gates. It cannot prevent them from returning after each eviction.

Or, rather, it could prevent all this, but only by becoming a visibly brutal force, and this would be another kind of defeat, since the British armed services and police want to maintain their image of patriarchal protectors; they do not want to appear to be batterers of nonviolent women. Greenham women expose the contradictions of gender: by being women they dramatize powerlessness, but they also disarm the powerful.

I came to see "woman" as a porous identity at Greenham—romanticized, celebrated, but also taken apart, transformed by an extreme situation. Feminism itself is bound to undergo change as it becomes a central term in new equations. Instead of seeking feminist consensus, Greenham leaves women on their own, abandoning them to radical independence—to life on the changing edge of gender. Very few women have ever been so entirely free of father, husband, or boss, or so entirely left to their own devices, even among themselves. I met women drunk with the pleasure of such unexpected autonomy.

Members of the Campaign for Nuclear Disarmament and other mixed groups have expressed dismay at what they see as the divisiveness of women-only actions like Greenham just at the time of deployment, when unity seems so necessary. It would be unnerving indeed to most of these well-meaning men if they could glimpse how profoundly alienated many women are from men's groups and the political process. Women tend to be gracious, to celebrate their children—both male and female—so the truth underneath is easy to ignore in the daily round. At Greenham, this truth wells out. Several told me if there were no place like Greenham, they couldn't imagine doing any political work at all. A woman taking an informal survey discovered that in one bus load of visiting women from a long, weary way off, 70 percent had never voted.

To experience the freedom of Greenham Common for a time is to recognize fully the burden of its habitual absence. There's an underwear ad in the London underground, "Underneath women are lovable." At Greenham, stickers read, "Underneath women are angry." At Greenham, women's anger finds a clear and suitable target: the male-dominated machinery of war. Refusing any longer to sustain this machinery by tolerating it, they also refuse the traditional relationship of women to men. And refusing to play by the old gender rules, they come to know the fraudulence of men's claim to protect women, keep them safe. As women have seen again and again, if they push the soldiers too far, the men stop pulling their punches, reverse their above-beating-a-woman attitude, and beat away.

Take the case of Blues, a very young woman who made the mistake of entering the base alone one night for an adventurous stroll. She came on a big machine, and delighted but mystified, she twiddled all its dials. The last one seemed to release some internal pressure, making an alarming gasping sound audible to a couple of soldiers nearby.

Unfortunately for Blues, she was wearing a leather jacket. The soldiers commented on this: "So, you're one of the tough ones." They beat her hard. When I saw her a day later, her face was a mask of wounds and her head was still throbbing from a bad crack on the skull. This was several against one, in the dark, cued by the permission implicit in "leather." The men threw Blues out through the gate, never charging her, since they would then have to name themselves as her arresting officers and face very serious countercharges.

The soldiers didn't kill Blues. Because she is a woman? Because the women are nonviolent? Because the orders are strict: no martyrs at the sensitive base? Because there are very few cruise missiles at Greenham Common and the others are being secretly deployed elsewhere, and if Blues were to find out where and sneak in there, then she would get the reception reserved for the real thing?

For whatever reason, this time the soldiers exercised restraint—walked up to a line and stepped back from it. But they came close enough to show the brutal, emotional, limitless force barely contained by institutional boundaries.

As I write, the Greenham network keeps changing, usually beyond the range of media reports. This very week the death of Greenham was announced once more, but when I called friends they only laughed. "Of course the women are still there." The water situation is desperate and benders have given way to still more primitive plastic shelters, but everyone is "quite cheery."

When I describe Greenham women, I often get the reaction that they sound like naive idealists detached from a reality principle about what can and cannot be done, and how. In a sense this is true. The women reject power and refuse to study it, at least on its own terms. But the other charge—that they are utopian dreamers who sit around and think about the end of the world while not really living in this one—is far from the mark.

In a piece in the *Times Literary Supplement*, "Why the Peace Movement is

Wrong," the Russian émigré poet Joseph Brodsky charged the peace movement with being a bunch of millenarians waiting for the apocalypse. Certainly there are fascinating parallels between the thinking of the peace women and that of the radical millenarian Protestant sects of the seventeenth century. Both believe that the soul is the only court that matters, the self the only guide, and that paradise is a humble and realizable goal in England's green and pleasant land. The millenarians offered free food just like the caravans now on the Common: Food, says one sign. Eat till You're Full.

But the women are not sitting in the mud waiting for the end, nor are they—as Brodsky and many others claim—trying to come to terms with their own deaths by imagining that soon the whole world will die. On the contrary, the women make up one of the really active antimillenarian forces around. President Reagan has told fundamentalist groups that the last trump ending human history might blow at any time now; the women believe that the dreadful sound can be avoided, if only we will stop believing in it.

Greenham women see a kind of fatalism all around them. They, too, have imagined the end, and their own deaths, and have decided that they prefer to die without taking the world with them. Nothing makes them more furious than the apathy in the town of Newbury, where they are often told, "Look, you've got to die anyway. So what difference does it make how you go?" These are the real millenarians, blithely accepting that the end is near.

In contrast, the women look very hardheaded, very pragmatic. They see a big war machine, the biggest the world has known; and, rather than sitting in the cannon's mouth hypnotized, catatonic with fear or denial, they are trying to back away from the danger, step by step. They refuse to be awed or silenced by the scale of modern war. Instead they say calmly that what was built by human beings can be dismantled by them, too. Their logic, clarity, and independence are endlessly refreshing. Where is it written, they ask, that we must destroy ourselves?

1985

Acknowledgments

I gratefully acknowledge the assistance of Theresa Bomford, Robert Bomford, Maria Jesus Gutierrez, Ellen Ross, Dick Glendon, Gwyn Kirk, Nesta King, and all those who granted me lengthy interviews—including Rebecca Johnson, Liz Beech, Helen John, Carrie Pester, Deborah Law, Elizabeth

Carola, Sheila Lunt, Lyn Briggs, Stephanie Leland, Tom Williams, Gillian Reeve. Thanks to the women of Hereford (Stephanie, Lyn, Sheila, Irene, Sue, Jennie, and more) for the splendid hospitality of their cookfire, Orange Gate, where we all—Olga, Kate, younger Lynne, Morna, Felicity, Fay, Alison, Amanda, Grace, Janey, and Nesta—harbored during the "10 Million Women" action.

Notes

1. E. P. Thompson, *Beyond the Cold War*, 2.
2. Whisker, "Essay." In *Breaching the Peace*, 34.

13

FEMINIST FUTURES IN THE FORMER EAST BLOC

This is an article about women—and about feminism in East and Central Europe—but I skip over the usual litany of women's post-1989 woes in the region for two reasons. First, this list has become a cliché much too fast. (No doubt you've heard it already: women's disproportional unemployment; the threat to abortion; the rise of nostalgic, traditionalist movements that use women to symbolize home, hearth, and religious revival; the loss of social services; the drastic drops in women's numbers in the new parliaments; and in spite of unemployment, the unchanged nature of working women's double shift.) Second, this comfortably familiar list hides the fact that very little public debating time, research time, political organizing time—East or West—is actually going into these issues. The list remains static, while the social reality, country by country, is extremely complex and undertheorized. Women's situation is too often treated—by politicians and social theorists alike—as unavoidable collateral damage, rarely as an indication of central problems, or a key point of intervention. So, what is actually happening to women is the buried body here. My question is, why does it stay buried? Why is the discussion of women so marginal, so hard to sustain?

Maybe I shouldn't be surprised at the way the variable "women" drops out of otherwise progressive conversations in the East and West. After all, these discussions, even in the West, are still relatively new and suffer from all kinds of underdevelopment. This dropping-out-of-women-as-category is common enough everywhere, a familiar complaint of Western feminists. Yet I am impressed by the way liberal, democratic ideas are being discussed in the East in a way that they could not be discussed here, where a fairly vigilant women's movement keeps interjecting women's different situation into every conversation, keeps insisting that "women" is a variable that introduces questions, whole realms otherwise ignored.

Given women's particular problems in East and Central Europe and the glaring inattention to these particularities, what are the prospects for feminist organizing there? Of course, feminist organizing can mean a number of things. It might start with something traditionally considered a women's issue—birth control or day care—then move from these to demanding women's participation in government or other places of power where women would work on all issues and from all points of view. This second move doesn't guarantee any particular outcome, since women don't agree, but the demand for participation puts women in the public sphere as actors, debaters, public people—a break with past prohibitions.

Still, another level of feminism connects women's interest with "difference politics" in general. Feminism, like antiracism, is a constant reminder of the unhomogenized nature of human societies; all difference politics demand that ideas of justice and citizenship start from a point of difference. They demand a rethinking of norms and categories. Finally, there is the feminism that is a critique of the gendered organization of social life—a critique that undermines the very notion of "women's issues," that rejects the idea that birth control or day care are naturally women's rather than men's concerns.

Whatever meaning of feminism you use, and whatever word you substitute for feminism to avoid the stigma attached to the term, any East-West discussion about women, or about gender, turns out to be a difficult, difficult conversation. In my effort to catalogue these difficulties below, I regrettably but unavoidably generalize, but perhaps generalization has its own value in this situation. Since 1989, the cultures in the region have begun a delirious rush to be apart, to establish difference, to separate their histories, to develop particularities of all kinds—different temperaments, different myths of origin. I don't wish to ignore this drive toward difference, but its effect is sometimes obfuscating for women's activism. As Maxine Molyneux, an English writer on Eastern Europe, has put it: The Communist policy on women was administered not only from the top down, but also from the outside—with no reference to indigenous culture or local conditions and wishes.[1] In fact, for better or worse, women from the East share a traumatic past and a memory of extraordinary survival strategies. Ironically, the current, often passionate resistance to feminism is itself a shared inheritance, a group feeling, possibly an effect of past homogenizations. Recognitions across a variety of borders are still possible, or so I hope. In any case, some of my generalizations are meant to foster them, to suggest commonalities in a world where people, though forced into one mold, were at the same time isolated from each other for decades.

Crossing the East-West border is quite a different case. Seeming commonalities often dissolve. Western feminists should never consider a project that doesn't originate from women in the region. To create a general plan in the West—however well-intentioned—reenacts the old structure of ideas from outside. A Western feminist entering this scene had better learn right away that she is not the first to arrive with an ideology crafted in another place and fostered by resources locally unknown.

Hence another difficulty in the East-West conversation about feminism is the temptation to draw East-West analogies. To some extent, such analogies are inevitable. The new, independent Eastern women's groups enter a world in which Western women's movements have been defining themselves for several decades, a world-historic condition that is simply a fact to be reckoned with—one way or another—as these new democracies look outward. Now that their isolation is past, East movements won't be able to evolve without reference to the ubiquitous ideas of global feminism and to the international phenomenon of large women's mobilizations.

All the same, analogies are of course misleading, often misdirecting the eye from the very places where the action may be in the new societies—say in entrepreneurship, or in the family, or in the wearing of lipstick in rebellion against a formerly drab world. To give one obvious but far-reaching example, the U.S. movement was fueled by an enthusiasm for making the private political—an unthinkable starting point for women in the East, where, under Communism, privacy was attacked, political life was supposed to be the only life, and everything was hauled into public scrutiny and control. In the East, building a wall around privacy was a common act of political resistance, a rebellion against instrumentalities of public power that was particularly available to women. Issues of public and private are central to Western feminist debates, but the East and Central European experience is a stunning occasion for rethinking the whole business.

Perhaps, if comparison is inevitable, and if it's not to be all a one-way projection, one might start the East-West feminist conversation with the distortions that arise from analogies; one might begin by assuming and facing common misunderstandings. As Romanian activist Doina Pasca Harsanyi has pointed out, everything needs explaining and translating, down to rival meanings for such mundane words as "restaurant," "day care," and "shopping."[2]

Here then, is my list of reasons why feminism is so fiercely resisted—or so resolutely ignored—as a political possibility in East and Central Europe. The list is polyglot, as befits such a complex situation. Categorical distinctions are less important here than the general atmosphere of denial when it comes to questioning gender arrangements. The list includes plain old sexism and conservative backlash, but also potentially useful anxieties about the limitations of identity politics and healthy resistance to the colonial incursion of imported concepts. As will be obvious, I respect some of these reasons for resisting feminist analysis and organizing far more than others, yet I put them all together in one heap because the important thing about this promiscuous, multivalent list is how long it is. Good reasons or bad reasons, everyone has reasons why this question of women is ridiculous, or special pleading, or not a priority, or dangerous, or wrongheaded, and on and on. The cumulative result is disturbing. Resistance to feminist thinking or organizing, however defined, seems to be over-determined. Cumulatively, the prohibition begins, almost, to look like a taboo.

Issue #1: The Community of Suffering

In countries where everyone is suffering a lot, it feels churlish, selfish, even vulgar to mention that women's suffering has its own particular qualities and forms—that women have separable grievances. Solidarity between men and women is treasured and remains necessary for survival. Reminders that women have a double day (four to five hours more work each day in one study) are countered with reminders of the special humiliation of being a powerless male. Women bypass this humiliation, presumably, since they never expect a role in public life. Individual solutions and personal loyalties were the great virtues under Communism. A generalization of suffering and endurance seems disloyal, like kicking your fragile—perhaps reliable—partner in the face.

Issue #2: Exhaustion

The exhaustion theme, very central in beginning debates, has already moved from center stage in discussions of women because it is now clear there will be no real pause for women. Though women are exhausted from the double day, and though they may want and deserve a rest after holding the world together so long, unemployment isn't leisure in a scarcity economy. Instead, women will be working with lower wages and fewer benefits and guarantees.

The exhaustion, though, is real. Any call to meetings, to volunteer political action, must reckon with how over-extended women are. Time and energy are precious and rare. Besides, why would one spend the few precious hours one may have on politics? This brings one to:

Issue #3: Disillusionment with All Politics

It is commonly felt that political life is a zone of corruption. The argument goes: private life was deformed by Communism, but it was more honorable, more satisfying than public politics. Women will now preside over the private, which is seen as the best and richest part of life. Only the worst people lust for politics after what that word has come to mean. Women are fortunate, at last, not to be "organized." Everything was political under Communism. Now women can represent something outside the political, another realm, hard to name, long denied.

We could discuss this reasoning as one more version of internalized sexism, familiar enough to anyone who remembers the fifties, a time of restoking the family, of recuperating from trauma, of withdrawal from the political. But it is also, under the circumstances, an understandable fear of groups, a distrust of politics, a clinging to informal but reliable networks, a resistance to the discredited word "organize." Indeed, many of the calls to action of U.S. feminism ring hollow in the East. They sound naïve, childish, idealistic, rhetorical—not resonant or possible. The idea that feminist demands are commonly known all through U.S. culture—even if they are resisted—is foreign, the other side of a vast organizing divide it's hard to imagine crossing.

Issue #4: Identity Politics

East and Central Europeans might well ask: Even if we accepted the idea that there might be a liberatory politics, a politics of free associations, civil society, grassroots organizing—why would we choose an identity politics, why would we wish to constitute women as a political group? Indeed, why should women in the East be interested in Western-style feminism as a mode of political struggle? Did it get Western women any of their demands? Do Western women have day care, do they have equal pay? Do they have constitutional guarantees—for example, like those in many Communist constitutions? In fact, Western feminism can be called a failure, particularly in material terms. If demands made through a shared cultural identity have made so little material difference, why bother? What's more, who needs another identity politics when one already has nationalism, ethnic conflict, painful searches for identity? It's hard enough to try to ask what it will mean to be Croat or Serb, Czech or Slovak—to this one should add the question of women Croats and men Croats? Difference politics is already baroque, choking, varied. No further variable need apply.

Ironically, while all those other ethnic and religious forms of identity politics were (at least overtly) repressed under Communism, the group "women" was the one nonclass identity long promoted by Communists. Corrupt female tokens were everywhere, powerless yet specially visible. They were women with niggling little powers that galled and irritated everyone. "The Women Question," was a sacred cow, yet most women—indeed, most people—had little say in anything, no chance to comment on their own condition. So now, while other identity politics flourish, feminism is rejected—partly because of good old sexism (Hurray! We don't need to include women anymore!) and partly because the Communist ideal of emancipation was hypocritical, puritanical, labor intensive, utterly insensitive to what the work of the double day actually includes. Emancipation was inert; this old, abstract ideal will not work well as a starting point for new thinking about gender.

A postscript about gender identity and research: in Eastern research, there's been a continuing reluctance to disaggregate data. Under Communism, one didn't use the variable "gender" since equality was achieved—no need to look any farther. In post-Communism, one doesn't disaggregate because women aren't an important category, or aren't different, or are so different as to be beside the point, outside the social argument, perhaps even a part of nature. In yet another formulation, some Czech women have explained that they don't want cultural discussions to be developed along gender lines because then women lose their majority, their human status, and become like a "minority." To mention the group "women" is to demote individual women to a subset of society, with a stigmatized status like Slovaks or Roma or Jews.

Fear of being demoted to a minority can be racist and often is. But it can also be a realistic assessment of the need to pull together, to construct a citizenship that doesn't depend on ethnic or gender identity. The idea that women need to become a group to fight the way individual women are relegated to the inferior category "women" has its tragic dimensions in a world where identity politics are so troubled, and where an old rhetoric promised equality without all this separation into interest groups, without all this enmity and grief.

Issue #5: Essentialism

A common, popular discussion goes like this: An unnatural Communism forced women to be like men (that image of the woman on the tractor). But there is a natural woman, a woman who can emerge now that Communist manipulations are past. At last, the free market and the true family can emerge—two states of nature, two examples of letting natural forces do their healthy, life-renewing work. "Equality" under Communism was universalist, blandly humanist, flat. "Difference" in this construction becomes a path into individualism. Essentialism, rather than seeming like a reductionist redefinition of a woman, is often equated with finally letting women flower as particular beings, with subjectivities, with private interests that cannot be defined by state interests. (There's a parallel here with Western feminist critiques of the false universals of liberalism.)

Yet accompanying this new privacy and subjectivity is an enduring public confidence in woman as symbol. For all the resistance to a political group called "women," there is very little critique of the naturalized category "woman," which includes all the familiar tropes from mother to beauty to sly, dangerous vixen. The essentialist category of "women" is intact for sexist purposes if not for political ones. Meanwhile, confidence in women as sane, decent, *hors de combat* provides real relief from anxiety, a promise of social continuity. Here at least is an identity one knows, an eternal woman with her permanent willingness to nurture, to make order, to love. Feminism in current scenes of economic and social distress can appear like a nemesis—or less grandly—like the last straw, an attack on one of the few certainties. And though men rather than women are more likely to see feminism as a threat in this way, women, too, feel pride in representing an anchor for everyone. Let men be the antennae for the disorienting newness of post-Communist society.

Issue #6: Symbols/Images

It would be a mistake to underestimate the power of hostile, sexist imagery to keep women in line, to keep feminism taboo. What social images are available to women? In Bulgaria, like everywhere in the former East block, active Communist women were called "iron women"—ugly, unfeminine, a cautionary tale to the young. Would men flock eagerly to public power if it were explained to them from earliest childhood that public power means giving up being seen as attractive, sexual, viable by the opposite sex?

But of course the very question is absurd, one more illustration of the asymmetrical situation of men and women. Their symbolic positions are not parallel. Women who wander out of women's metaphoric space pay a social and sexual price for any power they may gain as men do not.

Women have fewer plots, images, roles to play around with when they seek to be public people. They pay psychologically for this narrowing of personal possibilities. Of course, this is true in the West, too. Look at the gender scripts that dogged Anita Hill—grotesque phantasm, weak sister, Delilah bringing down the great man. She was the one sexualized by the public exchange. But at least Anita Hill had sympathizers, interpreters. A huge social dialogue swirled around her, lifting some of the humiliation. In the East, no such critical mass exists. One who breaks ranks with traditional womanliness is—as yet—still hideously alone, ridiculous, or monstrous. No doubt, soon, a brilliant graduate student will do a study of both Communist and dissident literature. I suspect a surprising confluence: these opposites will prove to agree in their distrust of women.

Finally, homophobia constructs the ultimate punitive image. Homophobes call active feminists "lesbians" and hope that social taboo, ignorance, and fear will combine to keep female anger tamped down, ashamed of itself.

Issue #7: Drab Feminism

"Equality" was dreary under Communism. Of course, there were oppressive gender divisions all along, but this fact was suppressed beneath a pretense, a dull surface of sameness. Now many feel that gender differences might become a zone for new pleasures. If gender is to be a variable, then let it mean sex-specific consumer goods at last—from sanitary napkins to makeup. As women from the East often point out, Western women can afford to criticize the market as sexist and exploitative. But in the East, people need everything, including the sense of play consumerism sometimes provides. Both feminism and consumerism make much of gender difference, but while feminism in the East feels dingy, a continuation of an earnest past, consumerism's account of difference seems new and blithe: "Vive la différence!"

Issue #8: Bourgeois Feminism

Western feminism is often dismissed in the East as relentlessly bourgeois in character. Its failures, its racism, its classism are cautionary tales. Many judge its constructions to be of little use. Western feminism can easily appear hedonistic, unserious, with its central images of pleasure and choice. It may seem at first that issue #7, a desire for consumer culture in the East, and issue #8, a disgust at Western-style bourgeois culture, are contradictory, likely to be felt by very different people. Often, though, these feelings live together. Communist education encouraged a dismissal of Western feminism as superficial, bourgeois. At the same time, the longing for consumer goods laid down another layer of feeling. These attractions and repulsions coexist in people's ideas about the always mixed and flawed "really existing Western feminism."

Issue #9: Social Services vs. Consumer Society

Western feminists often looked with envy at the social services Eastern and Central European women had. In most conversations, Eastern women are very critical of what they see as Western women's romance with these entitlements. The day care was drafty, over-crowded, far away. The health care often consisted of abortions and childbirths without anesthetic; often there was no contraception. The protective work legislation about hours and heavy lifting were paternalistic and limiting. The long maternity leaves tracked women out of the work force—often for years—lowering their pay scales and driving some into well-documented depression.

Of course, Western feminists argue in response that the services that came from Communist paternalism are nothing like the services an autonomous women's movement would demand. Yet Western feminism is often divided in theoretical discussions of protectionism. The whole business is a central problematic in feminism, a contradiction with its own special resonances in East and Central Europe.

Issue #10: Ideas of Past and Future

Women were overworked under Communism. But one cannot look forward to a glorious post-Communist future. That is the way Communists talk—the glorious future, the five-year plan, the people's struggle toward the good, the true, the just. (I hear the laughing voices of my new friends in the East, these superb ironists, these cynics; when they hear any of the pragmatic hopefulness or any of the visionary projections of U.S. feminism, they start singing party songs—"Our commune will have the biggest pig," etc.) Since, with the war in Bosnia on one side and economic crisis on the other, one cannot look with enthusiasm toward a future, paradigms of a pre-Communist past hold a kind of cultural allure, particularly for a traditionalist far right, but to some extent for everybody.

Which past will East and Central Europeans choose? A nineteenth-century past includes a traditional rural or a solid Biedermeier kind of family, but it also includes first-wave feminism—now totally obscured in historical accounts. An early twentieth-century past includes Communism's brief revolutionary feminist movement—Zetkin, Kollontai—though it leads quickly to that movement's brutal repression.

The female emancipation foisted on the Eastern bloc in the late 1940s had by that time little connection to its radical roots. "Emancipation" had become an instrumental industrial policy. The fact that almost all women had jobs remains earth-shaking, a powerful and useful cultural inheritance, but this past needs sifting. The legacy of a sort of fake feminism infuriates, even if it includes some tangible gains. Under Communism, women were living in a grotesquely gendered situation while being told that nothing needs to be said about their special case.

This enforced silence has left people with few analytical tools to look at women's continued, highly gendered experience. In the conceptual vacuum left by Communism, many find it liberating to kick away the fake feminism of the past, and this kick in the face of the old rhetoric can look like a rejection of the ideal of equality. I don't think it really is. A discussion of how the great-grandmothers, the grandmothers, and the mothers actually lived and the ideas they entertained about themselves will go a long way toward unearthing a variety of lost feminist movements, enabling a broader discussion of the meaning of the past and the possibilities for the future.

Issue #11: The Family

In discussions of feminism, many East and Central Europeans argue that the issue should be the family, not women. Rhetorically, women are seen not only as central to the family, but also as folded into it. In Poland in 1991, Anna Popovicz was fired from her job as head of the Office on Women and Family Affairs because she separated the "Women" from the "Family" by focusing on employment and abortion rights. Certainly, in times like these, when the family is a central means for survival, any women's resistance to being absorbed into the family can seem very threatening. Rather than seeing both men and women as needing the family and needing to protect its private interests, women continue to be seen as "the family" while men have free associations, alliances, and interests outside, without being called self-ish betrayers of those they love.

Issue #12: Feminism Is a Luxury We Can't Afford

As long as the drudgery of women is socially acceptable, feminism will continue to look like a luxury. Why pay women well or support socialized domestic services if women will drudge on for free? Shock therapy has become thinkable partly because it relies on the cynical assumption that women are manipulable, an unorganized group with low expectations; women are supposed to continue with their old, heroic endurance, to absorb the brunt of economic change resourcefully, without causing major unrest.

Hence old Communists and new governments are in essential agreement: Things go better if you leave women's work in the realm of the "natural." The "unnatural," women's liberation, has yet to be considered a necessity.

This list (which could go on and on) records histories, feelings, values that will surely shape women's possibilities in the changing societies of East and Central Europe. I wish finally to point out the cost to women in particular and to freedom in the region in general if the discussion ends here. I don't think anyone—East or West—can know what feminism will come to mean in East and Central Europe. It would be presumptuous to say, and precipitous. Yet the debates feminism fosters are profoundly relevant to these new societies.

What will the relationship be between public and private life and what should be the boundaries of those zones? For example, abortion needs to become more private, wife-beating more public. What social contract embodies that paradox? How much of daily life/domestic life should be socialized, supported in some way by decisions made by governments? Or by whom? Does the concept "civil society" ignore the central role the family has played and is likely to play in people's lives? Does the concept obscure aspects of experience that need theorizing? What does it mean to put women, at present largely disenfranchised, in charge of whole tracts of the social and ethical realm—to put them in charge of the care and education of children, to make them the keepers of the national honor, and other traditionalist propositions for virtue? What does it mean to expect a civil society to flourish that wastes the education of its women, disempowers them in the public sphere, yet asks them—these economically dependent, socially marginalized ones—to glue the realm of the social together?

In other words, who will the electorate be in these new democracies? Who will feel himself/herself to have a stake in public decisions, a chance to shape them? Since for historical reasons, quotas and affirmative action seem to be anathema in the region for a time, other forms of political struggle must be sought to address women's disadvantaged citizenship. Women's issues are often defined as peripheral, but this is dangerously misleading. As we have learned in the United States from the phenomenal rise of our own right wing, family values, control of the female body, pronatalism, and sexual Puritanism (including stigmas on gays and lesbians), gain crucial political territory for their advocates. First they're in churches and day-care centers, then they're in parliament. Why cede to the traditionalists the discussion of daily life?

The women's movement is one—only one—of the locations in which debates like these can become vivid for large numbers of people. In spite of the difficulties, a cross-fertilization between movements is crucial. Women's situation is pivotal in economic and social organization. To lose this dimension is to cede to the unconscious, to an ideal "nature," to the unspeakable, large parts of the social.

If we seek a genuine brake on the rapacity of free market thinking, feminist demands for social services, for recognition of differences, for basic health and welfare rights and entitlements become an important potential location for resistance. The unorganized are always the most vulnerable to cynical or instrumental manipulation. They can't produce social institutions that shape or interpret political experience. This is true, of course, in general, yet women's lack of a stake in public institutions is a particularly dramatic case of this general danger. New democracies shaped without the participation of women, and without any thought for women's issues, women's rights, women's freedoms, are no democracies at all.

Eastern Europeans are well placed to know what it costs to exclude people from the civil process, to leave large numbers outside of any control over public events. Women there may be exhausted from double and triple days, but there is reason to hope they won't stand for the new forms of overwork and powerlessness now being foisted upon them. Still, building resistance will take time; everything is changing so fast; no one is confident about the shape of things to come. When Jirina Siklova and I tried to open a bank account in Prague for a new Gender Center, the bank found the English word suspect. There is no word for "gender" in Czech. Later, when Jirina tried to deposit and cash checks, they asked if she were a madam, the "gender" center her brothel.

Finally, my list may be too depressing. Women's movements are cropping up everywhere in the region. Small and beleaguered as they may be, they represent one instance of the hope people in the East now have for themselves and their societies.

1993

Notes

1. Molyneux, "The Woman Question," 23–49.
2. Harsanyi, cited by Nanette Funk, "Introduction," 4.

14

FEMINISM TRAVELS

Cautionary Tales

As one of the founders of a small nongovernmental organization called the Network of East-West Women, I was preoccupied in the early 1990s with keeping a little list of the difficulties facing the often isolated and beleaguered Central and East European feminist colleagues who made up half the Network membership. The list might have been named "Regional Reasons Why People Reject Feminism" and it grew and grew, including reasons I respected and reasons I hated, but above all including a variety of reasons, a richness of reasons from every quarter of both public and private life. Dissidents had their rationale for disliking feminism and so did former communists, and on and on.

Of course, a shadow list of my own numerous difficulties as a feminist organizer in the United States was always running along parallel to my Central and East European one—but the differences were great and often illuminating, leading me to think at the time that an East-West conversation would give us all a new depth of understanding about our local and international situations. Different as we were, we were also all, precipitously, "postcommunist," a state of confusion I for one wanted to experience in the company of others.

When it was published and translated, my catalogue of difficulties was sometimes read as an erasure of feminist initiatives in the former Soviet bloc—which were in fact fast growing from the early 1990s and are continuing to grow now. But making the list was actually intended as an act of recognition of the knotty problems facing these fragile new movements. Feminists in the region had a discourse dilemma unfamiliar to their Western visitors: They couldn't start with a critique of the patriarchal family, because the family had been the bulwark of resistance to communism and was the often-beloved place of privacy, trust, and survival. Nor could they use the old language of communist "emancipation," because many remembered those old solutions to "the woman question" as crudely instrumental and hypocritical, not what women themselves had identified as being in their self-interest. Finally, they were tempted to embrace the general enthusiasm for new free markets, only to find that women's fate in these markets was often the dark side of the new dawn. But how were they to mount a popular critique of the very freedoms so many others were celebrating? Sour grapes—just when everyone seemed to be declaring a renaissance! These, then, were activists trying to use the category "women" against the grain. They were up against not only the new traditionalists in the postcommunist countries, but also against many of the new free market democrats, who like their women to be free and flexible—as in flexible labor pool.

In a series of valuable and suggestive pieces, the Hungarian historian Maria Kovács has tried to explain to her Western colleagues why all their assumptions about where to place "feminism" politically are unreliable when applied to the East. She has been building up a detailed diagnosis of the allergy to feminism so common in the region. In a description of the Hungarian political parties, she writes: "Our liberals-turned-libertarians reject feminism for its close relationship with welfare egalitarianism, while our egalitarian nationalists reject feminism for its close historical and philosophical relationships with liberalism."[1] In piece after piece, she has identified particularities of timing and association that have rendered feminist discourses as wanderers at best, and at worst as illiberal, racist, narrow, or Stalinist immigrants from some objectionable location on the political map. Like mine, Kovács's reasons-for-rejecting-feminism proliferated. As one piled the evidence up, the general result was clear enough: In Central and East Europe, resistance to feminism was over-determined. Feminism as a political movement was homeless.

Enter Western feminisms—or, rather, U.S. feminisms, to take the examples I know best. Each post-1989 East-West encounter has had its own dynamic, with successes and failures beyond the scope of this paper. But however different the two sides can sometimes seem to each other, the binary dissolves in the ironic fact that U.S. feminisms have arrived—with whatever exotic fanfare—trailing their own increasing marginality and conceptual confusion from home. As disparate Western feminisms move across borders in the accelerating round of international activity I will damply abbreviate as "globalization," the likelihood of wasted effort, misunderstanding, and even of what I consider damaging uses of the categories of gender analysis multiply.

U.S. feminist movements of the late '60s and early '70s were varied from the first, but—without always being conscious of this—they were all deeply embedded in the Civil Rights movement and in the New Left. Though this ideological legacy was full of contradictions, both Civil Rights and New Left ideas were end points of long strings of ideological thought and political experience, which gave structure and coherence to feminist desires and demands. Even when in these 1960s movements we argued angrily about ideas or strategies, we often shared a basic aesthetic of politics and a sturdy, confident critique of the prevailing social order.

Now, not a sentence out of any of our mouths or an expectation—conscious or unconscious—is unchanged by the breaking up of the great structuring belief systems of the Cold War period. Though some activists ignore the absence of a floor in the room in which they are toiling away at their former political tasks, and some are responding handily but abstractly with theories of hybridity, I want to pause a moment to discuss how odd U.S. feminisms can be these days. I want to mark a serious break in discourse, not the end of ideology, but a loss of currently useable ideologies. Like many other cultures of resistance that flourished before 1989, U.S. feminisms are often, now, unmoored from the deeper structures that formerly attached directional arrows to their work. Feminist activists who relied on Left constructions of future possibilities now need to reconceptualize what they want, and how to get it, in new terms, based on new conditions.

Indeed, feminism's Western "home" is breaking up, so that one might say that there is a parallel problem, East and West, with finding appealing, effective entry points for a feminist politics. In our homeless wanderings, there are many places where feminists may take refuge which can turn out to be no refuge at all, but places where feminism can lose its claim to being liberatory, socially innovative, or just. The potential illiberality of feminism can happen in big dramatic ways, or indirectly, in ways we aren't expecting. The obvious cases are well known: a racist feminism; a class-bound, elitist, or careerist feminism; a narrow, single-issue feminism without alliances; a puritanical, sexually repressive feminism, often advocating some form of censorship; a moralistic feminism; a feminism which asks merely for women's inclusion, not for more fundamental change. And the list could go on. I offer here, first, some examples of such limitations in the current diaspora of Western feminist ideas in Central and East European contexts and, second, a caveat against letting these weaknesses overwhelm the urgent project of finding newly vital entry points for feminism East and West.

In the following catalogue of ways in which Western feminisms circulate I do not mean to discount indigenous sources of feminism in Central and East Europe, or the former Soviet Union. On the contrary, there is a rich past which needs digging up. When one learns how, in 1948, the Czech Communist Party changed the locks on the door to the Independent Women's Building (in Prague, feminists are trying to get that building back), and how, in 1950, the party hanged the leading Czech feminist, Milada Horakova, one realizes the existence of a common heroic past, periods of mass mobilization followed by defeat that have been lost to memory, like the stories of so many other women's mass struggles. But, given this loss of memory about precommunist feminist debates, and the stigma on Stalinist emancipation rhetoric in the East, the powerful engines that are Western ideas take up a lot of conceptual space, accompanied as they often are with glamour or with foundation money. Local traditions provide interpretative frameworks, of course, but the diaspora of Western feminisms gives rise to contradictions that deserve attention if feminism is to seem worth struggling for either in the United States or elsewhere.

Examples of How Western Feminist Fragments Circulate in Central and East Europe and the Former Soviet Union

1. Gender as a Convenient and Often Over-simple Explanation for Complex Problems Sometimes in Central and East Europe, the category "gender" gains currency as a foreign import that holds out promise as an explanatory model. Often, though, it displaces other models or obscures them—most commonly "class," which in postcommunist thought is still a much discredited structure of explanation. In Osh, Kyrgyzstan, women organizers identified the gendered character of the new poverty: Where there had been seventy day care centers in 1992, in 1997 there were twenty, as women were pushed out of the work force and back into unpaid care of children at home. But the gendered nature of the new unemployment was a local adaptation to events happening very far away. Gender inequality is a necessary but not a sufficient description of the new immiseration in Kyrgyzstan. As a category standing alone it is both weak and misleading.

As Carole S. Vance has argued, one might include current human rights work on the trafficking of women as yet another example of how class sometimes gets obscured by discussions of gender.[2] The language of anti-trafficking campaigns often describes innocent or passive female victims who need rescuing. But one could describe the same phenomena very differently as a new form of poverty, as a new mobility of people and money, in which women make choices under terrible new economic pressures.

Take, for example, this exemplary exchange between a feminist from the United States and one from the Czech Republic: The Western feminist bemoans the line of young Czech prostitutes along the road near the border with Germany. The Eastern feminist responds that yes, there's a terrible new problem with the currency differential between Germany and the Czech Republic. The Western feminist thinks, "What low feminist consciousness!" The Eastern feminist thinks, "Why do these Western feminists see sexuality as the key to oppression?" Yet this idea, that sexuality is at the center of the new disempowerment of women in the region, is the one that garners attention and support funds from Western advocates, and therefore often becomes the main issue for women in the region as well. Trafficking is indeed an alarming problem, but kidnapping is already illegal. What is flourishing without much censure is the economic manipulation of women in the new order. It is easier to arouse outrage by antiprostitution campaigns than to construct a politics that criticizes the unregulated flow of capital and confronts women's further loss of social power both at work and at home. (Juliet Mitchell has described how the same displacement happened in England. When she first worked on women's issues in the early 1960s, she could not get labor figures disaggregated by gender. In the 1980s, after twenty years of feminism, the gender variable was everywhere and it was class that had become invisible in the statistics. She argues that feminist demands are often unselfconsciously complicit in the developmental leaps of capitalism, so that feminists need to be aware how their work articulates with other categories of social analysis.[3])

Related problems arise when the category displaced by "gender" is "race." Many Eastern feminists argue that racism is not a relevant issue for them—a familiar tragic error in the making. Many other Eastern feminists recognize that they may well be more like African American feminists and feminists of the South in their priorities and interests than like the mostly white U.S. feminists who seek contact with them. "Which Western feminism?" is always a useful question as Eastern feminists sort through various imports, which offer quite varied interpretative frameworks.

Nonetheless, self-conscious as one may be in one's borrowings, issues of race and ethnicity are particularly hard to translate from context to context. For example, I suspect that racism and ethnic hatred are not precisely the same kind of phenomena and should not be mapped on top of one another. The kinds of phobic prejudice faced by African Americans in the United States and Jews and Roma in Central and East Europe and the former Soviet Union are similar to each other and different in kind from the intimate sibling rivalries of many of the ethnic conflicts in the region. In each situation, "gender," "race," and "ethnicity" have complex, changing relationships with each other, and there are no shortcuts in the process of arriving at an inclusive politics. Western paradigms may or may not apply, though knowledge of past feminist failures to confront racism should sound a powerful warning bell.

2. Feminism as a Variable in Uneven Development

Western feminisms have produced long laundry lists of demands, but each item has its separate fate as it migrates into the discourses of other cultures. Take the liberal divorce law in Romania. One Romanian feminist lawyer expressed the wish to get rid of easy divorce in Romania. She observed that it was mainly men who wanted divorces, to escape their family responsibilities. Women rarely seek divorce, because a divorced woman is so disempowered in Romanian culture, so isolated, so ostracized, that the freedom is rarely worth it. Some Western feminists got depressed at the idea of a Romanian feminist campaign against easy divorce, and in the long run they are probably right that a no-divorce law is hardly a solution to women's problems in the family. But what the Romanian feminist was expressing was the inadequacy of legal reforms without the cultural and economic revolutions that would support women's independence. New Right women in the United States expressed similar criticisms of a feminism that they felt was stripping them of traditional protections without giving them enough in exchange. In Deirdre English's wonderful phrase, they "feared that feminism would free men first."[4] Feminism is a social revolution. Without general social discussion, consciousness raising, a public expression of pain and dissatisfaction, the letter killeth.

3. Problematic or Powerless Structures Authorized by Feminist Ideas and Values

Both Eastern and Western feminist organizers often congratulate themselves and each other for the invention of grassroots political forms that are more accessible and democratic than traditional politics. Indeed, in the former communist countries, it is an urgent task to invent new forms for politics, to develop civil society, free associations, the idea of voluntary public participation. However, the invention of voluntarism, and specifically of female voluntarism, in the East coincides with the dismantling of social citizenship and the decay of social entitlements there.

Now that the governments of Central and East Europe and the former Soviet Union are abdicating responsibility, the scene looks much more like the one in the United States, where private time and money are constantly filling in for government refusals to protect its citizens from ill health, poverty, or old age. This situation leads to various distortions of the potential value of NGOs in the East. Powerless, local nongovernmental structures are trying to compensate for the pain and chaos caused by failing governments. Since in the East there is little of the private money or the traditions of philanthropy that support this privatization of the social in the West, the small-scale women's NGOs so valued by Western feminists and Western funders often fail, reconfirming the general idea that women are politically and economically marginal and powerless.

To counter this trend, local feminisms would need to go against the current popular rhetoric of both the East and the West, that independence and small government are good, and that depending on the government is bad. Feminism would need to make what is in the East a counter-intuitive argument, that getting money and attention from government is necessary, that it is not a return to centralism, that resources from government can increase rather than decrease social freedoms. But such an argument is hard to make, given the so recent totalitarian past.

To avoid the failures they now face, some Eastern feminist NGOs construct themselves as enclaves, erecting bastions of safety against a larger exploitative situation. Or they build Western-authorized outposts, funded by Western sources. There is indeed useful work to be done in such outposts, but in general social supports for women's traditional tasks have suffered deathblows since 1989.

4. Gender as a Variable Emptied of Political Resonance

Central and East Europe and the former Soviet Union are ascriptive societies in which legitimization is a key value and a major theme of the transition from communism. Old structures of power and influence have fallen apart, but many of the formerly powerful have maintained their status regimes successfully under new names. One of the great sources of status is contact with the West, or with things Western. There is a (small) scramble to establish Western-style Women's Studies programs in universities. Though it is wonderful for feminist energy to establish new job pathways for women in the universities and in social policy agencies, Western feminisms can also function as the imported material that legitimize static elite enclaves. Mass U.S. women's movements were the initial source of energy and knowledge for American Women's Studies programs, and these programs claimed legitimization from those democratic roots for some years. But the East has much smaller, much more embattled movements. A university program could not currently gain legitimacy from the status of local movements alone.

Added to this difficulty is another: The very idea of an intellectual enterprise linked to a locally active political movement is anathema to former dissidents who were kicked out of universities for their refusals to toe party lines. The fantasy of a university with no politics whatsoever is cherished, so that when feminist research ideas knock on the door for entry, they must leave their ties to social movements outside or stay outside themselves. In this situation, Western high theory is touted as pure philosophy; Western social research loses its social roots and is translated as pure science; and Women's Studies professors swear on bibles held by more established male colleagues that their work has absolutely no bias, no social commitments, no ambition to influence politics.

5. Gender Difference as a Way to Restructure the Workforce

Efforts to find new entry points into the economy for women as professionals, as technicians, or as freelance operators in charge of their own time are all examples of effective feminist organizing against women's poverty. But it is well to heed some caveats: Verónica Schild has described how feminists who became professionals in Chile could sometimes weaken the poor women's grassroots movements they set out to serve.[5] And Juliet Mitchell warns that women are often allowed into new work situations first, just as they were the first in the textile factories of the nineteenth century. Like canaries in coal mines, they test the atmosphere and prepare the way for new work patterns. Mitchell argues that Western feminists have often been unaware of how their demands have supported larger, systemic changes in ways that were no part of their intent.[6]

Like many other Western partners, the Network of East-West Women has raised money to give its members computers and computer training. Sometimes the power and freedom this gives is a delight to Western organizers' hearts. At other times, the same organizers might well feel a frisson of anxiety: Have they merely offered a training program to prepare a new underpaid class for dreary office work to come?

As we seek new forms for work, we need to be aware of these larger patterns of change within which we shape our demands and desires. Women often want work that is part time, flexible, mobile. Be careful what you wish for. Mobility without security or benefits will surely be the prevailing form of exploitation for many workers in the future. The point is not to give up on the dream of mobility and flexibility—which are both values and work conditions that are already here to stay—but to recognize the need to bring these changes into politics, to establish new rights and protections under this new regime of fast-circulating capital.

6. Gender as a Grant

The English Anthropologist Julie Hemment has been studying the post-perestroika evolution of the Russian women's movement.[7] Her work is more rich and complex than I can summarize here, but one major theme is the distortions introduced by Western granting organizations. Because of the general distrust of controlling bureaucracies, people distrusted, too, a feminism clogged with the bureaucracy of foundations. One dispirited Russian feminist organizer told Hemment: "We used to live from party congress to party congress. Now we live from grant deadline to grant deadline."[8] Once again, the point is not that Western grants are intrinsically bad or politically contaminated. There is no pure money from any source. The point, rather, is to arouse skepticism about the travels of "gender" across cultural lines. Local feminists deserve much support as they face the inevitable difficulties of making an unfamiliar set of "gender" concerns visible and meaningful in their own communities. In worst case scenarios, foundation support merely makes the mysterious and untranslatable term "gender" fashionable, bandied about as a new way of talking, as in one Russian health activist's remark: "Prostate cancer is a gender problem."

Conclusion

I intend no intrinsic insult to contemporary feminist activity by describing these moments of ill fit or illiberality in the current dispersion of feminist categories. Rather, these are cautionary tales for committed feminists who hope feminist activism will prove agile enough, responsive enough to a changing situation, to last them a lifetime. Thirty years into the current wave of the feminist project in the West, anomalies like the ones I have been describing are everywhere. It is no fault of feminist movements that their categories have often been descriptive and politically productive, so that bits and pieces of feminist analysis now crop up in unlikely combinations. In the United States, for example, feminism floats around in the heads of right-wing senators, who use it to modernize their old song of seduction and sin; now they say that President Clinton's dalliance with Monica Lewinsky is a case of sexual harassment! Such acts of appropriation are marks of feminist success. In the long run, the dispersion of feminism into many different locations, no longer visibly linked by a passionately loud, publically named "movement," may be another proof of the staying power of feminist sensibility.

All the same, feminists are right to worry about the after-life of their initiatives, the long journeys of their ideas. How often have we asked for autonomy—only to be left alone, without support; or asked for participation in the market—only to be instantly grabbed up (if we are young enough, pretty enough, without children); or asked for mobility—only to discover that this means we need to keep moving, changing our skills and our entire lives every few years in order to keep up. Critical hindsight is of great value in keeping feminism alive, a project under constant reconstruction.

Finally, though, I have an even more urgent reason for exploring feminist migrations that seem to me to be wasteful or wrong-headed, beyond the project of self-awareness and critique. I want to forestall a move I see coming: Those political thinkers and activists with little personal stake in gender as a category on which to base thought and action will seize this time of dispersion and necessary rethinking as a chance to under-rate the importance of having an independent feminist movement at all. Using its current weaknesses as an excuse, these often otherwise progressive voices will argue that political movements based on identity were always divisive and dreary, and, now, thank heavens, they are dying.

Let us take a detour to the couch and listen to the patient: Feminism whined. Feminism complained. Feminism was an unlovely form of special pleading. Feminist movements were limited, flawed, aggressive, grabby, and angry. In short, feminism was a mother who was less than perfect, so let her go home and be heard from no more. In this time of renegotiations of almost all post–Cold War political relationships, this common willingness to let feminism disappear in both East and West signals a dangerous absence, a failure of new political discourses to register women's aspirations for economic and social equality.

Like all movements seeking a post-1989 meaning and *modus operandi*, feminisms are vulnerable—not least of all to internal self-doubts. The best course for feminists is to embrace the doubts, to embrace the "homelessness" of feminism. In the United States, I see the current feminist recognition of the differences among women, of our inevitable lack of unity, of feminism's fragmentation, as an advance. We are homeless in the positive sense that we are now out in the political world where no movement piety or automatic affiliation can be taken for granted. We now must construct our relationships with each other. Though women's movements have great potential for addressing basic problems facing the new market economies and for configuring strong new ways of demanding social justice, there is no reason to assume that a concern for women will inevitably lead to a powerful or useful politics. Feminism is not automatically a vanguard, an authority on what is to be done post-1989; nor is there anything solid or eternal in a commitment to feminism alone, or feminism in the abstract. Incomplete and in process as feminist projects now are, those who choose to call themselves feminists must seek alliances with other groups that, like ours, are inventing themselves in response to a swiftly changing context. In no way, though, should this call for feminist skepticism about the long-term value of our actions stop us from projecting tentative values as we move, case by case, decision by decision, to determine a political response to women's cumulative, multiple disadvantages.

Let me state the nature of the opportunity. "Gender" is not a nation to which anyone is required to migrate. It is, rather, a variable, a central one in the future ways in which labor, government power, and economic activity are all going to be structured—not to mention daily psychic life. Feminists have a long and distinguished history of debating the currently key contested concepts of public and private, and feminist initiatives and political forms have great potential for widening democratic participation. In the current inflation of rhetoric about "the global," it is easy to lose sight of the future actors who might demand social justice or call for fundamental changes. Just now such ambitious movements are on the defensive, uncertain about their future course. But, to take the example at hand, the current weaknesses of some feminist movements are no good reason to turn away from politically confronting the specific problems of women, or from building on feminist movements' accumulations of knowledge and power. Independent feminist movements can be of inestimable value. Are new forms of exploitation and political powerlessness to be contested—or not?

1999

Notes

I have learned much from various works in progress: Maria Kovács's evolving project on different forms of resistance to feminism ("The Egalitarian Appeal of Nationalism" [unpublished manuscript on file with the author]); Carole S. Vance's conceptualization of her Rockefeller seminar, the Program on Sexuality, Gender, Health, and Human Rights, offered at Columbia University, 1998–2001; Shana Penn's unpublished work on Czechoslovakia where I first read about Milada Horakova and other feminist histories from precommunist Central and East Europe; Julie Hemment's report on her dissertation work in Tver, Russia, at New York University's Center for European Studies, February 19, 1999; The New School's Victoria Hattam's forthcoming *Identification and Politics*, which has made me see the importance of the active choice of boundaries and alliances in the construction of any politics; and Joanna Regulska's discussions at the Rutgers University Center for Russian and East European Studies of local democracy in Poland and elsewhere, which suggest the various vulnerabilities of women's NGOs. An earlier version of this article appeared in Proceedings of the 93rd Annual Meeting of the American Society of International Law, March 24–27, 1999: pp. 35–42.

Finally, my thanks to all the members of The Network of East-West Women who are facing the difficulties described here every day with wisdom, patience, and dedication. (1999)

1. Kovács, "Ambiguities of Emancipation." Unpublished manuscript, author's file. Later published in modified form in *Women's History Review*.

2. Vance, "Innocence and Experience," 213–16.

3. Mitchell, "Reflections on Twenty Years of Feminism," 36.

4. English, "The Fear That Feminism Will Free Men First," 477–83.

5. Schild, "Market Citizenship and the 'New Democracies,'" 232–49.

6. Mitchell, "Reflections on Twenty Years of Feminism," 42.

7. Hemment, *Empowering Women in Russia*.

8. Hemment, *Empowering Women in Russia*, 67.

15

WHO ARE THE POLISH FEMINISTS? (SLAWKA)

I know (at least) something about how American women became feminists in the late 1960s, but how did it happen for my friends in Poland, who called themselves feminists in the early 1990s, making themselves utterly lonely in their suddenly changing society? True, they were eagerly sought out by a few Western feminists like me, but we were often as unequipped to understand them as the traditionalist Poles everywhere surrounding them.

I first met Slawka Walczewska in March of 1991 on Krakow's main square, one of the grandest public spaces in all of Europe. At that time, the prevailing color was grey. The vast rectangle of glorious buildings—dating from the twelfth to the nineteenth century—were beautiful in their bones but still melancholy in their crumbling details. I was seeking Slawka as one of the few self-proclaimed feminists of postcommunist Poland. In my pocket was the cash to buy her a ticket to the conference I was organizing to bring such feminists from the former bloc together to talk about their prospects.

I had a courtly guide, soon to be one of the up and coming young men of the new Poland; when he introduced us, Slawka treated me to the first of many feminist demonstrations which were later to take place on this monumental stage set. Zigmund took her hand as if to shake it, but his gesture turned into the elegant hand kiss, then still a common piece of Polish civility. Slawka's fine-boned face convulsed into a heraldic frown, a look of aristocratic defiance I have often seen since in Polish national art. She evaded the kiss as one might pull one's hand back from touching a hot poker.

Ah, hah, I said to myself. What have we here? Of course aware of the implications, I had nonetheless rather enjoyed this hand kissing in my few days in Poland. How quaint, how covertly sexy, how far from my New York problems with the social encounters between men and women who are supposedly equal. But here was someone who was freshly, absolutely furious at the every-day aesthetics of patriarchy. Embarrassed by Slawka's anger and alarmed by her strictness, I recognized this sudden refusal of ordinary, traditional life as the very stuff out of which feminist sensibility is made. Here was the raw material I knew so well, and I greeted this frowning woman with all my heart.

Since then, Slawka and I have paced the sublime square and the streets of Krakow, discussing feminist ideas. One day early in our peripatetic career, we entered the square to the sound of ecstatic violins; a folk troupe was dancing on an elevated wooden platform. We stood watching a long time. The women in their wide skirts twirled while the men opposite kicked and leapt. Then the men swung the girls. Then they all formed squares and the men and the women crossed and joined, bowed and parted, then joined again in couples for a final march, the eternal (fluttering) feminine on the arm of the eternal male hero. As Virginia Woolf said, you know you live in a patriarchy because it is *he* who suspends *her* in the air.[1]

When it was all over and the heartbreakingly lovely music had faded away, we exchanged such a look. "Maybe it's just impossible," she said. "This is all so old; how can it change?" We collapsed into wicker chairs at one of the outdoor cafes that ring the square, a perfect place to observe the promenade of he and she. Then, suddenly, in a turn half ironic alienation, half punch drunk confidence, we were hysterical with laughter. Yes, the dance was so strong, beautiful, joyous, seemingly timeless—but also so odd and unlikely. A shift in consciousness and now, when the gestures of standard heterosexuality were displayed on a plinth, they struck us as abstract and absurd, an artificial performance where nature meets art, like bear baiting. We argued about the boundaries of the possible for hours, but running parallel to the talk, our laughter was a new joint possession, a solvent we could not have rationally explained to anyone then, since our skepticism put us in the realm of the grotesque.

In Poland in 1991, the relationship between men and women was the most solid, clear, unambiguous, unquestionable human tie in a time when all other relationships were being remade. To live, as Slawka was living, in active opposition to the sacred dyad was to live, like all the dissidents before her, in the belief that everything could be completely different. Her daily commitment to another reality took not only courage but extraordinary imagination.

She was born in 1960 in Czestochowa, the city of the sacred image of the Black Madonna, at the height of the Gomulka years, the end of a small Soviet thaw, the beginning of stricter times—no travel, no letters. Her father, a teacher, was an engineer and a geographer. Rarely home when Slawka was growing up, he traveled all over Poland mapping the country's underground mineral resources. Her mother, also serious about work, was a teacher in a grammar school and attended to Slawka and her younger brother.

She was named Slawomira after her cousin, born twenty years before, in that very different moment, 1940. Slawka's uncle was then an officer in the Polish underground army. He had moved his wife and newborn baby to a village to be near him and the partisans he commanded in the nearby forest. This uncle is remembered as a peaceful man—clever and warm. (In 1944 the Russians sent him to Siberia for several years, and to Slawka's sorrow, he died in 1979, never to know the triumph of Solidarity the next year.) He named the baby Slawa for glory and Mira for peace. In the winter cold of that small village, with no medical care to speak of, in the midst of war, Slawomira the First caught a common infant illness and died. Slawomira the Second was supposed to live for both girls, to have a life of scope and heft, with freedom enough for two.

Slawka stores a favorite anecdote, her key to her parents. As a university student, she longed, like so many others, to see the forbidden Western world. After a long wait and the usual finagling, she finally got a passport that made it possible to leave Poland. She was on her way to England—in her mind a state that worked, a liberal democracy, where the free Poles had been during the war, and where freedom was still available. (She had read Orwell's 1984 in an underground Polish translation.) Getting there took three months; she had to earn hard currency on the way to cover her living expenses and to pay her parents back for the precious foreign money they had fronted for her, cash they had been stashing away illegally for years, $200. During this odyssey, her parents sent her a letter. Her mother wrote: Dearest Slawunia, Be careful. Wear warm clothes. Don't get ill. Be sure to eat. Come back soon. Her father wrote: My Dear Daughter, You are now on the way to the famous Albion, the center of the civilized world. I am proud you are so brave and doing such a journey. I always wanted to go there. Good luck on your travels.

This sounds as canonical a division of male and female as you can get; it's like the dance in the square—charming, and on the edge of caricature. But in Slawka these rival states are connected. Obviously, her father's yearnings for other cultures, languages, landscapes are one part of her inheritance.

She is hopeful like him, and like him, she believes in possibilities underground. From her mother comes a feeling of female sufficiency; the power of her mother's wishes seems somehow to have suggested the magic force of women in general.

But with her mother it has always been so difficult. In Slawka's earliest memories, her mother was already begging her "to change," an infinitive with many meanings—from wearing skirts instead of the more comfortable and freeing trousers to adopting some hard-to-name daughterly compliance. Why not carry a handbag? Use pretty handkerchiefs? Why take such long strides? Both parents were proud of her for fighting for her younger brother in the schoolyard, but they were anxious, too: Was this heroism female enough in a ten-year-old? She remembers her victories over the bullies with pleasure; one boy punched her in the face, and she responded with such sheer fury that he was scared from the field. Still, this was the end. The boys had so much training, she said; they were fighting all the time, learning technique. Regretting her lack of practice, she nonetheless took away from this last victory that if one is fierce and brave, one can win, even against the odds; to be certain is to win.

Slawka and her mother tangled for years. My mother, says Slawka, wanted me to change so much that I thought that I should come to her one day as a monster and say, "Look, I changed." Her mother only learned that Slawka was a lesbian when, at age 30, she brought home her new partner, the witty, brilliant, and beautiful Beata. Her mother refused to accept this new person into her life and asked that Beata go. So Slawka went, not seeing her parents for two years. As Slawka became well known in Krakow, her family began to accept her distressing feminism as a possibly acceptable identity. But just when this seemed settled, she began to publically advocate gay and lesbian rights. Once again her mother was embarrassed: Why couldn't she just be a feminist? The denial of Beata continues, rendering "home" a damaged place and "mother" a wound. Yet one day when Slawka was chopping cucumbers for a big soup and I asked her how she could possibly chop so fast, she gave a wry smile, her tribute to her mother, and to her mother's five sisters, a powerful female cabal still functioning across long distances of time and space, still loving the errant Slawka as their own beautiful, intelligent girl, who can no more be repudiated than they would cut off a hand.

I'm seriously studying Slawka now. How did she ever find her way into a feminism so passionate and fully thought through where there was no one else to talk to? Once, when she was helping her nephew of five to pee, he asked her if she also had a penis. She explained scornfully that she was finished with that phase—no doubt scaring the poor child half to death. (She remains capable of this kind of draconian message to young and poorly informed male children. Only last year, at Slawka and Beata's summer cottage, she told a seven-year-old boy she is fond of that, yes, the male hawk flying over our heads may be bigger than the female as he had proudly observed, but—in a voice of subdued threat and awe—the female bird is very, very *strong*.)

We are sitting in the apartment where Slawka and Beata moved when Slawka left home. It's an attic they renovated in a house built at the turn of the century for a new kind of person: unmarried middle class women with jobs who did not want to live at home. Slawka has written a brief illustrated monograph about these women's houses and once she took me for a grand dinner at one that was still going. It was like coming upon some nineteenth-century lace in a scented drawer. In fact, I now find it hard to believe that I really saw this world in the 1990s. Old, elegant spinsters (no term of opprobrium originally—just women who spin, or in this case work telephone exchanges) greeted us American visitors, fed us delicious food, showed us photographs of their independent youth. As we ate, portraits of permanently absent friends looked down on us, their hair piled high, their faces grand and dignified.

Simply, amazingly, Slawka had discovered the first wave of feminism in Krakow, had made friends with its survivors, had built this birds' eerie at the top of one of these women's early, free institutions. (Later she wrote a book, *Knights, Ladies, Feminists: Feminist Discourse in Poland* [1999], which describes this turn-of-the-century feminism.) Slawka and Beata's nest is a five-floor walk-up, all in wood, with windows opening into the tops of trees. These days they have a bigger apartment outside town, and I and other visiting feminists get to stay here, in a place where autonomous women have lived for a hundred years.

I say to myself at this point: Of course feminism is indigenous; all European countries had nineteenth-century women's movements. Slawka's feminism comes from the soil right here beneath this house, and I am merely a visitor without influence or interference—what a relief. I crave this kind of innocence, after so many years of being accused of bringing some Western pestilence to infect a healthy man-woman alliance in the East. But this restful fantasy of separation—the founding understanding of the Network of East-West Women, that we are clearly Other to each other—offers no real clarity about our ongoing relationship and gets undermined at once. Maybe it's the nineteenth-century ghosts who prompt me to ask again what I have asked Slawka so many times before: "Why *feminism* of all the dreams of liberation that were circulating around here? Why of all the possible formations, *that*? How did you even hear about it? Did it come from the communist rhetoric about equality?"

Slawka considers: no, not from communism. The excitement about women's emancipation was the experience of an earlier generation. For us, men ran things and women worked too hard; for us, communism meant only one thing: limitation. But she suddenly remembers where she did first hear about feminism, in a communist magazine in the '70s, in an article by a well-known Polish journalist, Daniel Passent. He had described a demonstration in New York by U.S. "feminists." Kate Millett had spoken and he made fun of her remarks. She was an older woman with grey, wild hair (already an offense) and she was arguing that women, blacks, and workers should unite. Ha, ha, a parody of "workers unite." How ridiculous, how childish.

The year must have been 1974 when Slawka was fourteen and in grammar school. She remembers her reaction to the article: "Long grey hair, telling something radical and new. Interesting." (In Slawka's English vocabulary, the word "interesting" is luminous, the highest praise.) So she decided at once to write a letter to Kate Millett. The first problem was taking the risk that someone might check the letter and see something suspicious in it. Then she had to concoct an address from the information in the article. Then she had to write something in her nearly nonexistent English: She could only send her greetings, and her wish to know something more. It was, she says, "a bottle in the ocean," and she didn't really expect a reply.

What must this letter have looked like to the people who received it, addressed to Radcliffe College, U.S.A. around 1975? I would love to find the person who recognized its importance and went to the trouble of putting together a packet with leaflets, group flyers, feminist catalogues. I want to know all that Slawka can remember about these ephemera straight out of the prime experiences of my youth. "I still have the catalogue. I've been carrying it around from one place to another for years. It should be here somewhere, in the apartment." She gets up and as if with a divining rod goes right to the shelf, presenting me with a large-scale book, *The New Woman's Survival Sourcebook: Another Woman-Made Book from Knopf*. I'm speechless; I have tears in my eyes. A record of the passionate proliferation of feminist activity of the U.S. Women's Liberation Movement in the 1970s is sitting on my lap in an attic in Krakow: where to find groups, with their names and manifestos;

where to find sensitive women's health care clinics—or witches' covens; where to get help defending against vaginal infections—or rapists. Everything, everything, in wild confusion on every page. Slawka points out an article called "Feminist Fiction." "I wondered about this—what could this mean? The word 'feminist' with the word 'fiction.' My English dictionary didn't help. In fact, with my English, I couldn't really understand any of it." Living in a communist country, she didn't have the concept "movement" either, but she had the sense that this was something big. Interesting! And not least interesting was the cover, an image by Judy Chicago in yellow and black of two outstretched wings. This was something sexual, Slawka understood. Freedom and sex in flight.

Slawka had treasured this book all these years and fed on curiosity. "When I met you on the Square in 1991, you were my first American feminist." I am secretly delighted of course, but instantly the old anxiety returns. How does U.S. feminism translate? Did she have reason to think it might be different from the European feminisms which, by that time, she already knew well? English and German feminisms were often more centrally, visibly focused on class. Did American feminism look good because consumerism looked good to new postcommunists? In fact when American feminists insisted on bringing up class, feminists from the East were often worried that this meant communism all over again. (A brilliant student at Warsaw University told me recently that if I had happened to begin the course I taught there in the mid-90s with a discussion of gender-with-class, she would have left immediately.) The Sourcebook was, among other things, a marketplace, an odd compilation of things to know, buy, do. Now that I was trying to look at the book from the outside, just what were the political movements manifesting themselves here? I was trying and succeeding in experiencing Slawka's bewilderment.

Obviously Slawka had had to project a feminism of her own onto her experiences in England and Germany. (Only West Germany, since in the '80s the East was afraid Poles might contaminate East Germans with the spirit of Solidarity.) Finally, her feminism made use of everything and was an invention of her own. I began to recognize Slawka as one of those early, creative organic intellectuals, like Shulamith Firestone or Jo Freeman or Cellestine Ware or Carol Hanisch or Martha Shelley or Cindy Cisler in the United States, who had started with the merest whisper heard on a street, an image noted in passing, a sense of wrongness which sought a name. Though there are two hundred years of ancestors, in times of quiescence, repression, or backlash their ideas recede from view, only to be rediscovered or reinvented by the Slawka Walczewskas of this world.

She told me that, from the first, she couldn't reconcile a sense of being herself with being what a woman was supposed to be. Putting the two together was an impossibility, making self-invention a necessity. Besides, she found it unfair and mysterious that her brother had privileges she had not. There was something terribly wrong with the world. Those who feel homeless can sometimes find the energy to withhold female assent, resist taking the required path. They seek out their own company and a way to live differently. If the time is wrong, they live Bohemian lives of one kind or another. If the time is right, they found movements. Being first, they pay a special price; they are ridiculed as misfits, trashed as leaders, disdained as dreamers, feared as extremists. They face these first lonely humiliations, and then, if the time is right, thousands of us come tumbling after.

In 1978, Slawka, then eighteen, began at Krakow's ancient university, the Jagiellonian, as a chemistry major. Though she hung on for two years, there was trouble from the first. She resisted the strict memory tasks, complained that there was no context, no meaning. On her exams, she began to talk about the social history of chemical discovery. Perhaps what this Polish romantic really wanted was to be an alchemist. Here was an early manifestation of her later infatuation with traditions of women's magical culture—a constant source of contention between her and me, not to mention a source of much mutual teasing and comic-ironic witch performances in the main square. How powerful can women be? In Slawka's book: infinitely powerful, capable of completely transforming reality. However small, very strong birds. However buried, precious ore.

In her small chemistry group, she said, "The sexism was terrible." One old, internationally known professor was willing to talk to her, but ultimately, to him, only men *need* to think. For girls it's enough to learn the formulas. Perhaps this is the first example of Slawka's originality as a public agitator: She made an exhibition of pictures created from the chemicals in the lab, called "Chemical Abstracts." After three days everything on the walls began to stink and burn.

In 1980, she changed her major to Philosophy. Did things get better? Suddenly, as I ask her this, the dark and guilty memories of a survivor surface in her: There were twenty students, mostly men. The few women were brilliant (necessarily in this competitive and elite milieu). One of them had a very high female voice. The men never heard her. A man would repeat her ideas as his own opinion and then everyone heard them. She became more and more "grey." She "died as a philosopher." Later, she became a librarian. Another gifted girl was incapable of fading; the alternative was to become crazy. She became a caricature of femininity, a sexy hoyden wearing raffish, aristocratic, hand-me-down clothes. She was trying to provoke, to capture their attention, and she ended as a grotesque all the men ignored. She never finished her degree, left Krakow for the provinces, takes care of her family, and does no professional work.

Once, a couple, both philosophy students, came to class with their newborn baby. The professor (a favorite of Slawka's) greeted all three warmly, then when it was time for the class to begin, he turned to the father: "You're staying for the seminar?" It never occurred to him that the mother might stay, or that neither could stay. These stories are so familiar that they are worth recounting primarily for what they tell about Slawka. At a time when such sexist culture was so common that no one noticed, she noticed. She grieved. She observed these gendered fates with a sympathy for the women that was not to be found, then, anywhere but in her singular heart.

Her own strategy for survival was to maintain a dignified silence. A few professors recognized her talent, but most of the time she traveled under the radar of male contempt for the female philosopher (oxymoron), respecting herself for her state of exile and cunning. Still, her invisibility and her empathy with the others created a rawness, a frustration, and then a need to fight—but how to avoid becoming yet another easily dismissed female type, the Angry Woman? How to win? She decided what she needed were words. She would organize with others to discuss, to seek the words to communicate "what is not okay." A small group of allies began talking among themselves "about women and men" in the mid-1980s. She was amazed when these new discussions aroused real anger and resistance in addition to the usual ridicule at the university. She maintained her dignity by developing her own syllogism: Philosophy should be a science in which all questions are good; the job is to ask questions about *anything*. But most of her colleagues refused to entertain questions about gender. Ergo, they were bad philosophers. Initially shocked by their closed-mindedness, she was ultimately freed by their attitude. Though they seemed powerful and authoritative, were they perhaps only a pack of cards? Their fear and derision disillusioned her.

And by this time she had begun to meet with women in Warsaw who had organized a women's film festival. This was Slawka's distant shout on the street: A male friend mentioned the festival to her in passing. What is a women's film festival? Interesting! In 1985, she found the organizers and was therefore one of the founding members of what may well have been the first independent, self-consciously feminist Polish women's group, the Polish Feminist Association. The group was an informal network that met in kitchens and held discussions very like the Consciousness Raising (CR) groups in the United States fifteen years earlier. Slawka loved the group and commuted three hours by train from Krakow several times a month; but she was frustrated, too, by the sequestered atmosphere that has always been one aspect of CR. She wanted this talk to be more public and to include growing numbers of women. So she persuaded the group to do their first outside action since the film festival, to join her and her Krakow colleagues in organizing a conference, "To Be a Woman?" ("The question mark," says Slawka, "carries the story.") Back at the University, no one had a better idea, so by default this became the subject of the official annual conference of the Jagiellonian students in philosophy.

The year was 1987 and the conference is a key moment in dissident history—if that story is ever to include women. Poland was just coming out from under the worst strictures of martial law and "To Be a Woman?" was one of the few public events around. But the reaction was disappointing. The question "To Be a Woman?" was odd certainly, but no one imagined the gathering to be subversive. Nobody cared, and only about twenty women and a few men—mostly the women's partners—attended. Yet Slawka marks this moment with pride. Later, every single one of those precious few did something memorable to build the women's movement that followed.

In 1988, Slawka organized the second feminist conference, "The Place of Women in the World of Patriarchal Culture." Here was a bold step beyond the question mark. Or rather the question was now peremptory: "What About Women?" The world was organized by men, for men. Is there a place organized by women, where women are heard? Are women absent from the whole history of culture? What about us?

Then, in 1989, everything changed. Slawka was tired of organizing conferences only a few would dream of attending. Like everyone at that startling moment when the roundtables began and new ideas were being discussed, she and her friends wanted a more public manifestation of their questions. They decided to write to Parliament to protest the draft of a new law that was to issue in the new, free society—a law against the right women had had since 1956 to get abortions, free and on demand. Here was the new society's payback to a church that had remained passionately anticommunist all through the years of repression. Women were an easy sacrifice to lay on the altar, an unorganized and powerless constituency, easy symbols of a return to "the normal." The irony of repressing them at the moment of general liberation was lost on nearly everybody beyond the small elites of feminists and their friends.

They wrote a letter: The antiabortion law is unjust; women are individuals who have the existential right to decide about pregnancy; they are not mere means to an end. Now, how to give this letter some weight? Interesting idea: Collect signatures! For two or three weeks, they solicited the town on the main square and at the university, and—against the grain of communist habits as this procedure was—several thousand courageously signed. After some days, a small group of Catholic students called in a priest who showed up at the main building of the university and asked at the table: Who sent you? (Unthinkable these young people had thought of this blasphemy by themselves.) Do you understand the meaning of what you are doing? Do you want people to kill each other in the streets without being punished? In conclusion, he told them: You will go to Hell for this. Slawka has vivid memories of this new kind of public exchange. She was ecstatic; here was the new freedom. She recalls how her group answered: Nobody sent us. This is important and we know what we are doing. As for Hell, let God decide about that, not you. (As Slawka is telling me this story years later, she teases me—a God-kicker—that the Goddess had given them different information about Hell.)

This letter, with all its signatures went to Parliament. No reaction, of course. But in Krakow, thousands had seen the protesters and talked to them. A public political life had begun.

After the dramatic break of 1989, feminists resumed their annual conferences. In 1990, the subject was "Motherhood: A Choice or a Duty?" Magda Schroda, much later to become the government plenipotentiary for women, was there and remembers the meeting as her first contact with feminists. This time eighty people came. The feminist movement was becoming visible.

In March of 1991, as soon as such a thing was possible, Slawka and cofounder, Barbara Kaszkur, registered an organization, eFKa (as a private joke, the same sound as the nickname for Eve, but officially the abbreviation of the Polish name, Foundacja Kobieca, Women's Foundation), which has been a home to feminist activism in Krakow ever since.

I know that so far this reads like one of the lives-of-the-saints: the early years. By and by, and inevitably, the story of feminism in Krakow thickened with the usual difficulties, limitations, and painful dissensions; also inevitably, Slawka played her part in all that. But it is also a part of the truth to let our moments of wild hope and joy rise up without their shadows. It is here, in the excitement of beginnings, on the main square, that my story and Slawka's began to cross.

2004

Note

1. Woolf, A Room of One's Own, 33.

16

"SHOULD I MARRY HIM?"

Questions from Students

In 1992, my colleague at the university, Elzbieta Matynia, started a summer school in Krakow where U.S. students and East Central European students could meet and exchange what they know, choosing two of four rigorous courses on such themes as democracy, nationalism, memory, cosmopolitanism. Just back from Dubrovnik and the founding of the Network of East-West Women (NEWW), I happened to be sitting in her office during the planning stage of the school. "Why not a class on gender?" In the context of my university, this thought could only be exotic and unexpected.

Elzbieta was surprised but intrigued. Indeed, why not? I made the case: the reorganization in Eastern Europe of absolutely everything including laws, expectations, and daily life; the repositioning of women as once again the symbolic keepers of the hearth; the disappearance of social services and government subsidies. The pace of change alone was enough to knock all identity sideways. My list went on and on. Always game and open-minded, Elzbieta included my gender course in the first year.

Sitting in this privileged front seat, I have been conversing every summer for twenty years with the young activists and intellectuals of the region, a spectator and sometimes participant in the high drama of accelerated change. For the first few summers, it was plain that we were teaching a new, young elite, the children of dissidents and intellectuals who were likely to become leaders in the now topsy-turvy situation where their parents' generation, recently in jail, were now in Parliament. Also during those early years, we at the Network of East-West Women sought out feminist activists for the gender course, people thinking on their feet and inventing new identities:

director of an NGO, organizer of independent associations, pro bono lawyer, journalist. At this stage, all of our students from the region had grown up under communism, and their educations and experiences were fundamentally different from their American colleagues in the school. "Difference" was no abstract matter. Our every encounter bristled with conflict and incomprehension.

But each year our students from the region changed. First those who grew up in communism; then those who were teenagers when the change came and could remember their parents' struggles; then those who were children in 1989 and knew the communist years only through family lore and popular memory. As I have watched from my perch, the generations have flipped by. (In the headlong pace which is postcommunism, a generation is about five years.)

Loss of memory had its own subjective timetable. The builders moved in early and Krakow became a vibrating site of urban renewal. "Do you mind the transformation of familiar landmarks?" I asked friends. "What! Everything is improving. Everyone is busy. Finally, foreign food in new restaurants! The sound of hammering is great!" I couldn't find in them a scintilla of nostalgia for the grey, utterly noncommercial city I had entered with wonder in 1991. Later, an artist, Karolina Kowalska, was to take a picture of Florianska, a main street leading out of the central square, and white out all the new commercial signs or ads. The resulting image was almost entirely white, with an occasional flash, a cornice or elaborate doorway still visible, half-buried reminders of the brilliant architecture beneath.

At some point in the mid-1990s, it seemed that no matter the generation, everyone's memory began to erode. Eyes front and few were grieving. Occasionally, as traces of the former time began to disappear, a few created little local museums of communism to hang on to disappearing objects. In Gdansk near the shipyard you can see a careful replica of a communist shop, only a few pieces of inferior-looking meat in the glass cases and spirals of fly-paper hanging from the ceiling. I visited the place with people old enough to remember. It was moving to watch them study its details, exclaiming over tins of beans and replicas of bad bread. In my first summer or two in Krakow, I had assembled things I needed from such shops, but each year more of them had disappeared. Where to get batteries now? Where to get tissues? The friends just laughed and piled me into the car. Everything I wanted was now at Tesco's, from yogurt to a mirror, from electrical appliances to a straw wastebasket.

Not everyone went quietly and happily into the land of consumerism tricked out with gargantuan posters of seductive women sucking passionately on long conical ice creams. The anarchists staged a protest at Tesco's by wheeling around the huge shopping carts, clogging the aisles, and buying nothing. But, finally, who could dispute the convenience? Most of the stuff for sale was cheap and ugly but had consumerism ever offered more? I can hear many friends from the East snickering at any privileged Westerner's critique: Here at least were aisles and aisles of tampons and soft toilet paper, lipstick and pretty, if shoddy, shoes.

Every year the regional students and the U.S. students became more alike. Wisely, Elzbieta stirred the pot by bringing in South Africans, Germans, Mexicans. This move toward cosmopolitan inclusiveness had a sort of United Nations effect: many voices, many lands. But during these years another tendency spoke even louder: globalization. With each passing year, country after country was experiencing privatization, a concentration of wealth, a euphemistically called "structural adjustment" away from entitlements, safety nets, and public social services.

Though the United Nations effect tended to obscure this gradual—and sometimes not so gradual—homogenization, the students themselves recognized each other's references, began to cite the same textual authorities, began to share similar ideas about what graduate school is for—to build an academic career based on free inquiry, a pathway rarely imagined in 1991 but also much narrower than the wild social yearning of that initial burst of energy and hopefulness.

Or let me put it this way: By the late '90s ambivalence about how to measure success had become common in all locations. Where was one to locate enduring values? Could Easties make use of the past as an anchor? Could Westies invent free spaces for idealism in a more and more harshly neoliberal world?

In the early 1990s, I was teaching ideas that were new to Easties. At the millennium, these ideas had traveled in various forms. Now the question was what to do with them. What, under the circumstances in which we found ourselves, would a feminist politics look like?

In the late '90s, I lend my Polish student Basia a copy of *Our Bodies, Ourselves*, the great, collectively written health bible of the U.S. Women's Movement. She returns it the next morning like a pestilent object. "What's wrong?" A response with fervor: "How can you call your movement ethical with this emphasis on pleasure and choice?" Ah, ha! I spend some moments digesting this critique. "Funny, I never ask myself if my movement is ethical. It's just not my word. Though in my activism I do seek the good in some sense. Is there an ethics in believing one can make things better? Belief that one can influence the direction of inevitable change does seem like an unprovable hypothesis; political activism does require some kind of faith."

We're so invested in this conversation that we are each drilling holes into each other's eyes. "If pleasure and choice aren't part of an ethics for you, what words would you use as guides for the good?" Without skipping a beat: "Duty and sacrifice." And there you have it, a ground base beneath hundreds of conversations I've had in Poland over the years. How can one lobby for the return of abortion rights if everyone's sense of women's goodness and rightness revolves around duty and sacrifice? But this small story has a sequel. Eventually, Basia wrote her dissertation about feminism. She now teaches courses in Gender Studies. I don't know what feminism and Gender Studies have become in her hands—and I don't presume to care. They are her new ground of professional identity and social action. Let versions of feminism travel around, borne by the flood of urgent new thinking which in postcommunism is reshaping a whole world.

In a summer in the mid-nineties, Reka is in my class. Smoldering and privileged, she is Hungarian. The feminist material in my course clearly fascinates her and disturbs her. She is engaged, but I get the feeling that she is feeling this excitement somewhat against her will. Finally, we get talking. When she leaves the school, she is going home to marry an American living in Budapest. I begin to sense her anxiety lies here; the gender class has been clouding her enthusiasm for this next move. I say nothing of course. An automatic suspicion of any and all marriages is the sort of programmatic feminism I detest.

Yet, clearly, there is a drama unfolding here, and in some way I have not sought, I am a player. The fiancé is coming to visit. Reka has written to him about the class. I tell her I look forward to meeting him, which by now, my curiosity aroused, I indeed am. But the boyfriend doesn't come to class; he is here in our castle, but makes no effort to see me. In chance encounters, Reka seems slightly embarrassed. It occurs to me that her fiancé is a rival! Never have I put any feminist pressure on Reka, so the idea that I'm toxic comes from this invisible other. Is he paranoid, or my god, here's another thought: She has told him all about the class—floating around key words such as housework, motherhood, public life, independence. I review these themes. As an American, he has of course heard about them. But his Reka, his foreign bride, has had no such questions running in her head until now. Living in Budapest, he has been able to find an eager, uncomplaining, uncontaminated mate. But no! She had to go off and take the gender class! (Ads on the Internet offer American men Russian brides: thin, because, the ads explain, they are hungry and without cars; compliant, because desperate; content with little, because innocent of feminist demands.)

After a few days, I am sure I will not meet the intended; our battle will remain safely invisible. But then, quite by chance, I run into the couple on that greatest of meeting places, Krakow's main square. The fiancé steps away, leaving Reka to greet me and gesture toward him. The game's afoot! I warmly insist on meeting the man she is about to marry. We walk over to him—and he cuts me dead! Now Reka is very embarrassed indeed. Who is this churlish fellow she is about to marry? He has acted like a naughty and sullen child. Alarm bells. I am feeling very concerned about Reka, but none of this is my business. The fiancé goes back to Budapest and the gender class continues, including occasional and always interesting challenges from Reka.

After the last class is over, I am sitting on the grass, exhausted but satisfied. We have discussed so much, learned so much from each other. I'm rehearsing in my mind a classroom exchange with one of the older students, which I will certainly dine out on in New York. The subject was sex and she told us that once after an arduous summer work detail, her period had stopped, and though she had never had intercourse, she assumed that she was pregnant. Such was the state of sex education in Czechoslovakia in the 1950s. They had taught her at school that sexual pleasure was bourgeois. Musing over such moments of revelation, I am suddenly interrupted by a stormy Reka. She plunks down beside me and begins in on me at once: "What am I supposed to do with all this stuff we've discussed? How can I go home now, knowing all this? You don't realize the harm you have done. You should consider the consequences."

I am taken aback. This becomes one of the turning points of my East Central European teaching career. Here is a serious charge. Where do all these hard-won feminist insights come from? Who are they for? How is one to construct a life in the glare of this information while one must still live in the same Budapest, with the same people, and the same limited prospects for independence?

Reka was enraged and I was instructed. *Lente, lente*. I formed new resolutions: Every class must not only include respect for the gendered lives people are actually living, a long-held value, but also must be taught at an emotional temperature that leaves room for the specific difficulties each one might well face at home. Every class must open up imaginable paths people might—but need not—take. An engaged feminist life has to be made thinkable as a response, say, to no abortion rights, or to gross unfairness in the workplace, or to lack of choice in sex or work or marriage. After Reka, for some years, I move much more slowly. Until the students themselves accelerate way beyond Reka's lonely desperation. Female narratives of limitation continue, but by the third classroom generation, students have heard about feminism as a potential source of resistance.

I apologize to Reka and tell her she is raising a question at the heart of any translation of feminist ideas from place to place. (I remember the feminist Romanian judge who told us in the Network of East-West Women law project that she was trying to abolish easy divorce. We were horrified but she explained: Only men use divorce. They wish to escape responsibility for wife and kids. Women rarely file for it since to be a divorced woman in Romania is so disgraceful and isolating that really it's never worth it.) Context is all, I tell Reka. Make a good life in the situation in which you find yourself.

Reader, she married him. But, that isn't the end of Reka's story—of course not. Two years later and I'm once again sitting on the grass outside our classroom, and here is Reka, paying the school a visit with a beautiful toddler in tow. I hug her, exclaim over the beautiful boy. But her misery is palpable. So? Once she was pregnant, her husband was never home. He skipped out every night to hang out with his friends. Once the boy came, things got even worse. He was actively hostile, wouldn't help with the baby, even called her a nag and a ball and chain when she asked him for help. She bore this for some months, then left him. Now she's a single mother looking for work. Luckily her mother helps her. Tears, terrible tears. It's ridiculous, I know, but I almost feel responsible. How could the old sob story be so unchanged? The compulsive repetition of women's entrapment causes me nausea.

God! Enough indulgence in the downbeat Reka lurking in my own personality! I rouse myself to face her sorrows. "Hey!" I say. "Look at this beautiful child. What a treasure you're taking away from the wreckage. And what a fool your husband is to want no part of him. And look at how young and smart you are. Your whole life is before you. No more one-act plays for women. You're not ruined. You are just at the beginning."

We discuss her depression, her prospects, her various support systems. Together we look for a secret source of vitality, the start of desire. I can see aloneness is too bleak, and I feel this terror of the loss of a safely partnered life myself, a vulnerability in my own and many women's lives. So no lecture now about glorious independence. Instead, I promise that she can choose a very different mate next time. Love, friends, work. We both want them all. We embrace and I wish her well.

Today's subject is motherhood, and at this moment the particular question: Who will take care of the children? We go around the room asking how each one imagines balancing childcare with work. A lot of the Americans say they don't plan to have children, a useless answer since 95% of American women eventually try to have children and 90% succeed. In contrast, those realists, the women from the region, assume they will have children and all give the same answer to the childcare question: Of course their mothers will take care of the kids. It's hard breaking this confident chain, a sort of group complacency that all is well and the American feminists are making a fuss over something the agile managers of the East have solved long ago. But Kinga from Romania is an outlier. She brings out: "But Ann said that now older women might stay active in the world. They won't just be exhausted all the time. They'll even have sex." Embarrassed silence. But surely their mothers won't have such a life. They will retire five years before the men, who will then die early; they will take care of their grandchildren.

I am amazed that Kinga has linked our discussions of women's and men's different life courses—not to mention our discussions of pleasure, choice, and sex—with the childcare question. How gratifying for the professor. "But Ann said . . . !"

Now the question has to change. Can we continue to expect women over fifty to spend the rest of their lives as their children's willing servants? Will they have other desires, better health, more mobility? Right now it doesn't look that way. Only young and pretty women are getting the new jobs (In Russia, job ads openly specify: "long legs.") Older women are bitterly complaining at being superannuated much too soon. Still, "Ann says. . . ." There is reason to believe that my young students may not be able to rely on the traditional solution even a few years down the road. For better and worse, families are moving, changing, sometimes falling apart. That screech owl Ann may be a harbinger of instability, changing wishes, different choices. Everyone is sitting very still contemplating Kinga's intervention. Ann says the future may include sex and action for older women and since Ann is active in the world, lover in tow, obviously sexually active, too, and in some cases older than their mothers, no one feels free to say a word against this thinkable future. A worried silence closes this motherhood episode.

The feeling of loss that pervades the room reminds me of two of my favorite Polish students, a gay couple, brilliant aesthetes who, at the time I first met them, were both living at home with their parents. "How has life changed?" I asked them—my perennial question in my quest to understand life over the precipice of 1989. But what I seek to know is always hard to tell. So many small shifts were slowly shaping an entirely new reality for Tomasz and Pawel as out gay men. Finally, though, Tomasz came up with a formulation: "We never had the books we wanted. We lived the life of the mind through friendships and conversation. Everyone hung out for hours talking; every birthday, anniversary, sunny day was a good reason to meet, drink, talk. Now we have the wonderful books we wanted, but we have no time to read them. The friends are dispersed or too busy to hang out. Instead of sitting around in each other's kitchens—private, intimate—now everyone meets in noisy bars and nightclubs. Having a good time is all about dancing and drinking. There's too much noise to talk. The old easy, slow pace is gone. Somehow, daily life is completely different." Telling this melancholy tale, suddenly Tomasz became aware that he was registering a loss; he hastened to say that certainly he didn't want the old days of stagnation and isolation back. Still, while returning his thoughts resolutely to the exciting present, he let slip, "There's a bit of desperation in social life now."

Vesna, from Croatia, one of the Network's leaders, was far more cutting on the subject of change. It was during the war that broke up Yugoslavia, which we all watched—and some Network members directly suffered—with such amazement. At a NEWW board meeting some of us Americans were talking about trying to make "social change." Vesna leapt on us: "Social change, social change. You Americans talk as if social change is naturally good, something you work for, as if it is not something overwhelming you can't control that changes *you*. No! Social change for us is this war."

Change comes, and who gets to name it? I am trying to chronicle rapid change in the region, which was often greeted in the West as the joyous triumph of capitalism. But, if I don't like this storyline, I'll need others. As an activist, I believe you can give a shove to change as it rushes by. But sitting at my desk, writing this, I'm a different, and more skeptical person. All I can say with any certainty is that the quality of my exchanges with individual others has made my life better and made action more thinkable. I simply don't know if the feminist activism we have shared in East Central Europe has increased the happiness of my students and friends. And how would they, themselves, rate happiness as a goal?

Take the case of Monika, wild and wonderful Monika. Tomasz liked my teaching in Krakow and invited me to lecture to his university students in

Lublin. I went. Though it was the late '90s, here it was like the early days all over again. A full room with boys making preening declarations about men's superiority, women's place, the idiocy of complaining about nature. In other words, the usual. (I flash on similar large meeting halls in Lviv, Prague, Wroclaw.) But I have my tricks; I use them; and we talk for a long time with not a single word from any of the many women in the room. That silence is also as usual—though it becomes less so as the years roll by.

And I know what will happen next. I declare the formal lecture and discussion over. I wait. And here they come, the girls, furtive but eager. They want to talk privately about these outré feminist ideas. Is there really something wrong with women doing all the cleaning, cooking, and care of children? By what authority can I claim there's a problem here? Such a refocusing of the lens of justice is both thrilling and scary.

One among them, with wild eyes and floppy red curls (as disheveled and charming as she is all these years later), is Monika. She has some urgent questions. Her boyfriend never helps her with anything. He won't pick up a dish or a dust rag. He's a lord of creation who depends on her for everything as, formerly, he depended on that loving slave, his mother. (I flash on one of my students in Krakow who was full of abstract theories about the strengths and weaknesses of feminism. He talked unintelligibly half the time, which greatly impressed the others, until the day we discussed housework. Each student told how housework was divided in his or her house. When it was our dear theorist's turn, he said that he had only just moved out from his childhood home to his own flat. Ah, ha! Everyone was eager to know how cleaning up after himself was going. So assertive and insistent were the girls in the class that he had to admit, a bit—but not very—sheepishly, that his mother comes round, cleans the new apartment, and takes home his laundry. Pandemonium. The girls never listened to him with quite the same awe and respect again. But he himself was essentially ungored. He didn't really see anything wrong with a busy scholar having a full-service female attendant.)

The peremptory Monika demands an answer: "Should I marry him or not?" I had to laugh. "A feminist is not a marriage counselor or a therapist or a fortune teller. How can I know if you'll be happy with this guy or not? I wouldn't dream of giving you advice." But this isn't acceptable: "I need help!" "Okay, okay, I'll send you some books to read."

The Network of East-West Women has had a Book and Journal Project since 1991, when we brought feminist books in our suitcases to the founding meeting. We were amazed by the hunger. Who in the West had this desperate longing for books? In the early years, it was all heavy suitcases and books sent by sea. (The books to Mongolia took a year; during the war, the books to Kosovo were sent back to New York by the hostile relay station in Belgrade.) Once I get home, I make a package for Monika. My mentor Dorothy Dinnerstein's *The Mermaid and the Minotaur*, of course, and what else? Pat Mainardi's perfect "The Politics of Housework"? Books about care, about balancing children and work? I don't remember, but I think probably Monika does. A few years later, she shows up as a student in the Krakow gender class. Neither a scholar nor all that interested in ideas, she bops through the course happily. "Well, did you marry him?" "Of course not. Wow, those books you sent! I read them and now I'm here taking gender class." "I'm sure it wasn't the books that broke your engagement off. It was your own good judgment." "Who knows?" Speculation is in vain, not Monika's thing at all.

Smart, fast, able to compromise and be practical without angst, Monika is now a player in the Plenipotentiary for Women, a department of Polish government that comes and goes depending on which party wins the election. She is also back and forth to Brussels, participating in talks at the European Union. I see her when she comes to New York, and I must ask her who her current boyfriend is. She has run through a number of men but hasn't felt satisfied for long with any. Feminist consciousness has made her finicky. Have raised expectations, mobility, and startling success lifted her beyond the reach of a mere mortal man? Like a traditional mother hen, I ask myself: "Who is good enough for our passionate, madly careening, vital Monika?" Her energy can move mountains, and I have great confidence in her. Marriage or not, children or not—those questions don't scare me for her—but I do so want her to have love as well as work, happiness as well as struggle. The travels of feminism: I'm constantly reviewing them—with excitement and doubt, with hope and unending anxiety.

2011

THE PERIPATETIC FEMINIST ACTIVIST/PROFESSOR SPENDS ONE DAY IN A SMALL CITY IN ALBANIA

I'm lecturing about feminism to seventy graduate students in the Social Work department. I have a fine translator and this gives me peaceful intervals to observe the class, mostly women but with a good sprinkling of men, all of them rapt. In this small city, feminism seems to be interesting news.

This is my second trip to Albania and by now I have some idea of what it might be useful to say: Women are people. To illustrate this deceptively simple point, I will tell them a story about a Ukrainian student I had some years earlier. He had faithfully attended my three-week course "Gender: Stable and Unstable" but had sat inert, speechless. Naturally, by the end, I was curious: I asked what the course had meant to him.

He told me that his mother had raised him and his brother alone. She had worked hard, and made many sacrifices. Everything she did was for them, the sons, to push them forward in life. He had never given her constant struggle a thought; he had assumed it was her duty. Now, after the class, it seemed possible that this had been love, something special. "I'm going to have to thank her now."

The arrival of feminist sensibility! (I had a private moment of communion with that mother. She wouldn't have recognized me, but nonetheless I was a fly on the wall the day her son thanked her.)

Editing out my huge teacherly pride in this story, I elaborate with a sense of urgency: These students are to be social workers in a new Albania, where all social service systems are crumbling and everything is going private. I describe how we all tend to assume that women are here to take care of us—feed us, clean up after us, give us support and solace. Women are our servants. We never think about it. It's their duty so we never say thank you. Women, I tell them, will be expected to take up the slack, fill in the empty spaces in the new Albania.

I've talked for twenty-five minutes, a short time by Eastern European standards. Students expect a long, at least partially unintelligible lecture to demonstrate seriousness after which they usually file out. Instead, I open the floor for discussion. After all these years I'm not surprised when not a single hand goes up. Inured to what I know to be both learned passivity and active fear, I wait. Mira Danaj, my smart translator, understands; she says nothing. We wait.

Finally, about half way back in the crowd, a young woman raises her hand. This is rare. It is almost always men who talk first.

"I do everything for my brothers. My mother is dead. I cook for them and clean the house. They tell me things they want done and I do them. I couldn't possibly change this."

I ask her, "What would they do if you ever refused, said you were too busy?"

"They would hit me." Suddenly, she and I are alone, our eyes locked as our dialogue proceeds.

"Would they hit you *hard?*"

A flurry of anxiety at this question. "The point isn't that they would hit me. It's that they would stop loving me."

Here we are in the unexplored country of feelings feminist sensibility cannot simply fix. I take a deep breath and launch in: "It's no part of the feminism I care about to expect you to give up the love of your brothers."

Her relief is palpable. She bursts out: "They sent me here to school. They protect me." Service and protection. Gratitude and love. These are old bargains, I say, rich, warm, familiar. It would be a vulgar and stupefying feminism that ignored the quality of life such traditions can sometimes deliver, especially now, in Albania, where the only religion is money, the public sphere is corrupt, and the shared social world so decimated that newly urban people throw garbage out their windows, expecting/waiting for a pick-up that never comes. One adorns and cleans only the inside, the often lavishly furnished family cave. There's the family or nothing.

"But," I say, with gathering intensity—and here comes a message, carried a long way, across an ocean, a sea, and delivered in the shadow of a mountain range which shuts out morning light—"you yourself can know what you are doing. You yourself can understand that bargain that your family and all the world established between you and your brothers from the moment you were born. Knowing this, and measuring the gains and losses, you may decide to raise any sons and daughters you have differently."

"And you won't be alone. It's all changing now. Albanians are living in new circumstances, which bend the old certainties out of shape. People hold on to the old family, but no one stays home for long. One in three Albanians, women as well as men, is away from home right now, trying his or her fortune in the global economy. You may have company if you seek new paths to a good life. To me, feminism at its best is about the good life."

End of lecture. My dear young woman is glowing; there are tears in her eyes.

At this moment, I am completely happy. The connection is everything. And I have rescued feminism once again from its potential for irrelevance and idiocy. Feminism and I are alive and well in Albania.

Now, the inevitable male hand goes up. This is a sclerotic, blustery, middle-aged man with a red face. Often I enjoy the crash that follows after such rhetorical heights. The return to earth is salutary. I am eager for whatever his question will be, hoping to make use of whatever comes: "What about the penis (pronounced pén-is)?" I couldn't have dreamed a more perfect sequel. For a moment, I consider various responses. But the delight of the moment seizes me and I laugh, not an insulting but a happy laugh. The whole class takes this as permission and joins in—men and women. I yell over the din, "Yes, good question! What about the body? So happy you brought that up!" A brief discussion on difference follows. Students ask interesting questions for another half hour, and then the crowd flows out, several students stopping to thank me, while the penis man rather shamefacedly comes up to tell me he knows feminism is okay. He was just joking. He's a musician and wants me to have his CD, Albanian folk music, the most ecstatic in the world. And here, at the end of the line, is the dear one with the brothers. We embrace. We observe each other's tears. Whatever we finally can make of it, we will remember our exchange all our lives.

2011

CERTAINTY AND DOUBT IN THE CLASSROOM

Teaching Film in Prison

When I first heard that my college had formed ties with a prison and that some of our teaching assistants were already offering college courses to inmates, I leapt to join on. Motive? Dare I say it? Boredom. Teaching well is always difficult, but I needed new kinds of difficulty. Feminism is everywhere and nowhere in my college students' lives; they are both ignorant and at the same time jaded about the whole business. I know what feminism can become for them, if I teach well. But what could it become in a medium-security prison for men who had been incarcerated for long periods, sometimes decades? I craved to know.

To my surprise, people praised my eagerness. Oh, how sacrificial, or how generous, or how public spirited. Odd. I thought we were all well beyond the fantasies of the sister of mercy. No one I know believes in disinterested altruism. Skepticism rules on the Left, casting doubt on any show of sympathy as covert imperialism. At the same time, with greater bluntness and scorn, neoliberals during the Bush years systematically emptied the prisons of all amenities, from gyms to education, from air conditioning to reasonable hope of parole.

I was skeptical myself, an emotion further developed in my conversation with my friend, the Lacanian analyst. "Ann, you're such an adventure tourist." To Marta, any illusion that one might "help" as a visitor from another world reeked of sentimentality: A white women arrives each week with a satchel and spends a few hours spreading light to a captive audience of black men.

"Besides," said Marta, "some of these guys will surely be psychotic." It occurred to me that after two decades inside some might indeed be insane, if they hadn't started that way. "So how do you recognize a psychotic in a classroom?" I asked her. "Psychotics don't doubt."

As far as Marta was concerned, my desire to teach in prison was absurd. But my confidence in her judgment took a hit when she connected what she saw as self-serving adventurism with my twenty years of feminist organizing in East Central Europe. True, I had sought adventure in the post-1989 me-lee, and also true: Traveling feminism is inevitably tangled in other forms of circulating power. But, I argued, willy-nilly, things come from outside, and people make use of what comes, even from tainted hands. Besides, there is no pure and ideal state of nature before a particular visitor arrives. There may indeed be no innocent, disinterested travelers, but capitalism had rushed in. Why not me, too, capitalism's feminist critic?

Still, this asserting of a potential value, even in adventure tourism, seemed a weak defense. I was both excited by the prospect of this new teaching and fearful that I wouldn't be able to discover some kind of authentic link with my students, something beyond the suspect reign of sympathy. I had eight months to obsess about this and so the process of designing the course began.

Distracted by all these doubts, I set my initial bar low. Whatever else the course might succeed in doing, I was determined that it would give pleasure. I was warned that though these particular students were culled by both the prison and a college selection process, some of them had weak writing and reading skills. If writing and reading were onerous, they would remain side activities. The main thing would be films: riveting, fascinating, beautiful, controversial. For one afternoon a week, we would watch great movies, then talk about them. I'm hypnotized by movies, utterly rapt, even when they are bad. I would allow myself to project this far, to imagine that at least some of the students are like me, carried away, happy to escape for a few hours from their current situation.

Next question: Which films? I decided that I would never use the word "feminism" but that I would organize the course around themes I know and care about and can therefore teach best. So, three clusters: Childhood. Manhood. Womanhood.

I spent months screening films. Each one would be vetted by the deputy in charge of prison outreach. The general rule was not too much violence and very little sex. It's hardly surprising how many films this eliminates. Because of students' uneven reading skills and what were likely to be bad screening conditions, it was risky to choose films with subtitles. The films would have to be in English and powerful enough to overcome the distancing devices imposed by low-tech prison life.

During this sifting process, I was working to develop another whole layer of meaning for the course, separate from the pure pleasure of watching diverting movies, separate from the raising of aesthetic and thematic questions, and separate from the need to find exciting material for debate. All that, yes! But, at some other level altogether, I wanted to hollow out a place where the complexity of human motive could be slowed down, carefully observed. Without presuming to educate anyone's emotions, I sought a way to show how art depicts our complex, layered inner life. As I explained it to friends when I asked them for help choosing the films, "I want to show that sometimes you hit someone, but really you're sad."

I allowed this aspect of my intentions to remain inchoate as I worked on the course, embarrassed by my secret goal of providing a sentimental education. Later, I was startled to hear the wonderful tough love counselor who taught the course before mine, "The Criminal Mind," bark out like an order to one of the prisoners, "You have no idea what you're feeling. Pay attention!" Paying attention—to the film, to art, to meaning, to one's own responses—this was to be the secret core of the course. I called it "Express Yourself" and everyone wanted to take it. "Why did you choose this class?" "Because I like movies," and "Because I want to express myself."

Here, finally, are the films:

Crooklyn (Spike Lee, 2006)
Spirited Away (Hayao Miyazaki, 2002)
Muhammad Ali: When We Were Kings (a documentary directed by Leon Gast, 2005)
My Son the Fanatic (Udayan Prasad, 1998)
In the Valley of Elah (Paul Haggis, 2006)
The Hurt Locker (Kathryn Bigelow, 2010)
The Times of Harvey Milk (a documentary directed by Rob Epstein and Richard Schmiechen, 1984)
Bad Day at Black Rock (John Sturges, 1954)
Dirty Pretty Things (Stephen Frears, 2004)
Thelma and Louise (Ridley Scott, 1991)
North Country (Niki Caro, 2005)
Speakout: I Had an Abortion (a documentary directed by Gillian Aldrich and Jennifer Baumgardner, 2005)

Iron Jawed Angels (Katja Von Garnier, 2004)

Pray the Devil Back to Hell (a documentary about women's organizing in
Liberia, directed by Abigail E. Disney and Gini Reticker 2008)

Day 1—Getting In

The correctional facility lies at the very end of an island, just off the road
near one of the biggest garbage dumps in America. Judging from the reading
I did before the first class, it seemed likely that in prison a central emotion
would be humiliation. On my first arrival, it was immediately obvious that
the mechanisms are relentless, even for the hapless volunteers.

The first problem was my purse. Why a mirror? To check the back of my
head. No, the prisoners might steal it, break it, and use the shards as weapons. No Metrocard. Because the prisoners might steal it, escape, and have
instant access to buses and trains. No chewing gum or lip gloss. These can
be used to glue up locks. Of course no pins. I had several floating around the
bottom of my big bag. Of course no cell phones or other means of communication with the outside.

The gate was a trial every week. *Surveiller et punir*, and I wasn't even an inmate. Why all these hair clips, hair ties, paper clips, makeup, string bags,
pills? Why not? "Because this is a prison." (Primo Levi asked a concentration
camp guard *why* he was forbidden to break off an icicle. "Here there is no
why.") Only once did a slightly more sympathetic guard confess to a real
reason. If they are lax, contraband seeps in, and then the doorkeepers are
blamed.

Once I had stripped my purse of all but a few amenities, and put everything in the visitor's outhouse locker room, I went through the metal de-
tector (of course setting it off), and eventually, got my hand stamped with
invisible ink. (I made the mistake of wearing elaborate boots only once; it
took five minutes getting them off and on again.)

One door opens, letting you in to show your hand stamp under a special
light, then it closes and another opens. I'm in! It's February, and a few, strag-
gly bits of grass and garden lie between me and the door to a long green
linoleum corridor called "Main Street."

A kindly, shambling man gives me an orientation: There are 67,000 inmates in New York State in 68 facilities. Most of the 941 prisoners now
here come from one of the five boroughs of New York City. Most have been
serving long sentences in maximum-security prisons. Being in this unit is a
sign—but not a guarantee—that parole is in sight.

The rules for volunteers are listed, and I must sign that I have read them. I must not give my address or phone number to anyone. No communication outside the class. There's an elaborate document about sexual harassment of prisoners by volunteers or staff, which as far as I can see boils down to no touching of any kind. No provocative clothing, like halter tops, miniskirts, plunging necklines, wrap around skirts. Nothing transparent. No heavy metal outfits or doo rags or T-shirts with provocative slogans on them, for example expressing racial hatred or "promoting crime, drugs, alcohol, or sadistic/violent, satanic, sexual, pornographic, vulgar, gang-related references."

The presumption is that anything might set a prisoner off. Vices beckon and all are forbidden. I register something I haven't thought about before: Freedom means you can have vices and bad habits and can reveal bad thoughts. Life here is pent up in ways that multiply as I make my way in. How conscious is the goal to punish through the humiliation of hundreds of small, meaningless rules and through an endless denial of all indulgences? The evidence certainly pointed to a constant effort to maintain discomfort at all times. I later learned that there is no air conditioning in the sweltering dorms in summer. The equipment is there, inmates told me, but the administration refuses to hook it up.

By the end, I get the message. These are criminals; most of them have been armed and violent; most of them would do drugs or drink or have sex or express rage if given half the chance; some of them are killers. Make no mistake, innocent lady volunteer. Like the guard at the gate says, "This is a prison."

Now we go to the classroom, which is dreary. The DVD monitor is locked up; the DVD player I must bring each time from the duty officer is for the moment without a remote. The room is much too bright to show films. ("Can I darken the room?" "Of course not!" "Can I cluster the chairs close together around the monitor?" "Of course not!")

All these months I've tried to imagine this situation. Who am I, here, and who are they? What voice will I have? Will I understand their voices? I interrogated several of the teaching assistants who have already worked here. One warned me that my being a woman is a distinct disadvantage. They will associate me, he thinks, with naggy high school teachers. From this conversation, I take away a new anxiety that I will remind them of an earlier stage of unfreedom.

The twelve men filter in. Though they dip in and out of the classroom, as far as I can tell, the group is eleven African Americans and one Hispanic, ranging in age from thirty to fifty. They are friendly, a few elaborately polite and happy to help sort out the mess, set up chairs. They are used to this level of chaos, both patient and gracious.

I simply start in. The voice I turn out to have is my own voice—loud, rhetorical, passionate, dramatic. I make no effort to imagine how to sound like them or to tailor my words to what I imagine they will understand or approve. On the spur of that terrifying moment, I decide that respect and professional distance lie in offering whatever it is I have in my own lingo. They can decide, then, to take it or leave it.

One of the students, Jonno, the Hispanic guy, remarks somewhat aggressively that I like to talk. I think to myself, "That one is going to be trouble." Several are silent, and that worries me, too. One in particular seems to me to be standing on his dignity, remote. I can only persuade him of my respect through my limited means, my eagerness, my clear devotion to the work at hand. If that's uncool, so be it. But at least the schoolmarm I am not. I quickly sense that my colleague's analysis was a mistake, perhaps a sexist assumption. My femaleness is obviously going to matter—I'm beginning to think it may even help me—but much more is at stake here. People in this room have their own urgent needs, their own eagerness that matches mine.

On that first day, there is one small confrontation, a mini-drama about gender and race. Several students call me "Miss Ann." Since my name is indeed Ann, it might seem that no harm is meant. I need only request that they drop the "Miss." However, mainly by luck, I happen to know that "Miss Ann" is a generic term used by black maids for the white ladies whose houses they clean and whose peculiarities they must endure. I say to the class, "Please don't call me Miss Ann. I know who Miss Ann is and this is *not* me." Several look startled. (We are to surprise each other constantly in the course of the semester.) They were so sure that a knavish speech would sleep in a foolish ear. Now they turn new eyes on me; they honor my knowledge with a few warm smiles and winks. The first fine filament of mutual regard. We're off!

I show Spike Lee's *Crooklyn*, and they are touched and delighted, some remembering playing those same street games in their own Brooklyn childhoods. We examine how this perfect coming of age story is put together, and I introduce and spell "*Bildungsroman*," a term Jonno eats whole and feeds back repeatedly.

The Class

The second class is a setback. There are endless technical difficulties before I can show them Hayao Miyazaki's *Spirited Away*, one of the most brilliant evocations of childhood I've ever seen. But it is animated and some suspect they are being patronized. It doesn't help that the deputy checks in and says, "What's this? Kiddie cartoons in college?" Still, a few like it, succumb to its weird magic.

I want them to see the fears of childhood and the gathering power the child has to do what's necessary in a world full of monstrous dangers and often equally mysterious helping figures. I am later to learn about some terrifying childhoods here, but this film is too strange. It fails to resonate. And because of all the technical problems, we have no time to mine the material.

The class really gets going in week three. I show the documentary, *Muhammad Ali: When We Were Kings*, about Ali's great victory over George Foreman in Zaire. I expect these students to adulate Ali and celebrate how he dances and dodges, always setting his own terms. And they do. Tyrone is particularly moved, and Lamar has a political analysis of the meaning to the black community of Ali's refusal to serve in the white colonial war in Vietnam.

The film is in love with Ali, and we all feel it. His beauty, his wit, the poignancy of his braggadocio and anxiety before the fight. But near the end of the class, Jonno says: "I was a boxer. I beat a lot of people. I was really good." The others look skeptical or indulgent. Jonno is tough and bellicose but also short. Then he goes on, "but then I beat a man to death twenty-five years ago. I'm a kind person, but when you're angry you forget they're a person. I'm not sure I want to go along with this boxer-hero thing." Real doubt, neither righteous nor pat.

The class takes a rhythmic pause, the former momentum arrested. I say I'm surprised but also interested to hear this criticism of officially accepted violence. Our time is almost up, but in those last moments, the question of violence, and how to think about it, is before us. Is violence simply human nature—nothing to be done about it? Is there a continuum between the worship of the strongest, toughest man in the world and what Jonno did one dark night? Some think yes, while others reject that kind of slippery slope thinking. Rival moral systems collide. What makes a hero? Does one need them?

Almost everyone is engaged now. There's a shared understanding that the course is going to be about things that are difficult, that matter, that connect with personal experiences they may or may not want to discuss openly.

The next film is *My Son the Fanatic*, taken from a short story by my favorite screenwriter, Hanif Kureishi. He can be relied on to set things going among people, to face the often regrettable truth about what one really feels ("my wife is ugly") and what one also is capable of feeling ("I feel sorry for my wife"). I love the film and am apprehensive about what they will think about this story of a humiliated but often decent Indian taxi driver in a bitter north England city, a convert to the pleasures the West offers—a mistress, jazz, good scotch, a sort of freedom from the family—but weighed down by a son disgusted by his father's English life, by English racism, and eager to invent a strict Muslim self to counter this immigrant humiliation he shares with his father.

I needn't have worried. And it is at this point in the course that I abandon any thought of hand-holding or patiently bringing people along. No. They have seen so much in the film. Jonno is an immigrant from Ecuador and knows all about it. And Harry moves right into an analysis of globalization and the complex economics of immigration policy. The forms of racism the film explores, subtle and unsubtle, are duly noted and the film's brilliance much praised. Though we argue loudly and intensely about point of view and where the film's center of gravity lies, all recognize a key moment in the father's plea to his son: "There is more than one way to be a good man."

So now we are in the thick of it—manhood and its various manifestations. How to be manly is a central question for every single person in the room. In his first paper, beautiful, restless Clayton, mesmerized by movies but drifty during discussions, writes that he can't be a man because he isn't in charge of a family; instead, at thirty, he's dependent like a child. I confront him about this idea and ask his permission to argue with him about it as part of class.

I don't think my passionate deconstruction of the romance of the *pater familias*—an ideal type who rules, takes care of his woman and children, and needs nothing from others—makes much of an impression on Clayton. He is committed to this terrible shame he feels, and my abstract ideas could never be enough to talk him out of it. And maybe he knows himself, is a critic of his own childishness. But others in the class are intrigued by my rejection of shame as simply what they all deserve. I'm arguing that outside and inside prison, there's a huge engine chugging out humiliation, like Clayton's feelings of failure, and we begin to discuss humiliation openly and ways one might resist feeling bad. "I know in all your classes and workshops you're being taught to take responsibility for what you've done, and I'm not saying no to that. But responsibility is different from shame. Shame rebounds. It often leads to shaming someone else. Being endlessly humiliated by rules and constraints and small injustices—how does it help? Best to see the endless tale of one's badness as an inadequate story, meant to make you feel like a worm. Okay, take responsibility, but also move on. Everyone is dependent; total independence is a myth. Outside, some men can pretend this isn't true; inside, you're reminded every day that you are under others' control, and that you need others to survive. Inside or out, dependency is the human condition."

This hectoring lecture hasn't convinced anyone, but quiet Elijah is taking it all in, nodding, looking excited about this demanding act of analysis. With my pontificating, we've arrived in the realm of Big Ideas. Everyone is listening, reserving judgment, registering doubt, considering whether or not any of this critique of humiliation actually applies to him.

The next two films are war films, In the Valley of Elah and The Hurt Locker. Now manhood takes a terrible hit. The son in Elah is utterly destroyed by the macho brutality of the Iraq War. He becomes a monster, and his equally blighted mates kill him for no particular reason. They're drunk, and have lost all moral compass. In The Hurt Locker, the hero defuses bombs. (Again, the scene is Iraq.) He is better at it than anyone else, taking insane risks. As we come to know him, we understand that he is addicted to danger and can never go home again. His constant return to Iraq is an expression of emptiness and desperation.

By now everyone gets it. I've put these films here to criticize the ideal of the lone wolf, the hero, the manly fighter. In Elah there's a moment of nostalgia for an earlier war when the father fought heroically. But Iraq is something else. We're lost; we need help; the hero has collapsed and become a monster. The lonely hero who defuses bombs is in fact a suicide in disguise.

I know that all this is unlikely to make a dent in the essentialist views of manhood and womanhood that often seem to prevail in the room. But these are belief systems with big cracks in them. Elijah, Harry, David, and Phillip have been working on themselves for a long time, self-consciously cultivating inner calm and wisdom. A different idea about manhood might be a lifeline. Who knows? Since they are near the end of their terms, the question of how to be a free adult outside (and how to avoid returning here) is in the air every minute. In a long teaching life, I have rarely encountered students with such intense motivation.

After each class, Marcus lingers. He never talks in class. He requires a private exchange. At first I balk at this, then think "why not?" He tells me he was the baby in a middle-class family, the indulged, spoiled one. He's soft all over and I can see the cosseted, darling baby he must have been. Soon up for parole, Marcus has been inside eighteen years for armed robbery (but no one was shot, he hastens to say). Trouble is, this is his second long prison term. In fact, he reluctantly acknowledges, he has spent most of his adult life in prison.

He has no intention of writing the four papers I'm assigning. Free as these assignments are, they are not free enough for Marcus. He has embarked on a long piece describing how deeply envious he is of his friends, now lawyers, professors, basketball players, while he has been stuck all these years, arrested.

The piece interests me. Again, the theme is shame. He remembers scenes from his brief, free life like a *halluciné*. He regrets not taking that stupid, boring job. Why didn't he seduce that woman who had a brilliant career and might have supported him? Instead, he always succumbed to the allure of the street. He lists what he briefly had without irony or self-criticism: money, fabulous clothes, lots of beautiful women. In his world, everyone agrees that the regular jobs available are a foolish waste of time—low paying, humiliating dead ends. The man worthy of respect lives in an entirely different economic system. After his first fifteen-year term, Marcus had returned to the glamour of hustling almost immediately.

"So," I ask him, "why do you think you'll resist the siren this time?" "I've found Christ." We contemplate this answer together for a long, sober minute. "And do you think Christ will be enough?" (I put no ironic spin on this question; I am feeling alarmed and deadly serious.) Again, a contemplative pause: "I don't know."

The next film was to be *Brokeback Mountain* but the deputy—for the most part a liberal and constructive guy—had rejected it for its homosexual love scenes, telling me, "Someone performing a homosexual act could claim he learned it in class." (I laughed, but this did no good.) I substitute a documentary I love, *The Times of Harvey Milk*. I announce to the class that at a certain point in this film, I always cry, not when the gay town supervisor Harvey Milk is shot but when the whole of San Francisco pours down the streets to grieve together, holding candles. Sure enough, the candles appear and I cry.

Everyone is impressed. I am still mourning this man. I am clearly devastated. What to make of this solidarity with a pouf, a fruit, someone so flagrantly public about not being a regular man? This is the class that establishes the wildness of the rest of the semester. We completely disagree, but there appears to be no price to pay. We are all yelling together. Homophobia meets resistance. Harry, my sophisticated autodidact who has read a great deal, startles me by saying "We call the police faggots to humiliate them, to bring them down a peg." Humiliation: Our theme again.

I go into a long explanation about how saying "faggot" affirms the world of contempt and unfreedom, how it, too, is a form of policing, to be avoided at all costs. Harry pays no attention to these arguments; he's not remotely convinced. Then I do something I've never done in a classroom before. I shout, "Harry, simply stop it! Never call someone, anyone, a faggot again!"

Everyone skips a beat. I realize how much trust we have already established because they recognize this as passion, not one more example of bossing prisoners around. Everyone goes berserk. Jonno shrieks that homosexuals are dangerous because they're too emotional, which makes everyone laugh because no one in the class is more emotional than hellion Jonno, ever proud of his Latin temperament. Elijah looks wise as ever. Okay. The word faggot is finished. Even Harry shrugs an acknowledgment. I win, at least for now, partly because they have come to believe I'll listen, am willing to not win at least some of the time. Wherever each one stands, we are all deeply moved by Harvey Milk's élan. Death for this lovable faggot is entirely wrong; the freak is the straight guy, the killer.

The class is over. Everyone leaves, except as always, Marcus. Then the dignified and usually silent David returns and asks for a private word. Reluctantly, Marcus steps out into the hall. "I just wanted to thank you for this film and this discussion. I'm gay and you can see what hell it is in here. Thank you." And he's gone. Now I have some reason to hope that whatever else happens after this, I haven't wasted my time and theirs. David's thank you makes me happy.

We finish up manhood with *Bad Day at Black Rock*, that perfect Sturges anti-Western, and the British *Dirty Pretty Things*, by the great Stephen Frears. The Western is an occasion to do some serious film criticism. We listen to film critic Dana Polan's commentary, analyze shots, theorize about the decay of a once idealized, heroic West. The good guy (Spencer Tracy), still a hero, bears the damage of war and the melancholy of the returning soldier (we have read Hemingway's "Soldier's Home"). This real man who has seen terrible violence is peaceable as long as possible and is finally violent only to save his life. Tracy is a complex, soulful hero who wins spectacularly. Once again, we discuss the centrality of this figure in our own culture, the good man who fights. His dignity requires no outward show. He cannot be humiliated. The shots of male groupings—there's only one woman, briefly, in the film—are gorgeous, grand Western tableaux, filled with rotten or lost men who no longer fit the heroic frame of earth and sky.

The theme of the good man who is violent in a bad world carries over to *Dirty Pretty Things*, where the mournful, illegal Nigerian immigrant breaks the law to do the right thing. Is it okay to break the law? Is part of the dream of heroism making one's own rules? Jonno from Ecuador says all these immigrants should have just stayed home. But Harry says that Western imperialism has ruined their homes, making everyone poor. Immigrants leave to survive; they become illegal while the real criminals, the imperialists, go scot-free. Some people are definitely drifting off at this point in the discussion, but Elijah the Silent is nodding vigorously. It's my opinion, though I have no direct evidence, that he gets everything.

Both films are riveting because they establish fully realized, dangerous worlds where heroes we love struggle to survive violence and racism. At one point I turn from the corner I sit in, the worst viewing position in the room with the most glare and reflection on the screen, and look at this small audience. They are rapt, every face still and at full attention. Whatever else, I know they are enjoying this—though early in the course, Harry said that he wondered if perhaps they watch too much TV, a form of narcolepsy. As every teacher who shows films knows, the class is dazed when the lights go up. It's always hard to get students to turn an analytic eye on what so mesmerized them the moment before. I worry about how much remains after the flickering glow fades but am reassured when the films start showing up in their papers and as points of reference in our discussions. The trance state may be a problem as well as a pleasure, but our eagerness to talk, or more accurately, to argue, seems to trump somnolence.

As we've been working through manhood, a parallel drama has developed. I've read their first writing—genre unspecified, length unspecified—mostly about childhood. Up from the usual student ruck, one brilliant and elegant piece appears—by Carl. He has a sharp critical mind judging from his remarks in class, but surely this paper is too good, too shaped, too literary. But why doubt this clever fellow, who could do well with even a few transcriptions of his remarks in class? My wish is to trust and admire him.

I mention my surprise to the deputy during our weekly encounter. I ask, could it be plagiarism? But they have no access to the Internet. "They call a friend who uses the Internet and then mails them the piece." I look surprised at the intricacy of this ruse and the Dep. laughs at me. "What do you expect? They're criminals!" We are laughing, but when he asks me the inmate's name, suddenly I decide to stall. "Let me investigate first." Carl will soon be up for parole. I'm horrified to recognize that I could do real damage here, become one of the cogs in the wheel of punishment.

At home, I type the most literary, sophisticated phrase from Carl's paper into Google, and the answer comes up at once: He has copied a published piece word for word.

So now what? Plagiarism is a serious offense that can get a university student expelled. Because of the specificity—and perhaps oddity—of my assignments, I've discovered only two plagiarists in forty years of teaching. How serious do I think this is? I discover that I think it is very serious, a self-defeating, foolish form of cleverness. But now that I am both dupe and witness, I also discover that I am unclear about my own attitude to the rules. Is it lying I object to? Theft of intellectual property? Theft is nothing new in the prison (I find it comic that inmates keep telling me to mind my purse), but how to handle this, my own case?

I see two possibilities. I can take Carl aside, tell him that at the college he would immediately fail the course and might well be asked to leave school, and tell him why people feel this is a serious matter, a break of trust within a community. Or I can bring the whole thing up in class, assume that this is a group tragedy, that anyone might be tempted to plagiarize, that there is something important for us all to discuss here.

I worry over this for two weeks, asking advice from friends who sink as fast as I do in the ambiguities of this power relationship. On the one hand, I would be treating this event as a private matter, not connected to the life of the group—a safe separation, probably having little effect on Carl. On the other hand, I would be humiliating him in public, just the thing I hate most about the prison regime—and the rule of racism beyond it.

As the group solidifies and the classes become more and more exciting, I begin to think we can handle this crisis together. I'm confident that the group will keep Carl's secret. I tell the class what happened, read them the "statement on plagiarism" (which I should have given them as part of my syllabus in the beginning), and explain why plagiarism damages both the perp and the class.

Carl makes a faint denial, which I ignore. Then an interesting thing happens. Rodney speaks up, and at some length. Rodney has been my techie, helping me deal with the wayward DVD player each week, telling me how to find batteries when someone has stolen them out of the remote to run a clandestine tattoo machine. But of all the students in the class, he has been the most skeptical. I early identified him as the one most likely to call

all of my enthusiasms girlish bunk. I considered going on the defensive, then decided here was an expression of freedom, the freedom to doubt the people they send to fix you up. I have been trying to accept without rancor his choice to undercut me with irony or mild scorn whenever he feels like it. I have been letting him know I respect his doubt, am willing to consider his disparagements as possibly useful interventions—or at least critiques I might well deserve.

He says, "Why you bring this up in front of the whole class? He can't learn anything this way. Why you don't talk to him alone, explain to him? You shaming him here. This don't help nobody."

I am deeply gratified to have this principled opposition get so fully expressed in my classroom. Without taking any credit for Rodney's fine character and with all my continuing self-doubt, at this moment I feel the class is a success. Again careful not to go on the defensive, I say that I had considered Rodney's position but had decided this was a group matter. No one wants Carl's chances at parole endangered, so this is a private discussion; we would work through this question by ourselves. Then I ask Rodney what he thinks we should do next. "Talk to the man privately."

I give the class a break and sit down with Carl in the empty classroom. "Why bother to cheat when the assignment was liberty hall? You didn't need to write more than one paragraph."

"I was busy with my parole application and couldn't get to it. And you said you didn't accept late papers."

I'm stunned. I've been telling students this for years: "We use papers as the basis for discussion, so no late papers—ever." How could I say such a stupid thing to these prisoners who have zero control over their time or their movements to computer room or library? In fact, why make a drop-dead rule like this for any of my students? Such a rule is born to be broken. And of course when people break it, I usually listen to their reasons and read their papers anyway, making a note: "Late." I try to project a double image, both strict and reasonable, a boundary setter, but one who can be flexible, fair.

But how can Carl know that he can negotiate with me, when the rules in the prison where he has lived for many years are so arbitrary and capricious? He has suffered from the rule of law and is justifiably wary and cagey. Though writing a brief paper would have taken less time than typing the longer stolen piece, for Carl, subterfuge feels better, safe. I apologize and resolve never again to declare an absolute deadline—here or anywhere.

But the problem with Carl doesn't disappear with my contrition. Surely he needs to learn that he can get to yes without lies or violence. He will need new strategies for dealing with the galling rules he will encounter outside. Letting him off the hook won't necessarily help him.

I'm pretty sure now, though, that I have made a mistake. It's not as if the world outside will reward Carl for innocence and goodness. He has to go back to the scene of stress and desperation that he came from, only this time he's a felon with most job opportunities off limits—unless he lies, and doesn't get caught. In the nineteenth century, prison was meant to discipline the inmate, train him to join the productive laboring classes. But now, in America, prison is a recessive enclave, a race-bound cul-de-sac. Grotesquely, monstrously, almost all the hundreds of inmates here are African American. The very few whites look strung out, hollow-eyed. Covered with tattoos and scars, they are the exceptions that prove the rule.

Of course, through self-conscious change and creativity—and with luck and a little help from their friends—some will find their way. But, talking to Carl, I feel the boundaries of race and class pinching at his quick heels. Almost inevitably, if he does get a job he will continue to be supervised, micromanaged, routinely humiliated, hence the constant interest of the street, of living outside the law. Outside, cheating might well feel like freedom, but with the irony that incarceration can be the ending.

Maybe I can save something from this catastrophe, offer Carl some practical protection? I can't help him save face, now that everyone knows, but I have useful information. "Carl," I tell him urgently, "surveillance has changed since you came inside twenty years ago. It took me three seconds on Google to find the source of your piece. Also, felons are now listed on the Internet." I see that this is interesting news and it registers.

When we're finished talking, I go out into the long corridor to bring back the others. They are all sitting there on narrow wooden benches against the wall, uncharacteristically silent and looking worried. This has been a big event and its meanings will keep evolving with the course.

As the semester winds along, Rodney's judgment that Carl is hopelessly shamed seems right. He rarely speaks now and has a haunted look. Exposure has been a trauma. Now I'm forced to consider that old question about the criminal justice system: Does the prisoner learn and change from the shock and shame of chastisement? The kind but constantly hectoring counselors I meet here think they are helping, but are they? I have no idea. I can hear Foucault laughing.

In any case, the group spirit seems to have survived this scary episode. Trust in me as primarily well-intentioned seems to hold. I am allowed my provocations, and people seem to know no harm will come to them if, like Rodney, they call me out, which they often do.

Carl writes two papers to substitute for the plagiarized one. The first is empty rhetoric about manhood. Man is tender; man is tough; man protects his womanfolk, etc., etc. The second paper is in another voice entirely. Here he tells in simple, eloquent language how his mother died, how angry he was, how rage and lawlessness ruled his life, how he killed a man in a quarrel over a gold chain, how he has tried to overcome his rage during these decades in prison.

The disassociation revealed in the gap between the two papers unnerves me. I tell him my opinion that the two papers come from different places in himself. How does he put such different stories together? Or, more simply, does he see that these are very different styles of writing? No real reaction or acknowledgment. Now it's clear that I am in way over my head. I have no idea what I am messing with or if I am doing harm. First do no harm. I leave Carl alone from that day on, weaving him into discussion normally as if all is well. But I do not really think all is well, and I now know my mistake with him is the least of his worries.

I have a reassuring counterexample of changing voices in Harry. His first paper makes me laugh out loud, then flood with sympathy. The autodidact is so brave and at the same time so disadvantaged: "Any attempts to examine manhood would also include exploring axiology, deontology, and praxicology. . . ." "I think that the son's dislike of his father's sequacious position . . . etc." I spend some time with my dictionary and make a note in the margin: "A position can't be sequacious."

What to do? There are some really interesting things in Harry's paper; he's the most sophisticated and well-read thinker in the room by far. Perhaps I need to persuade him that he doesn't need to impress me. But I decide to take another, more respectful tack. We sit down and I tell him it's a question of aesthetics (big word), of style (translation). Those long words in strings clog his prose and don't communicate all that well. I remind him of the story we read by Hemingway, and we discuss the historical development of American plain style. "Hardly anyone aspires to write like Hemingway these days," I say, "but use those long words sparingly; they go further that way." To my delight, his next paper is different, a limpid description of his early life, the appeal of the street, his first encounters with violence. He's still offering ideas, interpretations, generalizations, but the change is a triumph. I congratulate him.

We barrel into the last section of the course, Womanhood. The first film in the set is *Thelma and Louise*. Amazing how well this roady movie for women has held up. Its indictment of men is relentless, broad, and shameless. Jonno says, "The film isn't really fair to men, is it?" We all laugh at this understatement, but everyone seems to get the point of piling it on; what's more, they recognize the endless parade of male predators who ultimately bring down Thelma and Louise. Several see the male behavior in the film as simply realistic, things they themselves have done or seen done. I'm nonplussed by this reading of the film as realism. While I'm grateful for their lack of defensiveness, I begin to wonder if their untroubled acceptance of the film's events means they have no real criticism of all this egregious sexist behavior. Has the film's marvelous attack on macho, oppressive men failed to register? As the class ends, I remain uncertain.

The next week brings these questions back: *North Country*. This film is an exhaustive, faithful representation of how sexual harassment worked at a mine in Minnesota where a few women were hired for the first time, breaking the gender barrier. Once again, the indictments of men's unfairness and cruelty to women pile up. This time though, there's no playful exaggeration, no way to crack a smile as the heroine is raped, threatened, blamed as the problem, never recognized as the victim. The film is harrowing and the class is shocked. We're all on the side of the much-abused heroine when she finally wins in court. Several say they had no idea what this sexual harassment thing was all about; they consider themselves instructed, their consciousness raised.

Still, I am discovering how little I have dented their confident essentialism: men are men and women are women. Who am I to directly confront such a well-documented belief? The films themselves give quite mixed messages about this very matter. Gender may indeed be unstable as I occasionally point out, but they can easily counter that the difference keeps reasserting itself. Since I have never ever said the word "feminism" in order to avoid their dismissing me, I say nothing.

The next film is *Speakout: I Had an Abortion*. I love this humble documentary for how it shows that feelings about abortion are not particularly private. Historical context dictates emotions: In the 1950s, fear of disgraceful pregnancy, followed after the abortion by joy and relief. But by the 1980s, after years of backlash, the abortion decision is surrounded by anguish, guilt, doubt. Again, the men seem intrigued. Here is a different point of view, new news about the suffering of women. The stories about men running away from responsibility or accusing their pregnant girlfriends of sleeping around ring ominously true to the class. Rape stories, too, are no surprise.

But now Lamar makes an intervention which changes things here at the end of the course. Since the Harvey Milk episode, when he gave me a high five after the class, we've been friendly—a quiet feeling of camaraderie. We have already weathered an intense exchange over a story by Edward P. Jones, "An Orange Line Train to Ballston." I had said that dreadlocks in the story meant separation, independence, even rebellion and Lamar was furious. "That's what the parole board thinks. You better fix your hair before you go up." He attacked my inference that dreads mean rebellion. Maybe once upon a time; but now it's a style anyone might want. This reading of natty hair as a sign of aggression is nothing more than white fear of black men. I backed down completely. How had I allowed myself to forget the racist themes entangled in hair? Lamar was angry, and I learned from this anger, retreating with an apology he graciously accepted.

But now, after three weeks of films about the wrongs done to women, Lamar is angry in another way. "If my sister came home and said she was raped she better have a lot of scratches and bruises to prove it." In response, I try everything: Does this mean you think your sister asked for it, or liked it, if she doesn't show signs of being beaten up? Should she risk her life to avoid rape? And, more generally, what if she does like sex? Is that, too, a fault? I go into the double standard, and tell the old war stories about raped women needing witnesses and being blamed or disbelieved. Nothing works. Nobody joins in. Several have written papers about how the new, modern working girl has lost her maternal softness, her preciousness and charm. Implicit in all this is an indictment of female freedom. They're suspicious of it and feel betrayed. Their wives and girlfriends are outside while they are immured here. The women they praise, often poetically, are their endlessly self-sacrificing mothers.

Feminist that I am, I don't know what to do with this great weight of the group's shared experience and opinion. Lamar has a look on his face I've come to know. He is adamant and tremendously strong. I retire from the field, vanquished, and the class about abortion is over.

The next week I get an unexpected helping hand from the film *Iron Jawed Angels*. Hilary Swank plays Alice Paul, the suffragette who led the militants to victory with marches, pickets of the White House, and (here graphically depicted) prison hunger strikes. It's a galvanizing piece of feminist propaganda, historically faithful as far as public events go. The fact that women only got the vote in 1920, decades after black men, turns out to be new information. Now that we've moved off sex, that most ragged part of the self, suddenly the class is full of perfect, eager students asking questions about the history of the women's movement, really curious about this struggle that they are learning today has been going on for more than a hundred and fifty years. They ask for more and more detail. What is the women's movement like now? What's the problem, now that they have the vote? Disarmed and delighted by the energy they are bringing to these questions so central to my own life, I do what I have sworn not to do: I come out as a feminist, and what's more, as a feminist activist. Pandemonium! Phillip is accusatory. "Why didn't you tell us? Why didn't you teach us about this stuff?" But he is quick; a knowing look spreads over his face. "Oh, you *have* been teaching us about this stuff."

My cover blown, I wonder what difference it will make to the aftermath. Will what lingers in their memories be altered by this new knowledge that I have been a feminist mole in the classroom? Of course I will never know. I must think about whether or not to make this admission when, as I've already decided, I will teach here again.

The last class and the last film: *Pray the Devil Back to Hell*, a documentary about how Liberian women surrounded their parliament building and wouldn't let the all-male negotiators out, or any food in, until both sides agreed to sign a peace treaty to end Liberia's long civil war. Women heroes this time, and again radical, righteous lawbreakers. Does heroism look different when women do it? Here, there's a magnificent leader, but no violence, and the victory belongs to a collective.

But none of these thoughts get much play; this is the last class and the main thing on my mind is the pain of separation. I'm feeling it acutely, and I'm guessing maybe they are, too. I ask them about what they'll take away from all this, and of course this is the awful, teacherly kind of question no one can answer. But we're relaxed, chummy, a band that has been through a lot together. I recount my dream of the night before. The whole class was in the dream; I gave them all lots to eat, something that is absolutely forbidden, ("Can I bring in popcorn for the movies?" "Of course not!"); and then I left them, coming back too late to have a discussion. It was a nightmare about bad teaching and bad timing. "No," cries Jonno, "You were giving us food for thought." I'm so delighted. Our wild Dr. Freud has a beautiful interpretation of my dream. (Once Jonno said the class was like Ethiopia. I drew a blank, then took a leap: "Do you mean 'Utopia'?" Indeed, that was it.)

Elijah the Silent nods vigorously. Most of the few remarks he has made during the semester have been about numerology and apocryphal biblical texts. His belt is incised with occult symbols and mystical numbers, and he has corrected me several times about biblical references in the stories we've read. He's a scholar, and like me, he has a complex belief system that shapes his life. Looking at him fondly, I realize how much I myself have changed. Now all belief systems run together; they are what get you through the night. Belief in feminism, belief in Christ, belief in the sacredness of women (Clayton says they are as pure and perfect as water) and in women's perfidy, private moral systems, and dreams of renewal, conversion, redemption—all this is both invented and utterly real. Our beliefs are compelling; their force gives shape to the self and soothes it in times of suffering. I see our lives through a reverse telescope, hear a sort of distant din, the echo of the words we've said, the fights we've had. A dizziness comes over me from being so connected to the mental life of others.

Evaluations

I hand out two sets of anonymous evaluations, my private questions and the college's multiple choice. Later, when I read them, of course I'm gratified. Though they've made some helpful suggestions I plan to follow in the future, there's not a single negative response. They learned; they enjoyed; they felt heard; they really expressed themselves. Phillip has chosen to sign his form; he wants me to know this is him: "For three and a half hours every week, it was like not being in prison."

Since this is exactly what I most want to hear, all this praise backs up on me. They are more dependent on my good will than any students I've ever had. Phillip is particularly brilliant at the art of pleasing. Early in the course he praised one of the other teachers, a young artist I also like and admire. Then a worried look crossed his face. "But of course your class is the best." I didn't want him to have to say this, but he felt he had to. Being seen as good is the currency here. These students have been handpicked; they are good at being good. I wish I could signal to them that I don't require this much compliance, but perhaps—certainly since the Carl incident—they assume I do. And maybe, at some level, they are right. During my one visit to the Criminal Mind class, I saw students so angry and depressed they could barely speak. I have no idea how I would teach such openly angry, unwilling students.

My class has been very different. I have been privileged to work with people on the move inside themselves, clever strategists in a bad situation, bearing up under the stream of insult that is prison life. How earnestly I admire these men—their struggles, their patience, their solutions. Somehow, after years and years, they have kept themselves truly alive.

Graduation

As the last class ends they remind me that in three weeks there's to be a graduation ceremony. Everyone who has earned a high school equivalency degree or successfully completed a college class is to be honored in front of family and friends. The college hires a car and takes a bunch of us teachers out. The gate is as horrific as ever, and this time there's a crowd of visitors to witness the usual scouring of my purse.

We file into a big, bright common room and sit at tables. Everyone is dressed up and looks great. After a long wait, to which the people in this room are inured, the graduates file in to a swelling recording (amazing!) of "Pomp and Circumstance." The twenty-five high school graduates, who seem to be mostly in their twenties and thirties, are wearing bright red gowns with tasseled mortar boards to match, and our students, the college group, are elegantly dressed in bright colors or in white shirts and ties. The drab green they are always required to wear is gone for today. ("Green's not my color," Jonno once remarked sadly.)

We teachers are jumping around, straining to find our guys and waving. We get smiles and nods back, but everyone is very serious, very dignified. There are speeches, of course, including a nice one from the Dep. about how hard it is to study consistently in a prison environment and what an achievement this is.

When it's over, to our surprise, a rather good meal is served and it seems the rules about touching are suspended: We get to hug everybody. Carl, giving me his wary eye, introduces me to a pretty wife. I meet Rodney's wife and mother. I congratulate a mother who screamed when her son's name was called and his tassel moved from right to left, "That's my son!" The Dep. turns out to play vibes and several musicians join him. "No alcohol?" I twit him. "Of course not." It's a happy room.

I end up sitting at a table with Tyrone who has written his first poem for the course (a marvelous outpouring, "Am I a man?"). We're both high on the day, and he thanks me for the course, tells me he loved it. As always, my own sense of irony undercuts my enthusiasm for how well the course seems to have gone. I can't resist the promptings of my usual bad angel: "But Tyrone, do you think you learned anything?" His reaction is an important experience, a missing piece in my puzzle. He is clearly insulted. How could I ask him such a question? It's as if I'd slapped him. To doubt that the class is of last-ing value to him is, in effect, to doubt him, to cast mud on all those thrilling weeks together. I hasten to apologize; we hug.

A few years ago, one of the associate deans at the college went to a retreat and got hipped on the idea that we should do "outcome studies." The whole world was questioning the value (particularly monetary) of a liberal educa-tion ("Express Yourself," indeed!), and we were to respond to these doubts, find quantifiable ways to measure learning—and more ominously, failure to learn.

I don't know how it could be proven that these prisoners have learned something that will endure and be useful to them. Though I think that each week was momentous, revelatory, this is a common teacher's delusion. Sit in the back of your own classroom sometime—as I have—and discover how far away the teacher and her enthusiasms can be. There's no knowing where what we've said and been able to think will end up in the big, changing land-scapes of these students' tumultuous lives. The larger picture they will enter outside will push the material we've shared every which way.

But Tyrone was so sure it had all made a difference. On the evaluations they mentioned bits of new knowledge—several described with enthusi-asm those militant suffragettes!—and said that, yes, they had explored new ideas and learned how to look critically at movies. Of course we teachers fantasized how one might give them much more. The Good Prison would be a self-sustaining community with meaningful work and radical education. But that wasn't the prison we were working in. Perhaps it was defensiveness before my sophisticated friends with their charges of adventure tourism that created a divide I could not easily close: Foucault's take on prisons has long been my own—but that's no reason to insult Tyrone.

The Debate

In the course of the semester, the college debate team met the prison debate team. Harry is one of the stars of the prison team, which has never been defeated. Resolved: "The government should not finance higher education in prisons." The poor college students are stuck with the affirmative. What to do? They would never argue, as the Bush administration argued, that prison-ers are supposed to suffer. No perks for miscreants. These are well-educated, liberal college students, the critics of morally compromised enlightenment institutions like prisons. So they try to argue that the available education is tainted by the system, corrupt, and ultimately misleading. You can't dismantle the master's house with the master's tools, and so on. No school in prison means no indoctrination, no conformity, freedom from the man.

The prisoners are amused. (Harry thinks they are misquoting Foucault). They wipe the floor with the college team. It isn't just that the numbers are powerful—education cuts recidivism in half—but the inmates go well beyond claims that a prison education would make them into docile good boys who won't endanger anyone or return to prison. They want to be citizens, to join the debates of their times. Their rebellions so far have been forms of alienation. Now they want in. The system might be bad—all those prison-like, failing schools in black neighborhoods—but they want to be players, to have what the college students have—critique, Internet, and all.

At graduation, I miss Jonno. I ask around. "Yeah," says Rodney with his usual playful derision, "Where's your favorite?" (I thought I had hidden this well, but observant students always know). I tell him that by the end of the class he, Rodney, had become one of my favorites, too—the simple truth—and he seems to believe me for once. He tells me that Jonno, who was in for twenty-five years, has been released (joy!)—but was instantly deported to his native Ecuador. Was he an illegal alien all those years inside? Can they simply deport a foreign-born felon, whatever his status? Freedom had come to mean instant exile. I try to picture Jonno, whose parents have died, being suddenly landed "home" after twenty-five years of both toughness and intense inner struggle. His high spirits and vociferous arguments linger. I send him a mental message for travelers: However hard this is, may new happiness overcome regret.

Postscript: All names have been changed. Later, Carl got into a fight and, just before his parole date, was sent back to maximum security upstate. Marcus, too, went into solitary and back to a maximum security prison. Harry, Tyrone, and Clayton have, as people say at the prison, "gone home." Elijah has been very ill but is slowly putting himself together again with a possible release in 2013. Lamar, Rodney, Phillip, and David—who eventually came out to everyone—now flourish in a different college program, studying philosophy, literature, feminist theory, and, as they have reported, "critiquing everything." My college, short of funds, has closed the program.

2011

My consciousness-raising group (variously called The Third Street Circle or The Sex Fools), 1974 to the late 1980s. Left to right, front row: Alix Kates Shulman, Shaelagh Doyle, Ellen Willis. Second row, left to right: Bonnie Bellow, Cynthia Carr. Back row, left to right: Ann Snitow, Brett Harvey, Karen Durbin, M. Mark. Photograph: Dorothy Handelman.

Dorothy Dinnerstein, circa 1978.

No More Nice Girls demonstrates for abortion rights, Washington DC, April 1985.
Left to right: Joan Braderman, Carole Vance, Ann Snitow, Daniel Goode.

Attorney General Edwin Meese appointed a commission "to address the serious national problem of pornography" in 1985. Members of FACT sat in the front row with signs over their mouths that said "censored," and we demonstrated outside the hearings, performing a skit with some of us dressed up as Sex Cops and some of us as Ordinary Women. Our fabulous Sex Cops in police department drag were so convincing that when friends saw us on TV, they thought we were really being arrested. I'm in the center, an "Ordinary Woman" being censored.

My loft on Spring Street in Manhattan has been a center of event for feminist activism since 1985. Here, Carole Vance and I are welcoming participants to an international whores convention (1987). Why we are wearing flowered dresses we cannot fathom.

Rachel Blau DuPlessis and I at our book party for *The Feminist Memoir Project* (1998).

One of our many Take Back the Future demonstrations in the George W. Bush years: Holding the sign "Rotomo El Futuro Feminista," Temma Kaplan; in the center, Deborah Kaufman; holding the sign "Take Back The Future," Nanette Funk.

In the early 1990s, reproductive rights activists on both sides of the Atlantic were shocked that Polish women were about to lose their right to abortion, which they had had since 1956. In December 1992, No More Nice Girls demonstrated in front of St. Patrick's Cathedral on 5th Avenue in New York City with the support of the Women's Action Coalition drum corps. (For the few years the artists' group WAC existed, it was a brilliant resource for all feminist demonstrations.) In 1993, a very restrictive abortion law came into force in Poland. Center left holding the bird: Malgorzata Tarasiewicz; I'm on the right with the sign in Polish, "Solidarity With Polish Women." The artists who made these signs (in English and Polish) and the birds of freedom held up on poles are Hannah Alderfer and Marybeth Nelson. Photograph: Teri Slotkin Photography.

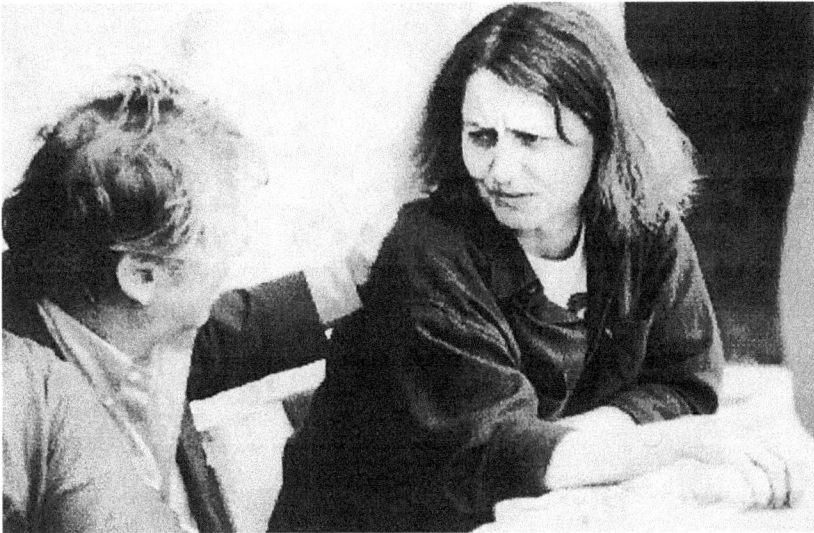

Slawka Walczewska is on the right at a Green Party meeting in Warsaw, May 2003. Explanation of the expression on her face: Daniel Cohn-Bendit has just said, "Europe is like a woman."

Visit to the home of Anna Walentynowicz (early 2007), who is credited with precipitating the Solidarity strike of 1980 in the Lenin Shipyard in Gdansk, which eventually led to the dissolution of communist rule in Poland. Left to right: Ann Snitow, Anna Walentynowicz, Malgorzata Tarasiewicz.

Teaching in Gdansk, Poland, 2010.

IV

REFUGEES FROM UTOPIA

19

INTRODUCTION TO REFUGEES FROM UTOPIA

Rachel Blau DuPlessis and I spent six years (1992–1998) pulling the pieces in *The Feminist Memoir Project: Voices from Women's Liberation* out of the humble, the busy, the still passionate, and the disappointed. All these writers were feminist activists in the United States in the 1970s, and they told tales of rapture and erasure. We were both teaching during those years, but the times had changed so much that, for our students, the memoirs we were gathering were snapshots of a lost utopia, a place from which they often felt time excluded them.

We fought hard against this mood, this reading of our book, writing pages and pages about all the ways and places in which feminism continued to grow and ramify. We rejected "narrative coherence" and "models of progress"—or decline. We said the essays were records of single voices; we had no wish to make a summing up. And, finally, we wrote: "We intend no elegy."[1]

Feeling desperation that the book might be read as "the past," fixed and canonical, we asked six others to read the whole thing and write responses to be included at the back. Though I have many favorite essays in *The Feminist Memoir Project*, in retrospect I find this move crucial to its usefulness as a representation of feminist sensibility—endlessly self-critical and always rethinking its concept of liberation.

This section ends with two of the many obituaries I've had to write in the last few years. I grieve over the loss of Shulamith Firestone (1945–2012) and Ellen Willis (1941–2006). Though their fingerprints are all over modern U.S.

feminist thought, that frame of reference itself is fading with time, a process I follow step by step here in "Remembering, Forgetting, and the Making of *The Feminist Memoir Project*." In this piece I attempt a taxonomy of the many ways women are commonly forgotten, including ways in which they themselves sometimes prefer to disappear. I urge remembering (the women active in Civil Rights, the generations of suffrage activists, the lost women founders), but I also, finally, accept forgetting. Nothing is more galvanizing than trying to learn from a next generation how they shape a life in politics now, and nothing more urgent than trying to join them as they struggle to Occupy our changing world.

Note

1. DuPlessis and Snitow, *The Feminist Memoir Project*, 21, 24.

REMEMBERING, FORGETTING, AND THE MAKING OF *THE FEMINIST MEMOIR PROJECT*

Rachel Blau DuPlessis and I, old friends from the women's liberation movement, discovered in the late eighties a shared indignation—and grief. The books about the '60s were beginning to come out. Histories mostly written by men who had been there, these books skirted the women's liberation movement with a finesse it was hard to quarrel with. One would stop the story before the movement came on the scene. Another would deal with it as an impressive side show—noises off. At around the same time in histories and general discussions, women's movements, along with a range of Black radical movements, were being corralled into a closed pen to keep in dangerously limited examples of "identity politics." The charge was that our movements had been chauvinistic in ways that the original democratic and civil rights movements of the earlier sixties were not.

Rachel and I recognized some truth in this critical analysis of some movement developments, but a kind of general constriction of meaning and empathy seemed to be at the heart of this critical writing. Had feminists and antiracists really claimed to be unified tribes, chanting about the wonderful true woman and the special beauty of Black? As we remembered the complex cultures of women's mobilization in the late sixties and seventies, ours had been a mass movement and had included multitudes. Our problem had not been nationalist claims and narrow interests. Rather, the movement initiated a wild proliferation of opinion and (often utopian) desire. We compared memories, and our sense was that what had lain just one step beyond the initial excitement of shared discovery was chaos. Chaos and skepticism about all fixed ideas of identity. Sometimes tribal, sometimes cosmopolitan, second-wave feminism had never been theoretically unified, and it always contained within it rival claims about feminism's subject and ground for analysis. Feminists differ fundamentally in their understanding of women's near universal subordination and most contemporary feminist thought has developed under the sign of difference.

Sometimes an activist's nightmare, this very instability has also been a source of movement strength. As Rachel and I were to write: "Feminism [has] constantly broadened its concept of liberation and deepened its recognition of the difficulty of achieving that liberation, the limitations of its own founding ideas."[1] The narrow accounts we were reading seemed to us a subtle form of dismissal. We felt both too soon forgotten and actively misremembered.

This paradoxical mixture of accelerated forgetting and distorted remembering raised questions for us about our own movement story, which we couldn't answer. What had we actually done, and even more elusive, who had we been? What trace of those actions and selves did we hope to leave behind? Would any of the sweep of our intentions survive us? Could the women's movement leave historical markers of itself that we ourselves could continue to identify with and approve? Or had our past been a brief utopian moment, separate from other experience, exciting, but destined to be essentially irretrievable—not only for others who were not there, but even for ourselves?

Around 1992, thinking of all this—the variety of the movement, its boldness, its erosion, the limited accounts of the sixties—with a primitive urge to record and save, Rachel and I put out a far-reaching call for memoirs of early second-wave women's movement activism. We asked people to describe what brought them into the movement, and we asked them to reflect on what they thought they were doing. We wanted them to add depth to memory and to explore the rich variety of interests that we remembered but couldn't find in the record so far.

We also began to seek explanations for what we began to recognize was an older habit of forgetting past women's mobilizations. What were the motors for forgetting what women do? Feminists seem to start from scratch every other generation, a pattern we could trace in Western history from the Enlightenment onward. We wrote that *The Feminist Memoir Project* was meant to stand "against historical forgetting."[2] This bit of brave rhetoric still rings for us, though it became obvious from the first that difficulties abound. Remembering was going to be much harder than we had thought. Could memoir make the journey into history? Memory and history were in some unstable relationship, and we were trying to intervene in a process we had only dimly grasped.

We began to conceive of *The Feminist Memoir Project* as both more and less than an accurate account of the movement that had so transformed our lives. Beyond any questions of faithfulness or fact, there was a tussle here, an agon of memory. Who would interpret the movement? Whom would memory serve? What atmosphere would envelop the movement in public retrospect?

As the memoirs came in and were subject to an arduous editing process, we came to think that the stories were best understood as a complex mixture of primary and secondary sources. Here were the actual activists, offering their fingerprints, tracings of who they were that hadn't changed and were still entirely recognizable after twenty years. Here were the voices of the kinds of people who made this particular, passionate attempt at changing history. That earlier time seemed present again in their words, like a scent suddenly released from a sealed bottle.

At the same time, these stories they told about themselves had already taken various hortatory shapes. Twenty years after the initial burst of intense experience, a number of narrative conventions had taken a firm hold. Here were tales of conversion or disillusionment, attempts at self-justification, confessions, rousing calls to act, to hope, to inspire, etc. At the same time, it became obvious that in the medium of this kind of direct memory, facts were shape changers.

After much discussion, we decided that any charges that these stories were interested narratives or that they were sometimes factually inaccurate were beside the point. Memory had inevitably done its selective, simplifying, distorting work. These pieces were both histories and polemics, both raw material and highly compressed narratives, fused together by political desire. Our writers wanted something from these histories, and we freely admitted, so did we. We shared a wish that memory might serve as a fountain of sustained future action. We had a political motive for building up a collective story that would prove enduring—and productive. Our first title for the book was "Live, From Feminism." The movement was not to be the past: "We intend no elegy," we proclaimed in our introduction.[3] Though this comment was, unerringly, a symptom that elegy was indeed one operable genre in this work, we wanted much more.

And, therefore, we feared: the thirty-seven pieces we had collected could easily blow away. We ended by calling the book *The Feminist Memoir Project* because we saw remembering as a group undertaking that would require more and more volumes. Ours would just be one of the first and would foster an ongoing project of remembering. In one of the response pieces we invited people to contribute at the back of the book, Ellen Willis expressed skepticism about this hope. She wondered what the next and future generations would make of these passionate effusions; the state of (revolutionary) mind they reproduced were rescued from a world of thought, feeling, and meaning that was, in 1998, as foreign as the mating practices of Hittites.[4] Feminist theorist Jane Flax had a similar response. She felt that the pieces, feisty and fighting as they were, nevertheless exuded a subtle atmosphere of trauma and loss. Like Ellen Willis, she saw the pieces as sealed off; their writers seemed to know their world was gone and only they were escaped to tell us.[5] No matter how many first-hand accounts we collected, a meta-question kept arising: Who would listen?

Of course, almost everything and everyone gets forgotten. We know hardly anything about the belief systems and—still more elusive—about the texture of how belief was lived in even the immediate past, for example in the lives of our grandparents. Hence, to remember is to swim against a great human tide. Cognitive psychologist and theorist of memory, William Hirst, poses this as a problem of what he calls "stickiness."[6] Many elements contribute to which memories are sticky, which get remembered both by participants and across generations. Some of these mechanisms can be seen as relatively neutral, like a tendency to remember red. Others can be classed as political: to remember is to craft a version of one's own story; to forget, too, can be an active, politically charged choice.

We began our work because it seemed to us that women in the public sphere, particularly active, feminist women, move on a fast track toward oblivion. I began to keep a list of the ways in which women's public acts disappear from the sustained public record. Beyond the universal obscurity shared by all, some of these barriers to memory arise from traits in women's cultural practices and movements themselves, while others arise in a tussle between active political women and their detractors.

History and Memory

Like many others, William Hirst makes the common, useful, if hard to sustain distinction between "history" and "collective memory."[7] History may tell us that women have been present as key players in any number of movements. Documents exist; first-hand accounts list their names. But collective memory of these movements is quite a different matter. People retell the past, knocking off edges that don't fit how the group desires to name and know itself. One might expect that remembering movements specifically for and about women would provide an exception; surely in political spaces where men are almost entirely absent, women must be memorable *faut de mieux*? But on the contrary. I have only to consult my high school textbook: the mighty U.S. women's suffrage movements of the nineteenth century were contracted to one paragraph, two names, one issue.

The first time Hirst and I discussed the problem of forgotten women's movements, I asked him, "so, why is women's past activism so much more invisible than men's?" He laughed: "Because we live in a patriarchy of course!" This flat-footed statement helps; it offers a starting point, an image of women speaking, speaking, speaking while listeners drift away. Women are rarely in charge of the story or in a position to insist on their centrality to the remembered significance of events. They have stories of course, but these are not often enough rehearsed, not inscribed on stones.

An example: William Hirst and I are colleagues at The New School, a university with a distinctively radical history. Over the years, I've heard this history recited dozens of times at convocations, graduations, formal dinners, awards ceremonies. This telling and retelling is a perfect example of the "collective memory" process. The New School identifies its founding moments as inspiring, heroic, and still resonant and moving in the present. The story produces a continuing pride and creates and re-creates a treasured identity. The founding moment was a rebellion against politically conservative, repressive, entrenched academics. Columbia University had fired some of its professors who had spoken up against the U.S. entry into World War I. Out of this bold nucleus of heroic *refuseniks* (of course all male—Columbia had no women professors) came The New School's first generation, dedicated to the proposition that first-rate social science should be a force in the world, that there was no contradiction between serious academic research and engagement in social action.

During my twenty-three years at the university I have always loved this story. But there were always bumps, rough places, glitches I was too busy to attend to. In their history of The New School, Peter M. Rutkoff and William B. Scott write the following sentence about Clara Mayer, student organizer and key supporter in the foundation of The New School: "[For] fifty years only Alvin Johnson played a more important part in the life of the New School."[8] What? But maybe she was merely a handmaiden, a typical role for women then and since? But no. Clara Mayer emerges in this account as a key shaper of The New School project.

And there were many others. One finds their names on The New School's founding document: Mrs. George Haven Putnam, Mrs. Willard Straight, Mrs. Charles L. Tiffany, Mrs. Learned Hand, Mrs. Henry Bruer, Mrs. Ruth Standish Baldwin, Mrs. George W. Bacon, with secretary Mrs. Victor Sorchan. One cannot easily discover their full names since until the sixties women continued to be cloaked in the names of their husbands. The fact remains: women were central. The school was founded in 1919, a culminating moment in feminist activism, the year before women voted in their first national election. And there it is, at the end of a list of subjects The New School intends to study: "Women in the modern social order."[9] Sixty-five percent of the students were women in the beginning. Seventy percent of the students at the relatively new undergraduate division, Eugene Lang College, are women now. Far from thinking that these facts require marking, many of my colleagues think that it is liberation enough that gender is not named, not marked. Women often keep their own names now. Gender should not matter; therefore it does not matter. *Point final.*

The problem for feminists is obvious enough and often repeated: to be in a marked category is a subordinate position, but pretending not to be subordinate doesn't actually erase the array of problems that form around gender difference.

William Hirst's research shows that the most effective way to make part of a story disappear is not, as one might suppose, to drop the story altogether, but rather to tell it again and again leaving out the part one thinks distracting, uninteresting, contrary to the central image or idea one treasures. It is another of his observations that groups seek a shared narrative; whatever doesn't fit fades from the account. And so it is with the story of The New School. Women's central position in the founding and development of the school has simply been dropped. There's an unsettling oxymoron in the concept of women-founders, something, perhaps, diminishing to our proud institution's glory.

The Black civil rights movement provides another example of displacement. No doubt The New School women had habits of self-abnegation and deference to male leaders. Women's self-effacement, fears, and the social price they pay for prominence are also elements in this story of forgetting. But African American women activists had even more reasons to be ambivalent about promoting themselves: they feared to damage the fragile, new-minted stature of movement men. Women were unquestionably central to the civil rights struggle, but when Rosa Parks wanted to speak at the first mass rally after the bus boycott that she initiated, she was told she had done enough. Instead, Martin Luther King, Jr. presided. Many of these effective, relentless, hard-working movement women live in memoirs but the readily available facts about them haven't been translated into national histories or collective public images. Here are some of the important people from the civil rights mobilizations of the fifties and sixties: Daisy Bates, Mary Fair Burks, Johnnie Carr, Septima Poinsette Clark, Dorothy Cotton, Georgia Gilmore, Thelma Glass, McCree Harris, Vivian Malone Jones, Diane Nash, Jo Ann Gibson Robinson, Shirley Sherrod, Modjeska Monteith Simkins.[10]

A different kind of example: Feminist theorist and psychologist Nancy Chodorow did a study of the generation of female psychoanalysts before her own, women trained in the thirties and forties in the wake of Freud, students of Karen Horney and Melanie Klein.[11] She asked these analysts questions born out of the feminist thinking of the seventies. To her dismay, her interlocutors completely rejected the terms and categories implied by her questions. They didn't think their gender had mattered at all. They didn't think the importance of the figure of the mother in psychoanalytic thought had any direct application to them beyond individual and technical questions of transference with particular patients. They didn't feel any special sisterhood or recognize a disadvantage shared with other women in the field. And on and on.

Initially, this was a story Nancy Chodorow didn't like. She was particularly worried that her interviews kept pushing her toward the conclusion that these mother figures suffered from false consciousness, an old and comfortable explanation feminists avoid for good reason: once again, stupid women don't understand their own situation, once again, they are the objects not the subjects of knowledge about themselves. But without using the explanation of false consciousness, where could Chodorow go while, in disbelief, she listened to her elders reject gender as an important category in their life histories?

She came up with an elegant solution to her problem:

> I came to conclude that my interviewees, rather than being gender-blind, had different forms of gender-consciousness than I and experienced a different salience of gender as a social category and aspect of professional identity. Gender salience became a central concept in my research.[12]

"Gender salience" is a useful concept for taking apart any illusion that "gender" itself is a stable, trans-historical category. Chodorow was looking for her own world of feminist thought in the self-understanding of these older analysts she valued, but her terms turned out to be much more historically specific than she had initially understood. "Gender" is not a freestanding identity, and for her interlocutors, it was a variable far less salient than "Jewish" or "professional-woman-who-is-also-a-mother." If feminists are right to see gendered identity as a changeable and contingent category, they must necessarily recognize variations in gender salience. Why would we expect an unchanging through-line in something so liable to manipulation, interpretation, absorption into any number of systems of meaning?

Well and good: But what if one were to add another variable to Chodorow's account, the surprising force in these women's lives of forgetting? Their mothers' generation was responsible for one of the largest drives for universal citizenship since the eighteenth century. Women's suffrage is one reductive way to name it, but the women activists who pushed for the vote wanted so much more. Some of them saw women as special, different from men, while others were skeptical on that point. But a collective sense of outrage at exclusion and restriction unified this struggle, keeping it alive for over seventy years. These militant women activists didn't call themselves feminists, but they shared a sensibility with Chodorow that the women of the thirties and forties she studied lacked. What had happened?

Not a single one of the interviews Chodorow quotes mentions or even faintly resonates with this dramatic, heroic immediate past. Many of these women were born in Europe or the United States before women could vote. Their mothers, active or not, had fought in one way or another for the space this first generation of professional women were to so confidently inherit. Yet not a scintilla of memory, of acknowledgment: that the generation of women before them couldn't go to school as they went to school; couldn't choose whether or not to be mothers as some of them had chosen; couldn't imagine a work world shared by both men and women. No echo, no gratitude, no continuity, no awe. Nothing. As Shulamith Firestone (1970) and others have argued, psychoanalysis closed down a broader discussion of politics, history, and women's place in both. Psychoanalysis has had its own role in the history of forgetting. It pathologized the relationship between generations, locating distortions and forgetting firmly in the realm of the private.

Who Wants to Forget Feminism?

These are examples of active, distorting forgetting taken at random. The New School and civil rights sagas emphasize the wish of the fathers to be the true and only begetters of public institutions and historical events. The saga of the psychoanalysts, who had no consciousness of the feminist struggle that created the professional space they inhabited, reveals the younger professionals' ambivalence about just how salient they wished their elders' struggles to be. Ironically, psychoanalysis provides a possible reading of this kind of forgetting between mothers and daughters. How else to emerge as a whole self, free of what Chodorow's fellow explorer of this territory, feminist psychologist Dorothy Dinnerstein, saw as the abjection of childhood, "the chagrins of the nursery?"[13] These analysts preferred a timeless sense of their position. Theirs was a genderless triumph. In these stories, it would seem that both men and women can collude in pushing women into the background in collective accounts of public events.

It is past disappearances like these that mark The Feminist Memoir Project with anxiety, with the anticipation that all these amazing works and days of the sixties and seventies will not be recalled a mere moment later, even as soon as in the lives of the sons and daughters. Indeed current forgetting is already far advanced.

Mary Hawkesworth made a study of the current, commonly repeated announcement of "the death of feminism" and came up with this stunning conclusion: there is no death of feminism. In fact, feminism is growing worldwide. What we are seeing, she argued in 2004, is not death, but the wish that feminism be dead, that it disappear.[14]

Susan Faludi had made a similar analysis in Backlash as early as 1991. The free women of the women's liberation movement had made everyone nervous. Faludi studied a wide range of popular and pseudo-scientific literature in the United States that warned women that if they proceeded along this path of rebellion, no one would love them; they would fail to have babies; they would die sad and alone. These admonitory texts were an invitation to forgetting: women, forget this folly; put the rage of feminism behind you; forget, and we will love you again, take you back into the fold.

The reasons for forgetting were over-determined and this backlash message offered a number of narratives from which the variously disaffected could choose. Sylvia Walby has catalogued some of these common scenarios of death and disappearance: some say feminism is over because it has succeeded.[15] (Feminists have gotten all they wanted and now can go home. Younger women don't feel the need to complain like their unlovely elders.) Others say feminism has died because it was narrow and self-absorbed, or internally incoherent, or in error about what women really want, or overwhelmed by catfights. (In other words, feminists killed the movement themselves because of limitations or mistakes; feminism died by its own hand.)

The idea that backlash itself has lowered feminist vitality rarely figures in these popular death announcements, but a number of feminist theorists have tried to measure the effect of such hostile or dismissive narratives on how feminism looks to a next generation. How much harm does a dismissive story—stripped of glamour and romance—do to the future?

Feminist psychoanalyst and Lacanian theorist Miglena Nikolchina offers a particularly devastating assessment of the situation: the-death-of-feminism party do not merely wish women to forget; they want women, the mother in women, to entirely disappear, to die so that we all may live—separate, whole, and beholden to no one.[16] Nikolchina argues that each generation of feminists thinks that this time women have made it out into the world only to have their public presence buried once again; the collective desire to bury the memory of women's power, presence, and influence trumps the facts of the record every time. Each time, women expect to be remembered at last, and each time, to their surprise, they are slated once again—by both men and women—for oblivion.

Scenarios like Hawkesworth's and Nikolchina's are not subject to proof. They are polemical accounts of a recurring injustice. What they introduce is a sense of urgency, an angry demand for active explanation. They recognize that forgetting women's social and political presence is normal, but they see this "normal" as a psychopathology of everyday life, a serious flaw in the collective project of culture. They hypothesize that, while forgetting is eternal, women's acts are more aggressively forgotten than men's. Women disappear with a difference. Thin as the record may sometimes be, the stories, symbols, and rituals in which the patriarch is the central character remain. He has left his trace, and willy-nilly—and with varying faithfulness—we contrive to weave him back into the stories we tell about ourselves.

How Forgetting Works

Minute by minute, memory by memory, how does it work? Only that which is most "sticky," to use Hirst's wonderful word, that which is most repeated, most narrated, most encoded in ritual, most elevated to the mythic or most shockingly, publicly traumatic survives as the story of who "they" were in the past and what "they" did. It helps if there are pictures. It helps if there are martyrs. It helps if there are charismatic and photogenic leaders. It helps if the story is clear and conforms in some way to already existing narratives people are prepared to hear.

The particular problems the women's liberation movement might have in relation to these rules-of-the-memorable are immediately self-evident. I remember our saying angrily to the press at those early rallies, "Don't take my picture!" We meant: We've been objectified enough. We hated the early images of feminist events showing cool chicks with short skirts who were so beautiful when they were angry. We carried this image-phobia quite far, not taking many pictures of each other, either. (The search for photographs to accompany The Feminist Memoir Project revealed a surprising lack. The contrast with the visual record of the civil rights movement—with its brilliant representations of heroes, martyrs, and key historical moments—was dramatic.)

To escape the usual disparagement, we also resisted being written about, refusing to be interviewed unless they sent female reporters. Sometimes the press raided the "research" pool, sending women out to cover us who had never had the chance to be reporters before. At other times men with microphones and cameras simply stormed away, leaving our events uncovered. We had no notion then of what, a mere moment later, everyone knew, that all ink is good ink, and that ink there will be—or else silence and invisibility.

Though our dream that the revolution would not be televised is still worth consideration, for the most part our refusals of representation were a losing game, expressing a utopian wish instantly defeated in a fast-expanding media universe. We felt our movement was earthshaking, but we had an underdeveloped sense of ourselves as historical actors. Grandiose as we no doubt sometimes were (and at moments the memoirs show this trait grandly), we were amateurs of self-promotion, neophytes as myth-makers, suspicious of what we saw as male styles of heroics. Because revolutionary moments seem to suspend time and are lived vividly, in a glistening present, memory seemed beside the point. We simply didn't register how much representation would come to matter.

Nor did we see any value in having charismatic spokespersons, like Martin Luther King Jr. The women's liberation movement eschewed leaders. Of course, like all movements, it had them, but they were endlessly savaged by activists who were fighting against the whole world of leaders, hierarchies, and elites. (The Feminist Memoir Project is full of stories of leaders attacked and chastened.) The egalitarian ethos of that time encouraged anonymity, teamwork, antihierarchical social structures.

One might well think that at least the women's liberation movement had the intensity of trauma on its side. After all, it had many martyrs, too. The victims of domestic violence, rape, and illegal abortions were rescued from the private dark where shame and the walls of home had long hidden them. But shame is glamour's antithesis; shame dies hard and forgetting is one of its prime expressions. When feminists brought these stories into the light, the fact remained that those who suffered or died were victims, not heroes. And they were so many! Too obscure to name (no list of names here), their situation was as common as dirt. With rare exceptions, suffering women remained relative creatures without individual, tragic fates.

These stories were not sticky while the backlash narrative had the clarity, simplicity, and power to alarm through a brilliant clustering of hostile ideas of what feminism is all about: ugly, bra-burning, man-hating, child-murdering, hairy, lesbians. This linked chain of words began as a relatively simple case of backlash. But such defamation has turned out to have a longevity the complex and diffuse movement itself lacks. By now, the ugly, man-hating feminist is a well-established figure of myth—one my students faithfully reproduce each semester as we begin our work of discussing feminism.

Hirst suggested to me that the disparity between the memory of the extraordinary social transformations arising from and parallel to the movement and the negative image of the horrible, miserable feminist arises from the movement's failure to promise happiness, a story with a readable ending. Feminist narratives are internally contradictory, diverse, reactive, unsettling, unclear. Feminists want a different world but have usually distrusted the closure of unity or happy endings. Though vital struggles continue, there is no beloved community once one has left the original commune of the seventies sisterhood.

These observations are not meant to name the faults in feminism. On the contrary, feminist values, and some of its best thinking, underpin the traits that also encourage forgetting. What, after all, is the feminist story? Women are all so different; we want freedom to do a wide variety of things. We have no sustainable identity as a group—nor do we want one.

What's more, feminism makes no promises. Feminism may be about freedom, but freedom is an empty set. Can feminism get one love, or security, or happiness? In contrast to traditionalist movements, which promise so much depth of feeling, does feminism keep you warm at night, provide you company in old age, offer a sustaining sense of meaning and purpose? Not only does feminism fail on all these counts, but it fails by design. Only in brief periods among a few groups was feminism meant to be an all-encompassing ideology, a full description of the world, a panacea for all ills, or a comfortable, permanent home.

Usually, feminism has been a disturber of the peace, a critique of our comfy resting places, a skeptic about what is usually on offer as happiness. Feminism is a complaint about oppression. Often accused of whining, feminists are constantly expressing a broad and persistent dissatisfaction with how things are generally organized. Feminist theorists often yearn for the unstable, indeterminate, and ironic. They are skeptical about mythical, enduring identities, heroes, magical coherence of any kind.

Feminism has few rituals to share with a next generation. It is nervous about any assertion of eternal verities about man, woman, god, truth. Though feminists often describe glorious utopian imaginaries—from men doing housework to an end of the house as we know it—it's hard to make those wishes stick as solid or real. Instead, what is apparent is that these women are unsatisfied. What, dear god, do they want?

The sticky, soothing story is the backlash story: the terrifying ugliness of female autonomy. Feminism is threatening. Though most feminists defend women's right to pleasure, they can't guarantee that pleasure will come with the collapse of known, deeply elaborated, mythically sanctioned identities.

Women are more forgotten than men, but feminists are suspicious of the ways in which men have achieved stickiness. The male narrative of creation and centrality and glory and autonomy is a story which feminism challenges at its root. Is there another form for remembering? Hirst tells me he thinks not, and I see no reason to dispute his conclusions. His research demonstrates that human beings remember badly: they need the help of simplification, the motive of self-serving teleologies, the false unity of sharing a story with the tribe. Revision is continuous and earlier structures of feeling are abandoned without leaving much trace. What remains in popular memory once the erasing tide recedes is, first of all, very little, and second, very unreliable and approximate. Stickiness depends on the distortions that are myth and ritual and is often sealed further by fear and trauma, death and martyrdom. Memory is a terror-monger; memory is faithless.

In *The New Yorker* as I write this, Ariel Levy is complaining that women are both the perpetrators and the victims of "cultural memory disorder."[17] Sometimes they themselves distort the record of what women have done. At the same moment, Gail Collins is being interviewed about her new book, *When Everything Changed: The Amazing Journey of American Women from 1960 to the Present* (2009); she is arguing that the colossal achievements of women and women's movements are not becoming part of what we call U.S. history. Nicholas Kristof and Sheryl WuDunn are on the stump recounting the argument of their best seller, *Half the Sky* (2009): Female babies are being aborted and women are being starved and terrorized and enslaved and murdered all over the world but this goes unremarked because it happens every day. How can something that happens every day be a crisis? Kristof and WuDunn try to sensitize their readers, to get them to register shock at what is ubiquitous, normal, generally accepted.

Each of these writers sounds the call: women are constantly forgotten. But there is small reason to think this outcry will alter the general process of forgetting. An undertaking like The Feminist Memoir Project can't build a bridge to historical remembering on its own. Though we hope we have created moments of "stickiness," we can't know how much we have succeeded. But in this act of collecting we have expressed a faith in a long-term project of change. Inequality lies deep, but most feminists share a belief that even such ingrained stories can shift. We gathered memoirs describing a fleeting moment in a long and slow process. Women are dissatisfied; they continue to express discontent. They are the ones most likely to herald that there is a relationship between what Dorothy Dinnerstein called "sexual arrangements" and "human malaise."

Our Utopia and the Future

Perhaps, finally, my outcry here about the forgetting of women is beside the point. Such a complaint can easily descend into a politics of ressentiment. After all the years I've spent in political movements, I've come to think that "I've-been-left-out" is one of our deepest-lying human emotions—right up there with rage, hate, and desire. Memory cannot repair loss and is only one aspect of continuity. Unlike religion, feminism does not demand eternal loyalty to unchanging beliefs—nor should it. The continuing density of sexism can be trusted to form its own reaction, and those who need some aspect of what has been the feminist project over the last several hundred years will keep reinventing it. This has already happened repeatedly and is happening all over the world as I write this.

Feminists now living have an understandable attachment to the bodily, animated particulars of their movement experiences. It is bound to be galling to discover that, in the usual course of things, these treasured, specific memories are not only as evanescent as foam but also, on their way out, subject to a sort of patronizing diminishment reserved for women's efforts to enter history. There is always the personal question of how to survive being forgotten or aggressively misunderstood. Inevitably, with longevity or luck, one outlives one's formative moment. In the case of those who were a part of ecstatic, hopeful, utopian movements, this common tragedy of the mismatch between an individual's life and the arc of history is likely to be particularly acute. For them, forgetting goes beyond personal loss to the loss of a whole world.

But one step beyond these feelings, that one's acts and words of protest have been specially chosen for neglect and insult, lies another more reliable experience feminists share: in modernity, feminism keeps returning. Though obscurity and abuse dog feminism, self-conscious feminist struggles are constantly finding new forms. Even if each return is greeted as if it were for the first time—the New Woman again and again—still she keeps coming. And she keeps bringing back some version of feminist resistance. Her central questions recur: What is it to be designated "woman?" Why does patriarchy keep insisting on this relatively fixed identity? How stable or unstable are gender categories and what have we to lose or gain in changing gender meanings?

Future feminists may develop a critique of the instability of gender that we cannot now imagine. They may say that continuity or discontinuity with the past are dangers to them not for our reasons but for their own. They may choose to define and ramify an activist feminist tradition because all historical through-lines have been destroyed. Our ambivalence about leaving a blood-line—records of leaders, martyrs, heroic triumphs—may develop new political meanings.

How much harm does it do when a particular manifestation of feminism fades from collective memory? In responding to my general consternation, Hirst explained that recalling earlier states of mind is one of the weakest links in human remembering. So let that old set of feelings go? Trust in whatever continuity feminism is likely to have over time? Be content to leave personal traces and records like The Feminist Memoir Project? Accept forgetting and at the same time try to create "stickiness" on one's own terms? After all, the power of patriarchy to sustain its myths, rituals, and emotions will continue to arouse women's long-term resistance to those selective stories.

The Feminist Memoir Project was intended to be a place where that tightly woven story of male domination and achievement could be shifted from central position and placed alongside other accounts of what the reality of then felt like. Though to talk back to forgetting is both difficult and, in some respects, doomed to failure, this unequal dialogue, this flash of presence of the Other, just might subtly change the story. Later tellers will determine what effect this try at telling had. Unless one believes in the eternal powerlessness of the Other, telling may be some small part of change, a part of a slow shift in the gender story in the longue durée.

Near the end of our time working on The Feminist Memoir Project I had this dream: I was in the stacks of a library climbing an unnaturally tall ladder past dark volumes upon volumes to an empty top shelf, on which I levered an unwieldy, bound copy of our book. I seemed to be saying to the book something like: stay there and wait for your readers to find you. The feeling was: this was the future. The future might find us obnoxious, unintelligible, grotesque. Or, perhaps instead, our exoticism would be exciting to them. They would read, misread, project upon us with their own purposes in whatever languages they would talk—and we would seem to listen.

2010

I thank Rachel Blau DuPlessis for the thorough editing she gave this piece and for the fine additions she made to it, though her account of what we were doing in *The Feminist Memoir Project* would be quite different from the story told here.

Afterword: Celebrating the Re-Publication of
The Feminist Memoir Project, Rutgers, 2007

An anecdote about my university, The New School:

Recently, I heard that the philosophy graduate students were meeting on their own, weekly, to discuss gender theory. Someone emailed me an ambitious ten-week syllabus. As the convener of what will eventually become a gender studies minor at The New School—and how hard this has been is another, related story—I went to one of the group's sessions.

I introduced myself as the person struggling to bring back some form of gender studies at The New School, and I asked them why they had organized the study group. Was it because they were frustrated that the philosophy department didn't have any courses in gender theory? No, said the group leader sternly. (No malcontent she!) No, this is a tradition in the philosophy department.

Let me unpack my exquisite ambivalence. It's an irony that the word tradition can so easily become a code word for forgetting the past. The original, radical philosophy students had started the student-run seminar in outrage that The New School supplies so few opportunities to study gender. They had called meetings, petitioned deans, held symposia critiquing The New School's attitude—all to no avail. These younger students didn't want to be associated with those quarrelsome, angry ancestors ten years older—if they even knew of them. In any case, the earlier group had failed—and let's confess, failure is damage.

But here's another way to tell this story: This new group wanted to study gender. Their syllabus was serious, multivocal, way beyond any charge of fashion or fad. They knew gender was important. The room was full of both men and women, studying this subject of value in an open way—no male grandstanding, at least none that I could see in the short time I was with them. When I was a graduate student, such a group could not have existed—not its subject, not its group dynamics. So the world changed. And remembering is not the word for this change. In fact, it is something else; call it a mark. What was thought, said, struggled over, agonized over has left marks and structures everywhere. Others live in the hills and valleys that are the triumphs and losses of the past.

These students don't remember. They are different—in texture and tone—from the irritated older ones. But difference is a sacred term in feminist theory for good reason. I may quarrel with their interpretation of their own present and believe that they should still be angry about the absence of support for gender studies in our university, but their sense of what their situation is and what is to be done will always be different from mine—a difference with great possibilities for productive thought. I wish the feminist past to be remembered, but I don't want feminism to be a mere memory. If we want a "tradition" of feminism, let it be this living stuff. Willy-nilly, these students are engaged in the development of gender knowledge. In their thoughts and acts they create part of the feminist present, mark out some of the ground for feminism's next moves.

2007

Notes

1. DuPlessis and Snitow, The Feminist Memoir Project, 18.
2. DuPlessis and Snitow, The Feminist Memoir Project, 23.
3. DuPlessis and Snitow, The Feminist Memoir Project, 24.
4. Willis, "My Memoir Problem," 482–84.
5. Flax, in conversation. Thanks to Jane Flax for extended conversations about The Feminist Memoir Project since 2000.
6. Hirst, in conversation.
7. Hirst, "Presentation to the Lang Freshman Class of 2009."
8. Rutkoff and Scott, New School, 34.

9. The New School founding document: *A Proposal for an Independent School of Social Science*, 13.

10. Barnett, "Invisible Southern Black Women Leaders in the Civil Rights Movement," 162–82; Olson, *Freedom's Daughters*; and Smith, "Meditation on Memory," 530–41.

11. Chodorow, "Seventies Questions for Thirties Women," 199–218.

12. Chodorow, "Seventies Questions for Thirties Women," 200–201.

13. Dinnerstein, *The Mermaid and the Minotaur*.

14. Hawkesworth, "The Semiotics of Premature Burial," 961–84.

15. Walby, "Backlash to Feminism," 156–65.

16. Nikolchina, *Matricide in Language*, 1–5.

17. Levy, "Lift and Separate," 78.

THE POLITICS OF PASSION

Ellen Willis (1941–2006)

Radical politics is about being happy, not about being good.
—*Ellen Willis, from a meeting in 2003, as noted by Leonore Tiefer.*

Genuine virtue is the overflow of happiness, not the bitter fruit of self-denial.
—*Ellen Willis, Don't Think, Smile!* (1999)

I believe that as the sexuality debate goes, so goes feminism. . . . Feminism
is a vision of active freedom, of fulfilled desires, or it is nothing.
—*Ellen Willis,* "Statement," Diary of a Conference on Sexuality
(1982, *suppressed by Barnard College, but intended as the program
for the Scholar and the Feminist IX Conference on Sexuality.*)

What it all comes down to for me—as a Velvets fan, a lover of rock-and-
roll, a New Yorker, an aesthete, a punk, a sinner, a sometime seeker of
enlightenment (and love) (and sex)—is this: I believe that we are all, openly
or secretly, struggling against one or another kind of nihilism. I believe
that body and spirit are not really separate, though it often seems that way.
I believe that redemption is never impossible and always equivocal.
—*Ellen Willis, "The Velvet Underground"* (1979)

Ellen Willis, my old friend and comrade in the women's liberation movement, died of lung cancer on November 9, 2006, at the age of sixty-four. This
shattering event heralds the obvious: in spite of the rare dynamism that characterized our time, the generation of U.S. women born in the 1940s and culturally shaped in the 1950s, who reacted with passion against that culture by
exploding into the civil rights, New Left, antiwar, and women's movements
of the 1960s, will soon be folded flat onto pages like this one, which you are
reading. Of this group of history-makers—women with raised expectations,
hungry for the world, utopian in their sudden release of new wishes—Ellen

was one of the very best minds. Given the ambition, brilliance, and sheer bulk of Ellen's written record, her relative lack of celebrity is a bad case, one of those examples of invisibility feminists have long identified as happening disproportionately to women.

Let me say quickly that Ellen wouldn't respond warmly to this kind of complaining. She would hear both whining and implicit scolding in it—two tones of voice and political stances that she hated. So already I'm at odds with her, as usual, and also as usual, beginning to see her point. What did she care about the state of her fame? The flaming work is out there for any-one who seeks it.

What did bother her, though, was the decline of what she stood for, the loss of the expansive ideas and culture of the sixties, when she took LSD, saw the unity in all things, and then—wonderfully, perversely—refused to see her acid visions as childish excesses but instead took them seriously as the hard-headed intellectual she always was. Out of the cauldron of those years she brewed a set of central, enduring principles: Rock and roll reaches for freedom and ecstasy, which we all want, in spite of our ambivalence, more than we want pain and fear. Utopian yearnings are rational, the deep expres-sion of human capacity. *Pace* to postmodernists, these yearnings are rooted in our species life. Though we are often caught in a vicious cycle of repression and retaliation, a destructive will to power is not an unchangeable essence of human nature. Equality is achievable, and so is freedom because, ultimately, terrified as we all are, we want these things. The desire for freedom is a power-ful force, which when mobilized in political life can move mountains. But we must also recognize the impediments to freedom; it is irrational not to take the irrational seriously, not to honor the force of unconscious fears. The "body armor" we live in is a sign of illness—by no means inevitable. Human wishes are our best birthright. Let no one scoff or be ashamed.

While yearning, she always saw how difficult is the path to delight. She never mistook an ecstatic moment with the Rolling Stones for a political transformation. She looked at the pop culture she loved without a scintilla of sentimentality. If she romanticized hedonism, which she sometimes did, I've always thought she got away with such abject love of cool because she herself was entirely incapable of being corrupted by it. Serious by character and social origin, she recognized in mass culture a world that offered—along with the schlock—the real ecstasy that she longed to enjoy. Our desire for sexual satisfaction and for freedom on the one side and our fear of these things on the other—on this great revolving contradiction Ellen founded her work.

The paradox at the heart of all Ellen's writing is that she remained true to her core, early ideas throughout her life, but she never turned them into holy writ or hardened them into unquestionable predictions. You could know these basic values of hers without having any idea where she would come out on any specific question. The suspense was delicious and her journalist's sense for the passing moment was often not only surprising but prescient. Each time she would start over from a position of radical doubt. And like many of the great masters of the personal essay, she interrogated herself relentlessly, probing for self-deceptions or wishful thinking. I find myself asking, as I watch today's news, what would Ellen say? Not knowing marks out the large territory of our loss.

Though Ellen Willis was often the crank and contrarian, the positive force of her will and wishes carried her beyond criticism into becoming a history maker herself. When I first met her in the early 1970s, she had already been recognized as one of the women's movement's most suggestive and daring theorists and had helped found New York Radical Women, and then Redstockings. These early groups claimed an independent authority for the women's movement, separating from the New Left without abandoning key Left values. Ellen's early movement writings were inspired; she simply insisted—while all were doubting—that patriarchy was oppressive to women and needed to be confronted on its own terms, not as a side issue in the fight against capitalism. No, there could be no revolution without a complete rethinking of sexuality, family, motherhood, patriarchal morality, domestic work, even of love itself and all that was usually assumed to be outside the realm of politics.

How obvious this sounds now, how raw and shocking then. The courage it took to demand a new place in history can no longer be imagined. The handful of women saying these things in 1968 dared to seem like aggressive monsters—silly, grotesque, embarrassing in their immodest wishes for significance. Ellen was among these few, and I never saw her waver, or equivocate, or apologize. Their radical thoughts were available to the mass of us who followed. We owe them our deepest gratitude.

By 1975, Ellen, along with many others, began to feel that radical feminism was becoming dangerously diluted by liberal feminism and by what came to be called "cultural feminism." In her careful account of movement history, "Radical Feminism and Feminist Radicalism" (1984), she tells this story and lays her claim to the importance of the radical phase of feminism, even while recognizing in hindsight its limitations. Though, as the political climate continued to worsen, she never indulged in the defeatism of nostalgia, she did write as early as 1979, "As the conservative backlash gains momentum, I feel a bit like an explorer camped on a peninsula, who looks back to discover that the rising tide has made it into an island and that it threatens to become a mere sandbar or perhaps disappear altogether."[1]

It was in those years, threatened by isolation, that a bunch of us returned to the technique she had helped invent, consciousness raising, as a way to think through what was happening to the radical feminist movement. When we were hard working, as we often were, we called ourselves "The Third Street Circle"; when delirious, for example at the founding of the zap action group No More Nice Girls, we were "The Sex Fools." In both characters we engaged in intimate political talk for fifteen years.

Three of us from our women's group convened at Ellen's house shortly after she died. We sat to keep her company until the undertakers came. We noted her always beautiful bones, the fine arch of her nose, the bruise she had gotten from falling downstairs in the last, hard week of her life—a life which, until the end, she had otherwise lived much as usual, writing lucid and original interventions and talking with friends and family.

She was the first of our group to die. What a privilege it was to meet with her—and with each other—once a week for fifteen years. We were a generation of women who had the good luck to love each other as comrades, as people who shared a public as well as a private world. This love was our luck, a gift from a great social movement. Such utopian uprisings of energy and hope leave all kinds of messages behind. Our way of talking, of experiencing our parallel lives, is one of the precious things we gained, the mark of our age. As I work my way through Ellen's hundreds of articles, letters to the editor, and unpublished manuscripts, I find the work wonderfully luminous and whole. In her leavings, I find an ineradicable trace of the times we shared.

2007

Note

1. Willis, "The Family: Love It or Leave It," 150.

RETURNING TO THE WELL

Revisiting Shulamith Firestone's *The Dialectic of Sex*

Shulamith Firestone's *The Dialectic of Sex: The Case for Feminist Revolution* has been reissued, after many mysterious years out of print. It was written twenty-five years ago, when the author was twenty-five and the modern U.S. women's movement was about three. Firestone was there from the beginning, first in Chicago SDS (Students for a Democratic Society), defying sexist catcalls from New Left men, then in New York, co-founding Redstockings and New York Radical Feminists, and co-editing the early, hot publishing ventures of the movement, *Notes from the First Year* (then the *Second* and *Third Year*.)

In those "Years," which have attracted metaphors like "explosion" and "revolution" and my own favorite, "mushroom effect," I didn't know the rules, so I reviewed *The Dialectic of Sex* on Nanette Rainone's WBAI radio show, "Womankind," even though I was in Firestone's women's group at the time, the "Stanton-Anthony Brigade" of New York Radical Feminists. Because of the bad, paper-hoarding habits of a lifetime I still have that review—which, alas, includes no mention that I was then closely acquainted with the author. My hopes to discover either prescience or idiocy (which I planned, of course, with hindsight to forgive myself) have both been disappointed on rereading this handwritten souvenir of 1970. There is, however, a more solid inheritance: I liked the book then and I like it still—if, inevitably, with a difference. Once again, I find it remarkable.

In the interval between my two readings, *The Dialectic of Sex* has remained famous—either for being radical or being outrageous—depending on who is (half) remembering it. From the first, it was demonized for some of its epigrams ("pregnancy is barbaric") or for some of its speculative practical suggestions (children should be raised by groups bound by seven-to-ten-year contracts because the family, like a genetic code, reproduces the domination of men over women and children). During the backlash years, conservatives used the book as a convenient proof of the dangerous madness of feminist desires. (They refuse to be mothers! They want babies from test tubes!) During those same years, some feminists used the book to show how short-sighted, overweening, or half-baked the early women's movement had sometimes been. (They refuse to be mothers! They want babies from test tubes!) Certainly a movement that was changing, testing its basic propositions, settling down for what looks like a long haul has used the book to measure distances: "Firestone promised us a rose garden; look how far we have come; we no longer believe in rose gardens."

No doubt Firestone invites some of these irritated readings. Her bold voice and sailing pace seem at odds with the enormity and difficulty of the change she is seeking. She is like a wonderful child who wants the moon, something big, bright, and at a distance she's not concerned to estimate. This sort of person appears (is created? is momentarily heard?) at the beginning of movements. Magnificent and stunned by insight, they tell us we must change our lives; the way we live is intolerable. Then they stagger off, leaving the less moonstruck but considerably brightened to try to live the insight out.

The ambition of the text has certainly been counted as one of its offenses: "Who does this little girl think she is?" She introduces almost the entire spectrum of subsequent movement interests in one big bang. She points out the limitations of Marx and Freud; she anatomizes the inner, often gendered dynamics of race and class; she compares the oppression of women and children (and finds them deeply analogous); then she goes on to make a chart of the great rolling dialectic of history from nomads to the disappearance of "culture" as we know it and the realization of the "conceivable in the actual."[1]

Even in 1970, I seem to have felt the scary undertow of this all-encompassing wave. I wrote: "Perhaps the reason membership in the women's movement is so often a painful experience is that the more we know, the more powerless and overwhelmed we feel. Knowledge doesn't turn out to be the instant kind of power we first expected it to be. In fact, the more conscious we become, the more lonely and naked we are in the middle of what we now understand to be an unfriendly situation." Unfriendly situation! This sort of mournful irony, this shy understatement of male intransigence is so far from Shulie's tone. She was a great leader partly because she eschewed such hedging. The risks she took opened a path. I took it and am eternally grateful to her.

Yet at some moments, *The Dialectic of Sex* wears the unassuming disguise of mere advice book. The prose bops along, with its summings-up of the little gender knots of daily life. Finally, though, there's always a trick; instead of the bromide that usually follows this now familiar kind of popularization, Firestone ends her snappy accounts of sexism with this warning: There is no private solution, dear reader, no short-term fix. There is only the revolution. Ann Landers from Hell, she makes mincemeat of the very concept "advice."

Her true genre is Utopia: "In our new society, humanity could finally re-vert to its natural polymorphous sexuality. . . . All relationships would be based on love alone, uncorrupted by dependencies and resulting class in-equalities."[2] "Good luck," I find myself thinking, but could this sarcasm be one symptom of the postsixties taboo on mentioning such far-off desires, such confident demands for structural transformation? We are allergic to utopia just now, often seeing any sweeping prefigurative thinking as falsely universalizing, naïve, out of touch with the hardness of power. Certainly Firestone's text is vulnerable to such criticisms. It can easily be dismissed as marginal ("cybernetic communism," ha, ha). Or her grand gestures, which clear families, races, classes from the board of history, can be dismissed as totalitarian. But this is to read the text out of its time. In an unequivocal voice now rare, Firestone simply insists that only fundamental reordering will change women's unfriendly situation, and that parts of that restructuring are currently imaginable in the West, while other parts are still only dreams.

The dynamism of Marxism, the flowing sixties atmosphere, and the gen-eral tendency of feminist utopians to dream of amniotic bliss—they all meet in *The Dialectic of Sex.* At that inspired moment, opposites—and barriers—seemed about to dissolve. The book is full of wishful fusions between con-tradictory concepts. For example, it begins:

Sex class is so deep as to be invisible. Or it may appear as a superficial inequality, one that can be solved by merely a few reforms, or perhaps by the full integration of women into the labor force. But the reaction of the common man, woman, and child—"That! Why you can't change that! You must be out of your mind!"—is the closest to the truth. We are talking about something every bit as deep as that. This gut reaction—the as-sumption that, even when they don't know it, feminists are talking about changing a fundamental biological condition—is an honest one. That so profound a change cannot be easily fitted into traditional categories of thought, e.g. "political," is not because these categories do not apply but because they are not big enough: radical feminism bursts through them. If there were another word more all-embracing than revolution we would use it.[3]

Typically, the protean Firestone is here the first essentialist feminist and the first social constructionist. She felt she could have it both ways, could claim the body as cause, as female prison, then could break the locks through social transformation. The pace at which modern Western societies seemed to be moving, the expansion of possibilities from the 1950s to the 1970s, lifted what Firestone saw as the heavy burden of biology off many women in the West. Biology-as-destiny was their past, but not their future.

Ironically enough, though feminist theory has moved steadily away from such biological determinism, feminists now have much lower expectations than Firestone's for the dissolving of "differences" like gender or race. These days, difference is either tolerated or valued as an axiom of political life. Contemporary feminists tend to be skeptical about the end of "othering."

Even with hindsight I find it hard to sort out my feelings about movement hopefulness in general. Feminism by its very nature demands such basic changes that none of its work would make much sense without an Enlightenment confidence in progress, without a belief in the human capacity to give conscious shape to ourselves. Yet part of what has happened to feminist thought since Firestone is the development of wise, rich doubts on these very matters. For those who remain feminist activists, these doubts are now baggage, the necessary, the useful impediments one carries with one on long journeys. I miss Firestone's avid joy, but I accept its absence as one by-product of the movement's longevity.

Now is a particularly good time to read or reread *The Dialectic of Sex*. Ten years ago it might well have seemed merely dated, with its confidence in "cybernation" and its brash social generalizations about male and female, black and white (and most objectionably at moments about homosexuality). A decade ago, the sixties were under vicious attack and even the most committed sixties people felt bitten, no longer in tune with sixties ardor.

But the wheel has turned again, and *The Dialectic of Sex* will now be exciting to a number of different sorts of readers. For those who are rereading, this is a period of memories and memoirs. Many feminist scholars and activists of a certain age have had their long, second thoughts, have put in their time in the necessary work of refining, revising, glossing, and pruning feminism, and may be interested in going to the well again to feel what that first energy was like.

Firestone felt herself to be throwing off a yoke, and in her first gallop, she wrote fast, wildly, freely. Those who came after have had to work at a slower pace, to take greater care. We police ourselves and each other more, while Firestone was shamelessly willing to generalize, speculate, make mistakes. To reexperience this unapologetic voice now is tonic.

For a new generation of readers, Firestone is movement history. Just what was it about the women's liberation movement that so took the culture by storm that—with whatever shortcomings, whatever waterings-down—it still has the power to interpret experience for millions? Young readers will sometimes think, "I already know this," then with some historical sense will, I hope, shake themselves and register that in 1970 no one knew any of it, even though it was all always already there to know.

For readers of whatever generation who have been following the feminist storyline, the book's precocity gives little gooses of surprise. For example, who remembers that John Berger's *Ways of Seeing* is fully anticipated in Firestone's dazzling chapter on culture? And move over Donna Haraway on cyborgs: "To grant that the sexual imbalance of power is biologically based is not to lose our case. . . . The 'natural' is not necessarily a 'human' value."[4] (Like Haraway, Firestone would rather be a cyborg than a goddess.) If her reading of Freud has been outdistanced, it is a pleasure to find here the still durable historical point that "Freudianism and feminism are made of the same stuff."[5] Indeed, for a text so famous for its iconoclasm, the book devotes a lot of loving attention to the masters and the past. Radical, it returns to founding texts. It is a love letter to Elizabeth Cady Stanton and Susan B. Anthony (in 1970, lost to history or scorned). It converses respectfully with Marx and Freud, and its hero is Simone de Beauvoir. It honors its dead and refuses the obfuscations of revisionists.

When one remembers that the feminist bookshelf wasn't a foot long in 1970, the fullness, clarity, and force of Firestone's feminism is simply amazing. (It's touching to see that her only source on childhood is the admirable Philippe Ariès and that she thinks there is no tradition of women's utopias. Today the library shelves are stuffed with feminist books on childhood and with feminist utopias old and new—and all in print.) She sought what roots she could find, and overnight she produced sturdy, waving green branches. Her analysis of women's daily experience—in love, in sex, in (mostly repressed) world-building—is as fresh and right as it seemed then; I regret to say this part of her work hasn't dated at all. To give but one example:

> The sex privatization of women is the process whereby women are blinded to their generality as a class which renders them invisible as individuals to the male eye. . . . Women everywhere rush to squeeze into the glass slipper, forcing and mutilating their bodies with diets and beauty programs, clothes and makeup, anything to become the punk prince's dream girl. But they have no choice. If they don't the penalties are enormous: their social legitimacy is at stake.
>
> Thus women become more and more look-alike. But at the same time they are expected to express their individuality through their physical appearance. Thus they are kept coming and going, at one and the same time trying to express their similarity and their uniqueness. The demands of Sex Privatization contradict the demands of the Beauty Ideal, causing the severe feminine neurosis about personal appearance.
>
> But this conflict itself has an important political function. When women begin to look more and more alike, distinguished only by the degree to which they differ from a paper ideal, they can be more easily stereotyped as a class: they look alike, they think alike, and even worse, they are so stupid they believe they are not alike.[6]

A hundred articles and books have since sorted through these painful paradoxes, major sources of female self-loathing, but here they are, in a witty, full-blown description on Day One. Firestone criticizes the false eroticism of this essentially bleak sexual landscape, but she draws back from the antipornography conclusions of a less insurgent, later time:

> In conclusion, I want to add a note about the special difficulties of attacking the sex class system through its means of cultural indoctrination. Sex objects are beautiful. An attack on them can be confused with an attack on beauty itself. Feminists need not get so pious in their efforts that they feel they must flatly deny the beauty of the face on the cover of *Vogue*. For this is not the point. The real question is: is the face beautiful in a human way—does it allow for growth and flux and decay, does it express negative as well as positive emotions?. . .
>
> To attack eroticism creates similar problems. Eroticism is exciting. No one wants to get rid of it. Life would be a drab and routine affair without at least that spark. That's just the point. Why has all joy and excitement been concentrated, driven into one narrow, difficult-to-find alley of human ex-

perience, and all the rest laid waste? When we demand the elimination of eroticism, we mean not the elimination of sexual joy and excitement but its rediffusion over—there's plenty to go around, it increases with use—the spectrum of our lives.[7]

So, sex, yes; beauty, yes; freedom, yes; an end to the boundary of gender altogether, yes—and to all boundaries. This was then. Our time is different, but this very fact is relevant evidence of the relentlessness and promise of change.

1994

Notes

1. Firestone, *The Dialectic of Sex*, 215.
2. Firestone, *The Dialectic of Sex*, 236–37, 264.
3. Firestone, *The Dialectic of Sex*, 1.
4. Firestone, *The Dialectic of Sex*, 10.
5. Firestone, *The Dialectic of Sex*, 50.
6. Firestone, *The Dialectic of Sex*, 168, 171–72.
7. Firestone, *The Dialectic of Sex*, 175.

V

THE FEMINISM OF UNCERTAINTY

23

INTRODUCTION TO THE FEMINISM OF UNCERTAINTY

Uncertainty always has an autobiography attached. As a young child, I had dyslexia and couldn't immediately read or write. Perversely, these two things were all I wanted to do. I struggled to proceed from the mysterious unclarity on the page toward a coherence that was alluring, but never final. In "Life Sentence: My Uncertainty Principle," I discuss how this commitment to the unresolvable made literature enchanting. Later, self-doubt became a value, a starting position for both writing and political activism.

Since this was my state of mind, Doris Lessing has always been a writer I needed. Her straight-ahead style conceals a belief in human limitation, confusion, and incapacity to willfully direct history. I have included here selections from some of the pieces I have written about her over the last thirty years. With dry irony, Lessing captures what it is to be a deeply political person with a constantly ambivalent attitude to the politics she imagines. Aggressively deflationary, she is also an architectural dreamer, a master builder—always constructing different environments where human beings might flourish. Or fail to flourish. She moves from the local to the planetary, trying to embody in fiction the insight Dorothy Dinnerstein was also seeking to explore: Human beings orient ourselves to a particular piece of reality to survive and achieve coherence, but ultimately we would have a better chance at survival if we could move more flexibly among the different layers of our consciousness. In other words, if we could learn to jump scales, we could both forage for a good lunch and protect the production of food on the planet. Lessing would like to believe in human agency, but her political yearnings are always checked by the long view she takes of everything.

After an ironic farrago about utopia, I end with a reprise of my beginning. I look at utopias and their shadows and try to affirm the political life without any illusion that one can know the long future of any political act.

In this book, I've explored "uncertainty" as a temperament, a political aesthetic, a counterweight to various forms of rigidity, false closures, or too-perfect dreams of unity or order. But I want to guard here at the close against any mapping of "uncertainty" onto a blithe disregard for the responsibility to shape one's feminist projects. Uncertainty as I figure it here is very far from "anything goes." On the contrary, it puts extra stress on the need to define—in each situation—what one is doing. I honor but also sometimes regret feminism's lability, particularly some of its current detours into private solutions far from any of the ideas about basic social changes that I care about. I get irritated and disappointed when, instead of ramifying as a political movement, feminist sensibility expresses itself in clothing styles or private "choice." As one student put it: "You did feminism, so now I can be an individual and not a woman. You struggled so I can choose not to." I loved this student's sense of new freedom and feared for her, too. Feminism is hardly a completed project she can count on in the years ahead.

Along with many other radical feminists who want fundamental transformations, I sit in my watchtower and monitor moments of political fragmentation, lassitude, and the many neo-liberal co-optations of feminist demands. Radical feminists may critique such detours but then we, too, must plot our course over shifting terrain. One's goals and political work can be forced into "liberal" or "radical" frames depending on context, and willy-nilly one crosses such conceptual borders in both directions many times. But this indeterminacy in no way reduces the need to shape a radical feminist identity and desire.

In an article from 1984, "Feminism: A Movement to End Sexist Oppression," which I have taught many times, bell hooks argues that the liberal goal "equality" is useless for feminists. She asks, "Since men are not equals in white supremacist, capitalist, patriarchal class structure, which men do women want to be equal to?"[1] This is one of the most mordant criticisms of liberal feminism ever written—and certainly the wittiest. She goes on to argue that any serious, committed feminism requires clear definition; feminism isn't whatever you want, but is a movement against all forms of domination—or it is nothing.

This is the feminism I continue to embrace, but the proliferation of feminisms since I signed on in 1969 are astonishing. Claiming a positive value for this indeterminacy is one way to demand that each manifestation of feminist politics define itself, affiliate with others, name short-term steps that may or may not be able to bring more sweeping, distant changes. Feminism requires not only definition as hooks says, but also constant redefinition and critique—a process hooks has undertaken for many years.

My mother, Virginia Snitow, a passionate feminist in both thought and action, used to beg me not to use the word "feminism." "It puts people off," she used to say, eager to persuade by whatever means necessary. I stick with the term because the stigma is exactly my point of entry, my starting place for provocation. I choose "feminist" as a radical name, with its transformative travels attached, and work toward solidarity with the company I find. But, *pace* Mama, it would be unmannerly to insist to others that only one word will serve our many related purposes.

hooks has her own way around this problem. She says one should not *be* a feminist, but should *advocate* feminism; "feminist" should not be an all-defining identity but a set of principles and goals, in other words, a politics. To many, public expressions of feminism have seemed narrow or culture-bound, but hooks says, one doesn't need to eat brown rice or denounce one's family to "advocate" feminism.[2] I admire this brilliant work-around, which makes space for many different people to include feminist ideas as part of a wide range of political work. Uncertainty is not synonymous with diversity, but they are relatives.

Finally, accepting not knowing is a way of acknowledging the complexity of all social history. We struggle to construct an account of ourselves, but can't fully trace just how our wishes have come to take their current forms. "Change" and "agency" are keywords, ambiguous, polyvalent, and unanchored. I'm certain of this: In my activist life, irony (comic whenever possible), doubt, and the unresolvability of questions about how to proceed have protected me from burn out. Not knowing how to place feminism collides with a feeling of urgency. Sparks fly, and I'm still fascinated: "What next?"

Notes

1. bell hooks, "Feminism: A Movement to End Sexist Oppression," 18.
2. bell hooks, "Feminism: A Movement to End Sexist Oppression," 29.

24

LIFE SENTENCE

My Uncertainty Principle

Nobody knows anything and they pretend they do.
—Doris Lessing, "The Other Woman," (1959)

This dyspeptic quotation, typed out, has been hanging more or less in front of my eyes for some years, on the corkboard above the writing desk. That sourpuss Lessing. What is she doing there for so long? To answer that, I discover, I have to go back to the beginning.

Learning to read: I remember it as a journey, linear, with stops long or short. I am trying to get somewhere, but the words point in different directions, so as I go, I take mental side trips, which only make the whole business even longer. My writing has everything to do with this early physical experience of reading, the climb up the line, the mysterious lull at a comma, the cliff at the end, the free-fall until one catches—if one is lucky—onto the next ledge down.

When I was five, all this overheated effort made desire more keen. I became a reader, then a writer, and a teacher of reading and writing. This is privileged work and people who don't like their jobs may find complaints about it irritating. At the same time, the difficulty of writing is a truism. Writers are always complaining to anyone who will listen; usually this means other writers. My students show alarm and disbelief when I tell them how many times they need to rewrite before a third party—not their teacher or their mother—would even consider reading what they've written. Most conclude that this job, writing, is no part of their life plan. How much I sympathize, since I can't easily help them. And among other pitfalls, writing is embarrassing, revealing each one's private, possible grammar. The shape of the sentence, and of the essay as a whole, is a complete confession: "This is the way I, I, I could find to do it, hence, this tells about my mind at work."

My first sustained experience of my own unavoidable grammar was writing a dissertation at London University. Always slow, I tried to cultivate perfectionism in lieu of pace. At the end of each sentence, I threw out a grappling hook to haul in what I hoped to persuade the world was the sentence that naturally and inevitably came next. I see now that from the first I was hopelessly skeptical about most claims of cause and effect, suspicious of artful structuring devices, leery of confident summations. But these temperamental doubts often felt like confusion. Asserting a unity I never felt, I developed the connectives editors love even now to cut from my work, little words to ease the reader along.

Before leaving off, I had written eight hundred pages, depressing my university examiner by my monstrous breadth of reference. When it came time to publish this endless effort to be clear, exhaustive, above reproach, I had to cut it precisely in half—a process undertaken in an old house, where the wooden worktable got gritty with sand. Reviewers have said of this book that I can be trusted about the novels of Ford Madox Ford. Lord, yes, I put in my time, and I cared as best I could, under the circumstances. Ford, who was as he often said, an old man mad about writing, got eighty books written. I, too, had written on and on, wondering where books come from in people. At the end, I was as stuck about the title for this study of modern irony as I had been about all the rest. How could I name it? *Ann's Bedlam? Drowning? Nobody Knows Anything?* The kindly publishers, used to revised dissertations, came up with and insisted upon the apt *Ford Madox Ford and the Voice of Uncertainty*. RIP.

Laborious as all writing is for me, it has never been quite like that again. The ordeal marked a shift. In future, I would have to find some other way—or ways—to get from place to place. If uncertainty and insecurity were my condition, then they would also have to be my subject and shape my work. If linear strings couldn't convince me, I wouldn't offer them to anyone else. If I doubted, then I would have to develop confidence in that doubt. At some point, I stopped waiting for things to get easier.

Still, on some level, I continue to write for that child who is learning to read and for whom things are never easy. I always have one hand out to help her along, trying to write only sentences I would like to read myself. My always ambivalent friendship with this faltering reader has its dangers: often she asks for the wrong kind of help, demands redundancy, tiresome explanations. She has stylistic agoraphobia, wants every open space filled in. She pretends that those little forward leaps—the jump cuts in the prose I like best—are too much for her. Sometimes she makes a shibboleth of clarity. Uncertain myself, I try to offer her what she needs; then conscience makes me explain that things aren't all that clear. Clarity is a flickering light, I tell her, not the answer, not to be mistaken for closure, or simplicity.

Like a comic caricature in Moliére, *l'écrivain fou*, my effort to be clear without false absolutes, arrogance, fatal simplifications leads me to elaborate— more, then more. Love or resist my primitive reader within, she is there, at the deepest level of my prose, making apposition, that grammatically hanging further explanation, my most constant writing tic—never one word where two will do. I live with these sentences, loose associations, increasingly complex clustering islands. Apposition floats; it breaks the forward rush. This gives me time to work the material around in rings. On good days, when I cut the writing down to half, the redundancy drops out of the circles; the clusters turn into grids and hold together in spite of their lack of a single narrative line.

I live with a composer, Daniel Goode, who has a piece called "Finding the Unison Sentence." A group of people are to start talking, each one talking continuously, all trying to find a sentence they want to say together. I used to think the piece was a failure, since the groups never came close to unison, petering out instead. But the composer suggested that on the contrary, perhaps the piece shows that there is no unison sentence. We speak (and write) very differently; only rarely can we raise one voice. (When should we?) Reading a few sentences of my mother's on a pad, I am struck by their similarity to my own cadences, the same invertebrate but dense structures. Maybe our typical sentences are in part an inheritance; surely they embody the history of what we could and could not do, of what happened to us, and how we managed.

All writers have voices they cannot elude; voice, like character and murder, will out. But most writers are also cannibals, trying to ingest what might be usable. It's a constant fight to write the sentences we dream of, working against the grain of our limitations. As I read, I'm always on the lookout for others' tricks, or for their beautiful solutions.

From my friend Chris I learn the transition "To be sure . . ."—a simple shift of ground I could never have found in my private store of combinations. To be sure, Chris derides the more assertive words "of course." "Of course," she says, is never true. (Certainly the words often flag the weakest part of an argument.)

Reading slowly, I notice how others work it. Olivia Manning: "One afternoon, while wandering about alone, Harriet met Yakimov and, strolling with him up University Street, took the opportunity to ask about some of the people they had seen in Athens."[1] How I envy this sentence, the property of the English novelists, with its confident internal transitions, its leisure, the double suspension of those present participles: first the "while wandering," then the loose "and, strolling." One afternoon, there was wandering, meeting, strolling, asking—none of these activities urgent, all snaking out into the special time which is English novel time, days (and sentences) that collect until, with a little shift, things are fundamentally altered.

Unfortunately, I can't ingest this sentence, product of a different world. I'll never have the ease to combine words at once so unheated and so riveting. And, more generally, though I love novels, I am instead an American essayist, writing analytically about social change. What models come to hand? I cruise around my library and find good sentences, sentences I might try for—flexible, muscular, complex without show.

Carroll Smith-Rosenberg: "But the scholar must ask if it is historically possible and, if possible, important to study the intensely individual aspects of psychosexual dynamics."[2] My shelves are full of sentences like this, which breathe, turn, and draw me into them. Also common in my library of course (though, why of course?) are sentences like this one of Stephen Heath's:

> Which is to say that in current ideological struggle it is not enough to assert in opposition women's relation to a non-genital, 'dispersed' sexuality, since such an emphasis (moreover close to Freud, who can talk of a feminine sexuality "dispersed over the body from head to foot") is a powerful representation of women from within, and as part of the existing oppression, woman as a kind of total equivalent of sex, her identity as that; the need is precisely to come back on the production of sexuality, women and men (the reduction of sexuality to genitality in their representation), and to understand the history of the subject in difference from there, in the social relations of its symbolic order, in a possibility of transformation.[3]

Where to begin? Why hang so many abstractions on such a weak armature? Why any of it—all those prepositional phrases? Perhaps I should feel friendly to Heath, since he tries to write as if he were speaking, uses loose appositions, gropes along a shapeless path, seemingly with all the lack of confidence I could desire. But I don't believe he's really the humble seeker this dreary sentence posits. Rather, he's with his clan, writing with his feet, and getting away with it. Such sentences are punishments for the uninitiated, and it is the powerful who are in the position to punish.

This may seem like the start of a now rather common diatribe against academic jargon, but that's not really a chorus I want to join. I assume that, at least for some, the rush to invent new vocabularies comes not so much from professional elitism as from a sense that current categories are breaking down. I'm never surprised that doubt has flooded in and washed out all the linguistic roads. One tries to be clear, faithful to what one has observed, yet, poignantly, in blow the questions, ruffling the prose: Clear to whom? True to whose observation? Are there rival clarities, inevitable unintelligibilities?

Both rhetoric and obscurity are annoying, yet just as I start to reject these writers, hating the way their sentences hector or exclude, I'm reminded that at least some jargon begins as oppositional language. Such language is by definition half achieved, even half-baked. A general snobbery about good prose is no help at all, since one is always thrown back on deciding, case by case, where a voice comes from and why it might be the way it is. The troubling opacity of another's words, categories, shaping gestures can be expressive, too, of our distance from each other. Though I am committed to the milling about, talking, straining—in other words to the quest for unison sentences, for unprovincial, shared communities—nonetheless, I do not believe in, or even want, one language, indivisible, and clear to all.

Yet I write, and all writing contains a miniature theory of order inside it. At the center of one's effort, certain clarities emerge. Doubt that asserts itself, that tries to be clear about itself—this is my lesson to my students, my writer's paradox. Mine will always be writing that puts lack, point of view, limitation—in other words my own speaking voice—in the foreground. The writing I care for most discovers its own edges, then discovers that even this self-reflexivity has edges, and on and on.

A social analyst with fewer crochets or qualms might say these words prove no more than that I am a Left-wing intellectual after 1989, living in a city, a postmodern situation, an American aftermath, or that I know the physics of my century, or that I am female, a feminist, with good historic reasons for my skepticism about authority, or that I was an anxious child, temperamentally uncertain. Sources for my private uncertainty principle proliferate, pile up, topple over. I accept them as the best explanations I can find, but my skepticism extends to them, too. Do I really know just when I skate out over thin ice, or just where my own edge comes up? Can I name my doubts as confidently as I thought? Maybe, after all, I can't find them, though they will find me. But surely, in all this, I have some company?

I believe (yes, this is a credo, an unprovable article of faith) that all writers and thinkers encounter ignorance as they write—whether they know it or not. Even at the center of the argument, their boundaries slice at the material, creating gaps and edges. In this, writing is like mortality. Or to be less melodramatic, here is my cliff, my childhood line of print, with the fall into what I don't know, can't master.

Writing, I am alone, yet with this wish for company; I am uncertain, yet with this wish for clarity. Hence Lessing: "Nobody knows anything." She's written thirty books about that! Much as I love to read urbane writing, writing with elegant plotting and satisfying closure, I seem to need most those writers who write on and on, spurred by an almost hysterical uncertainty. Exiled from the tradition into which they were born, the happy entitlements of the English novel, Ford Madox Ford is giddy and Lessing is dry with the awfulness of their loss, yet they seem very pleased with themselves, too, as they write, write. Words are their way of denouncing mayhem and of living in it. As far as I know, writing puts power and powerlessness together like no other experience. As far as I know.

1991

Notes

1. Manning, The Balkan Trilogy, 647.
2. Smith-Rosenberg, Disorderly Conduct, 59.
3. Heath, "Difference," 63–64.

25

DOUBT'S VISIONARY

Doris Lessing

Books discussed in these review essays:

The Children of Violence series (1952–1969)
Memoirs of a Survivor (1974)
The Making of the Representatives for Planet 8 (1982)
Documents Relating to the Sentimental Agents in the Volyen Empire (1983)
The Good Terrorist (1985)
Mara and Dann: An Adventure (1999)
The Story of General Dann and Mara's Daughter, Griot and the Snow Dog (2006)

We Are Overcome

People keep telling me they stopped reading Doris Lessing when she began writing science fiction. I want to seduce these readers back. Lessing's new book may help, but then again it may not. Though *The Good Terrorist* is a realist novel set in the crumbling but fertile London her old fans will fondly remember, Lessing keeps slapping the reader in the face throughout, hardly a come-hither gesture. I could try suggesting that readers imagine themselves dozing as their car accelerates toward a precipice; then they could love Lessing for slapping them.

Certainly, Lessing believes that we are at the edge; she takes it on herself to yell constantly, *Wake up, you're nodding off*. People seem more willing to listen when realism is the medium. They tend to see Lessing's science fiction as a vacation from terrestrial bad times. I want to persuade you: This is one writer who never took a vacation in her life.

All along, reports of the death of the realist have been greatly exaggerated. In recent years, Lessing has been experimenting with different focal lengths, swooping between bird's-eye and worm's-eye views, but her materials remain essentially the same. She wants desperately to know how the world works, how change happens, and how each person is a part of the whole. Sometimes she believes that the personal is political and she is content to show us daily life—resonating with history but tied down to consciousness. At other times, she throws up her hands in despair and decides it's ridiculous to hope the personal is tied to larger events by any reliable links at all. She sees chasms open between individual will and great social shifts. Volcanoes throw up mountains; ideas "move like tides," pushed into being by forces no one can grasp. But still she shows individual lives, if more briefly, tossing like corks on the great waves. In all her galactic fantasies, she is never talking about any world but ours, and this she does with an unmodified urgency.

The Good Terrorist is about politics in the conventional, limited sense of that word. But the recent Lessing novel that comes closest to it in didactic intention is the abstract science fiction satire, *The Sentimental Agents*, a novel that couldn't be further from *The Good Terrorist* in ostensible content or style. This is just another way of saying: Stick with Lessing. Her work—and obsessions—hold together.

Maybe the alienation people feel from Lessing's recent fiction has some of its source in her ambivalence about whether or not there's any story left. A while back, she stopped telling us the end is near and began saying the end has already happened. We're living on the last of the oxygen, sitting on the last patch of green grass, writing the final books. One novel in her science fiction series, *The Making of the Representatives for Planet 8*, is a minimalist chronicle of the last days of a planet. The cold closes in and the people, who in no way deserve this fate, drift off into a final, numb sleep.

When Doris Lessing calls a novel *The Good Terrorist*, we set our gears at once for her driest, most ironic voice. Such a naughty title promises a savage satire on marginal, underground political life, the life of mysterious "actions," unattributable explosions, "cadres," and "comrades." *The Good Terrorist* stirs a stick around in the reader's private mud where rhetoric, politics, unreasoned belief, and unconscious motive tend to settle at the bottom and are vegetating in shameless contradiction. Lessing is disgusted by the pretense at mastery of our species, which is coupled, as she sees it, with human ignorance and childishness. She's particularly contemptuous of anyone who still goes to demonstrations, joins partisan political groups, or is to be caught singing (with tears in the voice), "We shall not, we shall not be moved," or "We shall overcome." Lessing wants us to take note: We are constantly "moved" without much knowledge of how or why; we are far from "overcoming."

In the beginning, and in spite of the oxymoron of the title, Lessing's main character, Alice, is good in a number of homespun traditions of the term. She loves the unlovable, feeds the hungry, works without expectation of reward. As the novel opens, Alice and Jasper, her cohort and mentor during fifteen years of political activism, arrive at the door of a "squat," one of the many abandoned houses in London. This squat, once a solid turn-of-the-century family house, is now a sewer clogged by the rebellious and dispossessed. Here Alice, a child of the middle class, is to use her bourgeois confidence, respectability, and know-how in the service of a small sectarian group of communists who cling to the complex life of London like microscopic parasites.

Lessing has always loved this conceit: the world mirrored in a house. Her earlier novels *The Four-Gated City* and *Memoirs of a Survivor* centered almost entirely on women trying to keep a household together, cleaning, fixing, balancing rival family claims for mental and physical space. The action in these novels was women doing their ancient work under circumstances—the Fall of the West—that make housekeeping heroic and, finally, impossible. Alice, too, is one of Lessing's epic housewives, but with a difference: her housekeeping is vestigial, an automatic tic. While she builds and heals with one hand, she plots to tear this safe, ordered life down with the other. Alice the revolutionary is committed to kicking the nest from the tree.

Alice's "commune"—violently ironic word—stands for the dismantling of everything. Naturally, it can hardly keep itself together, call a meeting, or maintain agreement long enough to act. Yet everyone in the group shares a vocabulary, a set of assumptions, and a rage that the world of their fathers and mothers has left them a much smaller inheritance than they were raised to expect. They agree that this is a "shitty fucking filthy lying cruel hypocritical system."[1] When they throw oranges at policemen and are arrested for a few hours, they all yell "police state." They use their welfare checks for expensive take-out food and for transportation to far-flung radical battlefronts—Ireland, Moscow, and any factories with strikes (though in none of these places do they prove welcome). As Alice explains patiently to her mother, who has offered her safe haven all her life: "Don't you see that your world is finished? The day of the rich selfish bourgeoisie is over. You are doomed."[2] Then Alice steals her mother's carpet, her curtains; property is theft, so this crime is justified, forgotten, while the stolen curtains continue to emanate their mysterious childhood comfort at the windows of the squat.

Bubbles of narrative excitement start to pop to the surface of The Good Terrorist as the enormity of Alice's aphasia becomes clear. Alice, so kind, talented, and sensible, is a maniac. The unfolding of this surprise makes The Good Terrorist among the most intricately plotted of Lessing's novels. The suspense rises off the questions, "Who is Alice, and what will she do?" The gradual emergence of answers offers the chills and shocks of psychodrama. Lessing doesn't stint on the details, but she has begun to wonder if they might not be beside the point. After all, Comrade Alice, a privileged daughter of a loving mother, and another communard, Faye, once a battered baby, are both capable of the same aimlessly destructive act. What then, asks Lessing peremptorily, does differentiation, the individual life story, mean? She shrugs a bit regretfully at her glorious inheritance, the skills of the realist novelist, and tries to focus instead on the herd, the mysterious welding of unanimity, the shared words and attitudes among people who piously believe themselves unique.

For Lessing, Alice is above all a situation, a social location between the '60s and the '80s, between a cosseted childhood and a marginal, precarious adulthood. Parallel to Alice's story runs the exemplary counter-tale of Dorothy Mellings, Alice's mother. Her dry, sensible, independent voice is surely close to Lessing's. As Alice and her group move erratically toward what they call action, Dorothy moves steadily away from her former active political and family life, and begins in a very different way to dismantle the once so magically sustaining family house. Alice keeps returning there, surprised to see signs of packing, then terrified to find empty rooms. She simply fails to believe (what we slowly learn she has been told many times) that her mother, the linchpin of the world but now in fact rather tired and quite poor, has moved into a small and undistinguished flat. Nor can Alice take in that her mother, a radical all her life, is choosing to break those old social ties, questioning the revolutionary shibboleths of her own generation. Dorothy does not know what to do, but at least now she knows she does not know—Lessing's present ideal of the responsible position.

There are some people who know more, perhaps? Dorothy (and Doris) suspect there may be. Lessing has only to breathe on her fictional mirror once more and glimmering science fiction figures could start to form on her London streets, embodying alternative thoughts about power, action, and change. One may feel uncomfortable with the absolute and unironic authority she grants to her otherworldly heroes, the envoys of Canopus, but perhaps she indulges in this ideal to criticize the young who think that all evil lies in authority.

Once you know what to look for, there are many secret hints of Canopus on Alice's dreary turf: Decent policemen restrain sadistic policemen; bureaucrats work invisible miracles against depressing odds; small human exchanges demonstrate the nascent possibility of a kind and rational order. Even Alice's mental density is a clue: It's almost as if Lessing were saying to us, *You can see how stupid my characters are being. And since you can see it, perhaps there is something beyond their stupidity? Perhaps such stupidity is not really necessary* (beloved Canopean word)?

The Sentimental Agents (actually: *Documents Relating to the Sentimental Agents in the Volyen Empire*—as one small-city librarian said when I gave her this title, "No wonder we don't have it") is a megagalactic abstract of *The Good Terrorist*. On the planet Volyen, the most common and dangerous disease is "Undulant Rhetoric." Patients dry out in the Hospital for Rhetorical Diseases (quietly founded, of course, by the envoys from Canopus). Rhetorical illness erupts in ideas like, "If you're not with us you're against us," while good health equals a less strict good sense, embodied in the sentiment "There's no such thing as a free lunch." (All of terrorist Alice's lunches are cadged, all her rebellions sponsored by the world she says she hates.) Lessing is disgusted by Alice's call to arms, her wish "to tear it all down" and start over. She sends people to her imagined hospital because she doesn't want to hear any more crazy talk about broken eggs and omelettes.

It's hard to get specific about Canopean goals and practices because Lessing refuses Canopeans any rhetoric. One knows them by what they are not; one gets hints of what they are from what they do. They live thousands of years; hence, they take the long view of everything. They believe in evolution and wait patiently through millennia while herds individuate, carnivores learn to eat grass. At rare but crucial junctures, they put their oar in, giving a push—toward peace, order, and internal discipline without external authorities.

Sentimental Agents sets out Lessing's current formulations: The dangerous people are the ones who seek to be masters of an entirely new order after decimating the old, who believe they have a right to something just because they want it, who believe they can make social change in their own image without "a real knowledge of how things work, real socio-psychological laws." In contrast, Canopus lives in a humble understanding of the laws of social evolution without ever indulging in the pleasures of passivity. Struggle is necessary but not sufficient; one must find the path of the possible.

Canopus has its attractions, as the strong, silent type always does. But why, one may ask, is Lessing succumbing to fantasies of paternalism? Okay, no calling her "reactionary," a "fascist" for projecting a superior state of being onto the leader, but why is she so hard on any gesture toward political analysis? And are all calls for community inevitably manipulative and corrupt? Can it be that Lessing is saying the young are the problem, for not listening to their elders, or for not evolving beyond them fast enough? The radical rage of youth is always motiveless and self-serving in these pages, never socially authentic or transformative.

There are threads of this sort of carping throughout Lessing's recent novels, but she talks back to any reader's irritation, saying in effect: *If you conclude that my critique of political activism makes me a neoconservative, an old style anticommunist, a fascist, it's only what I would expect from knee-jerk thinkers like you middle-class, armchair radicals. What do you* MEAN *by those words? You haven't done any real thinking in years.*

Of course these insults hurt. In particular, it will upset Leftists that Lessing singles us out as the greatest monsters of rhetoric. *Sentimental Agents* is about sentimentality, posturing, self-indulgence, and ignorance in the Left movements that Lessing herself was a part of for decades. She saves the worst for her old allies, a practice that hardly would meet with the approval of her Canopean heroes.

I have a private imaginary picture of Doris Lessing in the 1980s. Here she is, fascinating, authoritative, mad with impatience, sitting alone, curling into herself with disgust because the tiles are rotting on the roof opposite, because a young person on the street outside slouches by instead of walking briskly, because dirt is piling up under the streets and if the sewers should fail, as they surely will, we all will be inundated with shit. Fastidious and alarmed, Lessing sits there imagining cataclysms prefigured in the little failures of maintenance that mean a society can't nurture or cleanse itself.

Parts of *The Good Terrorist* can sound like one of our real neocons, Midge Decter, a critic who explained the radicals of the '60s as youths who were overindulged in childhood and henceforth refused to grow up and face grim reality. But if rebellions are merely the temper tantrums of the children without oedipal restraints then adults represent a more ideal past: The past is solid, the present infantile, disappointing. This is a simplification as pernicious in its way as Alice's projection of all evil onto her parents and Mrs. Thatcher.

If this were all, readers might be justified in announcing Lessing's decline into a petulant dotage. But this is not all, not even a tenth. Her curiosity and urgency are both green: Collectively human beings know much more than we act on. Why? Canopus follows "The Necessity." Necessity for us will mean recognizing the situation in which we find ourselves—an extraordinary but fragile and unevenly developed species, on an equally fragile Earth.

These days, it seems that Lessing is angry at everyone and everyone is angry at her. I offer the proposition that we feel uncomfortable with the new Lessing not because she's changed or gone dull, authoritarian, or irrelevant, but because she has become increasingly uncompromising, experimental, and peremptory. She's been stripping layers of sugar off the pill for years. Now she's down to the bitterest part, the hardest to swallow. (Canopus may look like sugar, but look again. Heavy father comes closer.)

It's tempting to simply disagree, to point to the dandruff on the shoulder. She's left herself vulnerable enough, surely, burning bridges and insulting friends right and left. A real Jonathan Swift for now, she has power, and a sense of responsibility that never sleeps, until, after all these years, there can be weariness or offhandedness in the voice, the special detachment of the sleepless. When she seems to drift off into a dream of another world, we still can't do better than to sharpen our minds against her nightmares.

1985

Where Are We?: Lessing's Circular Tale of Human History

Books reviewed in this essay:

Mara and Dann: An Adventure (1999)
The Story of General Dann and Mara's Daughter, Griot and the Snow Dog (2006)

Human beings are divided; that's what Doris Lessing, genius of stripped down narrative, has come, once again, to tell. They are capable of building wonderful, complex worlds and feeling deeply for each other; they are also capable of mean-spirited betrayal and infantile destruction. They invent amazing things, then forget what they know. They fight fiercely to survive, then foul the nest they've made for themselves. But while this drama of self-division is going on, constantly repeating, a larger story is unfolding, which most of the time they barely notice: The ice ages come and go; seas become deserts, deserts become seas. Just when a great city seems secure and enters its maturity, the water comes and invades its foundations. Cities sink and take with them human memory. Bits and pieces are left to puzzle—and befuddle—future generations, who come along hundreds of years later, or is it thousands? Scrawled on a wall, words no one can read:

. . . truths to be self evident
Un vieux faun de terre cuite . . .
. . . be in England . . .
Rose, thou art sick . . .
. . . all the oceans . . .
. . . rise from the dead to say the sun is shining . . .
. . . to a summer's day . . .
. . . Helen . . .
Western wind, when . . .

In this return to science fiction with a pair of novels, *Mara and Dann* and *The Story of General Dann and Mara's Daughter, Griot and the Snow Dog*, Lessing tells the story of two children fleeing through a terrifying world of starvation, war, and cultural collapse. Mara and Dann, brother and sister, fugitives from a dying tribe, travel north through an Africa which is drying up (thousands of years from now it has become "Ifrik") but which is marked with messages from a more developed past in stone and metal murals, indestructible fabrics, and in some few crumbling objects—are they books?

The ancients seem to have tried to keep a record of the richness of a civilization, Yerrup, now under the ice, by building replicas—of Rome? London? But now the replicas themselves are under water, their roofs glimmering far beneath as Mara and Dann row over them.

The subtitle of the first book, *Mara and Dann*, is "An Adventure." When they start their journey, Mara is only seven and Dann four. They are raw human material, tested to the limit of endurance, running from wild water dragons and killer spiders the size of five-year-olds. They learn to be wary, to eat and drink almost nothing, to survive on the barest thread of possibility that somewhere, North, what was once desert (the Sahara) is now green again, flowing with water, and filling up with new cities.

As they travel and grow up, their journey has become so compulsive, so central to who these young people have become, that it seems impossible that they could ever arrive anywhere that could soothe their restless, anxious hearts—or the reader's long-suspended expectations. At the end of the first volume, they arrive. In her Introduction, Lessing says the story of the siblings questing across a continent is ancient, and in so far as this is an old tale, the design is complete when Mara and Dann discover that they are a princess and prince and that a crumbling palace awaits. But this is no ending after all. They must find a way to live, and by now they are so restless that human history itself is an inadequate frame for what they crave.

Time becomes the novels' central character. What makes Mara and Dann heroes in these strange and at times compelling books is not that they could be king and queen but rather that they glimpse a larger story. At the beginning of volume two, Dann is trying to travel in a little boat still further north, right up to the ice cap which was once Europe. Lessing places him on a cliff, deafened by the crashing of ice into the Middle Sea (the Mediterranean), which is filling up before him like an empty bowl. He witnesses the cascading of boulders as if geological time could be experienced by a single human being. And this is what Lessing is trying to do here—to depict eons so that we can see the big design in which we all live.

It's by turns a wonderful, odd, and maddening project. The problem with time as subject is the poor fit between the freezing and thawing of glaciers and the scope of individual lives. Of course, that is just Lessing's point. She wants us to play that game Martha Quest played in the *Children of Violence* novels (1952–1969): first to imagine our bedroom, then the street outside, then the city, then the country, then the globe, then the galaxy, then the universe. This game of expanding the context, changing the frame, stretching the human imagination to orient itself to large realities has always been at the heart of her work.

The first novel is told mostly from Mara's point of view, but lest we linger inside the scale of one human life, by volume two, Mara is dead and Dann is left as a reluctant leader of armies, admired for his sufferings, and marked by a tragic illness, which began in an early childhood trauma: a bad man tortured him and a second man, who looked exactly like the first, rescued him. Some basic mystery lies wrapped in this nightmare memory about the twinned nature of good and evil, the elusive mixtures of these elements in every human life.

Dann interests Lessing because he has glimpsed the ultimate intractability of human limitation: we are too ignorant, or soft, or desperate, or unimaginative, or destructive, or in denial to do much to save ourselves from either ourselves or from the ravages of nature and time. Dann is bored by our compulsive repetition. The foil for Dann's abstraction and angst is his faithful and adoring follower, Griot, the practical man who organizes armies, food, places to sleep, civic order. Because Griot cannot have the large-time, cyclical thoughts of his mentor, he is free to do what is necessary, to take the next step toward survival. Touchingly, eventually, Griot lives up to his name and becomes a storyteller. But it is the restless Dann who goes beyond narrative and gets the last word. Though Mara's daughter tells him they have finally ended "happily ever after," and though Griot points out that together they have developed here in the north a stable and nurturant polity, Tundra, which provides for everyone, there are rumors from the south of starving hoards who might invade. Griot says to Dann: "I can't believe they would be so stupid. Tundra is very prosperous, we provide stability for all the North-lands and to the south and east too. We grow so much food there are always surpluses for sale. We are an example to everyone. So there would be no advantage in attacking us. I mean, it would be too stupid."

And Dann replies: "Well, yes, Griot, it would certainly be stupid. I agree with you there."[3] These dry words end the pair of novels. Obviously there will soon be war. Lessing's verdict is in: How stupid we are. The genre of science fiction has freed her to say it from the top of a cliff, literally watching time crunch up civilizations even while they busily collude in crunching up themselves. She keeps returning to this mode because of the opportunity it gives her to pull way back and speak schematically, from on high, about how stupid, stupid, stupid it all is.

Who can argue? Are these wars really necessary? Isn't it obvious, they only make matters worse? Is it absolutely necessary for us human beings to squander our resources until nothing is left but nonbiodegradable flotsam? Can't we act out of good sense and intelligence, chaining ourselves to the mast in the midst of floods and confusion, restraining ourselves from doing stupid, destructive things?

And another question: Can great novels be written out of this cosmic boredom with human beings, this abstract dualism between good and evil? What does finally work in these books is Lessing's pace, her relentlessness: Abstraction and detail, ennui with the human story and fascination with just how it unfolds. She drags us with her through every excess of human striving and failing, through terrible suffering—the length of a continent. She earns the feeling of exhaustion with which she leaves us: Everything made—the houses, languages, civilizations—must be made again. The past never disappears, but it can easily become unintelligible in the span of only a few lifetimes. The solid melts and the security to which human beings cling is an illusion. Lessing's art here lies in a vivid depiction of the endless ups and downs of human stories, and the partial failure of the art lies in the weary simplicity of this message.

The good Lessing, who is a Jeremiah warning us of the inevitable results of human craziness, is the twin of the bad Lessing, who is above all irritated, delighted to throw up her hands and declaim: Here comes the ice, and boy, do you deserve it. (These books' twinning gestures can almost stand as an analogue for these two aspects of her sensibility—active engagement and angry disgust.) I've always been one of those who greatly values them both—crabby as they can be about stupid feminists, stupid Leftists, stupid young people, etc., etc.

In the 1950s, Lessing wrote, "Nobody knows anything and they pretend they do."[4] In the pretense, we get human striving, the miracle of personality, the drama of good and evil. In the ignorance behind the pretense, we get . . . a yawning question. In all Lessing's fictions, in whatever genre, she seeks first one narrative strategy, then another, to get a bigger picture, a larger reality than human beings care to contemplate.

When she was a child, Lessing's father told her, as they looked up together at the stars above Africa, that if humans blow up this world, there are plenty more. The cynicism and grandeur of his observation are both still with her. The *disjecta membra* of human history have fascinated her endlessly, while at the same time the more she observes the human situation, the less she grants authority to any account of ourselves we humans craft from our experience.

Lessing is certain that there is nothing more self-deluded than human certainty—and it is in that divided state of a grand knowledge undercut by the principle of doubt that she leaves us.

In Memoriam: Octavia Butler 1947–2006

For those who love feminist science fiction, someone important to our speculative pleasures has departed—shockingly early: Octavia Butler. Like Lessing, she was capable of making whole worlds collapse and of taking human beings over the edge of themselves into new forms of life. So, like Lessing, who kept writing away passionately, provocatively, until she was 94, how much one wishes that Butler, too, could have been afforded the time to take her particular sense of the dissolving boundaries of things into world after world. All who have followed her in imagination—and those who will in future—have sustained a great loss.

2006

Notes

1. Lessing, *The Good Terrorist*, 107
2. Lessing, *The Good Terrorist*, 18.
3. Lessing, *The Story of General Dann and Mara's Daughter, Griot and the Snow Dog*, 282.
4. Lessing, "The Other Woman," 190.

26

UTOPIA, DOWNSIZED

A Farrago

I got the picture a few years ago in a museum: The Jackson Pollocks—they were the past. The modern rooms looked as classical and distant as the Greek pots around the corner. That particular concentration of effect was over. Then the same feeling of distance came up in reading—was it T. S. Eliot? What was this wail of loss? Who could remember? While I wasn't really looking, the romance of an ending had simply ended, and a certain angst had bitten the dust. In the night, a sharp regret had slipped away and joined an illustrious company in the past.

Just one little problem, perhaps a private tic: What about the future? As most of my friends will tell you, human beings make whatever flickering meanings there are. And the glut that surrounds an urban person—wilted turquoise flowers at fruit stands, clogged drains, subway accidents—we made all of that, too. But are these particular artifacts inevitable? The utopians didn't used to think so. They proposed garden cities. They thought we live this way by a mistake that some insight, planning, maybe a little capital, could rectify.

But the postsensibility says no. If we make the world, we do it in ways not particularly reducible to reason or order. Desire is a construction it's hard to track, and meanings racket around or slip away; they don't stick inside words or intentions. Unity is a false god, and humanism a fantasy of accord that excludes. Better worlds? Watch *Star Trek*. But skepticism, irony, and rude remarks scuttle the conversation beyond this point. I asked the psychologist Dorothy Dinnerstein, a postmodern sensibility if ever there was one, what she thought of Utopia. She acted as if a bad smell just got into the room. "Is that like that concept we used to have, 'mental health'?"

So, do we pomos hope? Of course, yes—though not, ever, for final solutions. Our lowered and reshaped expectations mark a generation. At any hint of the high-flown we're gone, our Geiger counters for rhetoric in a naughty, laugh-track staccato.

But is our sensibility really so innocent of Big Ideas? On the contrary, we're constantly smuggling in bits of our own paradise: multiculturalism, say, or gender breakdown. Our deft escapes from the rigid binaries are in their own way the stuff of romance. Just beyond our aggressive anti-idealism, in creeps our own fantasy of the good. When pomos get tipsy, we see subjectivities all together in a dance; one gets to stand, for a moment, where the Other stood. No one at the party will confess to dreams of a common language, but we have our own daring enterprise in heteroglossia, a shared babbling in many tongues. Should we crush these secret illusions of escape from the prison of identity? Let's not, let's leave this wishfulness be. Viva our treasured (in some respects, questionable) belief in the breakdown between margin and center; the local and particular are the best ideological counters going to the new world order.

Fall asleep in front of the television. The scene keeps changing, the boundaries collapse, a Kurd refugee (no name), then Oprah, a parade of guests. Can't keep their stories straight, or separate. Somewhere here, beyond numbing, or the monochrome of meaningless variety—voilá, postmodern Utopia—a place where difference blooms.

During communism's farewell, anyone so foolish as to breathe a word of enthusiasm for planning or any kind of improvability can't dine out. In such a climate, what does postmodern social responsibility look like? In the future, will we succeed in distinguishing our "freedom" from the "free market," our skepticism about meaning from the "end of ideology"? Our clever adaptation to disorder—might it mislead us into demanding less?

In whatever directions the postmodern sensibility travels, it can claim credit for the early announcement that the old maps are gone. In spite of the mad insistence on borders in current politics, borders are not holding up well. The postmodern response is typically a conundrum: Irreducibly different, we're all connected (it's okay if you hear this as the New York Telephone jingle): there's hope for us, because we've come off our high horse, because we're more humble in our hopes.

1991

27

THE FEMINISM OF UNCERTAINTY: II

Feminist aspirations often look quite impossible, indeed outrageous. And naming feminist desires takes one to a far country: an end to all domination (bell hooks); an end to the common hatred of women (Dorothy Dinnerstein). At this point even equal pay, affordable day care, and easily available abortion seem far to seek, as if they too are distant utopian wishes. Feminism is at its most powerful when it combines both urgent, immediate need and larger aspirations for something different. Together, these dimensions sustain a long-term activism. And, sometimes, feminism has the power to create new cultures where people can live—partially, precariously, for a time.

Still, for better and worse, feminism is not a consistent ideology promising knowable ends or a panacea applicable in all situations. For example, is feminist sensibility useful for posthumanists? How will gender matter in new forms of political work? I believe feminism has great longevity, but only if it is a continuous shape-changer, capable of responding to new conditions and expectations.

In my piece here celebrating the twenty-fifth anniversary of Shulamith Firestone's *The Dialectic of Sex*, I registered surprise at the degree of hostility the text has sometimes aroused. The book is often misread as a practical guide to the future, with the inevitable anxieties such a literal blueprint would provoke. ("What, babies in test tubes?! She's a monster who doesn't believe in love!") Firestone dreamed of beginning afresh, of escaping the established order of life events. Of course she knew that starting afresh is impossible—but she didn't care. Read as a utopian vision, a passionate try at freeing us from the present so as to imagine an entirely transformed gender-world, the book continues to be endlessly suggestive.

I don't mean to forget the disturbing history of many utopian projects. My postcommunist friends laugh at the slightest drift toward a belief in that glorious day when the proletariat will rule and our commune will be perfect and have the biggest pig. And, more seriously, they remember various rivers of blood. I asked a Polish friend from Lublin why the Germans—fleeing the allies, the war essentially over—hurried in the last hours to kill the hundreds of Jews left in the city's fortress. He suggested that it was utopianism, the dream of a world cleansed of those vermin, the Jews.

I once pulled together a course about Utopias, Heterotopias, Dystopias—since it was a mystery to me why I was interested in a number of bad movies and in what Doris Lessing called "speculative fictions." At the start, the course was a failure. Utopia is empty, Other, easy to dismiss. In particular, the Good Worlds, those places always elsewhere, made the students irritable with their cascade of impossibilities and sexist lapses: "Hey, Ann, Sir Thomas seats the women on the outside of the communal table because it's their job to jump up when the baby cries." And beyond such obvious shortfalls, the internal unity of utopian spaces was too flat to give these urban, heterodox young any inspiration. Utopian, amniotic bliss may be a layer of everyone's psyche (indeed, I think it is), but this literature left my students dozing. Even the most literal or innocent student bloomed into a magnificent skeptic: "Hey, Ann, do they have good sex in Herland?"

However, the final, science fiction section of the course changed the atmosphere. Here, the perfection of utopia turned out to be what dictators want. These books were often ironic about stable definitions of pleasure or straight paths to progress. The entry of irony and doubt in these fictions seemed to free students from having to do that work. At last, they were willing to indulge in speculation. For the first time in the course, they entertained the idea that the impulse toward escape might be a valuable starting point for new thoughts. And rather than think of their earlier boredom with the utopias as a measure of utopia's worth, they entertained the idea that boredom itself might be an indicator of the insufficiency not only of fantasy fiction but also of their own wishes. As the German sociologist Siegfried Kracauer said, better to be bored than to seek mere distraction.[1] Boredom is a clue—founding a need for change.

Teaching like this is precariously positioned between activism and theory. The feminist/activist teacher knows she should never seek to reproduce herself or to plot clear paths forward—both impossible, even if she entertained such ahistorical and narcissistic wishes. But the classroom is an evocative stage set where ideas about identity and politics vibrantly appear. And action is poised in the wings—a postulate.

What I'm calling the utopian yearnings that I have been surprised to discover in some of the pieces here can't be located in any one place in the essays—a utopian state of nowhere—but, buried in much that I have written, I find some unstable but recurring hopefulness about making things better, with the term "better" tied to earth by a long balloon string—its length contested, dependent on context, elastic. Because so many feminist thoughts and acts include radical designs for a different world, uncertainty, doubt, skepticism—also rage and despair—are their inevitable accompaniments. But none of these disturbing states of mind cancel the fervent thought: People make change; it's never only a matter of macro forces which no one can predict or influence; we are, gulp, in some sense implicated in the construction of our world. Art is one way into imagining something different, activism another. Always people are imagining, wanting, and acting from somewhere in themselves, or rather from often unacknowledged multiple states of self.

This dream of agency can turn on one, of course, like that dream of the utopian Nazis in Lublin. It turned on me the week before September 11, 2001, when I gave the "Aims of Education" address at the university convocation. Hoping to inspire the students to think of themselves as potentially powerful actors in the world, I criticized all the prevailing ideas about macro forces, global markets, machines that know more than individuals can understand, etc., etc. I said that those current images of a vast spider web in which they are hopelessly caught is one construction of our situation—but there are a number of possible others. I offered the example of the then new International Criminal Court, which planned to hold individuals to account for the part they played in big events like wars.

A few days later, just blocks from where I spoke, nineteen men brought down the World Trade Center buildings, killing 2,977 people. No avoiding the fact that I was right: They took a dream seriously, they acted, they changed the world.

So, no romance here about personal power or about yearnings for alternative realities. No utopia without taking on some responsibility for its dark shadow, its possible negative consequences. And, to strike home at what I care about most, am I confident that any form of feminism is reliably safe, a well-marked path to changes I've said I want? Can feminism usher in the good life? Does it guarantee a loving bedfellow? Or collective rituals that warm the heart? Or more practically, as Falstaff asked about honor, can feminism "set to a leg"? Feminism is necessary but not sufficient; desire, pain, and lack break feminism's boundaries as they do all others. One can't ask feminism—or any other political movement—to firmly fix a better future.

All the same, I choose to be the fool committed to celebrating the power of political imagination. Whatever their uncertainty, I prefer unstable goals to cynicism. Finally, utopia is as much a site of agonistic forces as any cluster of unsettled political ideas. One needs to improvise. Then one needs to confront the nightmare version of one's wishes. Then one imagines again.

2014

Note

1. Kracauer, "Boredom," 331.

PUBLICATION HISTORY

The Feminism of Uncertainty: A Gender Diary Publication History

Information included for all previously published pieces.

I. CONTINUING A GENDER DIARY

Chapter 1. A Gender Diary
"Pages From A Gender Diary: Basic Divisions in Feminism." *Dissent* 35, no. 2
    (Spring 1989): 205–24.
Reprinted as "A Gender Diary" in *Rocking the Ship of State: Toward a Feminist Peace
    Politics*, edited by Adrienne Harris and Ynestra King, 35–74. Boulder, CO:
    Westview Press, 1989.
Reprinted in *Conflicts in Feminism*, edited by Marianne Hirsch and Evelyn Fox Keller,
    9–43. New York: Routledge, 1990.
Reprinted in *Legacy of Dissent*, edited by Nicolaus Mills, 303–32. New York:
    Touchstone, 1994.
Reprinted in *Feminism and History*, edited by Joan Wallach Scott, 505–44. Oxford:
    Oxford University Press, 1996.
Translated into Spanish in *Que son los estudios de mujeres?* edited by Marysa Navarro
    and Catherine R. Stimpson, 179–232. Buenos Aires: FCED Press, 1998.

II. MOTHERS / LOVERS

Chapter 4. Dorothy Dinnerstein: Creative Unknowing
"Introduction." In *The Mermaid and the Minotaur*, Dorothy Dinnerstein, xix–xxxiii.
    New York: Other Press, 1999.
Translated for Serbian edition of book.

Chapter 5. From the Gender Diary:

Living with Dorothy Dinnerstein (1923–1992)

Earlier versions of this piece appeared as:

"Thinking about The Mermaid and the Minotaur." Feminist Studies 4, no. 2 (June 1978): 190–98.

"The Mermaid and the Memories: Remembering Dorothy Dinnerstein." The Women's Review of Books X, no. 7 (April 1993): 7–8.

Chapter 6. Changing Our Minds

about Motherhood: 1963–1990

"Feminism and Motherhood: An American Reading." Feminist Review no. 40 (Spring 1992): 32–51.

A shortened version appeared as "Motherhood—Reclaiming the Demon Texts." Ms. 1, no. 6 (May/June 1991): 34–37.

Reprinted as "Feminist Analyses of Motherhood" and "Feminist Analyses of Motherhood: Timeline." In The Encyclopedia of Childbearing: Critical Perspectives, edited by Barbara Katz Rothman, 145–50. Phoenix: The Oryx Press, 1993.

Reprinted in Polish in Pelnym Glosem no. 3 (Lato 1995): 57–72.

Reprinted as "Feminism and Motherhood: An American Reading." Maternal Theory: Essential Readings, edited by Andrea O'Reilly, 290–310. Toronto: Demeter Press, 2007.

Chapter 7. The Sex Wars in Feminism:

Retrenchment versus Transformation

"Retrenchment versus Transformation: The Politics of the Antipornography Movement." In Women Against Censorship, edited by Varda Burstyn, 107–120. Vancouver: Douglas and McIntyre, 1985.

Reprinted in Caught Looking: Feminism, Pornography and Censorship, edited by Kate Ellis, Beth Jaker, Nan D. Hunter, Barbara O'Dair, and Abby Tallmer, 10–17. New York: Real Comet Press, 1986.

Reprinted in Moral Issues in Global Perspective, edited by Christine M. Koggel, 671–75. Broadview Press, 1999.

Chapter 8. The Poet of Bad Girls: Angela Carter (1940–1992)

Earlier versions of this piece appeared as:

"The Postlapsarian Eve." The Nation, October 4, 1986, 315–16.

"A Footman at the Door: Angela Carter's Last Novel." The Nation, April 20, 1992, 526–28.

Chapter 9. Inside the Circus Tent:

Excerpts from an Interview with Angela Carter, 1988

"Angela Carter, Wild Thing: Conversations with a Necromancer." The Voice Literary Supplement no. 75 (June 1989): 14–17.

Chapter 10. *The Beast Within:*
Lady into Fox and A Man in the Zoo, by David Garnett
Review of "*Lady into Fox and A Man in the Zoo* by David Garnett." *The Voice Literary Supplement* no. 42 (Feb. 1986): 8.

III. THE FEMINIST PICARESQUE

Chapter 12. *Occupying Greenham Common*
"Holding the Line at Greenham: The Revival of Direct Action." *Mother Jones* (Feb./ March 1985): 30–34, 39–44, 46–47.
Reprinted as "Holding the Line at Greenham Common: Being Joyously Political in Dangerous Times [1985]." In *Women on War: Essential Voices for the Nuclear Age,* edited by Daniela Gioseffi, 344–57. New York: Simon and Schuster, 1988.
Reprinted with new preface as "Greenham Common." *Occupy! Gazette,* no. 3 (December 2011): 20–24.

Chapter 13. *Feminist Futures in the Former East Bloc*
"Feminist Futures in the Former East Bloc." *Peace & Democracy News* 7, no. 1 (Summer 1993): 1, 40–44.
Reprinted in *What Can We Do for Ourselves?, Augmented proceedings of the East European Feminist Conference,* Belgrade 1995.
Reprinted in Polish as *Spotkania Feminstyczne,* followed by a symposium on the piece, 1995.
Reprinted in Russian in *The Women's Dialogue,* no. 9 (1994); no. 10, a symposium on the piece (1995); no. 11, my response to symposium (1995).
Reprinted in *Grappling with Democracy,* edited by Elzbieta Matynia, 209–17. Prague: SLON, 1996.

Chapter 14. *Feminism Travels: Cautionary Tales*
"Cautionary Tales." The Proceedings of the 93rd Annual Meeting of The American Society of International Law (March 24–27, 1999): 35–42.
Reprinted in a pamphlet titled "Lecture by Prof. Ann Snitow, Cautionary Tales: Teaching Feminism across Borders," Univ. of Lower Silesia AAE in Wroclaw, Poland, April 19, 2004.
Reprinted as "Cautionary Tales: Western Feminism in Postcommunist Europe." In *Transregional Center for Democratic Studies* 15, no. 2 (June 2005): 1, 5–7.
Reprinted as "Cautionary Tales." In *Women and Citizenship in Central and Eastern Europe,* edited by Jasmina Lukic, Joanna Regulska, Darja Zavirsek, 287–297. Aldershot: Ashgate, 2006.

Chapter 18. *Certainty and Doubt in the Classroom: Teaching Film in Prison*
"Dangerous Worlds: Teaching Film in Prison." *Dissent Magazine,* Summer 2011, 94–106.

IV. REFUGEES FROM UTOPIA

Chapter 20. Remembering, Forgetting, and the Making of
The Feminist Memoir Project

"Refugees from Utopia: Remembering, Forgetting and the Making of The Feminist
Memoir Project." In Memory and the Future: Transnational Politics, Ethics and Society,
edited by Adam Brown, Yifat Gutman, and Amy Sodaro, 141–57. Basingstoke:
Palgrave Macmillan, 2010.

Chapter 21. The Politics of Passion: Ellen Willis (1941–2006)

A longer version of this piece appeared as:

"The Politics of Passion: Ellen Willis, 1941–2006." Women's Review of Books 24, no. 2
(March/April 2007): 28–29.

Chapter 22. Returning to the Well:
Revisiting Shulamith Firestone's The Dialectic of Sex

"Returning to the Well" (Review). Dissent (Fall 1994): 557–60.

V. THE FEMINISM OF UNCERTAINTY

Chapter 24. Life Sentence: My Uncertainty Principle

"Life Sentence." The Voice Literary Supplement no. 98 (September 1991): 19–20.

Chapter 25. Doubt's Visionary: Doris Lessing

Earlier versions of the piece appeared as:

"We Are Overcome: A Vindication of Doris Lessing." The Voice Literary Supplement
no. 39 (October 1985): 5–9.

"The Long Version: Review of Mara and Dann: An Adventure and The Story of General
Dann and Mara's Daughter, Griot and the Snow Dog by Doris Lessing." Women's
Review of Books 23, no. 6 (Nov./Dec. 2006): 30–31.

Chapter 26. Utopia, Downsized: A Farrago

"Hope Trope (Post-Modern Utopia)." The Voice Literary Supplement no. 99 (October
1991): 19–20.

BIBLIOGRAPHY

Abzug, Bella, and Mim Kelber. *Gender Gap*. Boston: Houghton Mifflin, 1984.

Aguero, Kathi, Marea Gordett, and Ruth Perry. "Mothering and Writing: A Conversation." *Women's Review of Books* 5, no. 10/11 (July 1988): 29–30.

Alcoff, Linda. "Cultural Feminism versus Post-Structuralism: The Identity Crisis in Feminist Theory." *Signs* 13, no. 3 (Spring 1988): 405–36.

Allen, Jeffner. "Motherhood: The Annihilation of Women." In *Mothering: Essays in Feminist Theory*, edited by Joyce Trebilcot, 215–30. Totowa, NJ: Rowman and Allanheld, 1984.

Alpert, Judith L., Mary-Joan Gerson, and Mary Sue Richardson. "Mothering: The View from Psychological Research." *Signs* 9, no. 3 (1984): 434–53.

Anderson, Bonnie. *Joyous Greetings: The First International Women's Movement, 1830–1860*. New York: Oxford University Press, 2000.

Arcana, Judith. *Our Mother's Daughters*. Berkeley, CA: Shameless Hussy Press, 1979.

Arditti, Rita, Renate Duelli-Klein, and Shelley Minden. *Test-Tube Women: What Future for Motherhood?* London: Pandora Press, 1984.

Arnup, Katherine, Andree Levesque, and Ruth Roach Pierson. *Delivering Motherhood: Maternal Ideologies and Practices in the 19th and 20th Centuries*. New York: Routledge, 1990.

Atkinson, Ti Grace. "Why I'm Against s/m Liberation." In *Against Sadomasochism: A Radical Feminist Analysis*, edited by Robin Ruth Linden, Darlene R. Pagano, Diana E. H. Russell, and Susan Leigh Star, 90–92. East Palo Alto, CA: Frog in the Well Press, 1983.

Atwood, Margaret. *The Handmaid's Tale*. Boston: Houghton Mifflin, 1986.

Badinter, Elizabeth. *Mother Love: Myth and Reality*. New York: Macmillan, 1980.

Bamber, Linda, and Marianne DeKoven. "Metacriticism and the Value of Difference." Paper presented at the Modern Language Association Annual Meeting, Los Angeles, December 1982.

Barnett, Bernice McNair. "Invisible Southern Black Women Leaders in the Civil

Rights Movement: The Triple Constraints of Gender, Race and Class." *Gender and Society* 7, no. 2 (June 1993): 162–82.

Barrett, Michèle. "The Concept of 'Difference.'" *Feminist Review* 26 (Summer 1987): 28–41.

Barrett, Michèle, and Roberta Hamilton. *The Politics of Diversity: Feminism, Marxism, and Nationalism.* London: Verso, 1986.

Barrett, Michèle, and Mary McIntosh. *The Anti-Social Family.* London: Verso, 1982.

Bartlett, Katharine T., and Carol B. Stack. "Joint Custody, Feminism and the Dependency Dilemma." *Berkeley Women's Law Journal* (Winter 1986–1987): 501–33.

Benería, Lourdes. "Work and Culture: Meditations on Ivan Illich's *Gender.*" In *Work in the 1980s,* edited by Bengtove Gustavsson, Jan Ch. Karlsson, and Curt Raftegard, 121–29. London: Gower Publishing, 1985.

Benhabib, Seyla. "The Generalized and the Concrete Other: The Kohlberg-Gilligan Controversy and Feminist Theory." In *Feminism as Critique,* edited by Seyla Benhabib and Drucilla Cornell, 77–95. Minneapolis: University of Minnesota Press, 1987.

Benjamin, Jessica. *The Bonds of Love: Psychoanalysis, Feminism, and the Problem of Domination.* New York: Pantheon Books, 1988.

Bertin, Joan E., Counsel of Record. "Brief of the American Civil Liberties Union et al." amici curiae, *California Federal Savings and Loan Association et al. v. Mark Guerra et al.,* Supreme Court of the United States, October Term, 1985.

Bird, Kai, and Max Holland. "Capitol Letter: The Garland Case." *The Nation,* July 5, 1986, 8.

Bishop, Jacky, and Frankie Green. *Breaching the Peace: A Collection of Radical Feminist Papers.* London: Onlywomen Press, 1983.

Boston Women's Health Collective. *Our Bodies, Ourselves.* Boston: New England Free Press, 1971.

———. *Ourselves and Our Children: A Book by and for Parents.* New York: Random House, 1978.

Bridenthal, Renate, Joan Kelly, Amy Swerdlow, and Phyllis Vine. *Household and Kin: Families in Flux.* New York: Feminist Press, 1981.

Brodsky, Joseph. "Why the Peace Movement is Wrong." *The Times Literary Supplement,* August, 24, 1984, 942.

Broughton, John, ed. "Women and Moral Development." Special issue, *New Ideas in Psychology* 5, no. 2 (1987).

———. "Women's Rationality and Men's Virtues: A Critique of Gender Dualism in Gilligan's Theory of Moral Development." *Social Research* 50, no. 3 (Autumn 1983): 597–624.

Brown, Carol. "Mothers, Fathers, and Children: From Private to Public Patriarchy." Reprinted in *Women and Revolution,* edited by Lydia Sargent, 239–67. Boston: South End Press, 1981.

CARASA (Committee for Abortion Rights and Against Sterilization Abuse). *Women Under Attack: Abortion, Sterilization Abuse and Reproductive Freedom.* New York: CARASA, 1979.

———. *Women Under Attack: Victories, Backlash, and the Fight for Reproductive Freedom* (Expanded Edition). Edited by Susan E. Davis. Athene Series, no. 7. Boston: South End Press, 1988.

Carter, Angela. *The Bloody Chamber.* London: Victor Gollancz, 1979.

———. "The Fall River Axe Murders." In *Saints and Strangers.* New York: Viking, 1986.

———. *Fireworks: Nine Profane Stories.* London: Quartet Books, 1974.

———. "Notes for a Theory of Sixties Style." In *Nothing Sacred.* London: Virago, 1982.

———. *Nothing Sacred.* London: Virago, 1982.

———. "Peter and the Wolf." In *Saints and Strangers.* New York: Viking, 1986.

———. *The Sadeian Woman: And the Ideology of Pornography.* New York: Pantheon, 1978.

———. *Wise Children.* New York: Farrar, Straus and Giroux, 2007.

Catt, Carrie Chapman, and Nettie Rogers Shuler. *Women's Suffrage and Politics: The Inner Story of the Suffrage Movement.* New York: C. Scribner's Sons, 1923.

Chamberlayne, Prue. "The Mother's Manifesto and Disputes Over 'Mutterlichkeit.'" *Feminist Review* no. 35 (Summer 1990): 9–23.

Chavkin, Wendy. "Walking a Tightrope: Pregnancy, Parenting, and Work." In *Double Exposure: Women's Health Hazards on the Job and at Home,* edited by Wendy Chavkin, 196–213. New York: Monthly Review Press, 1984.

Chesler, Phyllis. *With Child: A Diary of Motherhood.* New York: Thomas Y. Crowell, 1979.

———. *Mothers on Trial: The Battle for Children and Custody.* Seattle, WA: Seal Press, 1986.

———. *Sacred Bond: The Legacy of Baby M.* New York: Times Books, 1988.

Chodorow, Nancy. *The Reproduction of Mothering: Psychoanalysis and the Sociology of Gender.* Berkeley: University of California Press, 1978.

———. "Seventies Questions for Thirties Women: Gender and Generation in a Study of Early Women in Psychoanalysis." In *Feminism and Psychoanalytic Theory,* 199–218. New Haven, CT: Yale University Press, 1989.

Chodorow, Nancy, and Susan Cantratto. "The Fantasy of the Perfect Mother." *Social Problems* 23, no. 2 (1976): 54–75.

Christian, Shirley. "Mothers March, but to 2 Drummers." *New York Times,* February 21, 1987.

Cixous, Helene. "The Laugh of the Medusa." *Signs* 1, no. 4 (Summer 1976): 875–93.

Cliff, Michelle. *Claiming an Identity They Taught Me to Despise.* Cambridge, MA: Persephone Press, 1980.

Cole, Ellen, and Jane Price Knowles, eds. *Woman-Defined Motherhood.* Binghamton, NY: Harrington Park Press, 1990.

Collins, Gail. *When Everything Changed: The Amazing Journey of American Women from 1960 to the Present.* New York: Little, Brown, 2009.

Comprehensive Child Development Act of 1971, S. 1512, 92nd Congress (1971).

Corea, Gena. *The Mother Machine: Reproductive Technologies from Artificial Insemination to Artificial Wombs.* New York: Harper and Row, 1985.

Cott, Nancy F. *The Grounding of Modern Feminism.* New Haven, CT: Yale University Press, 1987.

Dally, Ann. *Inventing Motherhood: The Consequences of an Ideal.* New York: Shocken Books, 1983.

Daly, Mary. *Gyn/Ecology: The Metaethics of Radical Feminism.* Boston: Beacon Press, 1978.

Daniels, Pamela, and Kathy Weingarten. *Sooner or Later.* New York: W. W. Norton, 1983.

Delphy, Christine. *Close to Home: A Materialist Analysis of Women's Oppression.* Amherst: University of Massachusetts, 1984.

Deming, Barbara. "To Those Who Would Start a People's Party." *Liberation* 18, no. 4 (December 1973): 24.

Dinnerstein, Dorothy. *The Mermaid and the Minotaur: Sexual Arrangements and Human Malaise.* New York: Harper and Row, 1976. Reprinted: New York: Other Press, 1999.

Donovan, Josephine. *Feminist Theory.* New York: Frederick Ungar, 1985.

Douglas, Susan J. "Otherhood." In *In These Times* (September 1989): 12–13.

Dowrick, Stephanie, and Sibyl Grundberg. *Why Children?* New York: Harcourt Brace Jovanovich, 1981.

DuBois, Ellen. "The Radicalism of the Woman Suffrage Movement: Notes Toward the Reconstruction of Nineteenth-Century Feminism." In *Feminism and Equality*, edited by Anne Phillips, 127-38. New York: New York University Press, 1987.

DuPlessis, Rachel Blau, ed. "Toward a Feminist Theory of Motherhood." Special issue, *Feminist Studies* 4, no. 2 (June 1978).

———. "Washing Blood." Introduction to "Toward a Feminist Theory of Motherhood." Special issue, *Feminist Studies* 4 no.2 (June 1978): 1–12.

DuPlessis, Rachel Blau, and Ann Snitow, eds. *The Feminist Memoir Project: Voices From Women's Liberation.* New York: Three Rivers, 1998. Reprinted: New Brunswick, NJ: Rutgers University Press, 2007.

Dworkin, Andrea. *Intercourse.* New York: Free Press, 1987.

———. *Right Wing Women: The Politics of Domesticated Females.* New York: Perigee Trade, 1983.

Eagan, Andrea. *The Newborn Mother: Stages of Her Growth.* New York: H. Holt, 1987.

Echols, Alice. *Daring to Be Bad: Radical Feminism in America, 1967–1975.* Minneapolis: University of Minnesota Press, 1989.

Edwards, Harriet. *How Could You? Mothers without Custody of Their Children.* Berkeley, CA: Crossing Press, 1989.

Ehrenreich, Barbara. "What is Socialist Feminism?" *Monthly Review* 57, no. 3 (July–August 2005): 70–77.

Ehrensaft, Diane. "Feminists Fight (for) Fathers." *Socialist Review* 20, no. 4 (October-December 1990): 57–80.

———. *Parenting Together.* New York: Free Press, 1987.

———. "When Men and Women Mother." *Socialist Review* 10, no. 4 (Summer 1980): 49.

Eichhorn, Kate. *The Archival Turn in Feminism: Outrage in Order.* Philadelphia, PA: Temple University Press, 2013.

Eisenstein, Hester. *Contemporary Feminist Thought*. Boston: G. K. Hall, 1983.

Eisenstein, Hester, and Alice Jardine, eds. *The Future of Difference*. Boston: G. K. Hall, 1980.

Eisenstein, Zillah R. *The Female Body and the Law*. Berkeley: University of California Press, 1988.

———. *Feminism and Sexual Equality: Crisis in Liberal America*. New York: Monthly Review Press, 1984.

———. *The Radical Future of Liberal Feminism*. New York and London: Longman, 1981.

Ellis, Kate. "I'm Black and Blue from the Rolling Stones and I'm Not Sure How I Feel About It: The Feminist Debate Over Pornography." *Socialist Review*, May–June 1984: 103–25. Reprinted in *Women, Class and the Feminist Imagination*, ed. by Karen V. Hansen and Ilene J. Phillipson. Philadelphia: Temple University Press, 1990.

English, Deirdre. "The Fear That Feminism Will Free Men First." In *Powers of Desire: The Politics of Sexuality*, edited by Ann Snitow, Christine Stansell, and Sharon Thompson, 477–83. New York: Monthly Review Press, 1983.

Epstein, Cynthia Fuchs. *Deceptive Distinctions: Sex, Gender, and the Social Order*. New Haven, CT: Yale University Press, 1988.

Evans, Sara M., and Barbara J. Nelson. *Wage Justice: Comparable Worth and the Paradox of Technocratic Reform*. Chicago: University of Chicago Press, 1989.

FACT (Feminist Anti-Censorship Taskforce). *Caught Looking: Feminism, Pornography, and Censorship*. Edited by Kate Ellis, Nan D. Hunter, Beth Jaker, Barbara O'Dair, and Abby Tallmer. New York: Linco Printing, 1986.

Faludi, Susan. *Backlash: The Undeclared War against American Women*. New York: Anchor Books, 1991.

Ferguson, Ann. *Blood at the Root: Motherhood, Sexuality, and Male Dominance*. London: Pandora Press, 1989.

———, ed. "Motherhood and Sexuality." Special issue, *Hypatia* 1, no. 2 (Fall 1986).

———. "Sex War: The Debate between Radical and Libertarian Feminists." *Signs* 10, no. 1 (Autumn 1984): 106–12.

Finger, Anne. *Past Due: A Story of Disability, Pregnancy, and Birth*. Seattle: Seal Press, 1990.

Firestone, Shulamith. *The Dialectic of Sex: The Case for Feminist Revolution*. New York: William Morrow, 1970.

Firestone, Shulamith, and Anne Koedt. *Notes from the First Year*. New York: New York Radical Women, 1968.

Fleming, Anne Taylor. "The American Wife." *New York Times Magazine*, October 26, 1986.

Folbre, Nancy. "Of Patriarchy Born: The Political Economy of Fertility Decisions." *Feminist Studies* 9, no. 2 (Summer 1983): 261–84.

———. "The Pauperization of Motherhood: Patriarchy and Public Policy in the United States." *Review of Radical Political Economics* 16, no. 4 (Winter 1984): 72–88.

Friday, Nancy. *My Mother/Myself: The Daughter's Search for Identity*. New York: Delacorte Press, 1977.

Friedan, Betty. *The Feminine Mystique*. New York: W. W. Norton, 1963.

———. "Feminism Takes a New Turn." *New York Times*, August 26, 1979.

———. *The Second Stage*. New York: Summit Books, 1981.

Funk, Nanette. "Introduction." In *Gender Politics and Post-Communism: Reflections From Eastern Europe and the Former Soviet Union*, edited by Nanette Funk and Magda Mueller, 1–14. New York: Routledge, 1993.

Gallop, Jane. *The Daughter's Seduction: Feminism and Psychoanalysis*. Ithaca, NY: Cornell University Press, 1982.

Garnett, David. *Lady Into Fox & A Man in the Zoo*. New York: Penguin Books, 1946.

Genevie, Louis E., and Eva Margolies. *The Motherhood Report: How Women Feel About Being Mothers*. New York: Macmillan, 1987.

Gerson, Deborah. "Infertility and the Construction of Desperation." *Socialist Review* 19, no. 3 (July/September 1989): 45–64.

Gerson, Kathleen. "Emerging Social Divisions Among Women: Implications for Welfare State Politics." *Politics and Society* 15, no. 2 (1986): 213–24.

———. *Hard Choices: How Women Decide about Work, Career, and Motherhood*. Berkeley: University of California Press, 1985.

Gerson, Mary-Joan. "Feminism and the Wish For a Child." *Sex Roles* 7 (September 1984): 389–99.

Giddings, Paula. *When and Where I Enter: The Impact of Black Women on Race and Sex in America*. New York: William Morrow, 1984.

Gilbert, Lucy, and Paula Webster. *Bound by Love: The Sweet Trap of Daughterhood*. Boston: Beacon Press, 1982.

Gilder, George. *Sexual Suicide*. New York: Quadrangle Books, 1973.

Gilligan, Carol. *In a Different Voice: Psychological Theory and Women's Development*. Cambridge, MA: Harvard University Press, 1982.

Ginsburg, Faye D. *Contested Lives: The Abortion Debate in an American Community*. Berkeley: University of California Press, 1989.

Gittins, Diana. *The Family in Question*. London: Macmillan, 1985.

Gleve, Katherine. "Rethinking Feminist Attitudes towards Motherhood." *Feminist Review* 25 (Spring 1987): 38–45.

Goode, Daniel. "Finding the Unison Sentence." Performance piece, circa 1983.

Gordon, Linda. *Woman's Body, Woman's Right: Birth Control in America*. New York: Grossman Publishers, 1976.

Gordon, Mary. "On Mothership and Authorhood." *New York Times*, February 10, 1985, *Sunday Book Review*, http://www.nytimes.com/1985/02/10/books/on -mothership-and-authorhood.html.

Gordon, Tuula. *Feminist Mothers*. New York: New York University Press, 1990.

Grabucher, Marianne. *There's a Good Girl: Gender Stereotyping in the First Three Years of Life: A Diary*. Translated by Wendy Philipson. London: Women's Press, 1988.

Greer, Germaine. *Sex and Destiny: The Politics of Human Fertility*. New York: Harper and Row, 1984.

Gross, Louise, and Phyllis MacEwan. "On Day Care." In *Voices From Women's Liberation*, edited by Leslie B. Tanner, 199–207. New York: Signet Books, 1970.

Gustavsson, B., J. C. Karlsson, and C. Rafregard. *Work in the 1980s*. London: Gower Publishing, 1985.

Hammer, Signe. *Daughters and Mothers, Mothers and Daughters*. New York: Quadrangle Books, 1975.

Haraway, Donna. "A Manifesto for Cyborgs: Science, Technology, and Socialist Feminism in the 1980s." *Socialist Review* no. 80 (1985): 65–108.

Hawkesworth, Mary. "The Semiotics of Premature Burial: Feminism in a Postfeminist Age." *Signs: Journal of Women in Culture and Society* 29, no. 4 (2004): 961–84.

Heath, Stephen. "Difference." In *The Sexual Subject: A Screen Reader in Sexuality*, edited by Mandy Merck, 47–106. New York: Routledge, 1992.

Hemment, Julie. *Empowering Women in Russia: Activism, Aid and NGOs*. New Anthropology of Europe Series, edited by Daphne Berdahl, Matti Brunzl, and Michael Herzfeld. Bloomington: Indiana University Press, 2007.

———. "Global Civil Society and the Local Costs of Belonging: Defining 'Violence Against Women' in Russia." *Signs: Journal of Women in Culture and Society* 29, no. 3 (2004): 815–40.

Herman, Ellen. "Desperately Seeking Motherhood." *Zeta*, March 1988, 73–76.

Heron, Liz. "Motherhood . . . To Have or Have Not? In *Changes of Heart: Reflections on Women's Independence*, 177–218. Boston: Pandora Press, 1986.

Hewlett, Sylvia Ann. *A Lesser Life: The Myth of Women's Liberation in America*. New York: William Morrow, 1986.

Hirsch, Marianne. "Mothers and Daughters: A Review." *Signs* 7, no. 1 (1981): 200–22.

———. *The Mother-Daughter Plot: Narrative, Psychoanalysis, and Feminism*. Bloomington: Indiana University Press, 1989.

Hirst, William, "Presentation to the Lang Freshman Class of 2009." Talk given at Lang College, New York, NY, September 6, 2009.

Hochschild, Arlie. *The Second Shift*. London: Viking Penguin, 1989.

Hoffner, Elaine. *Mothering: The Emotional Experience of Motherhood after Freud and Feminism*. New York: Doubleday, 1978.

hooks, bell. "Feminism: A Movement to End Sexist Oppression." In *Feminist Theory: From Margin to Center*, 17–31. New York: South End Press, 1984.

———. "Revolutionary Parenting." Reprinted in bell hooks, *From Margin to Center*. Boston: South End Press, 1984.

Hyde Amendment 1976.

Illich, Ivan. *Gender*. New York: Pantheon, 1982.

Jaggar, Alison M. "Sex Inequality and Bias in Sex Differences in Research." Paper presented at the symposium of Bias in Sex Differences Research, American Association for the Advancement of Science Annual Meeting, Chicago, February 1987.

———. "Sexual Difference and Sexual Equality." In *Theoretical Perspectives on*

Sexual Differences, edited by Deborah L. Rhode, 239–54. New Haven, CT: Yale University Press, 1990.

———. "Towards a More Integrated World: Feminist Reconstructions of the Self and Society." Paper presented at Douglass College, New Brunswick, NJ, spring 1985.

Jehlen, Myra. "Against Human Wholeness: A Suggestion for a Feminist Epistemology." Unpublished manuscript.

———. "Archimedes and the Paradox of Feminist Criticism." *Signs* 6, no. 4 (Summer 1981): 575–601.

Joffe, Carole. *Friendly Intruders: Childcare Professionals and Family Life*. Berkeley: University of California Press, 1977.

Johnson, Barbara. *The Critical Difference: Essays in the Contemporary Rhetoric of Reading*. Baltimore: Johns Hopkins University Press, 1980.

Kaminer, Wendy. *A Fearful Freedom: Women's Flight from Equality*. Reading, MA: Addison Wesley, 1990.

Kantrowicz, Barbara. "Three's a Crowd." *Newsweek*, September 1, 1986, 68–76.

Kaplan, Cora. "Wild Nights: Pleasure/Sexuality/Feminism." 1983. Reprinted in *The Ideology of Conduct: Essays on Literature and the History of Sexuality*, edited by Nancy Armstrong and Leonard Tennenhouse, 160–84. New York: Methuen, 1987.

Kaplan, Temma. "Female Consciousness and Collective Action: The Case of Barcelona, 1910–1918." *Signs* 7, no. 3 (1982): 545–66.

———. "Women and Communal Strikes in the Crises of 1917–1922." In *Becoming Visible: Women in European History*, 2nd ed., edited by Renate Bridenthal, Claudia Koonz, and Susan Stuard, 429–49. Boston: Houghton Mifflin, 1987.

Kay, Herma Hill. "Equality and Difference: The Case of Pregnancy." *Berkeley Women's Law Journal* 1 (1985): 1–38.

Kelly, Joan. "The Doubled Vision of Feminist Theory." In *Women, History and Theory: The Essays of Joan Kelly*, 51–64. Chicago: University of Chicago Press, 1984.

Kerber, Linda K., Catherine G. Greeno, Eleanor E. Maccoby, Zella Luria, Carol B. Stack, and Carol Gilligan. "On In a Different Voice: An Interdisciplinary Forum." *Signs* 11, no. 2 (Winter 1986): 304–33.

King, Ynestra. MARHO Forum, John Jay College, New York, March 2, 1984.

Klepfisz, Irena. "Women Without Children/Women Without Families/Women Alone." 1977. Reprinted in *Dreams of an Insomniac: Jewish Feminist Essays Speeches, and Diatribes*, 3–14. Portland, OR: Eighth Mountain Press, 1990.

Koedt, Anne. "The Myth of the Vaginal Orgasm." In *Voice's From Women's Liberation*, edited by Leslie B. Tanner, 157-65. New York: Signet Books, 1970.

Kovács, Maria. "Ambiguities of Emancipation: Women and the Ethnic Question in Hungary." *Women's History Review* 5, no. 4 (1996): 487–95.

———. "Ambiguities of Emancipation: Women and the Ethnic Question in Hungary." Unpublished manuscript.

Kracauer, Siegfried. "Boredom." In *The Mass Ornament: Weimar Essays*, edited and translated by Thomas Y. Levin. Cambridge, MA: Harvard University Press, 1995.

Kristeva, Julia. "Love's Heretical Ethics." *Tel Quel* 74 (Winter 1977): 39–49.

Kristof, Nicholas D., and Sheryl WuDunn. *Half the Sky: Turning Oppression into Opportunity for Women Worldwide*. New York: Alfred A. Knopf, 2009.

Lasch, Christopher. *Haven in a Heartless World*. New York: Basic Books, 1977.

Lazarre, Jane. *The Mother Knot*. New York: McGraw-Hill, 1976.

Lerner, L. "Chodorow's Reproduction of Mothering: An Appraisal." *The Psychoanalytic Review* 69, no. 1 (1982): 151.

Lerner, Michael. "Friends of Families." Organizing drive, California, c. 1979–82.

Lessing, Doris. *The Children of Violence* series. London: Michael Joseph, 1952–1969.

———. *Documents Relating to the Sentimental Agents in the Volyen Empire*. New York: Alfred A. Knopf, 1983.

———. *The Good Terrorist*. London: Grafton Books, 1986.

———. *The Making of the Representatives for Planet 8*. New York: Alfred A. Knopf, 1982.

———. *Mara and Dann: An Adventure*. New York: HarperCollins, 1999.

———. *Memoirs of a Survivor*. London: Octagon, 1974.

———. "The Other Woman." In *Stories*, 157–211. New York: Alfred A. Knopf, 1978.

———. *The Story of General Dann and Mara's Daughter, Griot and the Snow Dog*. New York: HarperCollins, 2006.

Levy, Ariel. "Lift and Separate: Why is Feminism Still So Divisive?" *The New Yorker*, November 16, 2009, 78–80.

Lorber, J., R. L. Coser, A. S. Rossi, and N. Chodorow. "On the Reproduction of Mothering: A Methodological Debate." *Signs* 6, no. 3 (1981): 482–514.

Lorde, Audre. *The Black Unicorn: Poems*. New York: Norton, 1978.

———. "Man Child: A Black Lesbian Feminist's Response." *Conditions: Four* 2, no. 1 (Winter 1979): 30–61.

———. "The Transformation of Silence into Language and Action." Paper presented at the Modern Language Association Annual Meeting, Chicago, IL, December, 1977.

Luker, Kristen. *Abortion and the Politics of Motherhood*. Berkeley: University of California Press, 1984.

Mainardi, Pat. "The Politics of Housework." In *Sisterhood is Powerful: An Anthology of Writings from the Women's Liberation Movement*, edited by Robin Morgan, 447–54. New York: Vintage Books, 1970.

Mairs, Nancy. "On Being Raised By a Daughter." In *Plaintext*. Tuscon: University of Arizona Press, 1986.

Manning, Olivia. *The Balkan Trilogy*. New York: Penguin Books, 1981.

Marks, Elaine, and Isabelle De Courtivron, eds. *New French Feminisms: An Anthology*. Amherst: University of Massachusetts Press, 1980.

Martin, Emily. *The Woman in the Body: A Cultural Analysis of Reproduction*. Boston: Beacon Press, 1987.

McBroom, Patricia A. *The Third Sex: The New Professional Woman*. New York: William Morrow, 1986.

McFadden, Maggie. "Anatomy of Difference: Towards a Classification of Feminist Theory." *Women's Studies International Forum* 7, no. 6 (1984): 495–504.

Miles, Angela. "The Integrative Feminine Principle in North American Radicalism: Value Basis of a New Feminism." *Women's Studies International Quarterly* 4, no. 4 (1981): 481–95.

Miller, Sue. *The Good Mother*. New York: Harper and Row, 1986.

Milkman, Ruth. "Women's History and the Sears Case." *Feminist Studies* 12 (Summer 1986): 375–400.

Minneapolis Ordinance (Ordinance to amend Minneapolis Code of Ordinances title 7, chapters 139, 141, drafted by Andrea Dworkin and Catharine MacKinnon), 1983.

Mitchell, Juliet. "Reflections on Twenty Years of Feminism." In *What is Feminism?*, edited by Juliet Mitchell and Ann Oakley, 34–48. New York: Pantheon, 1986.

———. "Women and Equality." 1976. Reprinted in *Feminism and Equality*, edited by Anne Phillips, 24–43. New York: New York University Press, 1987.

———. *Women's Estate*. New York: Pantheon, 1971.

Mitchell, Juliet, and Ann Oakley, eds. *What is Feminism?* New York: Pantheon, 1986.

Molyneux, Maxine. "Mobilization without Emancipation? Women's Interests, the State, and Revolution in Nicaragua." *Feminist Studies* 11, no. 2 (Summer 1985): 227–53.

———. "'The Woman Question' in the Age of Perestroika." *New Left Review*, no. 183 (September/October 1989): 23–49. Reprinted in *After the Fall*, edited by R. Blackburn, 17–77. New York: Verso, 1991.

Morell, Carolyn MacKelcan. *Unwomanly Conduct: The Challenges of Intentional Childlessness*. New York: Routledge, 1994.

Moynihan, Daniel Patrick. 1965. "The Negro Family: The Case for National Action." Washington D.C.: United States Department of Labor, http://www .dol.gov/dol/aboutdol/history/webid-meynihan.htm.

Ms. Editors. Theme of Issue: "When to Have Your Baby." *Ms.* (December 1986).

Navarro, Marysa. Grass Roots Meeting. May 3, 1986.

Newton, Judith, and Nancy Hoffman, eds. "Feminism and Deconstruction." Special issue, *Feminist Studies* 14, no. 1 (Spring 1988).

New York Radical Feminists. "Politics of the Ego: A Manifesto for N.Y. Radical Feminists." In *Radical Feminism*, edited by Anne Koedt, Ellen Levine, and Anita Rapone, 379–83. New York: Quadrangle, 1973.

Nikolchina, Miglena. *Matricide in Language: Writing Theory in Kristeva and Woolf*. New York: Other Press, 2004.

Nochlin, Linda. "Why Have There Been No Great Women Artists?" 1971. Reprinted in *Art and Sexual Politics: Why Have There Been No Great Women Artists?*, edited by Thomas B. Hess and Elizabeth C. Baker, 1–39. New York: Macmillan, 1971.

NOW. "National Assembly on the Future of the Family" Conference, New York, NY, November 1979.

Oakley, Ann. *Becoming a Mother*. New York: Schocken Books, 1980.

———. *Women Confined: Toward a Sociology of Childbirth*. New York: Schocken Books, 1980.

O'Barr, Jean, Deborah Pope, and Mary Wyer, eds. *Ties that Bind: Essays on Mothering and Patriarchy*. Chicago: University of Chicago Press, 1990.

O'Brien, Mary. *The Politics of Reproduction*. New York: Routledge, 1981.

Olivier, Christiane. *Jocasta's Children: The Imprint of the Mother*. New York: Routledge, 1989.

Olson, Lynne. *Freedom's Daughters: The Unsung Heroines of the Civil Rights Movement from 1830 to 1970*. New York: Scribner, 2001.

Omolade, Barbara. "It's a Family Affair: The Real Lives of Black Single Mothers." *Village Voice*, July 16, 1986.

———. "The Unbroken Circle: A Historical and Contemporary Study of Black Single Mothers and Their Families." *Wisconsin Women's Law Journal* 3 (1987): 239–74.

Peck, Ellen. *The Baby Trap*. New York: Pinnacle Books, 1971.

Peck, Ellen, and Judith Senderowitz. *Pronatalism: The Myth of Mom and Apple Pie*. New York: Thomas Y. Crowell, 1973.

Petchesky, Rosalind. *Abortion and Woman's Choice: The State, Sexuality, and Reproductive Freedom*. Boston: Northeastern, 1984.

———. "Fetal Images." *Feminist Studies* 13, no. 2 (1987): 263–92.

———, ed. "Workers, Reproductive Hazards and the Politics of Protection." Special issue, *Feminist Studies* 5, no. 2 (Summer 1979).

———. "Workers, Reproductive Hazards, and the Politics of Protection: An Introduction." *Feminist Studies* 5, no. 2 (Summer 1979): 233–45.

Phillips, Anne, ed. *Feminism and Equality*. New York: New York University Press, 1987.

Philipson, Ilene. "The Repression of History and Gender: A Critical Perspective on the Feminist Sexuality Debate." *Signs* 10, no. 1 (Autumn 1984): 113–18.

Pies, Cheri. *Considering Parenthood*. San Francisco: Spinsters Book, 1985.

Polikoff, Nancy D. "Lesbians Choosing Children: The Personal is Political." In *Politics of the Heart*, edited by Sandra Pollack and Jeanne Vaughan, 48–54. Ithaca, NY: Firebrand Books, 1987.

Pollack, Sandra, and Jeanne Vaughan, eds. *Politics of the Heart: A Lesbian Parenting Anthology*. Ithaca, NY: Firebrand Books, 1987.

Pollard, Vicki. "Producing Society's Babies." *Women: A Journal of Liberation* (Fall 1969). Reprinted in *Voices from Women's Liberation*, edited by Leslie B. Tanner, 193–98. New York: Signet Books, 1970.

Porter, Nancy. "Documenting Experience, Building Theory: Two Books on Mothering." *Women's Studies Quarterly* 11, no. 4 (Winter 1983): 44.

A Proposal for an Independent School of Social Science. New York: Marchbanks Press, 1919. (Founding Document of The New School, New School Archives.)

Pruett, Kyle. *The Nurturing Father: Journeys Toward the Complete Man*. New York: Warner Books, 1987.

Purdy, Laura M., ed. "Ethics and Reproduction." Special issue, *Hypatia* 4, no. 3 (Fall 1989).

Quindlen, Anna. "Mother's Choice." *Ms.*, February, 1988, 55, 57.

Radl, Shirley. *Mother's Day is Over*. New York: Charterhouse, 1973.

Rapp, Rayna. "The Ethics of Choice: After My Amniocentesis, Mike and I Faced the Toughest Decision of our Lives." *Ms.*, April 1984, 97–100.

Rapping, Elayne. "The Future of Motherhood: Some Unfashionably Visionary Thoughts." In *Women, Class, and the Feminist Imagination*, edited by Karen V. Hanson and Ilene J. Philipson, 537–48. Philadelphia: Temple University Press, 1990.

Regulska, Joanna. "The Political and Its Meaning for Women's Transitional Politics in Poland." In *Theorizing Transitions: The Political Economy of Change in Central and East Europe*, edited by J. Pickles and A. Smith. London: Routledge, 1998.

Renvoize, Jean. *Going Solo: Single Mothers by Choice*. Boston: Routledge and Kegan Paul, 1985.

Rich, Adrienne. "Compulsory Heterosexuality and Lesbian Existence." In *Blood, Bread and Poetry*. New York: Norton, 1986.

———. "Natural Resources." In *The Dream of Common Language: Poems, 1974–1977*. New York: Norton, 1978.

———. *Of Woman Born: Motherhood as Experience and Institution*. New York: W. W. Norton, 1976.

Riley, Denise. Lecture at the Barnard Women's Center. New York, NY, April 11, 1985.

———. *War in the Nursery: Theories of the Child and the Mother*. London: Virago, 1983.

Roe v. Wade. Supreme Court Decision 410 U.S. 113 (1973).

Rosenfelt, Deborah, and Judith Stacey. "Second Thoughts on the Second Wave." *Feminist Studies* 13, no. 2 (1987): 341–61.

Rossi, Alice. "A Biosocial Perspective on Parenting." *Daedelus* 106, no. 2 (1977): 1–31.

———. "Transition to Parenthood." *Journal of Marriage and Family* 1, no. 30 (1964): 26–39.

Rothman, Barbara Katz. *In Labor: Women and Power in the Birth Place*. New York: W. W. Norton, 1982.

———. *Recreating Motherhood: Ideology and Technology in a Patriarchal Society*. New York: W. W. Norton, 1989.

———. *The Tentative Pregnancy: Prenatal Diagnosis and the Future of Motherhood*. New York: Viking, 1986.

Rubin, Gayle. "Thinking Sex: Notes for a Radical Theory of the Politics of Sexuality." In *Pleasure and Danger: Exploring Female Sexuality*, edited by Carole Vance, 267–319. New York: Routledge, 1984. Reprinted London: Pandora Press, 1989, 1992.

Ruddick, Sally. "Maternal Thinking." *Feminist Studies* 6, no. 2 (Summer 1980): 342–67.

———. *Maternal Thinking: Towards a Politics of Peace*. Boston: Beacon, 1989.

Russo, N. F. "The Motherhood Mandate." *Journal of Social Issues* 32, no. 2 (1976): 143–54.

Rutkoff, Peter M., and William B. Scott. *New School: A History of The New School for Social Research*. New York: Free Press, 1986.

Sandelowski, Margarete. "Fault Lines: Infertility and Imperiled Sisterhood." *Feminist Studies* 16, no. 1 (Spring 1990): 33–51.

Schild, Verónica. "Market Citizenship and the 'New Democracies': The Ambiguous Legacies of Contemporary Chilean Women's Movements." In *Social Politics* (Summer 1998): 232–49.

"The Scholar and the Feminist VI: The Future of Difference." Barnard College, New York, April 29, 1979.

"The Scholar and The Feminist IX: Towards a Politics of Sexuality." Barnard College, New York, 1982.

Schulenberg, Joy. *Gay Parenting: A Complete Guide for Gay Men and Lesbians with Children.* New York: Anchor Press/Doubleday, 1985.

Scott, Joan Wallach. "Deconstructing Equality-Versus-Difference: Or the Uses of Poststructuralist Theory for Feminism." *Feminist Studies* 14, no. 1 (Spring 1988): 33–50.

———. *Only Paradoxes to Offer: French Feminists and the Rights of Man.* Cambridge, MA: Harvard University Press, 1996.

Segal, Lynne. "Back to the Nursery." *New Statesman,* February 1, 1987.

———. *Is the Future Female? Troubled Thoughts on Contemporary Feminism.* New York: Peter Bedrick Books, 1987.

Sevenhuijsen, Selma, and Petra de Vries. "The Women's Movement and Motherhood." In *A Creative Tension: Key Issues of Socialist Feminism: An International Perspective from Activist Dutch Women,* edited by Anja Meulenbelt, Joyce Outshoorn, Selma Sevenhuijsen, and Petra de Vries, 9–25. Boston: South End Press, 1984.

Sevenhuijsen, S., and Carol Smart, eds. *Child Custody and the Politics of Gender.* New York: Routledge, 1989.

Simons, Margaret A. "Motherhood, Feminism, and Identity." *Women's Studies International Forum* 7, no. 5 (1984): 349–59.

Sinha, Mrinalini. "The Age of Consent Act: The Ideal of Masculinity and Colonial Ideology in 19th Century Bengal." In *Proceedings, Eighth International Symposium on Asian Studies,* 1199–214. Hong Kong: Asian Research Service, 1986.

———. "Gender and Imperialism: Colonial Policy and the Ideology of Moral Imperialism in Late 19th Century Bengal." In *Changing Men: New Directions in Research on Men and Masculinity,* edited by Michael S. Kimmel, 217–31. Newbury Park, CA: Sage, 1987.

Smilgis, Martha. "Here Come the Dinks." *Time Magazine,* April 20, 1987, 75.

Smith, Valerie. "Meditation on Memory: Clark Johnson's *Boycott.*" *American Literary History,* 17, no. 3 (2005): 530–41.

Smith-Rosenberg, Carroll. *Disorderly Conduct: Visions of Gender in Victorian America.* New York: Oxford University Press, 1985.

Snitow, Ann. "Angela Carter, Wild Thing: Conversations with a Necromancer." *The Voice Literary Supplement,* no. 75 (June 1989): 14-17.

———. *Ford Madox Ford and the Voice of Uncertainty.* Baton Rouge: Louisiana State University Press, 1984.

———. "The Front Line: Notes on Sex in Novels by Women, 1969–1979." *Signs* (1980): 702–18.

———. "Mass Market Romance: Pornography for Women is Different." *The Radical History Review* (1979): 141–161.

Snitow, Ann, Christine Stansell, and Sharon Thompson, eds. *Powers of Desire: The Politics of Sexuality.* New York: Monthly Review Press, 1983.

Sojourner Special issue. "Motherhood is Political: The Ideal vs. The Real." 1987.

Spallone, Patricia, and Lynn Steinberg. *Made to Order: The Myth of Reproductive and Genetic Progress*. New York: Pergamon Press, 1987.

Stansell, Christine. *City of Women: Sex and Class in New York, 1789–1860*. New York: Knopf, 1986.

Stanworth, Michelle, ed. *Reproductive Technologies: Gender, Motherhood and Medicine*. Minneapolis: University of Minnesota Press, 1987.

Stimpson, Catharine R. "The New Scholarship about Women: The State of the Art." *Annals of Scholarship* 1, no. 2 (1980): 2–14.

Swerdlow, Amy. "Pure Milk, Not Poison: Women Strike for Peace and the Test Ban Treaty of 1963." In *Rocking the Ship of State: Towards a Feminist Peace Politics*, edited by Adrienne Harris and Ynestra King, 225–37. Boulder, CO: Westview Press, 1989.

Tanner, Leslie, ed. *Voices From Women's Liberation*. New York: Signet Books, 1970.

Taub, Nadine. "Defining and Combatting Sexual Harassment." In *Class, Race and Sex: The Dynamics of Control*, edited by Amy Swerdlow and Hannah Lessinger, 263–75. Boston: G. K. Hall, 1983.

———. "A Public Policy of Private Caring." *The Nation*, May 31, 1986, 756–58.

———. "Feminist Tensions: Concepts of Motherhood and Reproductive Choice." In *Gender in Transition*, edited by Joan Offerman-Zuckerberg, 217–26. New York: Plenum Medical, 1989.

Taub, Nadine, and Sherrill Cohen. *Reproductive Laws for the 1990s*. Clifton, NJ: Humana Press, 1989.

Taub, Nadine, and Wendy Williams. "Will Equality Require More Than Assimilation, Accommodation or Separation from the Existing Social Structure?" *Rutgers Law Review* 37, no. 4 (Summer 1985): 825–44.

Tax, Meredith. "Agenda for Meeting at Barnard." May 3, 1986.

Thompson, E. P. *Beyond the Cold War*. London: Merlin Press and END, 1982.

Thorne, Barrie, and Marilyn Yalom. *Rethinking the Family: Some Feminist Questions*. New York: Longman, 1982.

Trebilcot, Joyce, ed. *Mothering: Essays in Feminist Theory*. Totowa, NJ: Rowman and Allanheld, 1984.

Valeksa, Lucia. "If All Else Fails, I'm Still a Mother." *Quest* 1, no. 3 (Winter 1975): 52–64.

Vance, Carole S., ed. "Diary of a Conference on Sexuality," conference program for The Scholar and The Feminist IX, Barnard College, April 24, 1982.

———. "Innocence and Experience: Melodramatic Narratives of Sex Trafficking and Their Consequences for Law and Policy." *History of the Present: A Journal of Critical History* 2, no. 2 (Fall 2012): 200–18.

———. ed. *Pleasure and Danger: Exploring Female Sexuality*. New York: Routledge, 1984. Reprinted London: Pandora Press, 1989, 1992.

———. "Social Construction Theory: Problems in the History of Sexuality." In *Homosexuality, Which Homosexuality?*, edited by Anja van Kooten Niekerk and Theo van der Meer, 13–34. Amsterdam: An Dekker, Imprint Schorer, 1989.

Vogel, Lise. "Debating Difference: The Problem of Special Treatment of Pregnancy in the Workplace." Paper presented at the Women and Society Seminar of Columbia University, New York, NY, January 1988.

Walby, Sylvia. "Backlash to Feminism." In *Gender Transformations*, 156–65. London: Routledge, 1997.

Walczewska, Slawomira. *Damy, Rycerze i Feministki: Kobiecy Dyskurs Emancypacyjny w Polsce* [Knights, Ladies, Feminists: Feminist Discourse in Poland]. Krakow: Wyd. eFKa, 1999.

Wallace, Michele. *Black Macho and the Myth of the Superwoman*. New York: Dial Press, 1978.

Walker, Alice. *In Search of Our Mother's Gardens*. San Diego: Harcourt Brace Jovanovich, 1983.

Walkowitz, Judith R. *Prostitution and Victorian Society: Women, Class and the State*. Cambridge: Cambridge University Press, 1980.

Wattenberg, Ben J. *The Birth Dearth: What Happens When People In Free Countries Don't Have Enough Babies?* New York: Pharos Books, 1987.

Weideger, Paula. "Womb Worship." *Ms.*, February 1988, 54, 56.

Weinberg, Joanna. "Shared Dreams: A Left Perspective on Disability Rights and Reproductive Rights." In *Women with Disabilities*, edited by Adrienne Asch and Michelle Fine, 297–305. Philadelphia: Temple University Press, 1988.

Weisskopf, Susan Contratto. "Maternal Sexuality and Asexual Motherhood." *Signs* 5, no. 4 (Summer 1980): 766–82.

Weitzman, Lenore J. *The Divorce Revolution: The Unexpected Social and Economic Consequences for Women and Children in America*. New York: Free Press, 1985.

Wells, Julie. "The Impact of Motherist Movements on South African Women's Political Participation." Paper presented at the Seventh Berkshire Conference on the History of Women, Wellesley College, Wellesley, MA, June 1987.

Whisker, Brenda. "Essay." In *Breaching the Peace: A Collection of Radical Feminist Papers*, edited by Jacky Bishop and Frankie Green, 34–37. London: Onlywomen Press, 1983.

White, Evelyn C., ed. *The Black Women's Health Book: Speaking for Ourselves*. Seattle: Seal Press, 1990.

Williams, Wendy. "Equality's Riddle: Pregnancy and the Equal Treatment/Special Treatment Debate." *N.Y.U. Review of Law and Social Change* 13 (1984–1985): 325–80.

Willis, Ellen. *Don't Think, Smile!: Notes on a Decade of Denial*. Boston: Beacon Press, 1999.

———. "The Family: Love It or Leave It." *The Village Voice*, September 17, 1979, 29–35. Reprinted in *Beginning to See the Light: Sex, Hope, and Rock-and-Roll*, 149–68. Minneapolis: University of Minnesota Press, 2012.

———. "My Memoir Problem." In *The Feminist Memoir Project: Voices From Women's Liberation*, edited by Rachel Blau DuPlessis and Ann Snitow, 482–84. New York: Three Rivers Press, 1998.

———. "Radical Feminism and Feminist Radicalism." *Social Text* No. 9/10 (Spring–Summer 1984): 91–118.

———. Remarks at the NYU Symposium on the publication of *Powers of Desire: The Politics of Sexuality*, New York, December 2, 1983.

———. "Statement." *Diary of a Sex Conference.* Suppressed by Barnard College, but intended as the program for the Scholar and the Feminist IX Conference on Sexuality. 1982.

———. "The Velvet Underground." In *Stranded: Rock and Roll for a Desert Island,* edited by Greil Marcus, 71–83. New York: Knopf, 1979.

———. "Whatever Happened to Women? Nothing, That's the Trouble." *Mademoiselle,* September 1969, 150, 206–209.

Wilt, Judith. *Abortion, Choice, and Contemporary Fiction: The Armageddon of the Maternal Instinct.* Chicago: University of Chicago Press, 1990.

Wollstonecraft, Mary. *A Vindication of the Rights of Woman,* edited by Carol H. Poston. New York: Norton, 1975.

Woolf, Virginia. *A Room of One's Own.* New York: Harcourt, Brace and World, 1963.

Yeager, Patricia. "Writing as Action: A Vindication of the Rights of Woman." *The Minnesota Review* no. 29 (Winter 1987): 67–80.

Zelizer, Viviana. *Pricing the Priceless Child: The Changing Social Value of Children.* New York: Basic Books, 1985.

INDEX

abortion, 94, 109, 137, 199, 201, 233, 257, 285; affordability of, 58n50, 105, 126, 225; antipornography and, 126; demand for, 5, 10, 110, 123, 165, 231, 266, 269, 330; feminist defensiveness and, 99, 107–9; opposition to, 66, 200, 258; in postcommunism, 191, 200, 225–26, 231, 269; *Roe vs. Wade* and, 10. *See also* motherhood

Abortion and the Politics of Motherhood, 107. *See also* Luker, Kristen

Abortion and Woman's Choice, 107. *See also* Petchesky, Rosalind

Abraham, Julie, 61

Abzug, Bella, 25, 54n5

After the Fall, 10

Against Sadomasochism, 137. *See also* Atkinson, Ti Grace

Alcoff, Linda, 30–33, 54n17

Alderfer, Hannah, 77, 131, 269

Ali, Muhammad, 247

Alpert, Jane, 27–29

Althusser, Louis, 32

Anderson, Bonnie, 161. *See also Joyous Greetings*

Anthony, Susan B., 297, 301

antipornography, 7–9, 71, 73–79, 123–37, 267, 302; anti-antipornography and, 16; conservatism and, 76–77, 130, 134–37; Minneapolis ordinance and,

77–78, 123, 131. *See also Caught Looking*; pornography; sexuality

antiviolence movement, 73

antiwar movement. *See* peace movement

Ariés, Philippe, 301

Asch, Solomon, 83, 85

Atkinson, Ti Grace, 137. *See also Against Sadomasochism*

Baby M., 106. *See also* motherhood

Backlash, 283. *See also* Susan Faludi

Bacon, Mrs. George W., 280

Bad Day at Black Rock, 251. *See also* John Sturges

Baldwin, Mrs. Ruth Standish, 280

Balliet, Barbara, 61

Bamber, Linda, 31–33

Barnard Conference on Sexuality: The Scholar and the Feminist IX, 8, 74–78

Barrett, Michèle, 33

Bates, Daisy, 281

Benedict, Ruth, 83

Benjamin, Jessica, 90

Berger, John, 301. *See also Ways of Seeing*

biology, 87–88; ambiguity of, 29, 57n37, 144–45; childbearing and, 87, 101–3, 110–11; women and, 27–29, 31, 38–44, 52, 129–30, 183, 299–301. *See also* the body; difference; essentialism

Black Macho and the Myth of the Superwoman 104. *See also* Wallace, Michelle

Blake, William, 151

body, the, 29, 39, 43, 88, 101, 104–5, 123–24, 130, 186, 240, 300, 313; disembodiment and, 42–44; objectification of, 51, 77, 128, 132–34, 202, 302. *See also* biology; sexuality; social construction

Borden, Lizzie, 141–42. *See also* Carter, Angela

Breaching the Peace, 184. *See also* Whisker, Brenda

Brennan, Teresa, 90

Brodsky Joseph, 189

Brokeback Mountain, 250

Brown, Norman O., 83

Bruer, Mrs. Henry, 280

Buhle, Mari Jo, 90

Burks, Mary Fair, 281

Bush, George W., 241, 262, 268

Butler, Octavia, 326

Campaign for Nuclear Disarmament (CND), 183, 184, 187

Carr, Johnnie, 281

Carter, Angela, 8, 78, 139–52. *See also* *Fireworks*; *Nothing Sacred*; "Peter and the Wolf"; pleasure; *The Sadeian Woman*; *Saints and Strangers*; sexuality; William Shakespeare; *Wise Children*

Carter, Jimmy, 25, 54n5

Catt, Carrie Chapman, 10

Caught Looking: Feminism, Pornography, and Censorship, 77–78, 131. *See also* antipornography

Chavkin, Wendy, 42

Chesler, Phyllis, 106. *See also* *Sacred Bond*

Chicago, Judy, 222

children, 132–34, 150, 298, 321–22; childhood and, 3, 46, 101, 242, 246–47, 252, 283, 301, 321; mothers and, 23, 34–39, 47, 82–83, 88–111, 168–69, 234–36, 318–19. *See also* abortion; fatherhood; motherhood

Children of Violence series, 324. *See also* Lessing, Doris

Chodorow, Nancy, 87, 90, 104, 281–83. *See also* *The Reproduction of Mothering*

choice, 1, 91, 94, 128, 198–99, 230–31, 302, 308; career and, 111, 234; childbearing and, 98–100, 105, 107, 109, 226, 234;

forgetting and, 278; social location and, 46, 61, 137, 208, 233. *See also* abortion; motherhood

church, the, 11, 43, 53, 129, 202, 225

Cisler, Cindy, 222

civil rights, 44, 164; legislation, 124; movement, 7, 206, 274, 275, 280–82, 285, 293

Cixous, Helene, 104

Clark, Septima Poinsette, 281

Cliff, Michelle, 22

Clinton, William, 213

Cohn-Bendit, Daniel, 269

cold war, 91, 160, 163, 206, 213

Collins, Gail, 287. *See also* *When Everything Changed*

colonialism, 13, 63, 160, 247; sexism and, 36–37, 55n27. *See also* imperialism

Columbia University, 279

communism, 160–62, 192–201, 204–5, 210, 222, 270; emancipation rhetoric of, 196, 200, 205, 207, 221; memorialization of, 229; social services and, 199, 201, 210. *See also* postcommunism

consciousness raising (CR), 2, 5, 6, 21, 33, 34, 47, 51, 62–63, 125, 128, 137, 183, 208, 209, 224–25, 237, 257, 265, 281, 296, 298. *See also* New York Radical Feminists; New York Radical Women; Polish Feminist Association; Redstockings; Resolve infertility support group; The Sex Fools; The Third Street Circle

Contested Lives, 107. *See also* Ginsburg, Faye

context, 159, 308, 324; gender arrangements and, 26, 61, 134, 214, 232–33; importance of, 16, 61, 66, 208, 223, 90; reality shaped by, 84–86, 88, 257, 332

Corea, Gina, 99

Cotton, Dorothy, 281

Crooklyn, 246. *See also* Lee, Spike

cultural feminism, 27–33, 50, 295. *See also* radical feminism

cyborgs, 301

Daly, Mary, 30, 40, 136. *See also* *Gyn/Ecology*

Daring to Be Bad, 27. *See also* Echols, Alice

de Beauvoir, Simone, 83, 301

de Courtivron, Isabelle, 32

Decter, Midge, 321

Degler, Carl, 124

DeKoven, Marianne, 31–33
Deming, Barbara, 29
demon texts, 99, 101, 102
Derrida, Jacques, 32
De Sade, Marquis, 139–40. See also Carter, Angela; Philosophy in the Boudoir
Dialectic of Sex, The, 101, 125, 297–303, 330–31. See also Firestone, Shulamith
difference: equality vs., 38–46, 57n39, 57n43, 61–62, 127, 192, 195–98; importance of, 13, 48, 88, 124–25, 129, 135–36, 182, 192, 202, 229, 246, 286; as mark of subordination, 24–26, 31, 44, 195–96, 280; without politics, 104; race, class, and sexual, 2, 7, 16, 28, 41, 61, 71–75, 129, 207–8, 298, 300. See also essentialism; women
Dinnerstein, Dorothy, 5, 9, 54n3, 72, 80–96, 104, 105, 186, 237, 266, 283, 288, 307, 328, 330. See also The Mermaid and the Minotaur
Dirty Pretty Things, 251–52. See also Frears, Stephen
divides: critiques of, 59–61; feminist debates and, 11, 21–22, 26–47, 50–51, 55n21, 55n23, 56n33, 57n43, 59–62, 199
divorce, 6, 106, 107; opposition to, 209, 233
Drakulic, Slavenka, 160–61
Dreiser, Theodore, 149
DuBois, Ellen, 40, 124
DuPlessis, Rachel Blau, 16, 104–5, 268, 273, 275. See also The Feminist Memoir Project
Dworkin, Andrea, 29, 54n13, 77, 123, 136. See also Right Wing Women

Eagan, Andrea, 99
Echols, Alice, 27–28, 30. See also Daring to Be Bad
eco-politics, 13, 111, 183
education: feminism and, 2, 10–13, 228–30, 232–33, 238, 257–59, 223–26; politics and, 12, 32–33, 162, 201, 210–11, 229, 262–63, 331–32; prison and, 162, 241–43, 245–63; sex education 77, 134, 232
Ehrenreich, Barbara, 106
Eichhorn, Kate, 16
Eisenstein, Hester, 90, 110
Eisenstein, Zillah, 42. See also Radical Future of Liberal Feminism, The
Eliot, George, 149. See also Middlemarch

Eliot, T.S., 328
Ellis, Kate, 77, 124, 132
English, Deirdre, 110, 209
Epstein, Barbara, 124
equality, 31–33, 60, 72, 123, 126, 137, 200, 213, 217, 288, 294, 299, 308; communism and, 196–98, 207, 221; comparable worth legislation and, 56n33; compensation and, 31, 33, 56n33,195, 330; difference vs., 38–46, 56n30, 57n39, 57n43, 62, 127, 197, 198, 308; in law, 39, 41, 42, 107, 126. See also Equal Rights Amendment
Equal Rights Amendment (ERA), 98, 107, 126
essentialism, 22, 27–31, 43, 52, 57n37, 76–77, 104–5, 111, 124–27, 135–36, 164, 197, 201, 257, 249, 257–58; 275–76, 287, 294, 300; deconstruction and, 54n17; social constructionism vs., 28–29. See also biology; men; women
experience: context and, 85, 164, 193, 324; of men, 48, 72, 94, 110, 258; of women, 13, 24, 26, 28, 32, 34, 62–64, 94, 125, 130, 135, 185, 200, 298, 301–2; writing and, 64–67, 276–77, 310–11. See also motherhood
exploitation, 126, 129, 136, 198, 210, 212, 214

false consciousness, 63, 108, 281
Faludi, Susan, 283. See also Backlash
family, 40, 101, 102, 141–45, 205, 232–34, 248, 295, 297, 318–19; absorption of women and, 106, 200–2; divorce and, 209, 233; grandmothers and, 200, 234; nuclear, critique of, 46–47; postcommunism and, 197, 200–2, 205, 239–40. See also children; motherhood
fatherhood, 72, 84, 145, 218–19, 224, 282–83; Moynihan report and, 102; children and, 93–94, 109; mothers and, 93–95, 109–11, 233–34. See also family; motherhood
Feminine Mystique, The, 100–101. See also Friedan, Betty
feminism: backlash against, 16, 66, 71–72, 90, 103, 106–8, 126, 126–29, 194, 222–23, 283–84, 286–87, 296, 298; as bourgeois, 11, 13, 40, 43, 198–99, 230–31, 232; differences within, 8, 13, 16, 21, 31–32, 46, 125, 129, 182–83, 192–93, 206, 213–14, 275–76, 286, 291, 330;

feminism (continued)
disappointment and, 7–8, 13, 41, 44–45, 72, 127–29, 135, 195, 209, 273, 298; in East Central Europe, 10–11, 160–62, 191–214, 216–17, 219–22, 224–26, 228–40, 242; ephemerality and, 14, 33, 36, 60, 177, 221, 276, 284–85, 288–89, 291; ethics of, 108, 230–31, 240; future of, 2, 17, 76, 137, 199–200, 206, 214, 234, 277, 278, 284, 288–91, 328–33; generations of, 6–7, 9, 15, 16, 43, 46, 62, 76, 78, 90, 99–100, 125, 148, 184, 221, 228–30, 276, 278, 281–84, 287, 293–94, 300–301, 329; hostility toward, 4, 6, 184, 194, 197, 201, 204, 213, 232, 283–84, 286, 287, 298; individualism and, 36–37, 39, 41, 43, 60, 101, 194, 197, 302, 308; Internationalism and, 7, 159–61, 177, 193, 204–6, 214, 230; modern political movements and, 59–60, 195, 207, 211; nineteenth century, 36–37, 40–41, 76, 81, 110–11, 124–25, 128–29, 161–62, 200, 211, 220–21, 279, 282; oversimplifications of, 13, 16, 129, 184–85; race and, 28, 33, 41, 47, 49–50, 100–102, 182, 208–9, 221, 241, 275, 280–81, 300, 308; revivals of, 7, 76, 80, 283–84, 289; second wave of, 16, 21–23, 63, 80, 275–76, 293, 301; suburbs and, 3, 23, 46, 49–50, 65, 100; western, 22, 37–38, 43, 59–60, 191–93, 195–99, 204–12, 220–22, 230, 300. See also feminist activism
feminist activism: funding and, 208, 210–12; legal approaches to, 39, 77–78, 106–7, 109–10, 124–26, 135, 164, 209; necessity of, 1–3, 35–36; police and, 34–35, 164–65, 171, 175–81, 183, 185–88, 244–45, 267, 318; women's solidarity and, 22–24, 34, 37, 49, 164–65, 168–69, 183–85. See also feminism; peace movement
Feminist Anti-Censorship Taskforce (FACT), 8, 77–78, 131, 267. See also Caught Looking
Feminist Memoir Project, The, 16, 268, 273–74, 276–77, 283, 285, 287–90. See also DuPlessis, Rachel Blau
Firestone, Shulamith, 101–2, 125, 222, 273, 282, 297–303, 330–31. See also The Dialectic of Sex
Fireworks, 141. See also Carter, Angela
Flax, Jane, 87, 90, 278

Ford Madox Ford and the Voice of Uncertainty, 6, 311
Ford, Ford Madox, 311, 315
Foreman, George, 247
forgetting: feminist histories and, 7, 16, 200, 207, 273–91, 294, 301. See also memory
Foucault, Michel, 17, 32, 255, 262, 263
Foundacja Kobieca (EFKA), 226
Four-Gated City, The, 318. See also Lessing, Doris
Frears, Stephen, 251. See also Dirty Pretty Things
freedom, 66, 76, 82, 95–96, 104, 110, 129–30, 137, 195, 201–2, 205, 209–10, 258, 283, 286–87, 294, 308, 329; constraints and, 139–41, 156, 159–60, 187, 245, 254, 331; unconsciousness and, 142–43. See also choice; pleasure; sexuality
Freeman, Jo, 222
Freud, Sigmund, 8, 31, 83, 86, 88, 142, 145, 148, 150–52, 155, 259, 281, 298, 301, 313
Friday, Nancy, 104. See also My Mother/Myself
Friedan, Betty, 99, 100–101, 106. See also The Feminine Mystique; The Second Stage

Garnett, David, 78, 153–56. See also Lady into Fox; A Man in the Zoo
gender: free market and, 198–99, 202, 205; obfuscation of class and ethnicity and, 161, 206–8, 222; as shifting marker, 11, 33, 53, 84–85, 125, 128, 185–87, 212, 214, 257, 281–82, 289
gender studies, 34, 39, 290–91; programs, 4, 6, 66, 71, 210–11; term, 11; teaching 12, 15, 231. See also education
Gerson, Kathleen, 107. See also Hard Choices
Gilligan, Carol, 105
Gilmore, Georgia, 281
Ginsburg, Faye, 103, 107. See also Contested Lives
Glass, Thelma, 281
globalization, 193, 205–6, 214, 230, 248
Goode, Daniel, 312
Good Mother, The, 106. See also Miller, Sue
Good Terrorist, The, 316–22. See also Lessing, Doris
Gordon, Linda, 61, 104, 124. See also Woman's Body, Woman's Right
Gordon, Mary, 108
Grass Roots Movements of Women group, 34–36

Greenham Common, 7, 24, 160, 163–89;
    eviction and, 165, 171–73, 175, 187; fence
    and, 165, 175–79; media response to,
    170–71, 175, 177, 183, 188; militarism
    and, 163, 181; missile obstruction and,
    179–80; nonhierarchical community
    and, 176–77, 180–83, 187; public space
    and, 163–64, 172–73. See also peace
    movement
Gross, Louise, 103
guilt, 4, 94, 98, 108, 134, 143, 223, 257
Gyn/Ecology, 30, 136. See also Daly, Mary

Half the Sky, 287. See also Kristof, Nicholas;
    WuDunn, Sheryl
Hand, Mrs. Learned, 280
Hanisch, Carol, 222
Haraway, Donna, 101, 301
Hard Choices, 107. See also Gerson, Kathleen
Harris, Adrienne, 54n3, 57n37, 90
Harris, McCree, 281
Harsanyi, Doina Pasca, 193
Hartman, Mary, 124
Hawkesworth, Mary, 283, 284
Hawthorne, Nathaniel, 149
Heath, Stephen, 313–14
Hemingway, Ernest, 251, 256
Hemment, Julie, 212
Herland, 331
heroism, 9, 249, 251–52, 279, 318, 324;
    skepticism of, 247, 249, 284–87, 289;
    women and, 102, 108, 201, 219, 257, 259.
    See also men
Hewlett, Sylvia Ann, 106–7. See also Lesser
    Life, A
Hill, Anita, 198
Hirsch, Marianne, 90
Hirst, William, 278–89
Hochschild, Arlie, 106. See also Second
    Shift, The
homophobia, 2, 100, 198, 250–51
hooks, bell, 41, 100, 109, 308, 309, 330
hope, 7, 44, 48, 71, 85–86, 90–91, 96, 125,
    129, 135, 165, 203, 329; hopefulness and,
    1, 4, 5, 81, 199, 230, 300, 332. See also
    uncertainty; utopia
Horakova, Milada, 207
Horney, Karen, 281
House of All Nations, The, 149. See also Stead,
    Christina

humiliation, 10, 124, 185, 198, 223, 248–51,
    254; of men, 194, 250; of prison,
    244–45, 248–49, 253, 255; of women, 7,
    21, 44, 80–81, 136
Hunter, Nan D., 77–78
Hurt Locker, The, 249
Hyde Amendment, 58n50, 105

identity, 6, 53, 75, 99, 129, 228–29, 279, 329,
    332; as feminist, 12–14, 16, 45, 53n1, 161,
    219, 231, 259, 286–87, 308–9; identity
    politics and, 59–61, 194, 195–96, 213,
    275–76; as woman, 21–22, 26, 28, 30, 34,
    36, 39, 45, 61, 109–10, 182, 185, 187, 289.
    See also gender; Greenham Common;
    motherhood; sexuality
imperialism, 135, 180, 252; conceptual, 64,
    160, 194; sympathy as, 241–42
In the Valley of Elah, 249
Iron Jawed Angels, 258
International Criminal Court, 332

Jaggar, Alison, 42
Jagiellonian University, 223, 225; feminist
    conferences at, 225–26
Jaker, Beth, 77, 131
Jehlen, Myra, 11, 42
Johnson, Alvin, 279
Jones, Edward P., 258
Jones, Vivian Malone, 281
Joyous Greetings, 161. See also Anderson, Bonnie

Kahane, Claire, 111
Kaplan, Temma, 34, 55n24
Kaszkur, Barbara, 226. See also Foundacja
    Kobieca
Kelly, Joan, 25
King, Martin Luther, Jr., 281, 285
King, Ynestra, 22, 24, 37, 54n3, 55n24, 185
Kleckner, Susan, 164
Klein, Melanie, 83, 281
Knights, Ladies, Feminists, 220. See also Slawka
    Walczewska
Koedt, Anne, 125
Kohler, Wolfgang, 83, 85
Kovács, Maria, 205
Kowalska, Karolina, 229
Kracauer, Siegfried, 331
Kremlin, the, 181
Kristeva, Julia, 55n23, 104. See also Tel Quel

Kristof, Nicholas, 287–88. See also *Half the Sky*
Krueger, Heidi, 61
Kruks, Sonia, 61
Kureishi, Hanif, 248. See also *My Son the Fanatic*

Lacan, Jacques, 32; Lacanian psychoanalysis 30, 241, 284
Lady into Fox, 153–54, 156. See also Garnett, David
Lavender Menace, 125
Lavin, Maud, 61
Lazarre, Jane, 104. See also *Mother Knot, The*
Lee, Spike, 246. See also *Crooklyn*
Left, the, 3, 10, 83, 86, 106, 176, 183, 206, 241, 293, 295, 314, 321, 326; exclusion of women and, 24, 27, 36, 187, 275, 297
Lehrman, Daniel, 87–88
Lenin, Vladimir, 83, 151
Lerner, Michael, 106
Lesser Life, A, 106–7. See also Hewlett, Sylvia Ann
Lessing, Doris, 1, 5, 15, 307, 310, 315–26, 331. See also *Children of Violence* series; *The Four-Gated City*; *The Good Terrorist*; *The Making of the Representatives for Planet 8*; *Mara and Dann*; *Memoirs of a Survivor*; *The Sentimental Agents*; *The Story of General Dann and Mara's Daughter, Griot and the Snow Dog*
Levi-Strauss, Claude, 32
Levy, Ariel, 287
Lewinsky, Monica, 213
liberal feminism, 31, 42, 295, 308
liberalism, 60; feminism and, 40–44, 57n43, 104, 197, 201, 205, 209, 308. See also public sphere
Liberation Now!, 103
Lorde, Audre, 47, 102
Luker, Kristen, 107. See also *Abortion and the Politics of Motherhood*

MacEwan, Phyllis, 103
MacKinnon, Catharine, 77, 123
Mainardi, Pat, 237
Making of the Representatives for Planet 8, The, 317. See also Lessing, Doris
Man in the Zoo, A, 153–56. See also Garnett, David

Manning, Olivia, 313
Man Who Loved Children, The, 149. See also Stead, Christina
Mara and Dann, 323–25. See also Lessing, Doris
Marcuse, Herbert, 83
Marks, Elaine, 32
Martin, Janey, 185
Marx, Karl, 148, 150–52, 298, 301
Matynia, Elzbieta, 10, 228
Mayer, Clara, 279
McCarthyism, 3, 149
Meese, Edwin, 267
Melville, Herman, 149
Memoirs of a Survivor, 318. See also Lessing, Doris
memory, 85–86, 177, 229, 323–24; feminist archives and, 14–17, 64–65, 207, 222–23, 273, 275–91, 300–301; history vs., 278–79. See also forgetting
men: category of, 41, 73, 127–29, 136, 185, 186; domestic care and, 83, 90, 93–95, 108–11, 200–201; forms of manhood and, 248, 250; heroism and, 9, 217, 247, 249, 251–52, 279, 285; shame and, 185, 194, 248–51; violence and, 7–8, 24, 72–73, 76–77, 125–30, 134–36, 164, 169, 183, 187–88, 247, 249, 251–52, 257. See also family; fatherhood
Mermaid and the Minotaur, The, 9, 72, 80–83, 85–93, 95, 104, 186, 237. See also Dinnerstein, Dorothy
metaphor, 60–62, 95, 126, 135, 153–54, 198; doubleness as, 33; loopholes as, 61, 65–66. See also divides
Michnik, Adam, 4
Middlemarch, 149. See also Eliot, George
Miller, Jean Baker, 87
Miller, Naomi, 91
Miller, Sue, 106. See also *Good Mother, The*
Millett, Kate, 221
Milton, John, 151
minimizers: maximizers and, 27–28, 30, 50
Mitchell, Juliet, 42, 87, 208, 211
Miyazaki, Hayao, 247. See also *Spirited Away*
Molière, 312
Molyneux, Maxine, 192
morality, 83, 96, 128, 143, 150, 247, 260, 262, 295; moralism and, 8, 76–77, 124, 136, 185–86, 206; of women, 38, 51, 124. See also antipornography; essentialism

Morris, William, 151
motherhood: biotechnology and, 110–11;
  care for others first and, 38, 81, 95, 103,
  226, 236, 238–39, 258; experience of, 48,
  72, 93–95, 98, 105–6, 110, 233–34; fear
  of, 50, 81–82, 91, 101–2, 130, 219, 284;
  feminism and, 9, 21, 23, 35–37, 47–48,
  72, 97–121, 239–40, 295; infertility
  and, 98–99; motherists and, 34–38;
  peace movement rhetoric and, 23, 25,
  37, 168–69, 185–86; pronatalism, 9,
  47, 97–99, 202; race and, 47, 50, 100,
  102; refusal of, 97–99, 101–3, 107–9,
  283; sacredness of, 50–53, 107, 108–9;
  sexuality and, 140, 234; the state and, 42,
  90, 106–7, 109, 111; surrogacy and, 51–53,
  106. See also children; fatherhood; women
Mother Knot, The, 104. See also Lazarre, Jane
Mothers of the Plaza de Mayo, 35
Muhammad Ali, 247
My Mother/Myself, 104. See also Friday, Nancy
My Son the Fanatic, 248. See also Kureishi,
  Hanif

naivete, 4, 12, 28–29, 64, 188, 195, 299
Nash, Diane, 281
National Advisory Commission for
  Women, 25, 54n5
National Organization for Women (NOW), 106
NATO, 168, 180, 181. See also Greenham
  Common
Navarro, Marysa, 35, 55n24
Nelson, Marybeth, 77, 131
neoliberalism, 230, 308
Network of East-West Women, The
  (NEWW), 10, 161–62, 204, 211, 220,
  228–29, 233, 235, 236–37
New School, The, 11, 66, 279–80, 282, 290
New Woman's Survival Sourcebook, The, 221–22
New York Institute for the Humanities, 8
New York Radical Feminists, 2, 54n18, 297
New York Radical Women, 295
NGOs, 13, 161, 229; privatization and, 210
Nikolchina, Miglena, 284
No More Nice Girls group, 10, 50, 58n50,
  266, 269, 296
North Country, 257
Notes from the First Year series, 297. See also
  Shulamith Firestone
Nothing Sacred, 141. See also Angela Carter

Occupy Wall Street (OWS), 4–5, 163–65,
  274; sexism and, 164–65
O'Dair, Barbara, 77
Of Woman Born, 104. See also Rich, Adrienne
Only Paradoxes to Offer, 59. See also Scott, Joan
Our Bodies/Ourselves, 103, 230
Ourselves and Our Children, 103–4

Paley, Grace, 164
Parks, Rosa, 280–81
Passent, Daniel, 221
patriarchy, 2, 79, 88, 101–2, 109, 132, 142,
  217, 225, 239, 279, 284, 289, 295, 308;
  gender difference and, 27–28, 31, 63,
  289; motherhood and, 35, 94, 98, 99,
  104, 110–11; sex and, 75, 76, 136; the
  state and, 41–42, 187, 205
Paul, Alice, 258
peace movement, 9, 16, 49, 84, 86, 95,
  174, 177, 181–84, 188–89, 293; peace as
  "women's issue," 24–26; Vietnam War
  and, 9, 27, 49, 135, 247; women and, 7,
  22–27, 34, 35, 37, 38, 71, 164–68, 184,
  186; World War III and, 174, 180, 181. See
  also Greenham Common
Petchesky, Rosalind, 107. See also Abortion
  and Woman's Choice
"Peter and the Wolf," 142–43. See also
  Carter, Angela
Philosophy in the Boudoir, 140. See also de
  Sade, Marquis
picaro, the, 12, 159–62
Piers Plowman, 151
Platoon, 9
pleasure, 22, 75, 96, 125, 141, 144, 146,
  198–99, 234, 287, 331; of autonomy,
  15, 71, 143, 187, 222, 226; as bourgeois,
  198–99, 230–32; of film, 242, 252; fear
  and, 75–77, 141, 294. See also sexuality
Pleasure and Danger, 74. See also Vance, Carole
Polan, Dana, 251
Polish Feminist Association, 225;
politics, 3, 12, 21, 21–53, 160–61, 182–84,
  197, 205–6, 210–14, 277–79, 308–9,
  317–19, 332; aesthetics of, 5–7, 24, 90,
  151–52, 206, 209–10, 308; affect and,
  13, 16, 143, 294; affinity groups and,
  177; experience of, 24, 34–35, 63, 169,
  182, 202, 288–89, 307; motherhood
  and, 3, 34–36. 99–100, 105, 107;

politics (continued)
nonviolence and, 171, 178, 180, 183, 186–88, 259; rage and, 2, 5, 23, 44, 47, 50, 66, 71, 76–77, 80, 82, 94–95, 99, 108–9, 123–24, 128–29, 136, 185–87, 208, 216–17, 282–83, 290–91, 332; relation to the personal, 75, 99, 123, 134, 193, 195, 282, 295, 299, 308, 317. See also feminism; identity; the left; motherhood; peace movement
Pollard, Vicki, 103
Pollock, Jackson, 328
Popovicz, Anna, 200
pornography, 7–9, 73–79, 123–37; as violence against women, 7–8, 74–77, 124–26, 128–32, 134–36. See also antipornography; sexuality
postcommunism, 4, 5, 10–11, 161, 196–97, 199, 204, 231; church and, 225–26; freedom and, 201, 205, 209–10, 329; obfuscation of gender and, 192, 194, 196, 200, 207, 213; privatization, commercialism, and, 210, 228–30, 238; social change and, 234–36, 331; traditionalism and, 191, 200–202, 205, 216, 286. See also communism
posthumanism, 13; humanism and, 328
postmodernism, 33, 294, 314, 328, 329
post-structuralism, 30–33
Pottenger, Marty, 74
Powers of Desire, 8, 73. See also Stansell, Christine; Thompson, Sharon
Pray the Devil Back to Hell, 259
Pronatalism, 102
public sphere, 164; in East Central Europe, 193, 201–2, 205; men and, 7, 23, 26, 41–43, 48, 75, 81–82, 164, 183, 197–98, 200–201; relation to private, 41, 44, 75, 91, 195, 201, 205, 214; women and, 7, 25–26, 31, 34–35, 38, 40–44, 48–50, 65, 71, 110, 129, 172, 186, 192–98, 201–2, 226, 257, 278, 284–85. See also liberalism; women
Putnam, Mrs. George Haven, 280

queer theory, 13, 62, 79, 164

racism, 90, 196, 248, 252; feminism and, 13, 100, 129, 192, 198, 205–6, 209, 275; hair and, 258; prison and, 253, 255; sexism and, 37, 208

radical feminism, 2, 27–31, 77, 184, 186, 295–300, 308–9. See also cultural feminism
Radical Future of Liberal Feminism, The, 42. See also Zillah Eisenstein
Rainone, Nanette, 297
Reagan, Ronald, 8, 106, 124, 163, 168, 189; Reagan years, 77, 98, 107, 124
Redstockings, 63, 295, 297;
Reproduction of Mothering, The, 104. See also Chodorow, Nancy
Resolve infertility support group, 99
Rich, Adrienne, 38, 55n23, 74, 87, 104–6. See also Of Woman Born
right, the, 76–77, 105, 108, 126, 137, 202, 209, 212–13
Right Wing Women, 136. See also Dworkin, Andrea
Riley, Denise, 25, 26
Riot Grrrls, 16
Robinson, Jo Ann Gibson, 281
Rosenfelt, Deborah, 46–47
Rothman, Barbara Katz, 99
Rubin, Gayle, 76, 124
Ruddick, Sara, 54n3, 105–6
Rutkoff, Peter M., 279

Sacred Bond, 106. See also Chesler, Phyllis
Sadeian Woman, The, 139. See also Carter, Angela
Saints and Strangers, 141. See also Carter, Angela
Sarachild, Kathie, 27
scale, 1–2, 4, 84, 91, 189, 210, 307, 317, 324; of time, 320–26; of social forces, 180, 332
Scheel, Marti, 111
Schild, Verónica, 211
Schroda, Magda, 226
Scott, Don, 61
Scott, Joan, 59. See also Only Paradoxes to Offer
Scott, William B., 279
Second Shift, The, 106. See also Hochschild, Arlie
Second Stage, The, 101, 106. See also Friedan, Betty
self, the, 31, 39, 134, 260; autonomy and, 65, 101, 125; disembodied, 44; divisions of, 12, 84, 95–96, 185, 322, 332; knowledge of, 85, 91, 281–82; wholeness of, 93–94, 103, 283, 284

Sentimental Agents, The, 317, 320–21. See also Lessing, Doris

separatism, 24–27, 33, 46, 49, 54n6, 165, 183–84, 295

Sex Fools, The, 73, 265, 296;

sexism, 7, 35–37, 48–49, 63, 66, 73, 80–82, 126, 128, 130, 134–36, 164–65, 194–98, 223–24, 246, 257, 288, 297, 299, 330; images and, 128, 134–35, 137, 197–98. See also antipornography

sexual harassment, 128, 164, 213, 245, 257

sexuality, 9, 29, 37, 137, 150, 217, 313; censorship of, 8, 9, 77, 124, 131, 137, 206, 267; female pleasure and, 125, 130, 302–3; feminist discourses on, 8, 73–76, 88, 125–26, 208, 295, 299–301; male, 8, 76–77, 124–25, 127, 136; morality and, 40, 76, 124, 129, 136, 295; sexual freedom and, 48–49, 76, 79, 123–25, 129–30, 134–37, 139–40, 143, 234, 294; sexual imagery and, 74, 76–79, 124, 130, 134, 250; sex work and, 74, 207–8; shame and, 132–35, 143, 198, 232, 285–86; S/M and, 74–75, 137; violence and, 208, 257–58. See also motherhood; pornography

Sex Wars, the, 7, 8, 9, 75–76, 123; Pro-Sex Faction and, 16. See also antipornography; pornography; sexuality

Shakespeare, William, 91–92, 144–46. See also Carter, Angela

Shelley, Martha, 222

Sherrod, Shirley, 281

Siklova, Jirina, 202

Simkins, Modjeska Monteith, 281

Sinha, Mrinalini, 36–37

sisterhood, 2, 22, 27, 45, 52, 281; as undifferentiated, 31, 72, 129, 286; of motherhood 108

Sisterhood is Powerful, 103

Smith-Rosenberg, Carroll, 124, 313

Snitow, Virginia, 309

social construction, 28–29, 31, 59–60, 83, 104–5, 125, 129–30, 300. See also essentialism

socialism, 1, 16, 86, 151–52

Solidarity strike, 218, 222, 270

Sorchan, Mrs. Victor, 280

Speakout: I Had an Abortion, 257

Spirited Away, 247. See also Miyazaki, Hayao

Stacey, Judith, 46–47

Stansell, Christine, 8, 73. See also Powers of Desire

Stanton, Elizabeth Cady, 297, 301

Stanworth, Barbara, 99

Stead, Christina, 149–50. See also House of All Nations, The; Man Who Loved Children, The

Stevens, S.S., 85

Stimpson, Catharine, 27

Story of General Dann and Mara's Daughter, Griot and the Snow Dog, The, 323–25. See also Doris Lessing

Straight, Mrs. Willard, 280

Students for a Democratic Society (SDS), 297

Sturges, John, 251. See also Bad Day at Black Rock

Swank, Hilary, 258

Swerdlow, Amy, 23, 37, 54n3, 55n24

Take Back the Future, 4, 268

Tallmer, Abby, 77

Tanner, Leslie, 103. See also Voices from Women's Liberation

Tax, Meredith, 34, 55n24

Taylor, Katie, 74

Taylor, Louise, 90

Tel Quel, 104. See also Kristeva, Julia

Thatcher, Margaret, 171, 181, 322

Thelma and Louise, 257

Third Street Circle, The, 265, 296

Thompson, E.P., 181–82

Thompson, Sharon, 8, 73. See also Powers of Desire

Tiffany, Mrs. Charles L., 280

Times of Harvey Milk, The, 250–51, 258

Trotsky, Leon, 83

uncertainty, 1–6, 53, 67, 72, 128, 307–12, 314–15, 326, 332, 333; irony and, 6, 12, 199, 217, 226, 261, 287, 298–99, 309, 311, 331; mastery and, 317–18, 320–21, 328, 331; responsibility and, 308, 319; skepticism and, 1, 5, 12–13, 15, 33, 42, 62, 86, 95–96, 111, 135, 212, 214, 217, 223, 241, 275–76, 278, 282, 286–87, 299–300, 307, 314, 328, 329, 331–32. See also utopia

utopia, 273, 276, 288, 301, 307–8; dreams of, 16, 72, 86, 91, 130, 151–52, 188, 275, 285, 287–89, 328–29; limits of, 86, 134, 308, 328, 331–33; will and, 81, 300; writing tone and, 90, 101–2, 299, 301; yearning for, 1–6, 12, 212, 223, 293–94, 296, 299, 301, 330–33. *See also* uncertainty

Valeska, Lucia, 102
Vance, Carole, 8, 29, 73–75, 78, 124, 207, 267. *See also* Pleasure and Danger
Vindication of the Rights of Women, A, 43–44. *See also* Wollstonecraft, Mary
Voices from Women's Liberation, 103. *See also* Tanner, Leslie

Walby, Sylvia, 283
Walczewska, Slawka, 162, 216–27, 269. *See also* Knights, Ladies, Feminists
Walentynowicz, Anna, 270
Walker, Alice, 33
Walkowitz, Judy, 124
Wallace, Michelle, 104. *See also* Black Macho and the Myth of the Superwoman
Ware, Cellestine, 2, 222
Ways of Seeing, 301. *See also* Berger, John
Weitzman, Lenore, 106
Wells, Julie, 37, 55n24, 55n27
Wertheimer, Max, 83, 85
When Everything Changed, 287. *See also* Collins, Gail
Whisker, Brenda, 184. *See also* Breaching the Peace
Whitehead, Mary Beth, 51–52
Willis, Ellen, 29, 273, 278, 293–96
Wise Children, 143–46. *See also* Carter, Angela
Wollstonecraft, Mary, 43–45. *See also* A Vindication of the Rights of Women
Woman's Body, Woman's Right, 104. *See also* Gordon, Linda
Womankind (WBAI New York radio series), 64–65, 297
women: becoming men, 41–42, 48, 94–95, 186, 197; category, "woman" and, 11, 21–33, 45, 48–53, 59, 61–62, 73–74, 125, 127, 187, 191–92, 196–97, 200–201, 205, 289; experience and, 24, 26, 28, 32, 62–66, 94, 102, 135, 184, 200, 201, 223, 281–82, 301–2; invisibility of, 7, 25–26,

32, 36, 42, 47, 62, 64–65, 80, 94–95, 128, 130, 183, 191, 224, 274, 278–82, 285, 287–88, 294, 299, 302; private sphere and, 31, 40–41, 44, 46–47, 64–65, 75, 81–82, 105, 172–73, 193–95, 197–98, 200–202, 236, 282, 285, 302, 308; in psychoanalysis, 281–83; relation to men, 80–82, 92–95, 124–25, 127–29, 185–88, 217–19, 223–24, 236, 238–40, 257, 291; victimization of, 54n13, 76–77, 124–30, 135, 207–8, 285–86; "women's issues" and, 23–26, 192, 202, 208. *See also* gender; motherhood
Women Against Pornography (WAP), 74–75
Women Against Violence Against Women (WAVAW), 73
Women Against Violence in Pornography and Media (WAVPM), 73–74
Women in Sexist Society, 103
Women Strike for Peace, 23, 25, 37
Women's Action Coalition (WAC), 269
women's movement, 3, 14, 21, 27–28, 46–48, 59, 103, 123–29, 168–69, 191–93, 202–3, 211–14, 221, 225, 259, 275–76, 279, 283–85, 287, 293, 298, 301; prowoman line and, 63. *See also* feminism; feminist activism
Women's Pentagon Action, 174–75, 185
women's suffrage, 10, 40, 110, 125, 258–59, 274, 279; justice and, 42, 110, 282
Woolf, Virginia, 217
work, 26, 34, 39, 40, 46, 51, 56n33, 98–100, 125–27, 168, 194, 197, 207–8, 211–12, 220, 282, 330; domestic, 36, 56n33, 82, 106, 170, 201–2, 295; exhaustion and, 10, 82, 109, 174, 194–96, 202, 234, 319; motherhood and, 101, 103, 106–9, 111, 199, 233–34
Working Men's Circle, 3
World Trade Center: attack on 332
writing, 2, 12, 73, 97–98, 141, 146, 149, 166, 256, 317, 325; feminist history and, 5–7, 10, 62, 64–65, 71, 102, 273, 275–77, 293–94; labor of, 254, 310–15; plagiarism in, 252–56; trends in, 83, 90, 101–2, 299; women and, 149, 277–78. *See also* education; experience; memory
WuDunn, Sheryl, 287–88. *See also* Half the Sky